DONALD THOMAS was bor█████████████
Queen's College, Taunton, █████████████
received the Eric Gregory █████████████████ *Points of
Contact* (1963). His novels have brought Bonnie Prince
Charlie to the throne of Virginia in *Prince Charlie's Bluff*
(1974) and blackmail with murder to Victorian Oxford in
Belladonna: A Lewis Carroll Nightmare (1983). Biographies
include *Cardigan of Balaclava* (1974), *Cochrane: Britannia's
Last Sea-King* (1978), *Swinburne* (1979), *Robert Browning*
(1982) and *Henry Fielding* (1990). He has written widely on
censorship and is the author of its history in *A Long Time
Burning* (1969). As a writer of true crime, he devised and
scripted two series of the BBC programme *The Detectives* and
is the author of *Honour Among Thieves: Three Classic
Robberies* (1991). He is at present writing about Father
Ignatius, the Victorian miracle-worker. Apart from his
writing, he is Professor of English at the University of Wales,
Cardiff; General Editor of the Critical Approach series; and
Consulting Editor to Everyman Library.

THE MARQUIS DE SADE

Donald Thomas

BLACK SWAN

THE MARQUIS DE SADE
A BLACK SWAN BOOK 0 552 99499 5

Originally published in Great Britain
by Allison & Busby, an imprint of
Virgin Publishing Ltd

PRINTING HISTORY
Allison & Busby edition published 1992
Black Swan edition published 1993

Black Swan Books are published by
Transworld Publishers Ltd,
61–63 Uxbridge Road, London W5 5SA,
in Australia by
Transworld Publishers (Australia) Pty Ltd,
15–23 Helles Avenue, Moorebank, NSW 2170,
and in New Zealand by
Transworld Publishers (NZ) Ltd,
3 William Pickering Drive, Albany, Auckland.

Printed and bound in Great Britain by
Cox & Wyman Ltd, Reading, Berks.

CONTENTS

For Colin

ILLUSTRATIONS

The French Investigator: a modern view of Sade. *(Mary Evans Picture Library)*

The Condé Palace in Paris where Sade was born.

Saumane where Sade spent his childhood. *(Carol Thomas)*

The Horrors of the Inquisition. An illustration for *Aline and Valcour*, 1795. *(Weidenfeld & Nicolson Archives)*

The prison at Vincennes. *(Carol Thomas)*

Renée-Pélagie, Marquise de Sade.

The Marquis de Sade in the asylum at Charenton. *(The Mansell Collection)*

A manuscript in Sade's handwriting.

A *petite maison* of the 18th century.

The Beauties of the King of Butua's harem. An illustration for *Aline and Valcour*, 1795. *(Weidenfeld & Nicolson Archives)*

PREFACE

IN JULY 1990 AT ARCUEIL, the scene of Sade's most famous flagellation, the banners on the lamp posts and the Institut Marius Sidobre are out to welcome Nelson Mandela. ANC colours across the shabby urban street make past history of the rainbow-spray graffiti "Liberez Mandela" on the concrete walls of public buildings. Arcueil, the leafy retreat of the wealthy and the titled during the *ancien régime*, now looks like a badly bombed town from which a Maginot line of fortress-blocks is rising defiantly. The last creeper-covered villas of the nineteenth century are fighting it out with the southward march of high-rise Paris. Somewhere under the diggers and the framework of the steel-erectors are street names that survived until a few years ago. But the topography of Sade's Arcueil has vanished. Only a temporary yellow traffic sign points in the direction of the long-demolished *petite maison*, where he caused so much trouble. Appropriately, it says, "Deviation".

The world that Sade knew, where it survives at all, lies far to the south. La Coste, its château torn between restoration and decay, has an air of bourgeois chic. Where the constabulary of Louis XVI failed so often to hunt down the village's most famous son, middle-class tourism succeeds unerringly. Mazan remains a busy little town, an adjunct of Carpentras. The elegant bow-windowed "Chateau de Sade" still dominates the westward side. Yet change and decay have touched it too. This house of Sadean pleasure and passion fell victim to progress in 1929 and was turned into an old people's home. Saumane, the remotest of all his properties, is the most evocative of his presence. Perched on its rock above the adjacent valleys, it seems much as Sade would have known it. The village is still a single street, the church on its precipitous ledge at one end, the château and gardens crowning a slope at the other. It remains a place of silence and distant views, rock and bright flowers.

Of the prisons which survive, the great keep of Vincennes endures with a grimness that suggests Sade's ordeal within its walls. For much of the time since his confinement there, his books have been as much the victims of incarceration as their author.

This account of Sade derives from my illustrated commentary on his life and work in 1976. To write of Sade is also to write of his reputation and his effect on our time. He was, by repute, post-humously responsible for the Moors Murders and a good many lesser crimes. His name has been a moral shorthand either for the most loathed forms of human conduct or for romantic heroism under oppression. This book is therefore concerned with Sade present, as well as Sade past. While Arcueil rises in concrete above the rubble of the Arcadian village that he knew, those novels of his which were banned as moral poisons leading to madness or death now line the bookshop shelves with other mass-market paperbacks. In the light of his philosophical ambivalence, it seems appropriate that he achieved immortality by the skin of his teeth and by the labour of those few enthusiasts who devoted lives and livelihoods to the task.

In writing this book, I have incurred a number of debts of gratitude to the Bibliothèque Nationale, the Bodleian Library and the Taylorian Institute, Oxford, the British Library, the London Library, the Public Record Office, St Andrew's University Library, University College London Library, and the Library of the University of Wales, Cardiff. The passage on pages 168–9 is translated from the text of Sade's letter to Marie-Dorothée de Rousset in *L'Aigle, Mademoiselle . . .*, edited by Gilbert Lely, Éditions Georges Artigues, 1949.

My particular thanks are due to Peter Day, Susan Loden, Elfreda Powell, Ríona MacNamara, Paul Forty, Emma Worth, Michael Thomas and Andrew Wheatcroft, who have encouraged and assisted the completion of this book, both in its present form and as an initial commentary on Sade's life and work in 1976.

ONE

THE ACCUSED

1

ON 15 DECEMBER 1956, a criminal trial opened in Paris before the magistrates of the 17th Chambre Correctionelle. The proceedings occupied a long day of legal argument, before being adjourned at last in the winter lamplight of the Ile de la Cité. Even in the autumn of the Suez invasion and the Hungarian uprising, the trial in Paris was international news. Its participants included Jean Cocteau and André Breton, the great survivors of French surrealism, Jean Paulhan of the Académie Française and Georges Bataille, critic, novelist and iconoclast. The judgment of the Chambre Correctionelle was not announced until 10 January 1957 and the case was to continue until it reached a decision in the French Court of Appeal one year and four months later.

There was one absentee, who happened also to be the principal figure in the trial. As the public prosecutor remarked, this unquiet ghost was the true defendant. He had been dead for a hundred and forty-two years and his full name was Donatien-Alphonse-François, Comte de Sade. He seldom used the title of "comte", to which he succeeded on the death of his father in 1767. During his minority, he had borne the courtesy title of "marquis". It was as the Marquis de Sade that he preferred to be known. The title and the name lived on after his death as a synonym for sardonic sensuality and gloating cruelty. In the nineteenth century, with the advent of psychopathology, his name provided a general term for the most feared and hated of human aberrations: "sadism". It became one of the few words in the language of moral alienation whose meaning was never in doubt among ordinary people.

At every reference to the Marquis de Sade, the world paid attention and sensed a threat from his influence long after his death. Those who heard the name sometimes shuddered but seldom turned away. He had his champions among writers and artists, some of whom gave him the sobriquet of "The Divine Marquis". To the world in general, these men and their world of bohemian sympathizers appeared as a perverse minority.

The trial in 1956 had been precipitated by an edition of the collected works of Sade, issued by a relatively small publisher, Jean-Jacques Pauvert. He was known for editions of erotic fiction and his firm had caused a stir in 1954 with the publication of *L'Histoire d'O* by "Pauline Réage". This was described by Irving Kristol at the time of the Sade trial as "A Gothic tale of a woman, O, who, at the instigation of her lover, becomes the slave of a freemasonry of sadists, and who finds in the indignities perpetrated upon her a perfect contentment." By 1956, this modern novel had acquired a certain chic notoriety. It was not generally known that the author was Jean Paulhan's female colleague at Gallimard, Dominique Aury. He had written a preface for her book, as well as appearing at Pauvert's trial.

In 1947, Pauvert had begun issuing a limited edition of Sade's collected works in twenty-four volumes. By the time that proceedings were begun against him in 1953, the volume containing *The 120 Days of Sodom*, one of the novels to which objection was taken, had been available for five years. Some of the items in the collected edition would not have offended the most prudish reader. Others were considered so dangerous to the human mind that they had rarely been published in the two centuries since Sade had written them. Their erotic appeal was far less deliberate than that of a modern novel like *L'Histoire d'O* or that of commercial pornography in the 1950s. But their narratives appeared to be infused with a destructive contempt for civilization and society.

The four books which had caused the prosecution were *The 120 Days of Sodom*, *The New Justine*, *Juliette*, and *Philosophy in the Boudoir*. No one at the trial could specify their precise effect on the mind of an individual reader. In the nineteenth century it had been said that those who read the works of the "monster" ran a risk of destroying both their bodies and their souls. Girls were reported to have gone mad or committed suicide after reading Sade's works. In the 1956 hearing, the president of the court questioned Jean Paulhan as to whether he thought that Sade's fiction might have dangerous effects on its readers. Paulhan agreed that it might, laconically citing the example of one girl in his experience who had retired to a convent as a result of reading Sade's work.

Pauvert was charged with an offence against public morals in issuing the four titles, though the trial itself was something of an oddity, since he was not the first publisher of the books. Even as the proceedings continued from Chambre Correctionelle to Court of Appeal, the titles were displayed a few hundred yards away down the tree-lined elegance of boulevard du Palais. They lay on the wooden stalls that lined the banks of the Seine to nearby Notre Dame or faced across the river to boulevard St Michel. These were the paperbound translations issued by the Olympia Press of Maurice Girodias, "Not to be imported into the United Kingdom or the United States". *The 120 Days of Sodom* and *Bedroom Philosophers* were nonetheless reaching selected readers in London and New York. It was even thought worth dismembering the volumes and posting each section individually, so that it appeared like a letter. The black market London price for *Justine* in the mid-1950s was £8, the weekly take-home pay of the average worker.

The trial in Paris on 15 December began with an eloquent defence of press freedom by Pauvert's counsel, Maurice Garçon. Censorship in France was an easy target, governed by bureaucratic decree and a hint of the bourgeois authoritarianism to which Marshal Pétain had appealed. It was imposed by a state commission, the so-called Commission du Livre, set up by a legal decree in 1939 under the shadow of war. Books were referred by the police to this commission for a decision as to whether a prosecution should be brought. Its president was a judge of the appeal court. Its members consisted of an adviser to the appeal court, a representative of the Ministry of Education, a professor of law, a nominee from associations for the defence of public morality, and a member to represent the interests of large families. There was also a representative of the French Society of Authors, though the society was not allowed to choose who it should be. Not surprisingly, this commission took one look at Sade's more extreme fiction and sanctioned a prosecution.

Maurice Garçon, on Pauvert's behalf, appealed to the guarantee of press freedom laid down in the French constitution of 3 September 1791. By precept and example, he showed the futility, absurdity, and political malice which had characterized censorship in a century and a half of Gallic literary history. It was a powerful representation of the argument for absolute intellectual freedom, far more telling than any evidence given by his witnesses.

Pauvert, as publisher and defendant, was the first witness. It was likely that his case was a stone-cold loser from the start. If not, it soon became so. He began by announcing his duty to give the works of Sade to the French public, as texts of the greatest importance. This democratic right of free people to read their own literature was also the foundation of Maurice Garçon's argument. The president of the court then asked the publisher if Sade's books were not obscene. Pauvert agreed they were obscene but insisted that his editions were not an offence against public morality since he had issued them in limited numbers. It was almost the worst answer that could have been given. The defence of a limited edition not only contradicted the claim of a few moments earlier that Sade must be publicly available, it also conceded the prosecution's case in respect of the nature of the books. If the publication of Sade was an offence against the law, it was of no use to plead that the offence had been committed only on a small scale. As the president of the court pointed out, the fact that doctors and universities bought some of the copies did not make the books unavailable to the public.

Where Garçon crusaded, Pauvert sought a compromise that the law would never accept. Nor would the literary prestige of the witnesses rescue the defendant from the pit he had dug for himself. Either he was a small scholarly publisher beneath the notice of the law or he was the defender of the right of the people to read what they chose. In this case, he could not be both.

Despite the distinction of their names, his witnesses did little to help him. Jean Paulhan began badly when he tried to defend the "purity of destruction" in Sade. Courts of law are apt to dislike such concepts. Nor was it a valid defence to argue that other books not before the court were as corrupting as Sade's. No man is likely to be acquitted of a crime, merely because others have not been caught.

Georges Bataille, when asked by the president of the court whether Sade's philosophy was not destructive of all moral values, agreed that it was. Was it not dangerous, in that case, to let such books loose among the general public? Bataille denied this, saying that the novels were medico-legal documents. In any case, a general edition of Sade would not be dangerous. Bataille insisted that he had too great a faith in human nature to fear that men and women would put Sade's theories into practice.

"I congratulate you, monsieur," said the president drily. "Your optimism does you honour."

The two most eminent witnesses for the defence were not present in the flesh. Indeed, the second one was found not to be present in any form. Jean Cocteau's evidence consisted of a letter written to the court, insisting that Sade was a philosopher and a moralist.

"Did Jean Cocteau actually say that?" asked the president incredulously. It was clear that the letter would do little for Sade or Pauvert.

André Breton had made a statement on behalf of the defence but that had somehow got mislaid and was not available at the trial. With this unpromising revelation the case for the publisher ended.

The prosecution, while conceding that Pauvert had cooperated with the police, disputed the claim that he had truly published a limited edition. Public subscriptions had been invited and there had been magazine publicity. The volumes of the edition were sold openly along the Seine and advertising still continued. If Pauvert were acquitted, what was to stop him publishing Sade as a mass-market paperback? That was to happen a decade later, though Pauvert was not the publisher. Either Sade outraged public morals or he did not. That was the issue before the court and there could be no other.

Maurice Garçon had been right to attack censorship and repression, showing that public morality was not static but evolutionary. Garçon had been right, too, in his technical argument and in his attempt to win a trial by jury for his client. By contrast, Pauvert had been ill-advised to offer the illusory defence of a limited edition. The president of the court, a skilled player in the game, had beaten him on every point in this argument. Sade's more notorious works were either to be published or they were not. The object of a limited edition was to avoid prosecution or minimize the penalty rather than to win acquittal. Pauvert had failed in this. On 10 January 1957, the Chambre Correctionelle pronounced him guilty and fined him. Sade's four most objectionable novels joined the list of banned books.

The higher courts of justice pondered the collected works of Sade and came to a final decision in 1958. The unobjectionable volumes and the erotic or more mildly sadistic works were still published freely. Those four works, which filled fourteen volumes of the edition and had been the subject of the 1956 hearing, were to be suppressed.

After so much legal argument, the decision of the court was soon to be swept aside by a new freedom of publication in the 1960s. Sade's novels appeared without difficulty in France in "limited editions". But though these numbered copies might have a number stamped inside them, the editions were quite as large as unlimited editions, often running to five or eight thousand copies. English translations, bound in pink or yellow wrappers, had been sold at the bookstalls along the quays of the Seine throughout the 1950s as *Bedroom Philosophers* or *Good Conduct Well-Chastised*. Finally, the French texts were issued in mass-market paperback by such imprints as Folio and Livre du Poche.

Among the claims and counter-claims of the trial, the Palais de Justice was never free of its sardonic and vindictive ghost, inspiring the mind of the moralist with fear and fascination. The diseased and bloated body of the elderly author had been trundled to its unmarked grave in the cemetery of Charenton in 1814. In his novels and diatribes, the savage intelligence lived on. One of his most disquieting characteristics was the resilience of that mind which had not been broken by two narrowly avoided judicial executions, nor by twenty-seven years in the prisons and lunatic asylums of the *ancien régime* and the Revolution. From such experience blossomed an alternative philosophy of human conduct, composed secretly in the long months and years of confinement. In this new order of the Sadean universe, it seemed that there was to be no God, no morality, no affection, and no hope – only the extinction of mankind in a final erotic and homicidal frenzy. Murder, theft, rape, sodomy, incest and prostitution were to be the reasonable means to that end. But if Sade truly advocated such a system, it required no overthrow of the existing order to bring it about. In the darkness of the Terror and the savage justice of the Bourbons, he found inspiration on every side.

If this had been the dream of a lunatic, there would have been no collected edition and no trial in 1956. But Sade's interpretation fits with deadly precision a secular universe bereft of divine power, a society where reason can justify no other laws than those of nature. In his own age, the heroes and heroines of his fiction were frustrated in their grandest designs. To destroy the world was not yet in their power. In *Juliette* it is a matter of some regret to the heroine that she cannot destroy whole towns by bringing about an eruption of Vesuvius. Instead, she must be content with torturing a young woman and then throwing her to her death in the boiling lava of the volcano. Only later on is there some consolation in killing fifteen hundred people by poisoning a town's water supply. Yet by 1956, science had improved upon this, harnessing nuclear fission and bacteriology to provide for the destruction of all life on earth. Two centuries of scientific progress had made the ambitions of Juliette and her friends seem relatively modest by contrast with those of military strategists and their armourers.

It was argued, of course, that Sade's novels showed what the consequences must be if mankind chose to reject a world of divine moral order. But that objection served only to indicate the central ambiguity in his life, if not in his work. Whether or not Sade rejected a divinely ordered world, this obsession with Providence and the contorted phrases of blasphemy offered a strong argument to suggest that his greatest mania was religious rather than sexual. He was perhaps the only major writer in two hundred years to think the unthinkable and set down the conclusion in narratives which were regarded as unprintable in his own time as well as two centuries later. Voltaire had shown that all is not for the best in this best of all possible worlds. But even Voltaire's was a gentle voice by contrast with Sade's unveiling of a universe dominated by evil and destruction, where the men and women of reason indulge themselves in this brutal erotic prelude to the unlamented obliteration of humankind.

With the failure of the prosecution brought against *Lady Chatterley's Lover* in England in 1960, the defeat of prosecutions against this book and Henry Miller's *Tropic of Cancer* in the United States in 1959 and 1964, the way was open for Sade's works to be published more widely. In England, such editions as appeared were considerably expurgated, until the issue of *The*

120 Days of Sodom in 1989. In New York and Los Angeles, translations appeared in impressive volumes and without deletions, accompanied by declarations of their importance by academics and scholars. Sade's name, which had been prudently laundered from accounts of the Enlightenment or the Revolution, was now restored to its political and cultural importance, among critical and scholarly approval. The nineteenth century dismissal of him, which was summed up in Michelet's "frightening madman", now seemed comically precipitate. Indeed, his work acquired particular significance for the new generation of a revolution which the western world of the 1960s confronted.

Sade became a symbol to the 1960s, as he had done to Surrealists thirty years before. Yet the chief customers for his books were not intellectuals of the New Left. They belonged to a public which patronized such "horror" movies as *House of Whipcord* or the heterosexual sodomy of *Je ne t'aime moi non plus*. Their sub-culture reflected a hero exalted elsewhere in Weiss's *Marat-Sade* or by a critique of Fascism in Pasolini's *Salo: Les 120 Journées* in 1974.

The more popular revival of Sade's reputation was short-lived. He was not an adroit author of commercial pornography. His name, rather than his books, rang most resonantly to men and women who cared little for revolutions past or present. If such readers wondered whether the Marquis de Sade ever did the sort of things which he described in his novels, and if they heard that he had done, they may have dreamt more wistfully of the pleasures of being a French nobleman during the last days of the *ancien régime* than of the stern call to revolutionary violence.

2

Though Sade's fiction had crossed the English Channel only in a blander version, it was in England that his notoriety was renewed ten years after the trial in Paris. The crime and the nature of the proceedings were far removed in tone from the civilized debate of the Chambre Correctionelle. But, once again, Sade's name was invoked on both sides.

On 19 April 1966, at Chester Assizes, Ian Brady and Myra Hindley faced charges of murdering a seventeen-year-old youth, a boy of twelve, and a girl of ten. The bodies had been found in makeshift graves on the windswept moors of the Pennines, between Manchester and Huddersfield. Two more victims, a boy and a girl of sixteen, were also buried there but not discovered at the time. The location of the graves gave the case its name of the Moors Murders.

Not since the trial of Dr Crippen had an English murder case created such a public sensation. In no recent case of this kind in England were similar feelings of horror aroused by the nature of the crime. There was strong suspicion that the two accused were also responsible for the disappearance of another girl, aged sixteen, and a boy of twelve. The bodies of these victims were to be found more than twenty years later.

Even the sexual aberration which motivated the murderers would scarcely have accounted for the strength of public feeling and interest in the case. It was the behaviour and responses of the two defendants which shocked experienced police officers and journalists alike. Before killing the girl with whose murder they were charged, they had photographed and tape-recorded the acts preceding her death. The recording had been carefully copied, twice, so that in the following weeks they were able to play it over for their own amusement. During the trial it was necessary to play the tape again in open court as part of the evidence for the prosecution. The ordeal of listening to the victim's last moments was described by those who heard the tape as the most terrible experience that any judge, juror or policeman has had to undergo in a court of law.

The defendants seemed not only indifferent to the charges against them but almost to be acting under the immediate orders of some invisible spirit. His power was greater than any of the forces of law ranged against them. His name was mentioned and his views were given in evidence. A passage from Sade's fiction was read out on behalf of the attorney-general and eagerly reported. Soon the world was assured that these appalling crimes had been committed at the posthumous behest of the notorious Marquis de Sade.

Jean Cocteau and Jean Paulhan might speculate on the philosophical significance of Sade. The New Left might admire his revolutionary thought. Scholars and academics might hail him as the great discovery of recent studies in the history of eighteenth-century France. The officers of the Lancashire CID, however, were not much concerned with Sade's philosophical significance. They faced the consequences of his ideas at a more practical level. What might have been a routine crime of sexual assault had become a case of sex spiced by murder as a result of his influence. Or what might have been an abrupt act of murder had become a prolonged gloating over the victim, in imitation of the Divine Marquis. So, at least, it was argued.

The murderers had a library of books with which they were said to be obsessed. Many dealt with Nazism, and some were of the kind known in the trade as "sucker-traps", promising much on their lurid covers and delivering very little inside. Certain titles had been in print for many years and a few, like *High Heels and Stockings* or *The Kiss of the Whip*, were of more recent vintage. None of them stood in the least danger of prosecution for obscenity. "I suppose the titles are more sinister than the contents, if you were foolish enough to buy them," said Mr Justice Fenton Atkinson, the trial judge at Chester. "One was enough for me."

However, two books in the murderers' collection related directly to Sade. The first of these, by the distinguished anthropologist Geoffrey Gorer, was *The Life and Ideas of the Marquis de Sade*, first published more than thirty years earlier. It had been reissued as a paperback by Panther Books in 1964 and it was this version which the murderers possessed. The chapters deal generally with Sade's political and philosophical ideas, emphasizing particularly his indebtedness to the mechanistic theories of La Mettrie's *L'Homme Machine*, published in 1748. Geoffrey Gorer's book is no more pornographic in its choice of material than Bertrand Russell's *History of Western Philosophy*, which might have offered the murderers a "romantic" gloss on Nazism in its chapter on Rousseau. Indeed, as Gorer pointed out, Sade's sexual preoccupations are a hindrance to his novels rather than an inspiration.

The second book was an American translation of Sade's *Justine*. Despite its title, it was based on *The Misfortunes of Virtue*, Sade's first and least objectionable version of the story that he was to tell three times with greater elaboration. This translation was so bland and expurgated that it was sold widely in England by W. H. Smith and the major chains of reputable bookshops, even by those who had at first declined to stock a novel like *Lady Chatterley's Lover*. It might have been thought that such an introduction to Sade was likely to be a deterrent rather than a stimulant to the murderers' continued interest in him.

The public was left with an impression of the murderers as an evil young couple who had carried out their crimes as loyal disciples of Sade. This suited the sensationalism of the tabloid press and the moral preconceptions of those who saw Babylon reborn in the 1960s. But what precisely was the role of Sade in the crime and the trial that followed? It was certainly not of the kind which Restif de la Bretonne described in *Monsieur Nicolas*, where he reported that Danton read Sade to excite himself to new acts of cruelty during the Terror of 1793. At no time were the volumes which had been the alleged source of Danton's enthusiasm anywhere within the reach of the Moors Murderers. The evidence of their private pleasures indicates an inspiration closer to the commercial fetishism of *High Heels and Stockings* than to Sade's excesses. The careful snapshots of Myra Hindley in black underwear or displaying the marks of her partner's whip reflect the pulp eroticism of mid-century, which needed no assistance from Sade.

In all the publicity given to Sade as accomplice in the murder of Lesley Ann Downey and the other victims, certain truths were overlooked. It was not Brady nor Hindley but David Smith, the chief prosecution witness, who was first labelled as a reader of Sade. Smith had been present at one of the murders but was not prosecuted for any offence. He had copied out a "defence" of murder by Sade's hero in *Philosophy in the Boudoir*. This defence of murder as private justice was, in fact, Sade quoting Louis XV. Smith had not read the novel, of course, merely the quotation as it appeared in Geoffrey Gorer's book. The lines were next to others transcribed by Smith from bestsellers like Harold Robbins' *The Carpetbaggers*, "Rina was standing clad only in a brassiere and a pair of panties. . . . His hand reached up and touched her breast."

Despite the impression left by the mass-circulation newspapers and the moral commentators, it was the defence rather than the prosecution who gained most from Sade. Cross-examined by defence counsel Philip Curtis, Smith walked into the trap of admitting that he agreed with the atheism of Sade's heroes.

"The oath which you took yesterday, so far as you are concerned, is completely meaningless?" Philip Curtis asked.

Smith could only agree that it was, though even by discrediting him in this way the defence could do little for Brady or Hindley. Brady gave evidence that he had read Geoffrey Gorer's book and enjoyed it. So for that matter had reviewers in the *New Statesman* and the *Times Literary Supplement*. Brady admitted that he agreed with some of Sade's views or those of his characters but he did not agree that murder should be legal.

Yet once the name of Sade was mentioned, the Moors Murders acquired a new and more sensational character. The truth, as it was revealed in the trial, failed to sustain this. David Smith admitted to having a record of criminal violence stretching back for years before he had heard of Sade. Ian Brady was an illegitimate child of the Glasgow streets who never knew his father and whose mother left him to the care of foster parents. He lived with four other children in a tenement of the Gorbals, among the worst slums in Europe. As a little boy at primary school, he was known for his flick-knife and the manner in which he used it on cats and other animals. He had tied a classmate to a post, heaped newspapers round the child and set fire to them. By eleven, he was already practising his Nazi salutes and shouts of "*Sieg heil!*" Apparently, he needed no lessons from Sade.

In the debate which followed the trial, little was said about the fact that Brady had used an axe to kill his victims and that his experience with such implements came from working as a butcher's assistant. The slaughterhouse was as likely a breeding ground for violence as the library or bookshop. Yet those who deplored the presence of Sade's writing most loudly were silent on the trades of butchery or slaughter. There was a wide difference between reading about a murder and committing the crime. The difference between killing an animal and a human being was somewhat finer. Other voices condemned books on capital and corporal punishment in this private collection, preferring to forget that until only two years before the Moors Murders the state had trained and rewarded those who inflicted such forms of death or pain on its behalf.

The true danger of Sade's influence on the murderers, like the example of Hitler and Nazism, is simpler and more alarming. Under ordinary circumstances, the thoughts and desires which were to lead to the deaths of the victims would have remained confined within the mind of the potential criminal for fear of social disapproval or worse. But the potential criminal might discover, for instance, that his murderous instinct was apparently shared by the leaders of a modern totalitarian state, surrounded by mass admiration and fetishistic glamour. He might find that he was not alone, even in the sexual expression of that instinct. A famous French nobleman in the eighteenth century praised and even practised the things which appealed so strongly to his own imagination. A certain intellectual and moral respectability was apparently given to behaviour which would otherwise have been regarded as criminal or immoral. Sade, by his own account, used the crimes of his characters to illustrate his philosophy. The murderers, taking comfort from his very name, might seek to elevate their obsessions to the status of a philosophy, and then commit murder in pursuit of its goals.

Given the mentality of the Moors Murderers, an expurgated version of Sade's *Misfortunes of Virtue* and a study of his place among the *philosophes* of the eighteenth century provided the small amount of intellectual justification needed. It might equally well have been provided by ten minutes' reading of an encyclopaedia entry under his name. Perhaps that form of knowledge would have been more dangerous because it would have been easier to absorb.

Deprived of Sade altogether, the murderers would not have lacked alternative examples. In a not dissimilar crime in Chicago in 1924, Leopold and Loeb found their justification in Nietzsche, whose views would certainly have buttressed the admiration which the later criminals felt for fascism. The German philosopher's famous dictum, "Thou goest to women? Forget not thy whip!" summarizes at least one aspect of Sade's thought with cogent precision.

Crimes as brutal as the Moors Murders seem beyond irony. Yet there was an irony about the beliefs and characters of the perpetrators. Despite their admiration for the Nazi regime, that regime would have put them to death with expressions of abhorrence as powerful as those heard in England. Sade would have disowned them with the contempt which he reserved for the butchers of men and women during the Terror. Always conscious of his rank, such proletarian criminals would have earned little but disdain from him. Moreover, there was no greater irony than their ignorance of Sade as a man who saved the innocent from death and punishment, as a judge during the Revolution, and who lay in prison under the shadow of the guillotine for the crime of "moderation".

3

An author may be famous two hundred years after his death but seldom in the manner of Sade. The reputation of his books was stimulated by their systematic suppression and clandestine circulation. His own reputation was tainted and glamorized by the words and deeds of his fictional characters but also by half-told stories of the scandals that had made him a prisoner at Vincennes and in the Bastille. There was the savage beating of a young woman at his pleasure-house or *petite maison* at Arcueil, south of Paris. There was a homicidal orgy with a group of girls in Marseille. There were more private orgies which occupied him for the entire winter of 1774–5 in his remote château of La Coste. If such stories were believed, his private character was a match for the figures of his public fiction, revelling in every form of vice and crime, shrieking triumphantly like Saint-Fond in *Juliette* of the sublime achievement of simultaneously engaging in parricide, incest, prostitution and sodomy.

To the twentieth century, he was something of a new author. *The 120 Days of Sodom*, whose manuscript he had hidden in the wall of his room in the Bastille, disappeared during the turmoil of 1789. It was rediscovered at the end of the nineteenth century in the possession of a French family who had had it for many years. It was published at last in 1904. Much else had circulated only in restricted editions or, in some cases, not at all for almost a century. His name had given a word to European language, yet the man who bore it was seldom mentioned in any study of French literature or thought.

Sade also appeared belatedly as a hero of romantic revolution and literary rebellion. During his lifetime, some of his family and authorities of all persuasions hoped that by consigning him to prison or the lunatic asylum they would be spared further trouble from him. He had defied them, chronicling that defiance in volume after volume of denunciation and invective richly woven with scenes of sexual outrage that were calculated to be of the most scurrilous kind. So far as the authorities were concerned, his name and his works were intended for oblivion after his death. On 1 February 1835, the *Revue Aptésienne* refused to print his name when listing men of note in that area of Provence. Though the château at nearby La Coste had been the home of the Sades, the paper declined to speak of a figure of "such monstrous horror and infamy", whom it now pronounced guilty of murder. By such prudery, the article stimulated far more interest in him than a mere mention of his name would have done. On his books, it quoted Jules Janin: "There is nothing but bloody corpses, children snatched from the arms of their mothers, young women whose throats are cut at the end of an orgy." But those books, like their author, were destined to break the bounds of confinement, returning in scornful mockery of the social order that had condemned them.

With the addition by Krafft-Ebing of the term "sadism" to the language of psychopathology, Sade's immortality was assured. The man whom Henry James described with some amusement as "the scandalous, the long-ignored, the at last all but unnameable author" was established as a synonym for all that was worst in human conduct. His name was used at last to describe a particular class of murderers, torturers, tyrants, and those whose deeds were too loathsome to be listed.

The contagion of Sade is readily asserted. Perhaps he gave consolation of some kind to the defendants at Chester Assizes. On the other hand, Maurice Heine (1884–1940) was the man who gave Sade's unpublished manuscripts to the world, devoting his life and income to the study of his subject. Yet if Sade's writing affected him, he felt reason for gratitude. Heine became a pacifist, a communist who withdrew his support from the Soviet revolution only when he was appalled by its bloodshed, and a campaigner for the abolition of bull-fighting with its glamorized cruelty to another species. In the nineteenth century, Sade's "disciple" Frederick Hankey strove to follow a vegetarian diet because he detested the slaughter of animals for food.

Perhaps Sade casts a malign influence on the Moors Murderers and their kind. Or perhaps Théophile Gautier's defence still rings true from his preface to *Mademoiselle de Maupin* in 1835.

"Books copy behaviour: behaviour isn't copied from books. The Regency produced Crébillon, it wasn't Crébillon who produced the Regency. . . It's as if you were to say that the appearance of green peas brings the springtime. Quite the reverse. Green peas appear because it is spring and cherries because it is summer." More likely than either, the effect of each book on each reader remains unique. Sade's influence is determined by the field on which it falls.

Yet the power of the "unnameable" to inspire fear, loathing or horror has been impressive. The British Museum was once accustomed to classify "dangerous" books as "Cupboard" volumes, not to be seen without a special reason; the Private Case books which it omitted from its catalogue, and a Suppressed Books section, which was never to be consulted and which it did not even admit to possessing. But there was a rumour, chronicled by T. H. White, that the centre of the literary inferno was occupied by certain unpublished manuscripts of the Marquis de Sade. The Museum authorities, fearing the effects of such writing upon the mind of any mortal reader, decided that the documents were to be read only "in the presence of the Archbishop of Canterbury and two other trustees". The nature of the rumour is more instructive than the illusory existence of the manuscripts. From whatever infernal regions the spirit of the Divine Marquis may occupy, the story must surely have provoked a peal of derisive laughter.

TWO

THE GRAND SEIGNEUR

1

HIS BIRTH WAS AS AUSPICIOUS as it could have been. Close by the Luxembourg Gardens, where twenty years earlier men claimed to have glimpsed the Duchesse de Berry's naked supper-parties, stood the monumental arches and the grand courtyard of the Condé Palace. It was Sade's fortune to be born here on 2 June 1740, in the town house of one of the great families of France. The painted ceiling of the Princess de Condé's room, the *Baptism* by Albano, the tapestries, furnishings and carvings were among the richest collections in Paris. There was a fine library. The gardens were described in 1706 as showing "art and nature combining to produce the greatest embellishments", the trellis-work and the alleys with their ornamental arches being in the Dutch manner.

The masters of the palace were no less than the building. In the seventeenth century, Louis, Prince de Condé, had been one of the most celebrated military commanders in Europe, the news of his victories borne back to Paris or Versailles from Spain, from Holland and from Germany. The Prince's grandson had married a daughter of Louis XIV and, in 1723, had been briefly prime minister of the young Louis XV, as the Duc de Bourbon.

The power and influence of the Bourbon-Condé dynasty was formidable. It was even to outlast the Revolution and emerge again after the empire of Napoléon. In 1740, in the great house by the Luxembourg Gardens, "Monsieur le Duc", as he was known at court, lived with his wife, the Princess Caroline, and their four-year-old son, Prince Louis-Joseph de Bourbon. Among their companions at the Condé Palace was a young kinswoman of the princess. Her name was Marie-Éléonore and she bore the honorary title of Lady-in-Waiting. Not only was Marie-Éléonore allied to the house of Bourbon-Condé, she was also collaterally descended from the great Cardinal Richelieu. Her husband, Jean-Baptiste, Comte de Sade, was a soldier-turned-diplomat. He had been a staff officer and was said to have taken some part in secret negotiations with the English in 1733, as well as with the Russians. Publicly, at least, he was to be French envoy at the court of the Elector of Cologne.

The Comte de Sade's career as a diplomat gave his family name a certain prestige in the public life of France under Louis XV. Stolid and conventional in most things, he and Marie-Éléonore were of a type upon whom the young king and the fabric of the French monarchy depended. Yet despite an appearance of rather dull dependability, Jean-Baptiste, Comte de Sade, shared the vicissitudes of the public servant in a more brash and mercantile age. He was getting deeper into debt and saw the marriage of his son as a means of extricating his family from its difficulties.

Jean-Baptiste and Marie-Éléonore had themselves married in the chapel of the Condé Palace on 13 November 1733 in the presence of the prince and princess. Their first child, a daughter born in 1737, died in infancy. By 1739, Marie-Éléonore was pregnant again. When her husband left for his diplomatic duties at the court of Cologne, it seemed best for her to have the child at the Condé Palace. Indeed, the Sades' child, younger and therefore naturally deferential, might prove in time to be a suitable playmate for the little Prince Louis-Joseph. On 2 June 1740, the Comtesse de Sade gave birth to a son, her only child to survive infancy. The following day he was baptized at the church of St Sulpice as Donatien-Alphonse-François.

Far to the south, the child's family held positions of influence in Church and state. His father's next brother, Richard-Jean-Louis de Sade, had seen active service in Italy and was Commander of the Order of St John of Jerusalem. The younger of the comte's two brothers, Jacques-François-Paul-Aldonze, Abbé de Sade, was a worldly man-of-letters in Provence. He was to have the greatest influence on his nephew's early life. Of his father's sisters, four had given their lives to religion. Gabrielle-Laure was Abbess of St Laurent at Avignon, while Anne-Marie-Lucrèce belonged to an order in the same town. Gabrielle-Éléonore was Abbess of St Benoît at Cavaillon, where Marguerite-Félicité was a member of the Order of St Bernard. Only the youngest of the five aunts, Henriette-Victoire, had married. In 1733, she became the Marquise de Villeneuve.

Despite his father's financial difficulties, the heritage which awaited the newly born Marquis de Sade was quite as impressive in its way as the circumstances of his birth. In breeding and in wealth, the Sades had been one of the first families of France. But for their financial difficulties, they might be so again. There was a good deal of property in Provence, where the Sades had their origins. There were châteaux and lands east of the Rhône in the villages of La Coste, Saumane and Mazan. There was land on the far side of the river, near Arles, at the Mas de Cabanes. There was also property in Paris. In 1739, the Comte de Sade had inherited from his own father the Lieutenant-Generalcy of the provinces of Bresse, Bugey, Valromey and Gex with an annual income of ten thousand livres. These honours and the revenue would one day pass to his son. When the infant Marquis came of age, his eligibility as a husband for the noblest daughters of France would be beyond question. Moreover, the parents of a prospective bride would surely consider the proximity of the Sades to the throne, as well as the extent of their estates.

Jean-Baptiste had brought his family into the centre of French public life. The Sades were Italian long before, and Provençal by at least six centuries of residence there. In French life, the seventeenth century drew the admiration of Europe for the courtly splendour of Versailles. In the eighteenth century it was Paris itself which displayed the brittle artifice of fashionable society before the sharp scrutiny of the lampoonist and the laconic memoirist. Yet though the centre of power was now more evidently metropolitan, the predecessors of the Comte de Sade had had every right to think that they were much closer to the heart of European culture than any Parisian.

The château of La Coste stood high on a hilltop above a village of pale Provençal stone which was terraced on the lower slopes. Tall plain windows looked out across a wide and fertile plain, the range of the Luberon to the south and Mont Ventoux away to the north. Ten miles to the east was the little town of Apt. Twenty-five miles to the west was the Rhône and the ancient city of Avignon. The foursquare towers and walls of the great palace by the Rhône were a reminder of the days when the Popes had lived in exile at the heart of their Provençal enclave. In the fourteenth century, one of the granddaughters of Hugues de Sade had married the chamberlain of Pope Clement VII, while his nephew, Jean de Sade, became papal chaplain. Twenty miles west of Avignon and a few miles north of Nîmes, on the far side of the Rhône, lay that other estate of the Sade family, in the flat land of the Mas de Cabanes.

To the south of La Coste, thirty miles away across the range of the Luberon, stood the administrative centre of Aix-en-Provence. It was a town whose elegant classicism, handsome avenues and fountains made an almost frivolous contrast with the medieval solidity of the Palace of the Popes at Avignon. It was in Aix that the new Marquis de Sade would one day be summoned to answer for some of his more extravagant misdemeanours. Beyond Aix was the sea at Marseille, the city's reputation for sexual vice already sufficient to attract a young man whose tastes for the perverse or the sophisticated found too little immediate satisfaction in the hilltop villages. This world of the Sadean heritage was also close to the main route for Paris, along the Rhône. But it was equally well placed for the road to Savoy, Florence, Rome and the centre of southern European culture.

While the new world of Versailles and Paris, the urbane classicism of the eighteenth century, claimed the Sade parents, the manners and attitudes of the *grands seigneurs* in Provence appeared more akin to those of Renaissance princelings. The châteaux of the Sades at La Coste and Saumane were perched high above the river valleys and terraced vineyards, suggestive in some circumstances of a dramatic study by Salvator Rosa or the opening pages of a Gothic novel. At Mazan, however, the château was a bow-fronted mansion of seventeenth-century classicism, looking westwards from the edge of the little town across a fertile plain of vineyards and cherry orchards.

When the members of the Sade family surveyed their horizons from La Coste, Saumane or Mazan, they could not quite claim to be lords of all that lay before them. But it seemed that they possessed more than enough of it for immediate purposes. The Comte de Sade was in debt but his liabilities could scarcely equal the value of such estates. His son was to incur considerable expense in his wilder conduct. But even if the financial demands were considerable, he could live with safety and economy at La Coste, where he seemed to have little difficulty in attracting enough young women for whatever sexual dramas he proposed.

Traditionally, there had been a certain worldliness in the Provençal attitude towards sexual misdemeanours of Sade's kind. Secular and ecclesiastical authority alike anticipated Byron's comment in *Don Juan* that

> What men call gallantry, and gods adultery,
> Is much more common where the climate's sultry.

Accordingly, authority acted with tolerance. In 1319, for instance, a papal "tariff" was issued from Avignon, listing the prices to be paid as a penance by those who were guilty of various forms of sexual misbehaviour. A culprit who made unnatural use of a woman faced a steep ecclesiastical bill for his sin. In the case of similar conduct with a boy or an animal, the price was lower, since he had no alternative but to behave unnaturally on those occasions. There was a set rate for a man who murdered his wife. But if he murdered her in order to marry another woman, the amount was trebled, teaching him that he must not expect to get something for nothing. To murder a bishop, however, was a far more serious matter, much more expensive than killing a wife or making unnatural use of any species of partner. It was also more expensive than the cost to a woman of employing several lovers simultaneously. The notion of the tariff is instructive but it shows quite clearly that those who devised it would have had little to learn about sexual proclivities from the fiction of the Marquis de Sade four centuries later.

During the struggle for European supremacy, the private and discreet vices of individuals were not the matter of greatest concern to those who ruled them. The papal tariff of 1319 has an air of worldly-wise and easy-going sexual realism. But that was not to last. Robert Browning in *The Ring and the Book* gave life to the details of a "Roman Murder Case" of 1698 in which Count Guido Franceschini not only discovered that he would be punished for murdering his wife but that he would be executed for the crime. Sade's difficulties came not merely from beating some of the girls in his life or engaging them in unorthodox sexual acts. He did so in the middle of the eighteenth century, when such conduct was more likely to be complained of – even in the case of the lord of La Coste – and when such complaints might be listened to. While he looked forward to the overthrow of existing order by violent revolution, he felt aggrieved when the law called him to account for treating young women in the manner of a medieval autocrat.

At his birth in 1740, it seemed unlikely that he would eclipse the fame of his most celebrated ancestors. Despite the notoriety of his fiction, his reputation may be challenged by Laura de Sade, who married Hugues de Sade in 1325 and was identified as Petrarch's "Laura", the great figure of devotion for the sublime sonneteer of the later Middle Ages. According to Petrarch, it was in the church of St Claire at Avignon, on 6 April 1327, that he first saw Laura. She remained the inspiration of his poetry and of that platonic passion through which he expressed his adoration. Even after her death in 1348, she remained his idol, elevated to the status of a muse-goddess, as his friend Dante had honoured Beatrice.

There was some subsequent debate as to whether Petrarch's Laura was Laura de Sade, though the Sade family never doubted her claim. The uncle of the marquis, the Abbé de Sade, friend and correspondent of Voltaire, devoted himself to a study of his ancestress and her admirer. The result of his enthusiasm, *Mémoires pour la vie de François Petrarque*, appeared in 1764–67. The Marquis de Sade, who was consoled during his long imprisonment by the appearance of Laura in a dream, felt an equal loyalty to her. In 1792, when revolutionaries demolished the church at Avignon, he endeavoured to arrange that her remains should be transferred to a resting place below the château at La Coste. Characteristically, his enthusiasm for the overthrow of established order was tempered by a patrician distaste for the destructive mob, whom he denounced on this occasion as "brigands" and "imbeciles".

In Part V of *Juliette*, one of Sade's heroines, the Englishwoman Clairwil, remarks on the absurdity of respecting the dead. Even if this had reflected Sade's view, exceptions to this general rule were to be made in favour of sympathetic members of the author's own family, including Laura de Sade and Charlotte de Beaune, daughter of Gabrielle de Sade.

Charlotte de Beaune had no literary pretensions but an impressive list of lovers. Apart from her great beauty, which led to liaisons with Henri IV and the Duc de Guise, she became the favourite of Catherine de Medicis. In 1577, the year before her marriage, Charlotte was one of the naked ladies-in-waiting who attended the Queen Mother at dinner. The scene of these entertainments was the château of Chenonceaux, which Catherine de Medicis had extended in an ornate gallery at three levels, on stone pillars across the River Cher. Among the woodlands and ornamental paths of the riverside, this royal retreat in western France was one of the most enchanting buildings in Europe.

The Queen Mother was almost sixty and apt to behave like a delinquent headmistress with her young ladies. As if setting an example to Charlotte's descendant, there were games among the leafy parkland of the swallow-haunted Cher which culminated in one of the naked ladies-in-waiting being spanked by Her Majesty. The Abbé de Brantôme, publishing his account from the safety of Leiden in Holland, described the amorous and vindictive sports of the widowed queen among the trees or in the handsome apartments above the glittering waters of the broad shallow river.

> Unable to contain her natural lewdness, for she was a great whore, though married, widowed and very beautiful, she would make her women and girls undress in order to excite herself more strongly. I can tell you that they were the most beautiful ones who were undressed and that it pleased her very much to see them so. And then she would spank their bottoms with her open hand, producing great smacks and slaps, very roughly. With the girls who had misbehaved in some way she would use the birch. The pleasure she got from this was in seeing the movements and contortions of their limbs and their backsides, which, according to the way she beat them, produced a very strange and diverting spectacle.

"Sometimes," Brantôme added, "she did this to make them laugh and sometimes to make them cry. By such sights and the contemplation of them, she whetted her appetites so well that often she would go off and indulge them wholeheartedly with some strapping great fellow." Many of Sade's own set-pieces were no more outlandish. The old bawds of *The 120 Days of Sodom* had been matched by Brantôme's portrait of the queen who, looking out of her window at Chenonceaux and seeing a well-proportioned shoemaker making use of the wall to relieve himself, sent a page to bring him at once to a private place in the parkland.

The scandals of Arcueil or La Coste seem little different to the sports of Chenonceaux two centuries before. Charlotte de Beaune's service to the Crown suggests that Sade was carrying on – or reviving – a family predilection. But whatever its private indulgences, the public image of his family had been impressive. Since the emergence of the Sades in twelfth-century Avignon, they had exercised their fair share of ecclesiastical and civil power. A fifteenth-century Bishop of Marseille; a sixteenth-century Governor of the same city; a Bishop of Cavaillon; a Marshal of France, and a Vicar-General of Toulouse were on the whole more representative of family history than the ethereal Laura or the beautiful favourite of the sexually ambiguous Catherine de Medicis.

There were public lapses from time to time, including accusations of debauchery against Sade's uncle, the Abbé de Sade, who was supposed to be celibate. But there was no reason, among men of sense, why such charges should be allowed to tarnish family honour or impede the culprit's own career. A discreet withdrawal for a few months to a country estate, a token penance, a resolution to be more careful in future, were all the steps necessary as a rule to preserve a man's reputation in such difficulties.

Family honour stood in little danger from Sade's father. Jean-Baptiste, in his portrait by Nattier, appears solid and solemn. Carefully bewigged and correctly positioned, he gives no hint of the debts and obligations that had eaten away his own prospects. The strong features of the oval face, the aquiline nose, firm mouth and clear eyes have an air of dependability that only his financial difficulties were later to undermine. He retired from diplomacy, as he had earlier retired from war, endeavouring to lead a life of regularity and devotion on a small estate which he had bought near Paris. From time to time, he turned to the composition of rather windy dramatic verse. He had once written in verse to Voltaire, returning the great literary philosopher's compliment on the occasion of his marriage. But theatrical verse was one interest that anticipated the writing of his son, who turned to fiction more systematically after his failure as a dramatist.

The Comte de Sade was in no position to supervise the details of his son's upbringing. Yet, from his post at the court of Cologne, he could scarcely have wished for a more reassuring home for the child than the Condé Palace. While the Comte de Sade – and sometimes the child's mother – were away, young Donatien-Alphonse-François found himself in a situation that was to be familiar during long years of his adult life, that of being left to his own devices.

2

Sade's greatest crime, in the view of posterity, was the creation of a fictional world whose cruelty and sexual extravagance were a libel upon the society in which he lived. The truth was that the leaders of that society, in the name of moral example, devised the most ingenious forms of judicial cruelty and paid men well for inflicting them on other men and women, while crowds looked on as if at a circus of mortality. When Sade was seventeen, Damiens was executed with satanic ingenuity for his attempt on the life of Louis XV. In the name of law and morality, the victim's hair was seen to stand on end under such torment. Several hours later, by the time that the dismembered body had ceased to move and the excited crowds began to disperse, the hair had turned white. The fate of Damiens was exceptional in degree but not in principle. Even in the gentler climate of England the law still required that the Jacobite rebels in 1746 should be hanged by the neck, "but not till you be dead, for you are to be cut down alive; your bowels to be taken out, and burnt before your faces".

In continental Europe, courts had stipulated anxiously that a condemned criminal should not be allowed to die until the prescribed number of "nips" had been inflicted with red-hot pincers and the number of limbs indicated had been shattered by the executioner. Those who were merely beheaded or hanged were said to have been granted a "favour". When Sade's fictional excesses were deplored, it was seldom mentioned that he had denounced all punishment which did not morally reform the criminal or that he opposed the death penalty and had narrowly escaped execution for such heresy.

As a matter of delicacy, only men were executed in the most

demeaning fashion. Yet the public flogging and branding of women in England and France was commonplace. Indeed, the fate of juvenile prostitutes in Bridewell before the crowds of visitors prompted Edward Ward in *The London Spy* to remark slyly that such punishments were "design'd rather to feast the eyes of the spectators, or stir up the appetites of lascivious persons, than to correct vice or reform manners". It was also Sade's destiny, at one level, to challenge the self-righteousness of law-givers and law-enforcers. More specifically than Edward Ward, he depicted their most cherished moral arts as lechery and self-indulgence.

In terms of Sade's sexual imagination, almost all the vices which he chronicled were evident in the life of his society and his class. The reign of Louis XIV had reached an apogee of splendour among the wonders of Versailles or the military triumphs of Condé and Turenne. But, as the opening pages of *The 120 Days of Sodom* describe it, the quest for glory had ended in near-disaster by 1715. From Blenheim to Malplaquet, the armies of the Duke of Marlborough had routed those of France, destroying her prestige as the great military power on the European mainland. The wars ended, as Sade's novel begins, with the Peace of Utrecht. Bankruptcy and debauchery followed, both in fiction and reality.

The old king's final years were darkened by the death of his son, the Dauphin, and that of his elder grandson, the new heir-apparent. When Louis XIV died, the destiny of France passed into the hands of his nephew Philippe, Duc d'Orléans, as regent for the infant Louis XV. The late king had remarked of his nephew that Orléans was a walking advertisement for every type of crime. The regent's mother protested that her son had numerous talents, though she admitted that he had not the slightest idea of how to use them. Even a mother could not escape the evident truth of the regent's attitude to her own sex. He used a woman, she said, in the same spirit in which he used a *chaise-percée*.

The 120 Days of Sodom was to be a celebration of this post-war decade of disaster, a story of those who did well out of other people's miseries. Sade credits the regent with having tried to control the vices of the profiteers, but he endows his heroes with the vices by which Orléans was characterized, or at least by which he was made notorious. Just as the incestuous champions of his narrative contribute their own daughters to the shared harem, while continuing to make use of them for their own pleasure, so the regent had married off his daughters and then, most conspicuously with the Duchesse de Berry, was reputed to have become their lover. The Duc de Berry was not usually a jealous husband. But on discovering the nature of his wife's attachment, even he came to court and complained about it in very strong terms.

The regent was credited with having introduced a degree of religious liberty, absent under the more darkly orthodox regime of Louis XIV. Once the old king was safely buried, the prison doors were opened and the victims of fanaticism were set free. Yet the motive was indifference rather than toleration. It was common knowledge, for example, that the covers of Orléans' book of devotions concealed a volume of Rabelais and that, as Saint-Simon describes, he spent long nights toiling selflessly to raise the devil through the practice of black magic in its more seductive forms.

The regent's cynicism in religion anticipated that of Sade's heroes in *The 120 Days of Sodom*. But Orléans was exceeded in this by fashionable clerics, who not only yielded to their vices but saw no reason to conceal them. As the Abbé Servien pushed his way through the crowd at the Opera one night, a young gallant near him turned impatiently and said, "What does this bugger of a preacher want?" "Monsieur," said the abbé, "I am not much of a preacher."

If there was one cleric who provided a pattern for Sade's ecclesiastics, cynical in belief, avowedly corrupt in his public life, and perverse in his private sexual tastes, it was the Abbé Dubois. In his youth, he had been infatuated with a girl at Limoges. She refused to surrender herself to him except in marriage, and so Dubois married her. That seemed the end of his career in the Church. But the resourceful cleric returned to Limoges, drank the parish priest under the table, and destroyed the record of the marriage.

Dubois became a great favourite of the regent and was credited with having devised some of the less subtle entertainments at Orléans' supper parties. In one of these, a naked man and woman with legs clamped about one another's necks rocked as if on a seesaw, supported by the Abbé Dubois kneeling on all fours. As they rocked to and fro, the couple's bodies erupted rhythmically, drawing applause from the onlookers and appealing to the regent's taste for Rabelaisan amusements. Sade need hardly have looked further than the court of France for scatological inspiration.

The seesaw was certainly not the most sophisticated diversion in the regent's household. The beautiful Madame de Tencin, who was shared by Dubois and Orléans, endeavoured to raise the tone of the amusements. She first won the regent's attention by slipping into his bedroom before he retired for the night and posing naked on a pedestal as a living statue of Venus, awaiting discovery by the ruler of France. According to Sade, who gave his first female criminal in *Justine* the cardinal's name, the regent remembered his obligations to Dubois. Sade also recounts in his letters how a lady of noble blood once complained to Orléans that Dubois, in a moment of irritation, had told her to "get fucked".

"The cardinal can be insolent, madame," said the regent, looking at her carefully, "but he sometimes gives good advice."

In Sade's novels, as in life, libertines of the Dubois type not only escape the consequences of their immorality but are rewarded for it. In this, his fiction copied life rather plainly. Dubois became prime minister. To enhance the prestige of this position, it was thought fitting that he should be created a cardinal and desirable that he should succeed Fénelon as Archbishop of Cambrai.

Even in the easy-going moral atmosphere of the regency there were protests at this. Dubois was in theory a celibate and the world was prepared to overlook his lapses in the matter. But he had never bothered to take most of the necessary orders qualifying him for his new position. If he were consecrated Archbishop of Cambrai, it would be necessary to confer all these orders on him at once. The idea seemed preposterous. Indeed, it was sardonically suggested that a painting of the new archbishop's installation should be called, "The First Communion of Cardinal Dubois". Even this was challenged, on the grounds that Dubois could not be a communicant, having yet to be baptized. Dubois intervened to say that it was not unprecedented for a man to receive all the orders at once. It had happened in the case of St Ambrose. What was allowable in a great saint of the Church was equally valid for the inventor of the Rabelaisian seesaw. Then came the first half-suppressed sniggers at the absurdity of the parallel, the snorts of amusement, the guffaws of mirth. At last, even Dubois joined in the general merriment. He was consecrated Archbishop of Cambrai without further hindrance.

All that Dubois lacked to qualify for a place as principal protagonist in *The 120 Days of Sodom* or *Juliette* was evidence of some grosser criminality or homicidal passion. But what the new archbishop lacked was supplied, according to popular rumour, by the regent himself. Not without reason was Orléans known as "Philippe the Poisoner". In order for him to become regent, it was necessary for the Dauphin to die, which he did. It was desirable for the Dauphin's elder son to die, which he also did. There was strong suspicion that both deaths had been caused, or at least aided, by poison. There followed the fate of the Duc de Berry. Soon after he had come to court and protested about his wife's attachment to her father, the Duc de Berry called on her at Versailles. Having dined with her, he was almost at once seized by violent stomach pains and died soon afterwards, leaving the Duchesse de Berry once more at the disposal of her father.

In smaller domestic matters, the regent lived in a manner befitting a Sadean hero. He possessed a fine Sèvres dinner service, each piece of it ingeniously obscene and so remarkable as a whole that in the middle of the nineteenth century it was valued at £30,000. Like Sade's heroes, he was said to despise notions of religion and to take a particular pleasure in orgies that reflected this. In the cynical hedonism of his riposte to a reluctant girl, one can hear an anticipation of the dialogue between Sade's characters. The reluctant object of his passion vowed to the regent that he should never have her heart. Her heart, said Orléans, was something he would do without, provided that he might have the rest of her.

The influence which the court of France had upon lesser men and women, many of them the elder contemporaries of Sade, was formidable. Well-bred ladies were seized by an urge to prostitute themselves in remarkable ways. The Marquise de Gacé found her fulfilment among a party of drunken male admirers, before whom she danced as Salomé. When her final veil had been discarded, she was to be driven naked into the next room, so that a crowd of lackeys who were waiting in there "might do with her as they wished". Among churchmen, there were fit companions for Dubois. The Cardinal d'Auvergne could remember neither the Paternoster nor the Creed, while the private chapel of the Archbishop of Narbonne was said to offer incense, choral splendour and pornography with moral neutrality. But while the scandals of the Church echoed more loudly than those of secular society, it was at least the consequence of the Church having set itself higher standards than those of the court.

There was a distant relative of the Comtesse de Sade who enjoyed a reputation equal to that which the regent had earned. The Duc de Richelieu, a descendant of the famous cardinal, lived long enough to be amused by the indiscretions of the Marquis de Sade. Richelieu was a distinguished soldier who had fought against the English at Dettingen in 1743 and led the charge of the French household cavalry at Fontenoy two years later. He seized the island of Minorca from Admiral Byng in 1756. When the English decided to shoot their admiral, Richelieu chivalrously wrote an open letter to them, saying that the loss of Minorca was not Byng's fault and that he had done his best to hold it.

But there was a darker and more private side to this distant relation of the Sades. Like the regent, he was said to be a devotee of black magic and was accused of trying to raise the devil by feeding consecrated wafers to goats. A man was found bleeding to death at the scene of such an orgy of Richelieu's in Vienna, fatally injured in order to prevent him reporting what he had seen.

Richelieu's list of seductions was so extensive that he was widely thought to be the model for Valmont in *Les Liaisons Dangereuses*. Among his conquests were the Duchesse de Bourgogne and other ladies of the royal house. Mademoiselle de Valois, who married the Duke of Modena, proved difficult of access. Richelieu hired the apartments next to hers in the Palais Royal and had a secret passage constructed between adjoining fireplaces. His intrigues with royal ladies led to his first spell in the Bastille, where he received a consolatory visit from two of the princesses, while ladies of fashion in closed carriages drove mournfully up and down outside the great walls. Two of them, the Marquise de Polignac and the Marquise de Nesle, were said to have fought one another with knives to decide which should have preference in his bed. They were dragged apart but not before blood had been shed on both sides. In the course of such rivalries, Richelieu himself fought the Prince de Condé and the Comte de Gacé. He killed the Prince de Lixin and Baron von Pentenreider. Returned to the Bastille for another stay, he lived almost long enough to be guillotined, dying at the age of ninety-two, just before the Revolution began.

<h1 style="text-align:center">3</h1>

Such was the climate of aristocratic libertinage which had been fostered in Parisian society during the twenty years before Sade's birth. Even for a young nobleman with pretensions to virtue the path was narrow and perilous. To one who was inclined towards vice and sexual exploitation there was little impediment. Yet the contempt for virtue and the indifference towards private or domestic morality was a symptom rather than a cause of the old order's decay.

Greed and gullibility had done as much to destroy the basis of social morality as any form of sexual self-indulgence. Few ordinary men and women set up as imitators of the regent and his court, though the regency was popularly regarded as a good time, following the sombre last years of Louis XIV. It was a good time that cost many people their fortunes and even their lives, when Orléans sanctioned a plan for immediate national prosperity.

In 1718, the economic salvation of post-war France was entrusted to a Scotsman, John Law, who had hit upon the most seductive of economic principles. Wealth may be created or increased by printing money. Credit may be substituted for tangible assets. Law's bank was responsible for the Compagnie des Indes, which issued paper money or *assignats* to the value of a hundred millon livres in respect of its presumed assets. (Eighty years later, when Sade contemplated selling the estate of Mazan to Madame de Villeneuve, he demanded a hundred thousand francs but insisted that it must be two hundred thousand if paid in *assignats*.) In 1718, a madness of speculation seized the country. When it abated, two years later, the value of the additional bills which had been put into circulation was not a hundred million but two thousand six hundred million livres.

Not everyone was deceived or impressed by the scheme,

though few had the intelligent scepticism of Canillac. "Monsieur," he said ruefully to Law, "for years I have been borrowing money, writing promissory notes for it, and never paying the debt. And now you have stolen my system." But men and women more gullible than Canillac crowed with delight over the fabled riches which they had acquired and which were said to lie for the taking in the half-explored lands of the Mississippi. The price for a five-hundred-livre *assignat* rose with such speed that by the beginning of 1720, it stood at 18,000 livres. And then, as with the "South Sea Bubble" in England during the same year, the reckoning came. The precarious edifice of the Compagnie des Indes and its Mississippi scheme trembled. It collapsed with bewildering rapidity and its fall brought ruin more widely than had seemed possible. The effect upon the commerce and the morale of the nation was more destructive than the comparatively limited disaster of the South Sea Company in England.

The paper notes, which had been intended to bring wealth without exertion to so many French investors, were now worth no more than the paper itself. Some of those who held them decided that the best use for the bills was to stock the privy. One darling of society, Mazé, who had some reputation as an actress, took her loss more seriously. Carefully rouged and in flesh-coloured stockings, so that her beauty might be admired without unseemly exposure, she went ceremoniously to the Seine while her admirers looked on, and threw herself in.

Economic ruin came hardest upon those with most to lose. The Comte de Sade, like many patricians of his time, found that the general effects spread outwards from Law's catastrophe through the financial life of France until even the foundations of landed wealth were attacked. Great estates must be of questionable value if the tenants were unable to pay their master his rent. Nor was it a matter which he could deal with closely or systematically. The duty of a Comte de Sade was to serve his king in war and diplomacy rather than to administer widely separated estates. A lawyer or a bailiff might manage the lands, collecting rents and revenues on behalf of his master. It was not even necessary for that master to leave his duties or his pleasures in the capital.

The decay of the French economy and the encroachment of a new poverty upon the lives of ordinary families did not, of course, threaten the Sades with immediate bankruptcy. But the Comte de Sade's indebtedness increased and this, in turn, affected many of the decisions to be taken about the future of his infant son. Little Donatien-Alphonse-François must make a marriage of financial prudence, when the time came. Not that this need prove irksome. The Comte de Sade took marriage very seriously but he was perhaps not unaware of the current Parisian witticisms on the subject. According to one of them, it had been the custom for devout Christians in the early years of the Church to show their chastity by not making love to their brides for three nights following the wedding. "But nowadays," said the wits, "those are the only three nights when their wives ever see them."

The world of such moral ironies and social fragilities was every bit as much the child's inheritance as the estates of Mazan or Saumane and the hilltop château of La Coste.

THREE

THE CHILD'S WORLD

1

EVEN IN EXTREME INFANCY, Sade was to show, as he himself recalled in the fictional context of *Aline and Valcour*, that he was "proud, angry, and passionate" to a degree that would win him international notoriety before his life was half over.

> I was related on my mother's side to the highest nobility of France, and on my father's side to the most distinguished families of Languedoc. However, I was born in Paris among great wealth and luxury. As soon as I was able to believe anything at all, I concluded that Nature and Fortune had combined to shower their gifts upon me. And I believed this more firmly because of the stupid way in which people were always assuring me of it.

The little Sade, indulged and admired, acquired the traditional failings of an only child. He became the infant despot of his world at the Condé Palace. The death of "Monsieur le Duc" in 1740, at the age of forty-eight, was followed by that of his wife, the Princess Caroline, in the following year. The Comtesse de Sade now remained in the Condé Palace, guardian and governess, caring for the orphaned Prince Louis-Joseph and her own son, who was four years younger. But though Louis-Joseph de Bourbon might be the elder child, it was not his personality which dictated events in the Condé Palace nursery. The comtesse and her companions had good reason to observe with unease the development of her son's character. It was necessary, he wrote later, that everyone should yield to his will and submit to his childish demands. Having secured their accession to one set of demands, he would then change them arbitrarily merely in order to see his commands obeyed by his female elders.

Perhaps it seemed to matter less than he thought. There were always reasons for hoping that the child would outgrow his ill-natured and wilful inclinations. But then, in the summer of 1744, there was a nursery scandal. Sade and Prince Louis-Joseph, who was twice his age, had been playing together. It had been hoped that a gentle upbringing in a largely female household would impart a softness of manner and a lack of physical belligerence. This was a serious miscalculation, since it seemed only to irritate Sade's feelings against the rule of women and against matriarchy in its more precise sense.

On this summer day, the game the two children were playing became tiresome. There was a squabble. Louis-Joseph de Bourbon asserted his seniority both by age and social rank. The little Marquis de Sade thereupon flew at the older boy and began to beat him up with the energy of uncontrolled fury. So it was said. Sade was lightly built and, if anything, a little effeminate in his appearance. But the determination of the attack was unnerving. Prince Louis-Joseph, unable to defend himself against such an assault, endured what Sade called "a good drubbing". Only when the howls of Bourbon nobility brought some of the adults to the scene was the infant marquis dragged off his victim.

A fight between two children, even of the bluest blood, ought not to have counted for much. But the style and severity of Sade's attack led to a conference among the adults at the Condé Palace. The atmosphere was something like an expulsion from school, when none of the ordinary sanctions can meet the gravity of the offence. In that spirit of sorrowful rejection, it was decided that the four-year-old Sade must leave the palace. But where was he to go? The Comte de Sade had his duties at the Court of the Elector of Cologne. The comtesse would sooner or later have to join him.

A diplomatic mission was no place for an aggressive four-year-old. It was decided that Sade should be sent to Avignon to live with his paternal grandmother, for the time being. Accordingly, he parted company with his parents and the Condé Palace, arriving in Provence for the first time in August 1744. The village council of Saumane hastened to send an obsequious message, welcoming the troublesome infant to Provence as their lord and master.

Life in the elegant townhouse of the Sades at Avignon was agreeable, if only because Grandmother Sade misunderstood the reason for the boy's arrival. Knowing nothing of the rumpus at the Condé Palace, she assumed the role of comforter and consoler to a poor child bereft of his parents by their diplomatic duties. It was an agreeable exile. There were indulgent aunts, respectful cousins and playmates, including Gaspard-François-Xavier Gaufridy who was to be an attorney in the Provençal town of Apt, east of La Coste. Gaufridy also took on the emotionally exhausting task of being Sade's lawyer and was one of his most frequent correspondents. But in 1744 the old lady's pride in her grandson was misplaced. As Sade wrote from a prison cell four decades later, she attended to his demands with blind devotion. "She succeeded in strengthening all my faults." His grandmother discovered this for herself by the following year. The child's behaviour was intolerable and she could stand no more. Another guardian must be found for the little wretch.

Fortunately, Avignon was close to the three châteaux of the Sades: La Coste, Saumane, and Mazan. The Comte de Sade's youngest brother, Jacques-François, Abbé de Sade, occupied Saumane. In France, as in England, it was the custom of many families of rank to "give" one son to the Church. In the case of the Abbé de Sade, the Church had reason to view this generosity with misgiving.

Yet the Abbé de Sade, worldly cleric and biographer of Petrarch, was a far more sympathetic guardian to his nephew than the women of the Condé Palace or the unwisely indulgent grandmother at Avignon. The château of Saumane was some twenty miles north-east of Avignon. It was a further remove from the tamed landscape of the Luxembourg Gardens.

Saumane stood high and remote on a southern spur of the Vaucluse, looking out across the terraced expanse of Provence towards the blue distance of the Luberon and the last mountain barrier before the sea. The château at the northern end of the spur was approached up a hillside path from the village. Saumane itself was no more than a single street of narrow houses in pale Provençal stone, running between the square bell-tower below the château and the church at the far end. It was not easy of access, the land dropping steeply on either side to the wooded valleys below. The harshness of the stone was softened by the feathery pink of tamarisk trees and the blossom of cherry trees in spring.

In spiritual matters Saumane was directly subject to the papacy. In temporal affairs it was answerable to the Governor of Mazan, who was also Seigneur of Saumane. The Sades being lords of Mazan and Saumane, it had seemed appropriate to install the Abbé de Sade, who divided his life between Provence and the Auvergne. Despite the substantial ramparts of the château, which incorporated the rock of the hillside, the building and its grounds on their small plateau were a pleasant estate rather than a fortress. Saumane provided the abbé's creature comforts. He was able to devote himself to Petrarch and a fine library, as well as to the formal gardens and fountains of his home. Above the walls rose the layered green tops of umbrella pines. The château combined dramatic scenery and enclosed luxury in a manner that anticipated Silling as his infant nephew would one day describe it in *The 120 Days of Sodom*. Even the surroundings of Saumane added to the pleasures of nature and the prestige of the Sades. A few miles away lay the romantic gorge of Petrarch's isolation and the tumbling green water of the Fontaine de Vaucluse. Separated even from the single street of Saumane, the Abbé de Sade preferred to ignore the tiresome suggestion of celibacy, a discipline which he never contrived to master. When he died in 1777, the Sade family discovered that the Abbé had been consoled by a Spanish lady and her daughter, whose services he rewarded by selling them part of the estate at a bargain price. His nephew was left to get the property back as best he could.

At five or six years old, the young Marquis de Sade lived in surroundings that would have done credit to the wilder romanticism of lowering rocks and foaming water in Salvator Rosa's paintings, to the opening landscapes of the Gothic novel and, not least, to such settings of his own fiction as Roland's fortress, described by the heroine in *Justine*.

At four in the afternoon, we came to the foot of the mountains. At that point the road became almost impassable. We passed into the gorges and Roland told the mule-driver not to leave me, in case of an accident. We did nothing but climb and descend for more than ten miles and we were so far beyond any habitation or any clear road that it seemed like the verge of the universe. I felt a little uneasy, despite myself. Roland could not help seeing this but he said nothing and his silence troubled me still more. At last we saw a castle, perched on the crest of a mountain above a dreadful precipice into which it seemed about to fall. One could see no road leading there. The one we were now following was suitable only for the goats and was full of stones everywhere. But it brought us at last to this menacing lair, which looked more like a thieves' den than a dwelling of virtuous folk.

To a child of strong imagination, Saumane and its surroundings would easily evoke images of brigandage and dark practices of a kind that appealed suggestively to the eighteenth-century sensibility. When Sade infused sexuality into such practices and offered heroines to his brigands, he merely went beyond the point of suggestion, at which most novelists of the Gothic prudently drew back. The heroine's arrival at Roland's castle was in keeping with his transgression of such limits.

"I have brought you to serve the coiners, of whom I am the chief," said Roland, seizing me by the arm and forcing me across a little bridge which was lowered at our arrival and immediately raised again afterwards.

"You see that well?" he continued when we were inside, showing me a large and deep cave at the end of the courtyard, where four naked women were chained to a wheel which they were turning, "There are your companions and there is your work. Provided that you work ten hours a day turning the wheel and that, like the other girls, you satisfy whatever desires I wish you to submit to, you shall be given six ounces of black bread and a plate of beans every day. As for your liberty – forget it. . . ."

Sade's fiction was very nearly an exact contemporary of Ann Radcliffe's *The Queen of Terrors* in the circulating libraries of London and Brighton, Bath and Cheltenham. But the drawing-room and schoolmiss Gothic of the English middle class did not even hint at such sexuality as Sade's melodramas offered. His heroine describes, for example, the fate of Suzanne and the other young women chained to Roland's wheel.

If we were naked, it was not only because of the heat but the better to receive the strokes of the leather whip which our fierce master inflicted from time to time. In winter we were given pants and vest that were skin-tight, so that our bodies were no less exposed to the lashes of this rogue, whose sole pleasure was to beat us unmercifully in this manner.

Sade also writes in his fiction with an easy geographical knowledge of France, from Normandy to Marseille, from Bordeaux to the Rhine. He travelled on military duty and as a fugitive, recording descriptions of towns and landscapes which were to serve him well. His travels began when he was still a small child at Saumane. In the summer, the Abbé de Sade and his young nephew made a pilgrimage westwards across the Rhône and into the Auvergne. The abbé went to attend to his living of the Abbey Church of St Léger at Ebreuil. The little town lay between Clermont-Ferrand and Vichy, within sight of the heights of Puy de Dôme. St Léger was a foursquare romanesque church, its interior still decorated by frescoes of early apostles and bishops. Unlike Saumane, it stood among streams and meadows, just short of the first gorges of the Auvergne at Chauvigny. At Chauvigny began a land of rivers and dark hills, ancient and isolated mills perched here and there along the banks. Landscape again reflected the mood of the beholder. In Sade's case the image of the women at Roland's wheel found ample inspiration in such scenes.

When winter came on, the abbé and the child returned to Saumane. The roads across the high open plateaux were easily lost under drifts of early snow. If Sade needed a true progress to the château of Silling, where the heroes retire with their victims to celebrate the 120 days in winter isolation, the memories of a journey from Ebrueil to Saumane might have served him well. Once again, at home with his uncle, savagery of scene and luxury of provision combined as they were to do in fiction. Saumane in winter was isolated but the Abbé de Sade was able to assemble his comforts and to indulge his interests as an antiquary. For years he had remained preoccupied by his ancient documents and family records, happily pottering among those papers which would one day produce his great life of Petrarch, establishing beyond doubt the poet's indebtedness to Laura de Sade.

The child's sense of scene and drama was free to develop in

several years of semi-idleness. The mountain range, the steep wooded gorges and the swift rivers of the Vaucluse were infused by the excitement and promise of pleasure, tyranny and that uncontrolled self-indulgence in which the villains of remote châteaux might relieve their compulsions. The weeks of winter isolation were a time well suited for elaborating the dream, among the society of the abbé and his guests. Indeed, the structure of the château at Saumane – its underground vaults, fine stairway, gallery, apartments, casements piercing the massive lower walls above the valley – were to be characteristic fixtures and furnishings of Sade's novels.

In all these years with the abbé, the boy had little formal education. But he lived in a house where learning and antiquarian interest were instinctive. Moreover, his introduction to the life of rural Provence bore fruit in the shorter stories that he later wrote. These were tales derived, as he said, from the remote hilltop villages like Saumane and La Coste, some of the narratives having circulated as traditional folk humour. He wrote of communities living where the rocky slopes were so steep and the stone paths so precipitous that the goats could scarcely climb them, and where the sexual morals of the inhabitants were a match for those of the same goats.

In "The Married Preacher", he describes a priory near La Coste which was commonly regarded as a refuge for drunkards, womanizers, sodomites and gamblers. One of the "saints" of this hermitage was Father Gabriel, who took a fancy to a young wife in the village, Madame Rodin, "a little brunette, twenty-eight years old, with a saucy look and a round bottom". Father Gabriel, approaching the husband, swore that there was a man about to leave the area without paying back money that he owed the priest. Unless Gabriel reached him at once, it would be too late. Unfortunately, there was still one mass to be said. Rodin knew a little Latin, though he was not a priest. Would he be so good as to say the last remaining mass for Father Gabriel? Rodin's queries about the propriety of this were set aside by the most ludicrous assurances. While Rodin said the mass, the curé went to the young wife and satisfied her "more than once". Sade remarks that Father Gabriel, "being equipped like a stallion", had no difficulty in seducing "a young trollop of such a warm southern temperament".

When Rodin returned, Gabriel assured him that he had got what he wanted and had marked his victim on the forehead. As soon as the couple were alone, however, Rodin told his wife that he knew the curé for a seducer who had made a cuckold of some husband or other. He felt sure that it was the debtor who had been cuckolded and laughed heartily at such folly among married men. Then he told his wife of the mass which he had said in Gabriel's place. The young wife replied that she, too, had had a religious experience that morning. She hinted to Rodin that he must prepare himself to find her pregnant by means akin to virgin birth, as a consequence of this celestial visit.

If Sade as a boy lacked formal education, he was soon well versed in the antiquarian culture and worldly pleasures of Saumane and Ebreuil. It was later to seem as if the seeds of literary ambition and libertinage had germinated with equal success under the easy-going tutelage of the Abbé de Sade.

2

When the child was ten years old it was decided that his uncle's benevolent and scholarly example must be replaced by orthodox schooling. Perhaps this was as well. The household at Saumane was soon to be revealed publicly as a ménage of devotion to pleasure and a certain moral cynicism. Given the signs of violence and wilfulness in the child's character, he might benefit from a rigorous moral counter-balance to his years in Provence.

This was to be provided by a return to Paris and enrolment at the Collège Louis-le-Grand. The fortunes of the Sade family had changed somewhat and the son was even more a stranger to his parents than might ordinarily have been the case. The Comte de Sade had had a row with the Elector of Cologne in 1743, when the elector accused him of selling favours. It was not impossible that he had done so. On the other hand, the elector liked gambling but he also liked winning. Diplomats were advised to lose gracefully to him and perhaps the Comte de Sade had been tactless. Downright corruption certainly seems to have been out of character.

After the Comte de Sade returned to France, the comtesse decided to take up residence in the Carmelite convent of rue de

L'Enfer, where she lived until her death. When her son returned to Paris at ten years old, he was not to be under the immediate influence of either parent. Close to the Condé Palace, the Collège Louis-le-Grand was a school of social and intellectual prestige, run by the Jesuit order. Among its more distinguished pupils were Voltaire and Diderot in the eighteenth century and Baudelaire in the nineteenth. In the tradition of his age and class, Sade not only had his own rooms there but his own private tutor, the Abbé Amblet. The Abbé was to remain his mentor in adult life and, indeed, had the disagreeable duty of escorting Sade on his first journey to imprisonment. Sade himself, writing in middle age, named the Abbé Amblet as the first teacher of true intellect and principle whom he had encountered.

For the next four years, until he was fourteen, Sade remained at his school, deriving from it the benefits of order and system, which had been lacking at Saumane. He took easily to the demands of the curriculum and was to be described with some justice as one of the most widely read of all French authors. Indeed, the régime of the college lingered in his imagination, emerging three decades later in his fiction. History gave him the material and mathematics the obsessive structure underpinning the grotesque world of such books as *The 120 Days of Sodom*. His letters from prison used a system of personal mathematics, in which the figures of his calculations became potent and veiled symbols. In his fictional harems, the number of libertine heroes would equal the square root of the number of boys and girls serving them, or of the number of wives, bawds and gigolos who were to assist at the orgies.

The strict discipline and system of Louis-le-Grand were mirrored in the laws of such sexual despotisms as the château of Silling or the community of Ste Marie-des-Bois in *Justine*. Though devoted to the practice of perverse sexual indulgence, his palaces of pleasure are like strictly run schools and the demands made of the female slaves require in them the temperament of well-behaved schoolgirls. Like Swinburne and so many Sadean figures of the nineteenth century, the marquis offered a sardonic burlesque of moral education.

But the Collège Louis-le-Grand also offered pleasures that had been lacking in Saumane and Ebreuil. One of the chief recreations at the school was the performance of plays. Sade's enthusiasm for the theatre began early and continued throughout his life. He was to have little success as a dramatist and, on the surviving evidence, comparatively little talent or originality. But during his long imprisonment, he consoled himself by reading plays in the hope, as he said, that he might become a successor to Corneille, Racine and the great tragic dramatists of France in the seventeenth century. His gifts lay elsewhere but his ambition was stimulated by the heroic drama and the carefully chosen comedies which the Jesuit teachers encouraged their pupils to emulate.

After four years of formal instruction in ancient literature, religion, history and mathematics, Sade left the college. His next step was to acquire a certificate of nobility, establishing his ancestry. Armed with this, he exercised his right to enter the Light Cavalry School at Versailles. Though Europe was at peace, after the war of the Austrian Succession ended in 1748, he had chosen his career. Like his father, he would begin as a soldier.

It cost the Comte de Sade three thousand livres for his son's year at the military academy. On 5 December 1755, the boy was promoted from ensign to second lieutenant in the Royal Foot Guards. It was an unpaid appointment but it relieved the Comte de Sade from further expenditure on his son's education. All that could be done for Donatien-Alphonse-François had now been done. Despite his slight build and rather soft good looks, he seemed able to unleash enough suppressed ferocity to carry him through half a dozen battles. He needed only a war to prove himself. Monsieur de Castéra, a witness of this, wrote to the Comte de Sade saying that his son needed rather to be restrained than encouraged. Similar opinions were held by Sade's senior officers, one of whom noted of him: "Quite crack-brained but very brave."

Europe was still technically at peace when Sade became a second lieutenant in December 1755. But the British naval commander Admiral Boscawen, operating off Newfoundland, had already begun to interfere with French shipping in the north-west Atlantic. In a carefully registered protest, Louis XV withdrew his ambassadors from the twin courts of England and Hanover. By the spring of 1756 there were rumours of war as the French regiments marched south to Toulon, their port of embarkation on the Mediterranean, and eastwards in support of their Austrian ally against Frederick of Prussia. Faced with these preparations,

England declared war on France formally in May 1756, contributing Hanoverian troops and financial subsidies to the Prussian campaign. But France had won the initiative. Within days of England's declaration of war, the French fleet defeated Admiral Byng's squadron from Gibraltar, then seized Minorca and the British naval base of Port Mahon. On 16 June, France declared herself at war with England.

There was every hope that victory in what was later termed the Seven Years War would prove the salvation of France, of Louis XV, and of the patrician order. In place of moral cynicism, pleasure-seeking, and a drift towards political anarchy, evident since the death of Louis XIV in 1715, the nation faced the challenge of a fierce military struggle on three continents, tempered by the promise of a triumphant peace. The news from the Mediterranean was good. Reports from North America were better still. For all Admiral Boscawen's harrying, the French land forces and their Indian allies had so demoralized the English colonists that, as one British officer remarked, the French might take the whole of Virginia and Maryland simply by going there. As if this were not enough, the reinforcements crossing the ocean from England suffered two thousand casualties from the scourge of "gaol fever", the typhus spreading through the crowded transports from petty criminals conscripted into the ranks.

It was true that in Europe itself the English had attempted two landings on the coast of France, but they were thrown back on both occasions. The true theatre of European war was in Germany, where Prussia was fighting Austria. More specifically, the French army was campaigning in the Rhineland. Sade obtained a transfer to the Marquis de Poyanne's Regiment of Foot. Resplendent in his royal blue uniform with scarlet facings, the new subaltern rode with his men across the Rhine and into the plains of northern Europe.

Sade and his regiment were part of the army commanded by the Comte d'Estrées, confronting the defenders of Hanover under George II's son, the Duke of Cumberland, the "Butcher" of the defeated Jacobites at Culloden in 1746. Estrées crossed the Weser and brought to bear the entire weight of the French army upon Cumberland's regiments at Hastenbeck on 26 July 1757. The attacks on Cumberland's position lasted for three days and ended in one of the most decisive French victories of the long war.

Cumberland acknowledged it, signing a surrender at Kloster-zeven and evacuating his father's Electorate of Hanover. Horace Walpole wrote to his friend Sir Thomas Mann on 4 August 1757, describing the despair of George II on hearing of the battle. "What a melancholy picture is there of an old monarch at Kensington, who has lived to see such inglorious and fatal days!"

But as Sade describes it in his own account of the German campaign, the buoyancy of victory in 1757 was lost by the following year. In January 1757, he was promoted to lieutenant. At a more important level, command of the French army on the Rhine passed to the Duc de Richelieu and then, in consequence of a court intrigue by Madame de Pompadour, to the Comte de Clermont, a distant kinsman of the Sades in the Condé family. Clermont had little grasp of strategy. Worse still, he bore like a cushion the impression of the last person who had sat on him. On 23 June 1758 he confronted Ferdinand of Brunswick at Crefeld.

On the day before the battle, Sade had watched the antics of the cavalry as the Hanoverians chased the French out of the town, only for the French horsemen to return and evict the Hanoverians in what seemed more like a game than a battle. On 23 June, Sade and his men woke to find that it was no game. They were under attack by the main Hanoverian army and had only just time to form a regular defence. Even as they did so, the Hanoverian artillery opened fire from the front and on both flanks. There were gun-flashes and drifts of smoke ahead of them as Sade's men took up their positions. Loose earth spouted from the nearby impact of the shells and ragged gaps appeared in the line as the hissing cannonballs scythed through its ranks. It was a most ungentlemanly combat, not in the least like Fontenoy in 1745, when the French officers were said to have stepped across to their opponents and said: "*Messieurs les Anglais*, fire first."

Sade saw the Hanoverian attack coming upon the front and the right flank. Among those who were killed by it was the Comte de Gisors, son of the Comte de Belle-Ile, Marshal of France. Then Sade realized that these were only diversions and that the main attack was coming from the left, where his own carabineers formed part of the defence. There was a scrimmage whose outcome seemed to be decided only by brute strength. The opposing troops faced one another at close range, Sade reported, hacking and hewing with their sabres at one another's heads. The French line at this point was pressed hard. Help was promised but, in the confusion, no help came. Fresh Hanoverian troops burst from the wood ahead, bearing down in a charge to break the French defence. Sade claimed that his own part of the line held, that his men fought like lions with their sabres and drove back the elite of the enemy infantry. The position was held until nightfall. Then, under cover of darkness, the "shadow of an army", as Clermont described his force, began a slow retreat towards the Rhine.

After this, there was little for Sade to celebrate in the rest of the campaign. Though there were night attacks on the enemy, one of which yielded four hundred prisoners, the victories were elsewhere. Nor was there much hope of personal advancement in the army. Sade informed his father that he lacked the pusillanimity to pay court to men of influence or to flatter fools in order to ingratiate himself. Only once or twice did he succeed in bringing himself to the attention of his superiors. There was an occasion when he saved a deserter from being executed, after the man had been abandoned to his fate by his entire regiment. Sade attracted notice of a different kind when he ordered the firing of a triumphal salute to celebrate a French victory at Sondershausen. The gun was so ineptly laid that a shell went through the roof of a nearby manor house. Lieutenant Sade was obliged to publish an apology to the local council. In doing so, he tactlessly suggested that while the local dignitaries might be rather upset at the accident, they would surely understand and forgive him when they realized the natural jubilation of celebrating a victory by his nation over theirs.

Other news of Sade came back to France from his travelling companion Castéra, who reported that the young Marquis had proved "inflammable" when confronted by the local girls. There were no further details and, in any case, the effect of German girls on him soon ceased to matter. Sade remarked in 1779 that the best way to learn a language was to have a mistress to whom it was native. He had done this in Germany, choosing a fat jolly baroness who was a good deal more than his own age.

As the war turned against France and the casualties increased, there were vacancies in many regiments. In April 1759 Sade bought his captaincy in the Burgundian Cavalry. But the war, apart from routine cavalry patrols, was nothing to him after that. On his visits to Paris, keeping clear of his father and his childhood mentors, he took quickly to a life of sexual discovery.

It seems to have been a solitary and dispiriting existence in the end. "Friends, like women, are often found false," he concluded sourly. By his own account, he would sleep too much and get up late. Each morning he set out to look for a girl who could be hired for the day. By the evening, when he had satisfied his curiosity with her, he sometimes felt rather ashamed of himself. He was, after all, still a benevolent young man. But on waking the following morning he found that his passion burnt fiercely again and he began the search for that day's partner.

It was not surprising that news of this should reach his family, at a time when even the largest of European cities was still a town that could be walked end to end with ease. Sade thereupon had a bad attack of remorse. He wrote to the Abbé Amblet, confessing his folly and his thoughtlessness. Sade admitted that he had never loved any of the girls, which was no doubt true, and he now realized that none of them could have brought him happiness. These regrets might have been moral clichés to reassure the Abbé Amblet and the Comte de Sade but there was no evidence yet that the young man had indulged in the more extreme pleasures which were to bring him to public notoriety very soon.

Protesting his grief at the sorrow he had caused the Comte de Sade, "the kindest of fathers and the best of friends", the young marquis gave the impression of an essentially decent young man who had been led from the brink of ruin just in time. For the moment, he returned to war and the pursuit of glory.

But the queue for glory had lengthened considerably in his absence and the commodity itself was in short supply. The war, which had begun so promisingly for France, now threatened national catastrophe. By the attack on Quebec in 1759, the British had struck at the heart of French power in North America. In Europe, the military initiative had passed to the armies of Prussia and Hanover. The French army in the field seemed increasingly to decline the challenge to battle. This was scarcely surprising since the Duc de Choiseul, Louis XV's prime minister, had already begun secret peace negotiations with the English, which were not so secret as he might have wished. There was no purpose to the war and no enthusiasm for it. When it ended in 1763, Sade left the army, though not before the major of his regiment had spoken to a family friend, Monsieur de Saint-German, of the "dreadful things" of which Sade was guilty in his private life.

If the Comte de Sade paid less attention to this allegation than he might have done, it was perhaps because he was distracted by a greater scandal. The storm from which the Abbé de Sade's relaxed sexual attitudes had been sheltered in the privacy of Saumane now broke upon him in Paris. He had got on well in the game of ecclesiastical preferment, becoming Vicar-General of Narbonne and Toulouse. Yet his acquaintances, including Voltaire, had noticed that the new vicar-general's attitude towards young women lacked pure spirituality. He was particularly enthusiastic about his occasional excursions from Provence to Paris and, perhaps, his new sense of prestige in the Church got the better of his natural discretion. He reckoned without a new vigilance on the part of the police. Early in 1762, he had paid a visit to Madame Piron, a sexually versatile lady with a reputation for moral frailty. This, too, was a miscalculation. But the Abbé de Sade was ambitious to try the talents of Madame Piron in the company of her girl Léonore, who was a known prostitute. The agents of the police broke in upon the party and found the fifty-year-old Vicar-General of Narbonne and Toulouse deeply compromised with the two young women. Perhaps he had drawn attention to himself, though it seems to have been mere bad luck, on his part, that the establishment should have been raided on that night.

As it happened, the Abbé de Sade's period of detention was only a short one and no real harm was done to his personal or ecclesiastical reputation. Any suggestion that he must cease being vicar-general or that the living of St Léger d'Ebreuil should be taken from him would have then appeared as mere vindictiveness. All the same, it was advisable that he should retire to Provence until the gossip died down and that he should be more prudent on his future visits to Paris and Madame Piron. Voltaire had anticipated a scandal of this sort, viewing his friend's ecclesiastical career with genial scepticism in a verse letter.

> Behold the perfect minister!
> You shall love and you shall please,
> Triumphant always as you share
> The Church and Cythera, with equal ease.

The abbé had been a major influence and example in his nephew's childhood. His conduct may have removed the last of

Sade's hesitations in giving free expression to his own passions. If so, this was compounded by the Comte de Sade's decision to withdraw from the world and contemplate his own mortality, as the comtesse had already done. Indeed, he had some reason for his decision. The first signs of dropsy were upon him, the failure of vital organs was already allowing the accumulation of fluid. He sought relief, rather than a cure, from the waters of Plombières. Doctors might even sweat the dropsy out in a few milder cases. More probably the Comte de Sade would have to undergo "tapping", the drawing off of as much as ten or fifteen quarts of fluid at a time by means of a sharp trochar inserted into the abdominal cavities. The relief given by this remedy would be short lived. It would have to be done with increasing frequency and the patient's condition would grow inexorably worse.

Yet the example of the Abbé de Sade seemed one more proof that the pious order of Louis XIV had been swept away for ever. Political anarchy was coming and moral anarchy, even among the abbés, had already arrived. The tide of moral change moved with such rapidity that beliefs and loyalties which had once seemed immutable were now swept away like the fashions of a summer season. The public brothel and the private *petite maison* not only opened the gates on a sexual paradise, they offered a new philosophy of existence better suited to the age. Time was short and the "deluge", as Louis XV called it, was a mere quarter of a century away. Sade was to spend the greater part of that time in prison but in his periods of liberty he followed the prevailing fashion.

In his case, the perversity and cruelty which were alleged to inspire his sexual emotions seemed so powerful that, a year after his return from the war, the brothel-keepers of Paris were warned against him by Louis Marais, inspector of police in the city with particular responsibility for public morals. Marais visited Madame Brissault, a well-known brothel-keeper of the fashionable world with houses at the Barrière-Blanche and in rue Tire-Bourdin. Knowing that Sade was in Paris, Marais noted, "I have strongly recommended to La Brissault, without divulging further details to her, that she should not supply any more girls to accompany him to *petites maisons*." The *petite maison*, as a secret haven for the private pleasures of the titled and the wealthy, had become a symbol of well-heeled lechery. Its seclusion and security made it ideal for the excitements which Sade appeared to have in mind.

FOUR

The Philosophic Libertine

1

THE POLICE HAD BETTER GROUNDS than mere suspicion or rumour for their warning to Madame Brissault. On 19 October 1763, Louis Marais was confronted by a young woman of twenty, a fan-maker by trade. Though she was part of a shifting artisan population in the city, she had been lodging for some weeks at the Café Montmartre among the tall crowded buildings of rue Montmartre, north of the spacious grandeur of the Palais Royal and the Louvre. Jeanne Testard made too little money from her fans and in the evenings she supplemented her wages by working as a prostitute. But she was not an ordinary street-girl. She had an arrangement with Madame du Rameau, keeper of one of the smarter brothels in rue St Honoré, whereby she would cater for selected clients of the better class. Madame du Rameau's establishment, in the neighbourhood of the royal palaces, was what was known in the trade as an "introducing house". Jeanne Testard was a careful girl in the manner of exercising her profession but on the night of 18 October 1763 she had made a near-fatal mistake. Badly frightened by it, she had come to the police to tell her story.

That evening, at about eight o'clock, she had been taken to rue St Honoré, where a client was waiting for her. She was paid a handsome fee of two louis d'or to spend the night with him at his *petite maison*. He was a young man of aristocratic appearance. Without giving his name, she described him as fair-haired, slightly built and about twenty-two years old. The young man's servant, La Grange, escorted the girl to a hired carriage and she was driven across the Seine and through the darkened city to faubourg St Marceau, east of the Luxembourg Gardens. The carriage stopped outside a yellow-painted gateway and the iron railings of an elegant house where the young client took her to a room on the first floor.

He locked the door of this room, pocketed the key and questioned her about her religious beliefs. Then he began to boast of the acts he had committed with other girls, many of them involving blasphemy or sacrilege of some kind. During the course of this he appeared to brandish his fist at heaven and cried, "If you are God, let's see you take revenge on me!" It was certainly a challenge that ran through Sade's fiction of religious rebellion. Jeanne Testard was already unnerved before he opened the door to an inner room, which was to be the scene of the night's events. It was arranged as if for some obscene ritual with religious images and erotic pictures, several birch rods and five whips. At this point, the young woman tried to dissuade him from his purpose by saying she was pregnant. But this merely brought a promise from the young man to make unnatural use of her, as she demurely phrased it.

Far worse was the young client's other promise to employ the whips hanging on the black-draped wall. Some of these were exceptionally barbaric, their thongs tipped with metal which was to be heated before use. First she was to use one of the whips on him, then he would use one on her. She might perform her part in play but the young man showed every sign of being in earnest. However, as a courtesy, he would let her choose the one by which she was to suffer. Before they came to this, he proposed to perform various physical experiments upon her body, in order to watch its workings as he might have done with a beautiful and intricate machine. Douches and enemas were what he appeared to have in mind, among the ghastly surroundings of the black inner room. He never doubted for one moment that she would submit to sodomy or any other preliminary demand, for that was his least expectation of her.

Had Jeanne Testard been a more sophisticated young woman, it might have crossed her mind that the whole thing was an elaborate joke, perhaps imitated from the schoolboy antics of the Hell Fire Club in England, whose members represented the bluest of blood and the most lethargic of political heavyweights. Rites of that sort were sometimes undergraduate iconoclasm but more often they were amateur theatricals that had little more excitement than the humdrum pages of the drawing-room

Gothic novel. In this case the young woman took the sensible view that she was locked in a room alone with a dangerous lunatic who meant every word that he said. He did not talk about whipping or sodomizing her as if it were a prank. Indeed, when he had done all these things to the girl, his only security would be in silencing her. Jeanne Testard might be lucky not to end up in the river with her throat cut. If that happened, it was unlikely that Madame du Rameau of the "introducing house" in rue St Honoré would implicate herself in the crime by coming forward to tell her story. The girl would be just one more body in the Seine.

Jeanne Testard controlled her terror sufficiently to try to talk her way out of her predicament. By this time the young man had produced pistols and a sword, assuring her that she must die unless she submitted to his commands. She coaxed him back on to the subject of sacrilege and promised him that, though her physical condition prevented her from obeying all his present commands, she would become his assistant in black magic. She would, for example, meet him at seven o'clock next Sunday morning and accompany him to mass. They would conceal the consecrated wafers given them by the priest, return to the sinister room and indulge in a memorable orgy. She would surrender herself more energetically to such perversities than she felt able to that night. This pleased the young man sufficiently to stop him talking about the whippings and the other diversions he had planned for her just then. Though there was no sleep for the young woman, she knew that if she could delay for long enough, Madame du Rameau's hired carriage would be calling to take her home. When it arrived at about nine o'clock in the morning, Jeanne Testard persuaded him to let her leave the house, still promising to meet him on the following Sunday. This was agreed and the young man now gave her a piece of paper with his signature on it, which she could not read.

That afternoon she went to the police. But the Paris police of the 1760s, like their London counterparts, consisted of officials who lived in their own houses. On the first two occasions, when Jeanne Testard called, she was told that the police were out. It was not until the evening that she was able to make her statement.

None of the details of the story taken alone would identify the young man as Sade. Nor, indeed, was there any evidence to corroborate Jeanne Testard's version of events. She would have been expected, for example, to insist that she never agreed to an act of sodomy since that was a crime for which she as well as the perpetrator might be burnt at the stake. The criminal code specified that this penalty was to be exacted from the woman who permitted such an act as well as from the man who initiated it.

The appearance of the young client and of his *petite maison* certainly suggested that he might be Sade. His defiance of heaven's vengeance, as though half hoping to incur it, and the nature of his sexual tastes make the identification stronger still. Divested of satanic paraphernalia, the acts which he proposed were of the kind for which he employed young women during the next dozen years. Sade was certainly in Paris. He had left Echauffour in Normandy, a hundred miles west of the city, on 15 October for a meeting at Fontainebleau with the prime minister, the Duc de Choiseul, in search of preferment. His period of military service was over and it was not unreasonable to expect that he might be found some diplomatic post, as his father had been. By 18 October, he was certainly within reach of the introducing house in rue St Honoré and the *petite maison* in faubourg St Marceau.

Louis Marais and his colleagues had one specific piece of evidence, the paper on which the young man had written his signature. Sade was arrested on 29 October and held on the authority of Antoine de Sartine, Lieutenant-General of Police, while the details of the incident were forwarded to the king. In the case of a nobleman, Louis XV might prefer to deal directly with the matter. Three weeks after his son's arrest, on 16 November, the Comte de Sade wrote to his brother the abbé at Saumane. The marquis had rented a *petite maison*, furnished on credit. There he had engaged in what the comte described as a *débauche outrée*, which so shocked the girls involved that they felt obliged to make statements to the police. The king was informed that such conduct should be punished with extreme rigour. Sade had been imprisoned in the Château of Vincennes, on the eastern edge of Paris. He was not tried nor sentenced and was to remain at Vincennes only until his family decided which prison might most conveniently be chosen for him. The Comte de Sade urged his brother to deny the truth of the story, if it should begin to spread in Provence, and not to say anything to Sade's aunts. As matters stood, Sade was to be transferred from Vincennes to Normandy, "so that it will be easier to destroy any rumours that may spread".

Even before this, on 2 November, Sade himself had written from Vincennes to Sartine. It was not the letter of a rebel or blasphemer but of a penitent – true or false. "I deserve Divine vengeance," he wrote. "My only occupation is to weep for my faults, to hate my sins. Alas! God may crush me without giving me time to acknowledge and feel them." By an irony of repentance, the young man now recognized that it was his neglect of the sacraments which had brought him to his present plight. He begged to be allowed a servant and suggested one who had set foot in his *petite maison* at Arcueil on only a single occasion.

In the course of the letter, Sade also refers to a book whose immorality now caused him trouble with the police. It had presumably been found and confiscated at the time of his arrest but there is no evidence that it was his own work. Certainly, the reference to the book does not suggest that he was arrested for a crime that had nothing whatever to do with Jeanne Testard. It indicates a second offence which he feared would be held against him, perhaps the possession of some pornographic volume which, like the "impious" prints which the girl reported seeing on the black-draped walls, belonged to his private collection. Twenty years later, while he was a prisoner at Vincennes, Sade wrote to his former tutor, the Abbé Amblet, about his first attempts at writing. He remarked that he made a good deal of money out of what may have been an erotic novel in the style of Pietro Aretino and none at all from his plays. What the earlier piece may have been, we do not know. His references suggest that it dates from the time of his travels in Holland during the autumn of 1769.

The letter which Sade wrote to Sartine on 2 November 1763 suggested that he was less a blasphemer than a joker, that indeed his antics in the *petite maison* had less to do with satanism than with the fancy-dress games that had been instituted ten years earlier by the Hell Fire Club in England. Sir Francis Dashwood, Lord Sandwich, John Wilkes and George Selwyn had been among its more prominent members, meeting first in the ruins of Medmenham Abbey on the Thames and then in excavated caverns on Dashwood's estate, near his fine Palladian mansion of West Wycombe. The proceedings were more like a costume ball than a black mass, the only moment of true terror being that at which Wilkes suddenly let loose a black baboon among his friends as they tried to raise the devil by flickering candlelight. The truth of the proceedings was summed up by an entry in the account book of a famous London brothel-keeper, Charlotte Hayes. "June 18, 1759. Twelve vestals for the Abbey. Something discreet and Cyprian for the friars." Like Sade's *petite maison*, the Hell Fire Club was as much a sexual gymnasium as a temple of devil-worship. Its *Idolum Tentiginis* was provided for the young women to ride, a hobby-horse with the head of a bird turned backwards and its beak shaped as a phallus.

Such rituals in England were able to masquerade as a ribald form of anti-Catholicism. Sade could scarcely plead this excuse. However, his penance was accepted. On 13 November, Louis XV signed an order for his release from Vincennes. The young lord was ordered to return to Echauffour where he would live under moral surveillance by his family. Yet there was a further cause for the shock felt by those who read of his conduct with Jeanne Testard and other girls. For six months, the Marquis de Sade had been a married man.

2

By 1763, Sade's relationships with young women were divided between those in which he hired partners for his private obsessions and others in which the girls represented an ideal of platonic or romantic courtship. It seemed that there was a dualism in his character and that he went to the grave with it unresolved. He had shown no inclination towards marriage and, indeed, he was to write to his aunt, Gabrielle-Éléonore de Sade, Abbess of St Benoît de Cavaillon, on 22 April 1790, insisting that his main reason for marrying had been to have people around to look after him in his old age.

Yet by the spring of 1763, almost twenty-three years old, Sade was at least prepared to consider candidates for the role of marquise. In March he visited Avignon, in pursuit of Mademoiselle

Laure-Victoire de Lauris, the daughter of an old-established Provençal family. For her he felt the greatest and most genuine passion of his early life. The Comte de Sade, his own health failing and eager to see his son settled, encouraged the courtship. There seems no doubt that Sade intended marriage. At the same time, the relationship was far from platonic. In a letter written to her from Avignon on 6 April, Sade pretends to great jealousy and threatens to reveal the secrets of their sexual intimacy to any rival that he may have. Mademoiselle de Lauris, then twenty-two years old, seemed an admirable choice as the future Marquise de Sade. The romance between the couple got no further than an engagement but she was to remain Sade's mistress.

April 1763, during his visit to Provence, was the occasion of Sade's first appearance at La Coste as his father's heir. The celebrations for his arrival were organized by his aunt, Madame de Villeneuve. The château of La Coste had been transformed from a hilltop fortress to a patrician residence by a former owner, Claude de Simiane, in the last years of the sixteenth century. The building passed to Sade's grandfather a century later. In its new form, it was reached by a massive exterior stone stairway from the upper level of the village on the north-east side, or by a gentler approach to the south-west through the olive and almond groves that had been planted in alleys to give shelter from the sun and the Mistral.

On that April day in 1763, Sade and his party arrived from the little town of Apt, across the plain to the east by way of the Roman bridge, the Pont Julien. He was met by a cavalcade of horsemen and flowered carts, ribboned shepherdesses and young men with cockades in their hats, pet lambs decked out with flowers and favours. In a scene that might have come from *The Marriage of Figaro*, there was an address of welcome and a peasant chorus was sung. The entire procession swept on and up to the château where there was a banquet and a ball to conclude the celebrations. Sade was to be in residence at La Coste on almost a dozen occasions before the prison of Vincennes closed upon him finally in 1778. The most flattering attentions among the welcoming party came from a girl of sixteen, Marie-Dorothée de Rousset, who was to be Sade's companion at the château fifteen years later.

Whatever Sade's difficulties, the village of La Coste remained loyal to him until the shift of allegiances brought about by the Revolution a quarter of a century after his arrival. La Coste, in 1770, had 430 inhabitants divided into 110 families. It also had a tradition of intellectual dissent, far removed from that of Catholic obedience in southern Europe. Religious dissent had been common in the village during the sixteenth century and in 1663 it had been necessary to ban Protestant worship. Under Louis XV such worship was tolerated so long as it did not appear obtrusive. Pastors held services in barns or in the fields round the village. Yet by the 1770s, when the forces of law descended upon La Coste, it still seemed that the incorrigible Marquis de Sade and the troublesome Protestants might be equally the objects of the search.

While Sade was in Provence during the early spring of 1763, his father had been considering other possibilities. It was plain that the family finances now depended on the young man making the right marriage. Among the bridal candidates on the Comte de Sade's list was Renée-Pélagie, the twenty-year-old daughter of Claude-René Cordier de Launay, Président de Montreuil, who presided over the Court of Aides, and whose function was to raise money through taxation in order to provide subsidies or welfare payments for those in need. The Comte de Sade met and liked the Montreuil parents. They were the best and most honest type of people in his view.

The Montreuil family was in no way comparable with the Sades in nobility but its financial standing was a good deal sounder. As the Comte de Sade remarked, Renée-Pélagie had only one sister, though there was also a girl of three, and an even younger boy, with whom to share the immediate family inheritance. She also had a childless aunt. Her mother, Marie-Madeleine Masson de Plissay, Présidente de Montreuil, came from a family which had been successful in public life and had amassed an impressive fortune. She and her husband were able to afford a socially advantageous marriage to a more ancient line, so that the triumph of the Montreuils might be displayed to the world. The Sade family was impeccable in its lineage and it was probably as close to an alliance with the royal house of Bourbon as the Montreuils might ever hope to get.

Renée-Pélagie's inheritance was likely to be over two hundred thousand livres and indeed, one hundred and sixty thousand livres awaited her on her marriage. Sade himself might look forward to an annual income of some forty thousand livres after his father's death.

In more romantically sensitive times, the decision taken by the Sades and the Montreuils might have precipitated an emotional scene or two, a passionate refusal, perhaps even an elopement. But Sade took the news with philosophic calm. Marriage was not synonymous with sexual love. Mademoiselle de Lauris might remain his mistress in Provence, while Renée-Pélagie de Montreuil was his wife in Normandy or Paris. In Paris itself, his enthusiasm for the theatre was exceeded by his eagerness to be the lover of some of its actresses. For the most part, his sexual pleasures with young women of the theatre and the ballet were orthodox enough. But he must have reflected that the fright or bewilderment of street girls confronted by his proposed sexual melodramas was, after all, frustrating. Far better, perhaps, to interest an accomplished performer in the dark games that he chose to play. If he could confine his activities within these bounds, it seemed unlikely that his family would trouble themselves much further.

Renée-Pélagie de Montreuil was a striking brunette, tall and stately with dark eyes of great beauty, though rather plain in her facial features. But her younger sister, Anne-Prospère de Launay, offered a physical and emotional contrast, fair-haired and blue-eyed, more lively and even frivolous in her manner. Though she was to become the more withdrawn, studious and enigmatic of the sisters, Anne-Prospère at first looked and acted younger than her age, with something of the air of an inexperienced schoolgirl at eighteen. She showed a tendency to hero-worship and seemed apt to flirt with her future brother-in-law. In his letters, Sade later recalled an incident at this time, when the family was visiting the Château d'Evry. A child was in the path of a runaway carriage and, at the risk of his own life, he had dashed out and snatched it from danger. A drama of that sort, before the eyes of Anne-Prospère, could have done no harm whatever to the reputation of the gallant young cavalry officer with whom her family was now united.

Just before the marriage, it was alleged that Sade had tried to get the contract altered with a view to marrying the younger sister rather than her more statuesque and phlegmatic elder. Any suggestion of an exchange of partners was dismissed by Madame de Montreuil. Perhaps there was something in her future son-in-law's suggestion that put her on her guard. Anne-Prospère's youth and eagerness were appealing to Sade. But it was as yet only in the harems of his imagination that girls of her kind, though still in their early teens, played a vivid and unwilling part in the orgies and the horrors.

Madame de Montreuil herself was to be a decisive and sinister influence in Sade's life, by his own estimate. To the world at large she had what her son-in-law called charm enough to attract the devil and, in her physical charm, there was a reminder that she still appeared in the prime of life, young enough to have a child of three. Despite the hostility that Sade felt for her, she was described by Sade's friend Mademoiselle de Rousset as lively and seductive. She was petite, witty, energetic and impressed the Comte de Sade as being good company. She joined in Sade's enthusiasm for amateur theatricals and, at her brother's house in April 1764, took part in two plays with Sade and Renée-Pélagie. There was nothing dull or old-fashioned about her. Better for Sade, perhaps, had there been. Unfortunately for him, she also represented a new generation of patrician womanhood, practical and hard-headed in matters of finance and reputation. She might be slow to disapprove and condemn. Once she did so, she was likely to be implacable.

Her misgivings may have begun early but, when confronted with the first scandals of Sade's *petite maison*, she appeared to take the view that boys will be boys. Madame de Montreuil at this time still had the air of being what later ages would have called a "sport" or a "woman of the world". After the incident with Jeanne Testard, she wrote to the Abbé de Sade on 21 January 1764 assuring him that she felt no animosity against his family. "It only requires your nephew to make up for the past by giving no cause for reproach in the future." Like her daughters, she then joined with enthusiasm in Sade's amateur theatricals. Of far greater concern to the Montreuils, in the months following the wedding, was evidence that the Comte de Sade was edging closer to bankruptcy and that it would prove increasingly difficult to get from him the money that he had agreed to pay to his son.

The Sade family sent out a steward dressed in black and carrying a sword to deliver the wedding invitations. The ceremony took place in Paris at the church of St Roch in rue St Honoré on 17 May 1763 with all the pomp of an occasion to which Louis XV had given his blessing. St Roch had been built in the neoclassical style during the reign of Louis XIV, with veined red marble down its pillared aisles and apse, domed vaulting and a sense of Roman grandeur. Close to the royal palaces and the pleasures of the city it was an appropriate scene for a wedding of fashion. The marriage contract had been signed two days earlier at the townhouse of the Montreuils in rue Neuve du Luxembourg, close to the Condé Palace and the scenes of Sade's childhood.

Under the marriage contract, the Montreuils were to provide a home for the couple at Echauffour and in Paris. The Comte de Sade made over to his son the properties of La Coste, Mazan, Saumane and the Mas de Cabanes. However, there was a cash deduction which reduced Sade to being able to live in the properties without doing much else. The Abbé de Sade, who lived at Saumane by his brother's invitation, continued to do so. All too soon, however, there was bickering over the Comte de Sade's contribution to his son's finances. The comte had resigned the honour of being lieutenant-general of his four provinces so that his son might succeed him in the titles. Though there was honour, the lieutenant-general also received a useful income of ten thousand livres from the king. Now there was a squabble between Sade, supported by Madame du Montreuil, and his father. The young man insisted that money was due to him from the lieutenant-generalcies for the previous three years.

In the quarrel over money, according to the Comte de Sade, the son took the part of his wife's family against his own father. The old man called in vain to see him, while Madame de Montreuil was made welcome every day. Time and chance were overtaking the family of the former soldier and diplomat. The last of the Sade elders, the indulgent grandmother at Avignon, had died in 1762. The Comte de Sade himself was now in poor health, the dropsy gaining on him and his enthusiasm for life gone. His wife had withdrawn to the Carmelite convent. Though he had lived to see his son married, he was to die in four more years. At least his death spared him the greatest of the scandals attached to the family name.

In the aftermath of the wedding the Présidente de Montreuil

behaved with something like gratitude and affection towards Sade as a young man who had opened the ranks of nobility and even royalty to her daughter. There was no doubt that the young husband was genuinely fond of Renée-Pélagie and that he treated her well. Even the damage done to his public reputation by the Jeanne Testard scandal was soon repaired. Under his new titles he was received by the high court at Dijon, on a summer day in 1764. With pardonable exaggeration, he assured those present that it was "the happiest day of my life". He took the oath, swearing to follow the example of his colleagues in dispensing justice and to be a pattern of conduct in the sight of the virtuous and ungodly alike. In the years that followed he was to be the recipient of criminal justice far more often than its dispenser. His marriage continued to prosper. Though Renée-Pélagie was brought to bed of a still-born child in 1764, the couple presented Madame de Montreuil with three grandchildren. Louis-Marie de Sade, the elder son, was born in January 1768 and attended at the baptismal font by the Prince de Condé and the Princesse de Conti. A second son, Donatien-Claude-Armand, was born on 27 June 1769 and a daughter, Madeleine-Laure, on 17 April 1771. Towards the two boys, Mademe de Montreuil was to show commendable devotion, matched by a possessive jealousy that was the cause of considerable trouble.

3

Six months after the wedding the first blow to the marriage had fallen, when the Sades and the Montreuils were informed of Sade's arrest in Paris on 29 October 1763. The honour conferred on him at Dijon in 1764, a gift from his father, helped to balance this. Madame de Montreuil had been uneasy at the scandal. Yet she had believed, as she wrote to the Abbé de Sade, that marriage was having a settling effect upon her son-in-law and that he had the makings of a steady and responsible husband for Renée-Pélagie. Before long, however, his offence proved to be more than a single impulsive act of debauchery. If Louis Marais's warning to the brothel-keepers of Paris on 30 November 1764 was to be believed, there was a considerable police dossier on Sade's activities.

Yet even in 1763, there had seemed to be hope. To the Governor of Vincennes, the imprisoned marquis expressed his earnest regret. He asked only to see his wife and, if that were permitted, to be led by that sweet creature back to the path of righteousness from which he had so lamentably strayed. To Sartine, Lieutenant-General of Police, he acknowledged that he had deserved his imprisonment. He asked to be allowed to see a priest and insisted that his arrest and detention were acts of God's grace which should make him search his conscience and reform his behaviour for the future. Any suggestion that Sade had become an outcast among his peers was absurd. On 16 March 1767, he and Renée-Pélagie joined the king and queen, the dauphin and his sister, the princesses and the counts of Provence and Artois as witnesses to the marriage of the Comte de Coigny and Mademoiselle de Roissy.

Sade was to spend a good deal of time in the unfamiliar surroundings of northern France. When he was released from Vincennes in 1763, it had been a condition of his freedom that he should live under the supervision of the Montreuil family at Echauffour. The carriage that brought him through Paris on a day of early winter drove out through Versailles and began a hundred-mile journey on the road that ran to Argentan, Vire, Mortain and the hills at the base of the Cherbourg peninsula. Echauffour was short of that, though it was a journey of several days. The long undulating road passed through forest on either side, the trees invested with a shadowy and suggestive Gothic gloom in their arches and pathways. At the little crossroads town of L'Aigle, the carriage turned north for several miles, coming at last to the Montreuil estate and the plain stone manor house of Echauffour set among woods on a hill that looked down on the village and across the fields and distant forest ridges of lower Normandy.

It was quite unlike Provence, though the secrets of the forests were reflected in Sade's fiction as plainly as the hilltop châteaux of the Vaucluse. The long and narrow house stood within walled gardens. There was nothing picturesque about its white walls and steep roof. It was the centre of a prosperous agricultural community, its fields and barns as characteristic of northern Europe as the vineyards and olive slopes of La Coste or Saumane were of the south. To the north of Echauffour lay the English

Channel, to the south of La Coste the Mediterranean. In all the conflicts of Sade's life that lay ahead, this cultural division was to play its part.

Sade and Renée-Pélagie had adjoining bedrooms at Echauffour, looking out across the sweep of forest to the south. A few feet away from them, Anne-Prospère's room looked over the parkland and the avenue of trees on the northern side. While the younger sister might regard her brother-in-law with pride and affection, there was no suggestion of any but a subconscious sexual attraction between them at this stage. After six months of living quietly at Echauffour, Sade was allowed to leave in May to attend the high court of Dijon in his official capacity as a provincial lieutenant-general. While he was there, he spent some time reading manuscripts of the late Middle Ages in the Chartreux convent. These manuscripts contained historical episodes of France in the fourteenth and fifteenth centuries. Sade was interested most of all in the dramas of murder, treachery and torture during the civil strife and political instability which characterized the reign of Charles VI and his queen, Isabelle of Bavaria. During the days of his spring visit to Dijon, he took notes from the manuscripts, turning them into an historical novel in the last year of his life, *Isabelle of Bavaria, Queen of France*. It was as well that he made his notes in 1764. When the Revolution came, both the documents and the monuments of the Chartreux were destroyed in a moment of republican zeal. Sade, putting aside any allegiance to the new order, described the action as "the imbecilic vandalism" of the time.

From Dijon, he returned to Echauffour by way of Paris, staying until September 1764. The order requiring him to live on the estate in Normandy was then revoked. Once more the wide road from L'Aigle to Versailles lay open. If it was difficult for the police or the Montreuils to keep track of him, this was because Sade now hired lodgings in the city and Versailles, making use of them for one night at a time, in company with the girl he had chosen. His *petite maison* was at Arcueil, a few miles south of Paris among newly cultivated parkland which had become a setting for the villas of the noble and the wealthy. Louis XV himself had set the fashion with his own establishment, the Parc-aux-Cerfs at Versailles. A royal harem was chosen for him from girls whose task it was to ensure that Louis's enthusiasm was exclusively for their sex and not, as some feared, for his own. The most famous of the girls was the fifteen-year-old Louise O'Murphy, who fills Boucher's canvas, sprawling naked and face-down on the silks and velvet of a sofa, her legs languidly far apart and her bottom displayed in a manner of which Sade might have approved.

In such a moral climate as this, Sade was unlikely to find himself harried so long as he misbehaved with discretion. Though his name still appeared in the reports of Louis Marais, the memory of the Jeanne Testard scandal was no longer of great interest to the police.

Sade now took as his mistress in Paris an eighteen-year-old actress from the Comédie Italienne, Mademoiselle Colette. She had the reputation of being rather juvenile in her appearance and extremely licentious in her conduct. At first he shared her with the Marquis de Lignerai, but Lignerai soon gave up his claims to the girl and she became Sade's exclusive sexual property. By the end of 1764, the vigilant Marais reported that Colette slept with Sade on three nights of the week. Sade had written to her on 16 July 1764 assuring her, in lines of formal insincerity, that it was difficult to see her without loving her and impossible to love her without saying so. Though she might not know his name, he informed her that his servant was standing by to bring her reply to him.

Mademoiselle Colette was offended by his audacity, or pretended to be. Sade sent her another letter on the same day, promising her that he was at her feet and anxious to make good the offence. When they quarrelled, six months later, it seems that she threatened to make his letters public. In an abrupt change of tone, Sade demanded their return, though assuring her, "A woman's vengeance is always contemptible and it is only to show you the truth of this that I write to you now without fear of the consequences."

Marais and his spies kept watch on Sade's dealings with actresses and ballet-girls. Nor was Marais in any doubt as to what Sade was doing on the other nights of the week at his *petite maison* in Arcueil. A number of girls, picked up by the marquis's valet in central Paris, were taken there from time to time and whipped for the pleasure of the master of the house. The constable of Bourg-le-Reine, just south of Arcueil, noted that these whippings of the girls brought to the house were a frequent diversion of Sade's. But as no complaint was made by the victims, there was little that could be done. It seems likely that the girls in question had suffered worse at the hands of the law without being paid the louis d'or with which Sade rewarded them afterwards. To many of them it was a month's wages, though Sade's valet would deduct the amount he had spent on hiring a carriage to fetch them and take them home. Beyond that, the stories of scandal were for the most part vague.

However, Jean-François Vallée, the public prosecutor for the area of Arcueil, was an exact man by profession. He gave details of an evening in early February 1768, when Sade's valet set off for faubourg St Antoine, a working-class district round the Bastille, in the east of Paris. This was a necessary recruiting ground since, as Marais reported in the previous autumn, on 16 October, the more fashionable brothel-keepers whom Sade had patronized now refused to let him have girls for this purpose, "knowing what he is capable of". Sade had turned to those young women who were "less scrupulous" and could be persuaded by his servants. On this February evening, the valet returned with four girls, some of them perhaps new to Sade's soirées. They were taken into his room where the melodrama unfolded. The girls undressed and were whipped by him, singly or in a tableau. Whether Sade had intercourse with them, or by what means, Vallée did not know. However, when his evening's excitement was over, the marquis provided dinner for them all. After this, and possibly after further scenes of "debauchery", the valet was instructed to take them back to the city. The public prosecutor ended his affidavit by agreeing that Sade paid them through his servant, as a gentleman would, but added that the servant kept back three of the twenty francs to cover the cost of transporting them.

There was not much to be done. By the time the news reached Vallée, the identity of the girls would have been impossible to establish. In any case, there was no suggestion that they had been forced to submit against their will. It might seem foolish or unusual that a girl would consent to a punishment, regarded elsewhere as the vengeance of the law, without having committed any offence. If she chose to, there was an end of the matter. And however reluctant some or all of the girls might have been, stronger evidence of this was needed. That news of the activities came so specifically was apparently the consequence of Sade's meanness to drivers of hackney coaches. Sometime earlier, he had had a quarrel over the fare with one of them who had come out to Arcueil and during this he had struck the man. The revelations of his perverse pleasures on that February evening in 1768 may have been a result of the same coachman or one of his colleagues trying to level the score.

Though it caused a more powerful sense of outrage among his neighbours at Arcueil, Sade's preference for employing several girls in an evening's activities no doubt gave them a sense of safety in numbers. It even put him at a disadvantage, since he could hardly sustain the number of physical acts which were necessary to bring his erotic daydreams into reality. He advocated in his fiction a variety of methods and recipes for restoring potency to the solitary hero besieged by a selection of young slaves. As he suggests in a footnote to *Juliette,* a girl who serves such a man must know just how to use her hands or lips, or to apply warm cloths. The man himself must be expert in the internal and external use of spirits.

In practice and in fiction, his dramas led to the involvement of his own male servants as assistants and surrogates of the hero. The casual orgy became a staged drama, though the acts were real enough, with Sade dictating in detail and in advance how the plot was to develop. The use of other men, obedient to the hero's commands in their approach to the young women, is a central device in *The 120 Days of Sodom.* The *fouteurs* have no real part in the scheme of things except to act as proxies for their masters, giving life to those teeming suggestions which the sight of such a beautiful harem inspires in the minds of its social superiors.

Sade was rumoured to be employing boys as well as girls in the *petite maison* at Arcueil. Though they may have been his assistants with the girls from faubourg St Antoine, the implication of bisexuality and its development in him was soon evident. La Mierre, of the Académie Française, went to a dinner party and found himself sitting next to Sade, whom he described as "one of those charming creatures whose merit consists in entertaining the men and boring the women with tales of sexual conquest, sometimes real but often invented". La Mierre had had more than enough of his neighbour when Sade turned and asked him, in an off-hand manner, who was the best-looking man in the

Académie. La Mierre replied coldly, "I have never thought about it. Personally I have always considered that masculine beauty was of interest only to the type of people whose name is not mentioned in polite society." The snub was much applauded by those who believed that Sade had added the corruption of his own sex to the exploitation of the other.

4

Sade continued to draw a distinction, even if it was not absolute, between those mistresses with whom he shared more orthodox pleasure in his Paris apartments and those girls whom he hired for the evening at his *petite maison*. Young actresses like Mademoiselle Colette were quite willing to accept a retainer of twenty-five louis a month for sleeping with him and at least taking part in those fantasies which his own sexual compulsions required. But they were no part of the harem of hired girls at Arcueil. There was no suggestion of multiple copulation, whippings, douches, enemas and the other amusements of those evenings in the seclusion of his own house. It was generally the case that such a man lived his married life in Paris and kept his *petite maison* for his indiscretions. Sade used his Paris apartments for his indiscretions and kept his *petite maison* for forms of debauchery which the law, understandably, classified as "*outrée*".

By the end of 1764, in his twenty-fifth year, Sade's reputation was such that many of the brothels in Paris had closed their doors to him, encouraged in this by the police. Some of the girls had been whipped at Arcueil and there was talk of sodomy. It never reached the level of legal accusation, since the girl herself had as much to fear from the law. But at the beginning of 1765 Sade was too preoccupied with other matters to care much about brothels and their inmates. He had grown bored with Mademoiselle Colette and replaced her by Mademoiselle de Beauvoisin.

At eighteen, Mademoiselle de Beauvoisin was a girl of great beauty who had been in the keeping of the Comte du Barry. She had trained as a ballet dancer for the Opera but her stage technique was said to be less impressive than her presence in a bedroom. She and other ballet-girls were among Sade's mistresses at the time, including Mademoiselle Le Clair, Mademoiselle

Rivière and Mademoiselle Le Roy, all of the Académie Royale de Musique. Promiscuity was almost part of their profession in the atmosphere of the ballet school, according to the philosopher La Mettrie. In the case of Mademoiselle Beauvoisin, Sade may have been attracted by her reputation for distributing her sexual favours to women as well as men. Who better than such a young woman to procure others for his entertainment? Moreover, she had two houses for this purpose, one of them conveniently situated in rue Saint-Honoré, the other in rue des Deux-Écus.

In the summer of 1765, Sade was obliged to visit La Coste. The business of the estates and the collection of revenue required his presence. He was expected to make an appearance as Lieutenant-Governor of Mazan, an appointment which his father had held and for which Sade himself was now drawing a salary paid by the royal exchequer. There was approval in Provence when it was heard that he would be accompanied by his young wife. The couple were received by the villagers in June and the hilltop château was a scene of entertainments staged by Sade for his neighbours and guests. At Mazan itself, the fine bow-fronted house looked out across the flat vineyards and cherry orchards which stretched in a patchwork landscape to Carpentras in the west. His summer was divided between the romantic château above its village on the hill of La Coste and the elegance of the townhouse at Mazan.

The Marquise de Sade joined in her husband's amateur theatricals at La Coste in the summer of 1765. In the north gallery of the hilltop château, Sade found an outlet for his frustrated ambition as dramatist and director. Those who saw the marquise giving rein to her dramatic talents were impressed by her brunette beauty, though she was neither as tall nor as regal as they had expected. Indeed, it was surprising that she should forget her rank to the extent of performing in such a manner. The Abbé de Sade came over from Saumane and met her at one of the summer banquets at La Coste. And then the scandal was revealed. The woman whom the visitors and villagers alike had honoured as the Marquise de Sade was Mademoiselle de Beauvoisin. Sade had been anxious to take her to La Coste and explore her talents in his private theatre. How better to do this than to present her as his wife, who was in truth at Echauffour? It was unlikely that many of those to whom Mademoiselle de Beauvoisin was presented

69

would have the least idea of what the Marquise de Sade looked like. And if the real marquise should accompany her husband to La Coste in a future summer, it would be a brave tenant who accused her of imposture.

The Abbé de Sade, at least, had realized that this young woman could not be his nephew's wife. For the time being, it seems that he kept his secret to himself. But there were inconsistencies in her conduct and manner that led to rumours. The rumours spread until they reached Echauffour. In Provence, Sade's aunt, the Abbess de Cavaillon, wrote him a letter of reproof. In his reply, Sade made no further attempt to disguise the identity of his mistress at La Coste. Instead, he tried to turn the tables on his aunt by reminding her that she had not been so morally squeamish when her own sister, presumably Madame de Villeneuve, was living there openly with a lover. "Did you then regard La Coste as being a place under a curse?"

Sade's mother-in-law, Madame de Montreuil, was roused by the news that had reached her. Yet her first onslaught was directed against the Abbé de Sade, whom she accused of having been to La Coste, recognized the deception, and of having kept the truth to himself. She insisted that Sade's other secret infidelities were an injury to her daughter and herself, but his subterfuge with Mademoiselle de Beauvoisin was an insult to the whole of Provence. In tones of reproach verging on self-pity, she added that she and her family had worked hard to silence the earlier scandal and to promote her son-in-law's interests. The escapade with La Beauvoisin was all the thanks they had received for such efforts. But the Abbé de Sade, seeing himself about to be cudgelled by the Montreuils on one side and the Abbess of Cavaillon on the other, side-stepped them both by announcing that he had not been to the banquet at La Coste and had never seen the lady who was his nephew's companion there.

Leaving the two families to their quarrel, Sade took Mademoiselle de Beauvoisin back to Paris, concealing his movements from his father and the Montreuils. But there was a further reason for his secrecy. During the period since his release from Vincennes, he had contracted debts in almost every direction. Not only was he a debtor but the son of a debtor, not to be bailed out by future inheritance. His father could give him little or nothing and his privileges of rank made him a spender rather than an earner. His creditors and their bailiffs now joined the long trail of policemen, mother-in-law, plaintive girls and angry men, all of whom had accounts to settle with the infamous young nobleman.

But though Sade excused himself from returning to Echauffour, on the grounds that he was establishing his position in society by tracing his precise ancestry, he had neither abandoned nor forgotten Renée-Pélagie. Nor had he put from his mind her younger sister, Anne-Prospère. Safe among the forests and hills of lower Normandy, Anne-Prospère still nourished something like a schoolgirl's passion for the handsome young marquis. Indeed, her family seemed to reinforce this trait subsequently by sending her off to a convent near Clermont as a "canoness". It was not a renunciation of the world, since fees were paid and she was free to marry. Instead, it seemed a curious extension of a scholastic regime into adult life. Yet in the 1760s, Sade's very misconduct appeared to feed the girl's half-conscious jealousy of her elder sister's legal entitlement to his sexual favours. Anne-Prospère was not yet Sade's mistress but her appearance in that role was only a question of time. In the view of Krafft-Ebing, the two sisters at Echauffour were one source of inspiration for the two most famous sisters of Sade's fiction – Justine and Juliette. In this interpretation, Renée-Pélagie was the meek and submissive wife, her upbringing a reflection of conventional virtues. From Anne-Prospère's attachment to him Sade might have fashioned the thrill of a feminine and incestuous sensuality.

Despite the disapproval of the Montreuils, Sade was later to employ both sisters in his theatrical exercises at La Coste. The power of manipulation which this gave him certainly matched his own dramatic and semi-incestuous fantasies in a collection like *The Crimes of Love* or the more sardonic use of wives and daughters in *The 120 Days of Sodom*. Even while separated from the Montreuil daughters, cultivating the talents of Mademoiselle de Beauvoisin or the girls who entertained him in his *petite maison* at Arcueil, Sade's letters to Renée-Pélagie encouraged a sense of sexual anarchy among the young women of Echauffour. The tone of such letters also suggests Sade's sardonic satisfaction in tearing the veils of conformity and moral prudence by which the sexual self-awareness of the sisters had been protected. Renée-Pélagie never showed her husband less than tenderness and solicitude but in the following decade she threatened to refuse all further correspondence from him. It was under the guise of anthropological discovery that Sade's more outrageous visions and suggestions were shared with her. He was also to make good use of this in his philosophical novel *Aline and Valcour*.

In his subsequent letters he wrote with enthusiasm of the King of Assam, waited on by a harem of several hundred girls. From these he chose some who were merely to be flogged for his amusement and others whose heads would be used for sabre-practice. He also described, as an example of domestic economy, the Mogul with a stable of a dozen young women on whose backs he rode every day, mounted on a howdah, as though riding an elephant. But Sade points out that the emperor, by the standards of his own religion and culture, was a man of piety. On the death of a prince of the blood, he always showed his grief by killing every one of the girls with his own hands, however sexually appealing he found them. This ritual was a token of his respect for the dead prince, even though he was then put to the trouble of replacing his entire collection, who would occupy him until the death of another royal personage.

Such conduct, Sade remarked laconically, was regarded with moral approval in the culture where it occurred. It illustrated the absurdity of trying to set up an absolute or universal morality. And then, as if the Montreuil sisters were potential subjects of such a regime, he assured them that the Mogul emperor and his imitators had a far more rational system for governing their women than any yet devised in Europe.

In 1767, withdrawn from the world, the Comte de Sade died. He had lived apart from his wife for some years and was now discovered to have left debts of 86,000 livres. It was evident that the young couple and their children were to be dependent on the Montreuils. Sade himself had an income of 10,000 livres a year as an absentee provincial governor but this was far from adequate and, in any case, had not been paid at all for the first four years.

Sade later suggested that he had seen little of his father during childhood. To the Abbé Amblet he described him as "the kindest of fathers and the best of friends", though this may have been the rhetoric of filial duty which the abbé expected. After his father's death, Sade continued to use the courtesy title of Marquis de Sade rather than that of Comte de Sade, which he now inherited. It suggests, at least, a wish to distance himself from his father's memory.

His relationship with Mademoiselle de Beauvoisin was less straightforward. He broke off their affair, patched up the quarrel and then quarrelled with her again. She had become pregnant by one of her lovers but was no longer so in December 1765 when she became the mistress of the Duc de Choiseul. During this time a succession of ballet-girls had shared Sade's bed, though there is no indication that they allowed themselves to be employed in his more extravagant sexual games. In the aftermath of his elder son's birth in 1767, Sade bought the favours of a professional courtesan at Paris and took into his keeping a ballet-girl, Mademoiselle Le Clair.

At the age of twenty-eight, his life had achieved an equilibrium of lechery and tedium which was characteristic of a good many patrician Europeans in mid-century. It might have been predicted that he would decline through relatively inoffensive libertinage to tranquillity in his middle years. Such was the appearance of his conduct on 3 April 1768.

FIVE

ROSE KELLER

1

THE COBBLED CIRCLE OF PLACE DES VICTOIRES, an equestrian statue of Louis XIV railed off at its centre, was a Parisian tribute to the Roman circus. The streets entering it divided the circle into segments of tall patrician houses with mansard roofs and arched window embrasures on the ground floor. Just north-east of the gravelled spaces and arcades of the Palais Royal, place des Victoires was on the verge of royal residence. Its tall, uniformly designed houses with their pilasters and handsome porticoes scarcely made it an area for the poor or destitute, except when they asked for charity.

April 3, 1768, was a Sunday, indeed it was Easter Sunday, which added a further resonance to the events of that day. The grand circle of houses with their tall windows and doorways made it a promising pitch for an appealing beggar. A young woman, Rose Keller, had gone there for that purpose. She asked a man for money and he gave her some. Sade was the next man on foot to cross the wide cobbled circle. She described him as a dapper, slightly built figure in a grey riding-coat, wearing a muff and carrying a stick. He was also carrying a hunting-knife. It was just after nine o'clock in the morning. Rose Keller was the young widow of a baker and now an unemployed cotton-spinner. She claimed that she had been to mass shortly before the events leading to the outrage began. A native of Strasbourg, she spoke French with a strong accent and not much sense of grammar. There was, at least, scope for misunderstanding.

Having seen the first man give her money, Sade came up to the young woman. According to Rose Keller, he asked her if she would like to earn some more by accompanying him to Arcueil for a *partie de libertinage*. Rose Keller, by her own account, replied that she was not that sort of person. It seemed to her that the rebuke had its effect upon the young nobleman. He changed his tone and asked her if, instead, she would like a job as chambermaid in his *petite maison* at Arcueil. She agreed to this, which suggests that she was either extremely naïve or less than accurate in her story. Sade's version of their meeting was that he had offered her money in exchange for sexual favours and that she accepted it without argument.

Whatever the conversation between them, he now took Rose Keller a short distance to a room near the new market. It was a second-floor room, apparently his own, decorated in yellow damask and furnished with armchairs and a chaise-longue. He told the young woman that she must wait while he completed one or two errands. An hour later, Sade returned with a hired carriage. They drove southwards across the river and out of the city, past the Luxembourg Gardens and the observatory which marked the beginning of a suburban Arcadia. The road to Arcueil lay between fields and wooded hills in the little valley of the Bièvre. Arcueil itself was two miles short of the administrative centre of Bourg-la-Reine, the southern landscape closed off by a majestic aqueduct that spanned the valley.

The road by which Sade and Rose Keller approached the village led over a simple stone bridge and into the little street with its Cross of Arcueil and its Church of St Denis. Arcueil, like Twickenham in the age of Pope and Walpole, offered seclusion to the rich or noble of a great metropolis. It was a place of high walls and quiet villas, formal gardens with lakes and tree-lined walks, ornamental arches and nude statues of antique inspiration. This suburban idyll had been popularized by such visions as Jean-Baptiste Oudry's picture of 1744, *A Mirror of Water in the Gardens of Arcueil*.

To the left of the road that ran southwards through Arcueil lay rue de la Fontaine. The carriage turned into it and stopped at the gates of one of the walled gardens. Sade's *petite maison* was, for the most part, a long single-storey building, though it had attic rooms with dormer windows and the main floor was raised above the cellars which were at ground level. Sade led Rose Keller up the driveway, then made her wait at the servants' entrance while he went round through the main door. The servants' gate opened into a little garden.

Sade let her into the house, whose vestibule opened to the courtyard on one side and the garden on the other. From this they passed through a dining-room, its two sideboards set out with glassware and dishes of decorated porcelain. There were three casually furnished rooms beyond this, looking out on to the garden, and then a bedroom with corner cupboards and desk. Sade evidently chose one of the intermediate rooms, with basket-chairs and two beds. He said something about going to find food and drink, leaving Rose Keller in the room. When he returned, Sade said, "Come down, my love," and led her out across the garden again. They entered by another door and she found herself in a closet. It was dark and a little sinister, the only light coming from four panes of glass high in the wall and barred on the outside. Sade told her to undress. When she asked why, he reminded the young woman that he was going to amuse himself with her. There was an argument which, by Rose Keller's account, ended with Sade giving her the choice of taking off her clothes or else being killed and buried in the garden.

Locked in alone, Rose Keller began to undress but kept her shift on. When Sade returned, she alleged that he demanded to see her naked and with his own hands pulled the shift off over her head. Then he bundled her into an adjoining room. At its centre was a day-bed, upholstered in cotton of a red and white pattern. He pushed her face-down on this, tying her hands and feet to it with hemp cord and also tying her round the waist. He then put one of the narrow bolsters across the back of her neck, so that it was difficult for her to see what was happening behind her.

Sade went back to the closet, took off his clothes and put on a sleeveless jerkin. He also bound up his auburn hair with a hand-kerchief, so that it should not fall about his face during the exertion. Before he began, he stood where Rose Keller could see that he had a birch-rod in his hand.

In her own version of the ordeal, he began by using the birch upon her, then used a stick of some kind and, finally, sat on the calves of her legs to stop her struggling while he cut her buttocks with a knife, pouring melted wax into the incisions. Rose Keller insisted that she had been beaten seven or eight times. When she cried out, Sade showed her a knife and told her that he would kill her unless she kept quiet. She begged him not to kill her, since it was Easter and she had not made her confession. Her captor told her scornfully that he would hear her confession himself before he despatched her. Then she claimed that Sade emitted a series of cries. Presently he cut the cords which bound her to the day-bed. He took her into the closet and brought some water for her to wash with, as well as some eau de vie to apply to the marks he had made. When she had dressed again, Sade produced bread, meat and wine. He took her back across the garden to the first bedroom she had entered and locked her in. Before leaving her alone, he promised that he would set her free that evening. Rose Keller asked him not to keep her too long, fearing that she might not get back to Paris before dark and might have to sleep by the road.

The structure of the house was such that, though this room was raised over the cellars, it was not far above ground level. As she looked from the window, hoping to find a way of escape, she swore that Sade appeared in the garden below and shook his fist at her. But she was undeterred and managed to unfasten the window. Taking the covers from the two beds, she twisted them into a makeshift rope. When there was no one below, she climbed out and down to the garden. It was then that one of Sade's servants saw her. He shouted after her, telling the young woman to come back. His master had not paid her for her services and the money was waiting. But Rose Keller took to her heels, outdistancing the servant. She scaled the garden wall and dropped down into the street on the other side. The worst of her escape was in grazing her wrist as she came down from the wall into rue de la Fontaine.

2

Such was the story of her ordeal which Rose Keller was soon giving to the world. Sade's version differed by making her a willing partner rather than a victim. He even maintained that Rose Keller was a consenting, if not a very willing, partner in the beating he had given her. In place des Victoires that morning she had agreed without hesitation to his suggestions and had known exactly what lay in store for her at Arcueil. He insisted that he had not tied her down on the day-bed, since there was no need to. She undressed and lay down of her own accord. In his own version he had used a whip of knotted cords rather than a birch-rod. He had never used a knife. As for the "wax" which she claimed had been poured on to her abrasions, this was an ointment which he had applied after whipping her. Though his version of events seemed questionable in general, in certain details it was the more probable.

Whether Sade or Rose Keller spoke the truth, another scandal in his life was now inevitable. If Rose Keller was to be believed, that scandal would also constitute a crime. It was about half-past four on the afternoon of Easter Sunday when the young woman, whipped and bedraggled, her clothes in disorder, dropped down from the garden wall into rue de la Fontaine. The first person she saw was Marguerite Duc, the wife of Jean-Baptiste Sixdeniers, wine-grower of Arcueil. Rose Keller's shift was torn and part of it was hanging down. Madame Sixdeniers saw her take a pair of scissors from her pocket, cut off this torn piece of shift and wrap it round the hand which she had just grazed during her escape. Rose Keller told her story at once. Madame Sixdeniers and two other women of Arcueil examined her shortly afterwards. They did not find, as the victim claimed, that her shift was bloodstained. But they found the marks of a birch on her buttocks and the backs of her thighs. There were traces of a substance which might have been white wax, though not the red wax which Rose Keller also claimed had been used on her. Whether the appearance of white wax was consistent with Sade's claim to have used an ointment of some kind was not yet investigated.

Whatever the truth, there was evidence of a crime. Even if Rose Keller had been a consenting partner, Sade might have been called to account. It would be no defence to a charge of murder that the victim had consented to it. Whether a defence of this sort could be sustained in the case of such accepted harm as Rose Keller had suffered was debatable. In practical terms, a *partie de libertinage* of this kind was usually a discreet and patrician affair which never came to the attention of the law.

By this time, the authorities at Bourg-la-Reine had been alerted. On the following day, Monday 4 April, Rose Keller's deposition was taken at the Château d'Arcueil. From then on, she seemed prepared to tell her story to anyone who would listen. She was examined by the surgeons, including Dr Le Comte of Arcueil, who confirmed her ordeal in general but not in particular. She had not been cut with a knife. She had the marks of a birch on her buttocks and adjacent to them. The marks were raised here and there but the skin was not broken. There were no marks on her wrists, ankles or waist to suggest that she had been tied down on the day-bed. Either she had been a willing accomplice in her own beating or else Sade had so terrified her that she had placed herself as he commanded and had remained there without resisting.

Indeed, Rose Keller's story grew less plausible in its details the more it was investigated. There was a considerable area of uncertainty as to what Sade had done to her. She had seen him holding the birch beforehand but the bolster on her neck meant that she could feel but not see what he did after that. To those who thought she was exaggerating or misrepresenting the incident, it was a matter for some scepticism that a young woman who claimed to have been thrashed to a state of collapse had still possessed agility and presence of mind sufficient to shin down the outside of the house, outpace Sade's servant, scale a wall and make good her escape into the street.

But if Sade spoke the truth, he did not lessen the scandal. As the public prosecutor at Arcueil, Jean-François Vallée, now revealed, the young marquis had been giving this bourgeois Arcadia a bad name for some time. That was his greater crime. As for Monsieur Coignet, an Arcueil magistrate, or the clerk to the justices, Charles Lambert, such men were not amused at having a scapegrace like this twenty-eight-year-old nobleman for a neighbour. Nor did Sade conceal his opinion of these self-important upholders of the law. They were men, he wrote in his story "The Mystified Magistrate", who showed themselves "more easily moved to compassion for the whipped bottom of a street-girl than for the people they called their children yet whom they allowed to die of hunger." These magistrates were humbugs in office, determined "to prosecute a young soldier who, returning from the sacrifice of the best years of his life in the service of his prince, found no other reward on coming home but humiliation prepared for him by these – the real enemies of the country he had just been defending."

In his novel *Aline and Valcour*, published in 1793, he praised Rome, Naples, Venice and Warsaw as cities which dealt more sensibly with such matters than Paris or London. In these cities, if prostitutes complained of having been whipped or otherwise ill-treated by a client, the court would ask if they had been paid by him. If not, the man was ordered to pay. "But if they have been paid and complain only of such rough usage, they are threatened with imprisonment on the next occasion that they assault the ears of the court with their indecent clamour. Change your profession, they are told. Or, if you like your present occupation, accept its discomforts."

Such fanciful self-dramatizing in his fiction appeared as an afterthought. In his letters, Sade's denunciations were bitter in their contempt for Sartine and the police as well as for the Montreuil family. In 1763 he had written to Sartine expressing his remorse for the Jeanne Testard incident. Privately, Sade despised the man. Writing to his servant "La Jeunesse" in 1780, he named Sartine and the Montreuils as friends of whores and supporters of the brothel trade. "They will stand solidly behind a whore and throw a gentleman into gaol on her behalf for twelve or fifteen years without a qualm." Three years later, he assured Renée-Pélagie that the police would tolerate any infamy, "provided one respects the backsides of whores . . . because the whores bribe them and we don't".

In the hours that followed his birching of Rose Keller, his principal aim was to avoid arrest. At six o'clock on Easter Sunday evening, Sade was already preparing to leave Arcueil for Paris. From Paris he would go into the country, as far as possible from his pursuers. In this he followed the most sensible course of action. Staying put and owning up would do him no good. As every schoolboy knows, the best course on difficult occasions is to become as scarce as possible until anger has cooled and moral indignation grows wearisome. With the passage of time, interest in Rose Keller's allegations would dwindle. If Sade could keep out of the way for a twelvemonth, he would probably be able to return to Paris – if not Arcueil – in safety.

This was evidently the belief among the Montreuil family as well. On 19 April, Henri Griveau, bailiff of the high court of Paris, arrived at the townhouse of the Montreuils in rue Neuve du Luxembourg. Sade and Renée-Pélagie had their Paris apartment in some of its rooms but there was no sign of the fugitive. Though Griveau had a warrant for the arrest of Sade and for his detention within the medieval walls of the Conciergerie on Ile de la Cité, he left empty-handed, remarking that Sade was not even the owner of the furniture in the rooms where he lived.

But Madame de Montreuil and her daughter were already at work on a more direct and productive course of action. Rose Keller must be bought off. There was much about her story which suggested that she was prepared to exploit her ordeal to the limit. In her financial and social situation, that was entirely reasonable but it also gave Madame de Montreuil her chance. Despite the difference in rank, both the mistress of the grand house in rue Neuve du Luxembourg and the unemployed cotton-spinner were moral realists. Before the week was half over, Renée-Pélagie began work on her mother's behalf.

Early on Thursday 7 April, four days after the incident, the family lawyers came to rue Neuve du Luxembourg. Having discussed the matter, Claude-Antoine Sohier, legal representative of the Montreuils, went to Arcueil with the Abbé Amblet, Sade's boyhood tutor. Lambert, the clerk to the justices, took them to the room where Rose Keller was sitting on her bed, complaining of her condition and insisting that after such an ordeal she was in no state to make her own way in life. Visitors and victim understood each other. There was no difficulty in getting Rose Keller to name a price for withdrawing her complaint against Sade, though it was plainly going to be expensive. Sohier asked if she would take money. Rose Keller said without hesitation that she would. She demanded three thousand livres. Sohier told her it was exorbitant. He offered eighteen hundred. Rose Keller refused. The lawyer and the abbé returned to Paris and then came back. At length, the two parties split the difference and a sum of twenty-four hundred livres was agreed on as the price of Rose Keller's silence. It was more money than she could have earned in the next few years. She also demanded and got seven louis d'or to pay for medical preparations in respect of her injuries.

3

The case against Sade seemed less ominous, though the warrant for his arrest remained. He had less to fear, however, and it might have seemed best to surrender to the law and get the matter settled. It was not a mistake that he ever made again. On 8 April he was arrested and taken to the château of Saumur on the Loire by royal command. This intervention was the first indication that while he might not face a criminal trial, he could easily be detained as a prisoner at his majesty's pleasure by virtue of *lettres de cachet*. For the time being he was still treated as his rank demanded and as a man whose word of honour was respected. He was taken to Saumur with his friend and tutor the Abbé Amblet in charge of him, rather than a military escort.

Life at Saumur was not entirely disagreeable. Sade had freedom of movement within the walls of the fortress and dined with its commandant. On 12 April, he wrote to his uncle, the Abbé de Sade, of the "unfortunate events" which had overtaken him. He assured the abbé that his family had stood by him, working for his release, and had been able to arrange for the Abbé Amblet to accompany him to Saumur. Sade still talked and wrote like a boy quietly expelled from school for some peccadillo. The authorities took the offence more seriously. At the end of April, Inspector Marais arrived with orders from Saint-Florentin of the royal household to take him to imprisonment at Pierre-Encise, near Lyon.

Marais informed Saint-Florentin that Sade was surprised to see him and still more surprised at the news of his transfer to Pierre-Encise. But he was to be treated with the deference due to his rank. At Pierre-Encise he was promised the same privileges that he had enjoyed at Saumur. But Marais explained that, in the light of Sade's crime and the punishment it deserved, the authorities thought the regime at Saumur too "relaxed".

Marais travelled south with his prisoner. At Dijon and Lyon, as well as at Saumur, he found that Sade's thrashing of Rose Keller was the talk of the day. Sade regretted nothing, except that he had been caught and punished. As Marais reported to Saint-Florentin, the prisoner firmly denied that he had ever done anything worse than use a whip on Rose Keller. It had not entered his head to cut her with a knife. He "could not imagine who had employed the creature to make such a complaint and he was certain that if the high court ordered an examination by medical experts, no sign of a cut would be found".

His protests did him no good. The stories that circulated grew more lurid with every repetition. By the time that Restif de la Bretonne recounted the drama, twenty years later in *Nuits de Paris*, three murders were part of the narrative. Rose Keller became an innocent girl whom Sade lured to his secret torture chamber. He took her down to a cellar where several conspirators were waiting to watch the victim put to death. "What earthly use is she?" Sade insisted in this version. "She is good for nothing. She must serve as the means by which we penetrate the secrets of the human anatomy."

> She was fastened on the table. The Comte [de Sade], as the one who would dissect her, examined every part of her body, calling out the discoveries of his anatomical investigation. The woman uttered the most terrible cries. The conspirators withdrew to send the servants further off before beginning the dissection. The unfortunate woman broke free and escaped through the window. She reported seeing in that room, where she was made to undergo these surgical attentions, the corpses of three people.

Not for the last time, Sade was to discover that his fame related less to who he was or what he did than to his reputation. In an age of Gothic fiction, designed to chill the blood of middle-class womanhood, he seemed to bring to life the villainy and to inspire the agreeable shudder of revulsion which heightened the pulse-rate of the schoolmiss and her mama alike.

But the readership for Sade's atrocities ranged far wider than drawing-room fiction. By 26 April the Rose Keller scandal had been reported in the Dutch press, beginning at Utrecht, followed on 3 May at Leiden. The dowager Comtesse de Sade complained from her convent retirement that the Dutch papers were describing the details of her son's indiscretion "in the blackest colours". England was soon alerted. On 12 and 13 April, Madame du Deffand, doyenne of Paris salons, had written to her correspondent, Horace Walpole, about the infamous "Comte de Sade", whom she correctly identified as "nephew of the Abbé who wrote a life of Petrarch". No less than her successors, she coloured the story with a judicious mixture of moral outrage and furtive relish. She described Sade's encounter with the girl in place des Victoires.

> He questioned her at length, expressed his sympathy, and to relieve her poverty offered her the post of caretaker at his *petite*

maison near Paris. . . . On her arrival, the Marquis showed her every nook and cranny of the house, and finally conducted her to an attic, where he locked the door and made her strip. She threw herself at his feet, begging him to let her go, since she was a respectable girl. But he drew his pistol and ordered her to obey him, which she did. Then he tied her hands and flogged her until she bled. Taking a box of ointment from his pocket, he rubbed it into her wounds and left her lying on the floor. . . . He did not return until the following day, when he examined her wounds, saw that the ointment had worked, seized his knife and cut her all over her body. He rubbed more ointment on her and went away again. The poor girl managed to free herself, escaping through the window to the street below. It is not known what damage was done to her in the fall.

With the publication of Walpole's letters in the nineteenth century, Sade's reputation was established. When the culprit was called to account for his actions, Madame du Deffand assured her correspondent that Sade had behaved more like a satanic madman than a violent criminal. "He gloried in the unheard-of shamelessness of his crime, and actually boasted that it was a noble action, by which he had revealed to the world an ointment that would heal all kinds of wounds immediately."

On 3 May, Saint-Florentin advised the Montreuils against any attempt to appeal to the king on behalf of their son-in-law. In the circumstances, they would have little chance of success. The imprisonment at Pierre-Encise lasted a further five weeks. Then Sade was brought from Lyon to Paris on 8 June to answer the charges against him.

Sade was present in the Chambre de Tournelle of the high court of Paris, where he was summoned to appear, on 10 June. It was evident that he had requested the right to be there and to clear his name, which the king had agreed to. Questioned by Jacques de Chavannes, King's Counsellor, he repeated his own version of events. On meeting Rose Keller in place des Victoires, he had "explained his intentions". She had undressed willingly at Arcueil and he had undressed at the same time. When she was naked, "he had told her to lie down on the day-bed but had not tied her". After that, Sade insisted, "he had whipped her with a whip of knotted cords but had not used a stick, a birch, a knife nor Spanish wax. On the reddened parts, he had used a small amount of ointment containing white wax to heal the abrasions, admitting that he had whipped her four or five times."

What may have sounded like a reasonable explanation to Sade had the tone of a damning confession in the ears of the judges of the Chambre de la Tournelle. How could he have continued to whip the young woman as she cried out? Sade parried this by explaining that "she had not uttered a single cry – and if she had done, she would have been heard by everyone in the house". Counsel for the king persisted. Even if she had not cried out, how could he bring himself to continue whipping her when he could see the marks already inflicted on her? Sade admitted that he could see "that the strokes she had received had caused inflammation. That was why the ointment was used." He conceded that after he had used the whip two or three times, she complained that it was hurting her. He had used it only once after that.

Finally, he answered that no price had been agreed for this ordeal before the young woman disappeared from the *petite maison* but that they had remained on good terms until he last saw her. Rose Keller's only concern was that she should be able to get back to Paris in good time that evening. The implication was that she thought she could get more money from Sade by compromising him than by accepting payment before she left.

In the eyes of the court, Sade's defence was no defence at all. But the nominal penalty by which he purged his guilt was, to say the least, trivial. He was ordered to pay ten livres, the money to be used to provide bread for other prisoners in the Conciergerie.

That was far from the end of the scandal or of the penalties inflicted on Sade. A day or two after the hearing in Paris, he was escorted back to Pierre-Encise as a prisoner of the king. Under the system of *lettres de cachet*, he might be imprisoned at the king's pleasure without sentence being passed by a court. Sometimes it was the king or his ministers who wished to put out of the way a political opponent. But *lettres de cachet* were also used as a mark of royal favour to influential families who wished to dispose of one of their members. The Montreuils might well feel that their son-in-law would benefit from the lesson of a few months at Pierre-Encise. He had been saved from a major criminal prosecution but he was not to expect that such salvation was without price.

Madame de Montreuil had written to the Abbé de Sade on 26 April, after Rose Keller's complaint was withdrawn, assuring him that his nephew's misconduct now appeared as "an act of folly or libertinage which one cannot excuse but which is stripped of all the horrors that had been added to it". On 13 June she added that he had purged his guilt, so far as the high court of Paris was concerned. As he had told the court, the king had granted him *lettres d'abolition*, by which the charges against him were set aside. But, as Madame de Montreuil also informed the Abbé de Sade, her son-in-law had been returned to Pierre-Encise by royal command, "for as long as the king thinks it proper to keep him there."

Sade had not been without friends from his own family and its allies. The Abbé Amblet had sworn to the Arcueil magistrates that Sade was a decent young man who had been popular at school, though quick-tempered and high-spirited in his pleasures. More to the point, the abbé had gone to the *petite maison* on 9 April, at Renée-Pélagie's request, to bring back silverware and prints which might be either valuable or incriminating. He had found nothing there to support the complaints that Rose Keller had made. There was even a story, published in 1779, that the Montreuils had tried to bribe the investigating magistrate at Arcueil but that he had been driven to take action by his superior who had bought a house in the neighbourhood.

New of the scandal had spread with the speed of a best-seller. Rose Keller's ordeal was trivial by comparison with those women like Katharine Bellenden whom the Bow Street court in London sentenced to be publicly whipped until she bled for stealing a kettle. It was insignificant by comparison with the horrors of Damiens' execution or the ripping out of men's bowels on Kennington Common in 1746 after they had been cut down still living from the gallows. Yet the story, like a moral fable, caught the imagination of contemporaries. As a drama, it appealed by the trappings and settings of the scene. Even if Rose Keller was an unwilling participant, the degree of physical suffering was less than that routinely inflicted by contemporary dentistry or by surgery when patients were "cut for the stone" without the benefit of anaesthetic or "tapped" for quarts of fluid. The ordeal of amputation was such that the poet John Dryden chose to die rather than submit to it.

But Sade claimed attention by the implicitly sexual character of the whipping he inflicted, scarcely an ingredient in the more brutal and public flogging of criminals. The abduction and captivity of the woman, the isolation and the secrecy turned a routine episode of debauchery into an erotic melodrama and a social parable. As rival versions of the Rose Keller story spread, it was not surprising that men and women shuddered with horror or quickened with curiosity, sensing that Bluebeard and Gilles de Rais might live again in the person of the unspeakable Sade.

He remained a prisoner at Pierre-Encise for five months. It was not more arduous than his brief spell at Saumur. But he was a prisoner, none the less. Renée-Pélagie made her way to Lyon at the end of August with permission to visit her husband. But, at that time, it was indicated that she had better prepare him for a long stay there.

The ghoulish exaggerations of Restif de la Bretonne and his nineteenth-century imitators reflected the contradictory versions of the Rose Keller story. Forensic evidence throws doubt upon her version of events at Arcueil but does not acquit Sade of assaulting her. Was she a willing victim? She claimed that he had first asked her to join a *partie de libertinage*. She refused. But she agreed at once to become his chambermaid, which was traditionally one of the most sexually hazardous occupations for a young woman. During the hour she waited for him to return with the hired carriage, she did not change her mind.

Whether or not she was a consenting partner was a question on which the case turned. It is just possible that she and Sade had each told a version of the truth. When he suggested a *partie de libertinage*, it may well have evoked images of a group of men and women, where Rose Keller would be at the disposal of a number of strangers. It was natural to be frightened or wary at the implications of this but, in her present circumstances, to consent to intimacy with the young nobleman who had apparently taken a fancy to her, provided that he was the only one. With no idea of precisely what awaited her at Arcueil, Rose Keller might have been willing to go there with him alone. To become a seduced chambermaid perhaps seemed better than her present role as beggar.

Whatever her reasons for consenting, the woman who had been begging in place des Victoires on the morning of Easter

Sunday was to acquire a larger sum of money by the following Thursday than she could have earned by years of toil as a cotton-spinner. In that light, her story was not so much a Gothic horror as a social irony.

4

Sade's view of the injustice, which he claimed had been done him, was bound to appear ludicrous. And yet he had surely been the victim of a certain degree of bad luck. The sexual extravagance of aristocrats and courtiers during the ten years preceding the Rose Keller scandal had made it necessary for a moral check to be put on such behaviour. Sade presented himself as a plausible scapegoat. His crime had involved an element of Gothic perversity, far removed from the more elegant lechery of court and parkland. It had overtones of impiety. The crime had occurred on Easter Day, though Sade would presumably have taken the opportunity on any other day. The whipping of Rose Keller was even seen as a deliberate parody of the scourging of Christ, though the nature of Sade's act was overtly sexual in his dealings with the young woman. By promising to act the part of a priest, hearing the confession of his naked captive before putting her to death, Sade appeared to set the seal of sacrilege on his offence. It was entirely possible that he never spoke such words and that the encounter with Rose Keller was mere opportunity. But it was convenient that he should be seen in a more sinister role.

Far better that Sade should suffer as a symbol of what Horace Walpole once called "flagrancy" than that the general malady should be too closely investigated. Louis XV was still a popular monarch but it was desirable that his subjects should not know too much about him. When he escaped assassination, recovered from a serious illness, enjoyed his triumph from such military adventures as the capture of Fribourg or the battle of Fontenoy, the crowds cheered and admired. They might not have applauded the disturbing preference for boys rather than girls, which he showed as a young man. Folios of prints offering shepherds and shepherdesses in passionate heterosexual encounters were left conspicuously for the young monarch to find and browse through. But still he did not quite seem to catch on to the general truths of sexual conduct.

His advisers did their best by rounding up the boys to whom he appeared most attached and sending them away. The king was puzzled. He asked why his young friends were no longer in attendance. He was told that they were dismissed for vandalism, for pulling up palings in the royal parks. They were *arracheurs des palissades*. The story and the phrase caught the fancy of those who heard it. For years after this, a man's reputation might be tainted by calling him an *arracheur des palissades*.

It had been thought best that the king's sexual education should be supervised by the Comtesse de Toulouse and undertaken in detail by Madame de la Vrillière, a mature woman of great beauty and considerable experience. The experiment was a success and the discovery of the delights which such women offered was the great experience of the king's life. The repeated proofs of his passion which he gave his young queen upon their marriage seemed as gratifying as they were unexpected.

Louis's attention wandered to the seraglio of potential mistresses which surrounded him. He picked out the three Mailly-Nesles sisters, the Comtesse de Mailly, the Comtesse de Vintimille and the Duchesse de Chateauroux. Van Loo's portrait of them, naked as the Three Graces, shows a classical elegance of dark eyes and braided hair with their bodies carefully proportioned by the artist. The eldest appears more heavily built, the younger two slighter and more virginal. Louis's ambition was said to be to sleep with them simultaneously, enjoying quasi-incestuous pleasures which were very much of the kind exploited by Sade in *The Crimes of Love* as well as in his franker fiction. The scandal of this royal entanglement became more widely known. One day, when the Comtesse de Mailly entered the fashionable church of St Roch, where Sade had been married, a group of ladies began to talk loudly of the ease with which one might take her for a common whore. She crossed over to them and said pleasantly, "Mesdames, since you know so well what it feels like to be a common whore, do not forget me in your prayers."

The king's pleasures were soon to be governed by his most famous *maîtresse en titre*, Madame de Pompadour, who dominated his life from 1745 until her death in 1764. Knowing that her own physical charms must fade, she retained the king's affection by acting as mistress of ceremonies and employing girls for him who remained subservient to her. In 1755, as France prepared for another war, his villa at Versailles, the Parc-aux-Cerfs, became the most famous *petite maison* of all. It was a retreat where Louis was attended by the girls whom Madame de Pompadour and others provided for him. His taste developed rather like Sade's, towards young women of undistinguished origin, shopgirls, seamstresses and others with an inclination for selective prostitution. He masqueraded among them as a Polish gentleman consoling himself by such pleasures. The truth was soon revealed when one girl began rummaging through his pockets, from force of professional habit, and discovered letters addressed to His Majesty from the King of Poland and a Marshal of France.

The Parc-aux-Cerfs was sometimes reserved as the exclusive residence of a single girl. This was the case with its most famous tenant, Louise O'Murphy, the Louison, who achieved immortality in that painting of Boucher's where she perches saucily over a sofa, naked, face-down and with thighs casually parted.

This cult of the *petite maison* opened the way for a new genre of painting and decoration, which seems like a light-hearted anticipation of certain scenes in Sade's fiction. It encouraged bric-à-brac that were sometimes more vulgar than erotic. There was the trick chair, which can scarcely have been used in earnest. It operated by a concealed spring as soon as the female victim sat upon it. Her arms and legs were held fast. The chair reclined, taking her with it, until she lay on her back with her legs raised and parted. In an age when skirts fell clear and nothing was worn under them, the invitation to her partner was less than subtle. Since the device required that the "victim" should cooperate by sitting at just the right angle, the chair was far more of an entertainment than an aid to the unskilled ravisher.

Few *petites maisons* could boast such trinkets as the erotic dinner service made at Sèvres for the regent of France but there was no lack of erotic ornamentation on tableware. Soup dishes were designed so that, as the level dropped, the scene on the bottom of the dish became clearer. It might be a cameo of copulation or a Rabelaisian motif. One design showed a peasant girl kneeling with her elbows on the ground and her hips raised. The force of the blast emerging behind her turns the sails of a windmill at a little distance. *Spiritus flat ubi vult*, says the motto, "The wind bloweth where it listeth." Shepherdesses with breasts of improbable perfection made love with shepherds on cups and saucers; nymphs and satyrs danced and coupled on the lids of snuff-boxes; teams of girls on enamelled lockets joined their heroes in an unending variety of "spintrian postures", as multiple copulation was euphemistically termed.

Painters reflected the same preoccupations, seeking slight pretext for the portrayal of female nudity and sensuality. For the benefit of male patrons, there was much emphasis on the behaviour of women when closeted alone together. Boucher depicts a girl ostentatiously washing her genitals in the presence of another. The action was sufficiently ambiguous to offer a second interpretation of the picture.

An easy route to popularity for the painter was the cliché of women bathing, one Venus emerging naked from the water and falling into the arms of her assistant. The suggestiveness of a painting like Greuze's *The Lady Friends*, in which the hands of the half-naked girls are just beginning to stray, was well-calculated to appeal to the patron of the *petite maison*. The object of so much artistic labour was not, as its enemies supposed, to drive a man or woman wild with lust that would not be denied. It was, rather, to infuse an eroticism which lingered in the air like perfume, civilizing lust as well as promoting sensuality.

The artist, if not his patron, attributed sexual awareness and eagerness to women of all ages. In Coypel's painting, *Jeux d'enfants à toilette*, the participants are playing with adult cosmetics. One of the children has glued "beauty spots" on her skin. Those on the face are close to her eye, a signal traditionally given by the sexually adventurous woman. She holds up her skirt to show other beauty spots placed on her hip. It was certainly common for a woman who wore such beauty spots to place them in a way that would lead her lover on, but the girl in the picture looks too young to have a lover. However, to put such anomalies into perspective, it need only be recalled that Madame de Bonneval was picked out as a likely mistress for Louis XV when she was nine years old.

By the time of Sade's imprisonment in 1768, however, it was

the style of life rather than the style of art which caused most criticism of the *petite maison*. There had been a violent incident at one dinner-party, where members of the Condé family were present. Some of the men stripped a young woman, Madame de Saint-Sulpice, who was pregnant at the time. Using a lighted candle they tried the experiment of seeing whether, as one contemporary verse termed it, they could make the smoke go up the chimney. Madame de Saint-Sulpice claimed to have been an invalid as the result of their attentions and her death followed but her tormentors were never brought to justice. The perpetrator of this horror was the Comte de Charolais, uncle and tutor of Sade's kinsman, the young Prince de Condé. He subsequently killed a servant whose wife resisted his sexual demands. It was he to whom Sade alludes in his suggestion in *Philosophy in the Boudoir*, when he opposes capital punishment, that murder should only be punished privately by murder. Charolais asked Louis XV for a pardon and Sade quotes the king's answer. "I pardon you but I also pardon him who will kill you."

Even among those who would have recoiled at such illtreatment of the girls they hired, extravagant behaviour was not hard to find. It was not particularly uncommon for a man like the Prince de Conti to hire ballet-girls and then, as one of them complained delicately to Sophie Arnould, to treat them as though they had been little boys. The banker Peixotte made demands that were no less bizarre. As a preliminary to his bedroom pleasures he required the girl to parade on all fours with a tail of peacock feathers fastened into a pearl sheath behind her. But the unfortunate Peixotte was the victim of an elaborate revenge on one of these evenings. As the performance was proceeding, the girl's accomplices burst in, pretending to be the police. They informed the banker that his only hope of pardon lay in making a full written confession. Overwhelmed by the bogus police-raid, he did as they instructed. To his dismay, the confession was then printed and hawked all over Paris as a best-selling pamphlet.

When set beside the most outrageous or brutal episodes of the *petites maisons*, Sade's infliction of several strokes with a whip on Rose Keller seems almost unremarkable. Even at court, when Madame du Barry succeeded Madame de Pompadour, she would have a girl whipped if it took her fancy. The penalties inflicted by the law of France certainly suggested that physical damage was not to be condemned in itself. The appalling torments suffered by such men as Damiens or Jean Calas, accused of murdering his son, were merely extreme examples of this. It is hard to imagine, for instance, that the spectators who attended the birching and branding of a young woman like Jeanne de la Motte were moved by an abstract concern for the French legal or penal systems. The culprit had forged the queen's authority for the purchase of a valuable necklace and had then disposed of it to her own advantage. She was condemned to be stripped, tied to the back of a cart and birched by the executioner. Then he was to brand her on each shoulder with a "V" for *voleuse* or thief. When she was untied from the cart after the birching, it required six men to hold her as she bit and scratched at the executioner. It was as much as they could do to brand her at all without caring too precisely where the mark appeared.

Despite the greater cruelties of public justice, the scandals of the *petites maisons* had become an embarrassment. Sade's conduct at Easter 1768 was precisely of the kind that could be punished without causing too much disturbance to the social order and yet giving the impression that something had been done. Thereafter, the girls and the procurers, the patrons and the artists, would continue business as usual, though perhaps with a little more discretion.

Sade remained a prisoner at Pierre-Encise through the summer of 1768. It seemed likely to be much the same sentence as that served by the Duc de Richelieu, a means of reforming a man of useful qualities rather than degrading him to the rank of criminal. There was a hopeful sign in August when Renée-Pélagie, who travelled to Lyon, was allowed to visit her husband. It came to nothing. She was warned in consequence that she had better prepare Sade. Louis XV was extremely displeased by the acts of libertinage of which the young nobleman had been guilty and had no intention of ordering his release.

It came as something of a surprise when Renée-Pélagie was told in November that she might visit Sade as often as she wished. Then, for no apparent reason, the king ordered Sade's release on 16 November. It was a conditional release, requiring him to go to his estate at La Coste and remain there. Sade accepted this restriction and the doors of his prison opened. He had inspired such confidence in Madame de Montreuil, the Abbé de Sade, Renée-

Pélagie, and all those who were concerned for him, that they believed he had learnt his lesson. He was now to be a model husband and a pattern of patrician decorum. They did not yet know that Sade was still privately cursing Rose Keller, scornful of the law and its officials who prized "the backside of a whore" above his own liberty. On a mid-November day, he rode out of Lyon towards Avignon and La Coste.

SIX

THE SENTENCE OF DEATH

1

THE ROSE KELLER CASE was a far more public controversy than the Jeanne Testard incident. Yet Sade's return to La Coste was certainly not that of a man in disgrace. His prospects were no worse than those of the Duc de Richelieu, who had spent a little time in the Bastille for his scandalous sexual behaviour. No one thought the worse of him when he came back victorious from Fontenoy or from his defeat of Admiral Byng at Minorca.

As for Sade himself, libertinage still seemed a pastime rather than an occupation. No more than the verses he wrote was it yet the main business of his life. He was a public figure, the young and personable Lieutenant-General of the provinces of Bresse and Bugey, Valromey and Gex, the first two being territories over which his cousin, the Prince de Condé, had the highest authority under the king. Sade was conscious of such honours but regarded them as a stepping-stone to the great ambition of his public life. He had been retired from the army at the peace of 1763 but had not yet given up hope of getting back into it again. He wrote to the Prince de Condé, urging him to intercede with the king so that the colonelcy of a cavalry regiment might be conferred upon the younger cousin.

Sade was that most unfortunate of men, seized with the ambition to be a soldier at a time when a great war ends. Moreover, the thrill of mounted warfare and particularly of a cavalry charge had an intensity and glamour unsurpassed even by the excitements of the *petite maison*. It was absolute and decisive, its greatest days yet to come. The charges of mounted regiments like the Scots Greys at Waterloo or the Light Cavalry Brigade at Balaclava offered an even chance of death or glory to the participants. Such occasions had something of the quality of a great symphony in performance.

The appeal of this to Sade was understandable. So much of his character was to be seen in terms of sexuality or a bulldog defiance of personal injustice that other aspects were apt to be overlooked. He was a slight, excitable figure (1 metre 68 centimetres, or 5 feet 6 inches in height), moved to fury or desire with equal facility, far less a bulldog than a terrier with its teeth sunk into the ankle of its tormentor. The glamour, excitement, colour and sophistication of life in a smart cavalry regiment, whether among comrades in battle or among the ribboned elegance of peace, seemed tailor-made for him. But Sade had been born too late for Dettingen or Fontenoy, too early for Wagram, Iena or Waterloo. His share of such excitements in northern Germany had been meagre enough. Shortly before the Rose Keller scandal broke, he had been given the rank of captain-commandant of cavalry. It was more than he would have hoped for in the months following the Arcueil incident but the truth was that there was no cavalry for him to command.

At the first opportunity in 1768 he left La Coste. Though forbidden to live in Paris by the king's decree, Sade exaggerated an attack of piles from which he had suffered and pleaded that he must seek medical attention for the fistula. He was allowed to stay just outside Paris, so long as he kept himself to himself. By this means he was at hand when his second son was born in June 1769 and christened Donatien-Claude-Armand. Unless the child was almost two months premature, he was evidently conceived on one of Renée-Pélagie's visits to the prisoner of Pierre-Encise, which suggests that Sade's confinement there was not very restrictive. This time, the infant was baptized in the presence of his family. The days when members of the royal family attended such celebrations by the Sades were now past.

Later that summer, on 24 July, Sade announced that he would be rejoining the Burgundian Cavalry with the active rank of captain. The regiment was then stationed in the little river-town of Fontenay-le-Comte, some thirty miles inland from the flat Biscay coast, just above La Rochelle. Sade arrived at the beginning of August and presented himself to the officer temporarily in command. He was astounded to be told that he was not wanted. It was not a question of his military record or abilities. The acting commander of the regiment was not prepared to serve with a man who did such things to young women as Sade had done.

Though he held a non-active commission, his requests to be given a full captaincy were everywhere rebuffed. He pestered the minister of war until, at last, he was given the honorific title of Marshal of Cavalry, largely because his father had held it before him. But the title also removed his claim to a captaincy in the Burgundian Cavalry, sparing its colonel any further visits from the eager and unwanted volunteer.

While Sade travelled in search of military preferment, Madame de Montreuil had resumed her correspondence with the Abbé de Sade in a spirit of exasperation. The Comte de Sade was dead and if anyone was to exercise moral influence on a young man of Sade's kind it was presumably to be his uncles. The elder of them, Commander of the Order of St John of Jerusalem and Prior of Toulouse with a Parisian home at St Cloud, had little to do with him. The comfortable Abbé de Sade might have appealed to his nephew's better nature, as one who had been his guardian. But the abbé had felt the anger of both sides in the Mademoiselle de Beauvoisin imposture at La Coste three years before. He seemed disinclined to intervene now.

It was not just a matter of indolence, as Madame de Montreuil seemed to think. Despite his reputation as a genial old lecher, the estrangement from his nephew was growing more marked. His own pleasures did not include tying girls down and thrashing them. Indeed, he was soon one of those who expressed the view privately that the young lord was a maniac who ought to be locked up. And so, for the moment, Sade remained beyond Madame de Montreuil's influence, trying to purchase a commission in a smart regiment, which might easily cost ten or twenty thousand livres.

Money was a source of dispute in its own right. In her letter of 2 March 1769, Madame de Montreuil informed the Abbé de Sade that his nephew had already spent seventeen thousand of the twenty thousand livres which came from her daughter's marriage portion. The money had been spent largely on the pleasures of the *petite maison*. During their marriage he had "eaten up" a total of sixty-six thousand livres by his "casual amusements", a debt still to be paid.

Though exiled from the attractions of Paris, Sade continued to travel a good deal. During September 1769, ten months after his release from Pierre-Encise, he went to Holland. Its libertarian atmosphere may have appealed to him but he was struck by the dull and phlegmatic character of Dutch society. At least, he said, the theatres were passable. If his claim to have visited England is valid, then it seems probable that it was an extension of his travels in Holland. It was in England that he recalled seeing a transcript of the trial of Joan of Arc, which he later drew upon when writing his novel *Isabelle of Bavaria*, as well as in an unperformed stage tragedy in the manner of Racine and Corneille. Sade found his sources in the Royal Library, by which he presumably meant the collection which George III gave to the British Museum as the King's Library.

Where did he get the money for these travels? In January 1782, Sade was to write to his former tutor, the Abbé Amblet, revealing the existence of what may have been an erotic novel, "written with the pen of Aretino". It was published shortly before he left for Holland. He gives no further description of it beyond saying that the money earned from it paid for his pleasures in one of the great cities of France and enabled him to live for two months in Holland. At the risk of spoiling the story, it has to be said that Aretino's principal title was as a satirist, "Flagello del Principi". That being the case, Sade may perhaps have been rewarded for an act of literary and political partisanship, scurrilous rather than erotic.

In 1790, J.-A. Dulaure, in a brief biographical list of former aristocrats, reported that Sade had travelled as far as Constantinople after his release from Pierre-Encise. He may have done but there is no evidence beyond this report. During his absence, Renée-Pélagie and her sister Anne-Prospère remained in Paris and Echauffour. On his return from the tour of Holland both Renée-Pélagie and her sister went to live with him at La Coste. In consequence, Sade's last child, his daughter Madeleine-Prospère, was born in April 1771.

In the light of the enthusiasm with which Sade's fictional heroes debauch their own daughters and the energy with which they argue that a daughter is her father's sexual property, his own attitude towards Madeleine-Laure seems instructive. He showed her little affection, let alone sexual desire. He remarked that she was plain and stupid and, in the event, she displeased him almost as much as his second son. It was one more caution on the error of supposing that Sade's fiction necessarily mirrored his own acts or even his specific desires.

He was briefly arrested for debt in 1771 but released from Fort-l'Evêque in Paris on 9 September after being detained there for eight days. Soon after this he was busy at the château of La Coste. Like his heroes in *The 120 Days of Sodom* he withdrew for the winter to his fastness, above the steep roofs and the narrow ways that ran between the limestone houses of La Coste. His playthings were not young slaves abducted for sexual experiment but a group of actors and acrtresses who were to perform in his private theatre. During the winter of 1771–2, he lived out his fantasies on the stage as he was later to do in the pages of his fiction. On 20 January 1772, he produced one of his own plays in this private theatre.

In the spring of that year, Sade engaged seven actors and five actresses at Marseille, as well as the leader of an "orchestra". Plays were performed from May to October, alternately in the private theatre at La Coste and the bow-windowed salon of the fine neo-classical house at Mazan, or in its raised garden with a backdrop of summer fields to Carpentras and the Rhône. Most of these plays were in the theatrical repertoire, though at least one was written by Sade himself, *Le Marriage du Siècle*, in which he, Renée-Pélagie and Anne Prospère played parts with the hired actors and actresses. From Madame de Montreuil came further protests at the manner in which the family money was being squandered.

Madame de Montreuil had heard something of this summer season of theatre. When she expressed unease at the indecent part which her two daughters might be made to take in these spectacles, her misgivings seem to have been caused less by the plays than by the two sisters being on an equal and familiar footing with a company of actors and actresses. Sade was not interested in amateur theatricals as mere self-entertainment by the bourgeoisie. In its more professional form at Mazan or La Coste, Madame de Montreuil would certainly regard the stage as an inappropriate place for the daughters of Echauffour.

Before the winter of 1771–2 was over, Sade had persuaded Anne-Prospère to share his bed. It had certainly happened before the matter became semi-public the following summer and may have occurred much earlier. The younger sister was the more enigmatic of the two, withdrawn and secretive in one respect, yet more sexually adventurous in another. Whatever Sade's reputation as the man who planned unnatural acts with Jeanne Testard in a black-draped room or who whipped Rose Keller, Anne-Prospère's feelings seemed unaffected. Renée-Pélagie remained the witness of an affair which was, indirectly at least, incestuous. Whether she was more accomplice than witness was to be a question of debate. She made no apparent attempt to interfere in the pleasures of her husband and her sister. For Sade himself, as his stories in *The Crimes of Love* suggest, the depravities of incest were as moving as any of his dramas with Jeanne Testard or Rose Keller.

Life at La Coste went on this way until the spring of 1772 began to turn to summer. South of the village ran the hazy outlines of the Luberon range. Beyond them was the leafy administrative town of Aix-en-Provence with its fountains and avenues, its rococo elegance and prosperous mansions. To the south of that was the city of Marseille.

Towards the end of June 1772, Sade set off for Marseille with his valet Latour, taking up residence there in the Hôtel des Treize Cantons during the week of 21 June. Whatever other business may have brought him to the streets of the great port, one of his appointments was to entertain a company of actors to supper on the following Thursday, 25 June.

A fortnight later, the capitals of Europe heard of a murderous debauch contrived by the same infamous Marquis de Sade who had flogged Rose Keller and promised to cut her up alive. In some accounts, the latest outrage rivalled the most violent sexual excesses of the Roman emperors. Five years later the *Mémoires Secrets*, attributed to Bachaumont, still spoke of a splendid costume ball given by Sade for the best society of Marseille. At the height of the festivities it became evident that the satanic master of ceremonies had poisoned the chocolate which his guests had drunk. Soon the ballroom and the streets around it were filled with prostrate men and women, groaning and writhing in their last agonies. But there was a more demonic element in the story. A good many of the women had unwittingly taken a milder poison. They did not die immediately. Instead, they came leaping out of the ballroom, tearing off their clothes, seizing the first available partners in the great port and begging for sexual relief. The demon marquis had put them into such a state of "uterine frenzy" that they must either find such relief for their desires or go mad.

It is possible to imagine that Sade might have been flattered by such an account and gratified by the moral chest-beating which he had inspired. But the story matched his future fiction rather than his present life. There had been a truth behind the drama and scandal at Marseille. But what was it and how had it come about?

2

Sade had certainly gone to the city in search of pleasure. He had always regarded the girls of Provence as passionate, warm-blooded and more willing to join in extravagant sexual games than the cooler women of Paris. Nor was it difficult to find them. Marseille had been partly rebuilt in the seventeenth century. The handsome classicism of the Canebière, where hemp had once been grown by the rope-makers, now ran through the centre of the city to the basin of the old port. To the east of this, the long stretch of rue de Rome and the smaller rue d'Aubagne carried traffic towards Provence and Italy. It was in the little streets between these two, almost in sight of the masts and rigging of the harbour, that Sade found a hunting-ground for girls who would cooperate in the realization of his fantasies.

A nobleman did not, of course, search the hot and narrow streets himself. On Thursday 25 June it was the valet Latour, apparently with Sade directing the encounter from within his carriage, who visited a girl of eighteen, Marianne Laverne, at her lodgings in rue d'Aubagne. Latour was dressed in blue and yellow, like a sailor rather than a valet, but his message was plain. Marianne Laverne recalled that, "He said that his master only came to the town to have some fun with the girls and that he particularly liked them young." The statement later sworn by her described the proposed arrangement. Sade "would come the next day, Friday, at eleven in the evening. He would have come the same evening but as he was having supper with some actors, he could only call on the following night at eleven."

Latour himself came back to the house on Friday evening, only to find that Marianne Laverne was out. She had gone for a boat-trip. But he found another girl who lodged there, Marianne Laugier, twenty years old. He suggested that Sade should come to the house next day and amuse himself with several of the girls simultaneously. This was agreed. But when the next morning came, Latour once again appeared alone. He explained that Sade thought the house in rue d'Aubagne was too conspicuous and that he had arranged to use the apartment of Mariette Borelly. At twenty-three, Mariette Borelly was a little older than the others and a natural choice as mistress of ceremonies. Her apartment was nearby, on the corner of rue des Capucins, at number fifteen in rue d'Aubagne. By the time that Marianne Laverne and Marianne Laugier got there, they found another girl of twenty, Rose Coste, who called herself "Rosette". The apartment was on the third floor of the house and other than Sade, Latour and the four girls, there was only a servant-woman in the kitchen.

Sade arrived, wearing a grey dress-coat with a blue lining. Like any would-be cavalry officer, he wore his sword and carried a stick. As the director of the drama, anxious to rehearse his cast, he began the first act. He took a fistful of coins from his pocket and promised them to the first girl who went into the bedroom. Marianne Laverne won the race. Sade and Latour followed her and locked themselves in. Sade told the girl to undress and lie on the bed with Latour. She later said that she lay there "with" Latour, whom Sade encouraged with one hand while he whipped her with the other. The point of Latour being on the bed was evidently that she was performing face-down on top of the valet while Sade roused her with his whip.

When this episode was over, Sade produced a small box of crystal bound with gold. It contained some pastilles of sugared aniseed. He persuaded the girl to take them. The sweets would have a carminative effect, he said, as she swallowed seven or eight of them. Presently he would either watch Latour sodomize her or do so himself. According to her statement, Marianne Laverne rebelled at this suggestion. The law would do nothing to her for allowing herself to be whipped. On the other hand, to permit herself to be penetrated in the way Sade suggested was to risk a death sentence. Even if she did not reject his suggestion, it was advisable for her to say that she had done so. He then invited her to whip him as a variation but she lacked the resolve to do it. Already the orgy was beginning to dwindle into banality.

Irritated by the girl's incompetence, Sade told her to go and get a broom. This was sent for from the kitchen. When it arrived,

Sade handed it to her and told her to use it on him as a birch. Marianne Laverne tried it for a while and then complained of a stomach ache. She went off to find a glass of water. Such everyday inconveniences were never permitted to impede the erotic fantasies of his fiction.

By this time, an air of general grumpiness rather than ardent sexuality seems to have hung over the proceedings. Marianne Laverne was in the kitchen complaining to the servant about her stomach ache. Latour and two of the girls, Marianne Laugier and Rose Coste, were standing about waiting for something to happen. Sade was in the bedroom alone.

It must have been with an urge for retribution that Sade summoned the mistress of the apartment to the bedroom. He told Mariette Borelly to undress and bend over the end of the bed. When she had done so, he began using the broom on her as a birch. Those outside waited patiently while Sade put his energy into beating the young woman. At last it seemed that events had measured up to his expectation of the morning's pleasures. Presently he stopped and abruptly told her that she must use the broom on him while he stood by the mantelpiece and kept a tally of the strokes, cutting the numbers on the wood with his knife. Indeed, he kept a tally for the entire team, his grand total coming to more than eight hundred.

Just as abruptly, he told Mariette Borelly to lie on her back and made love to her in the most orthodox and unimpeachable manner. She later gave evidence that Sade was sodomized by Latour during this. Perhaps he was, though her accusation was unsupported and Sade's attitude towards homosexuals, expressed in his Italian journal three years later, casts some doubt on whether the bisexuality of his fiction from 1785 onwards reflected his own past experiences.

Rose Coste followed Mariette Borelly in the bedroom. When she was lying naked on the bed, Sade told her that Latour would now "make use of her behind". Rose Coste swore that she had refused. There was some argument at this but she was a good girl and was not to be persuaded. Instead, she lay on top of Latour and had intercourse with him while Sade birched her.

There remained only the other twenty-year-old, Marianne Laugier. When she had undressed, Sade fondled her and told her that he still had twenty-five strokes with a whip to give. She was to be the recipient. He produced a spiked whip and the girl, in a panic at the sight of it, tried to get out of the room. But at this point they were joined by Marianne Laverne, whose stomach ache was easier after drinking a cup of coffee in the kitchen. Sade insisted that she and Marianne Laugier must eat some more of the wind-producing sweets. Marianne Laverne refused. Marianne Laugier took some without enthusiasm.

Marianne Laverne had dressed by now but Sade locked the door before he and Latour put her prone on the bed. Sade lifted her skirts and studied her behind hopefully. For want of anything better, he took the whip and beat her a second time. The proceedings apparently ended with Sade sodomizing the reluctant Marianne Laverne. The other girls alleged that while this was happening Latour, whom Sade referred to as "Monsieur le Marquis", treated his master "Lafleur" in the same way. Whether this was true or was a means of trying to rescue Marianne Laverne from a possible death sentence by making her an unwilling victim was not clear.

Sade gave each girl six livres and arranged that they should have another party that evening. Later that afternoon, Latour went round to rue d'Aubagne to invite Marianne Laverne and Marianne Laugier to come with him on a boat-trip. They refused. Though Sade had intended to visit them, he was delayed by a visit from the actor, Sebastien de Rosières, whom he entertained to supper. By the time this was over, he was obliged to take pleasure where he could find it. Latour went out at nine o'clock and encountered Marguerite Coste, a young woman of twenty-five, outside the doorway of her house in the little rue St Ferréol le Vieux, which ran between rue de Rome and rue d'Aubagne. Sade was due to leave Marseille for La Coste the next day and was intent upon a final night of amusement.

Marguerite Coste was willing. Latour returned to the Hôtel des Treize Cantons and informed his master. As soon as he could, Sade disengaged himself from the supper with Sebastien de Rosières and made for rue St Ferréol le Vieux. Sade and Latour must have made an odd sight that evening, the tall valet dressed as a sailor beside the short dapper figure of his master in dress-coat and silk breeches, wearing a sword and carrying a gold-topped stick to ensure a safe passage through this part of Marseille after dark. They arrived at the house and Sade went into the bedroom with the girl alone. He divested himself of stick and sword, then sat down on the bed. Taking the crystal box from his pocket he offered Marguerite Coste one of the aniseed sweets. She took it and ate it. He offered her another.

Without ado he explained that he wished to "play with her behind", a euphemism which concealed little, and that there were certain other unusual pleasures in which they would spend the night. Marguerite Coste refused, though accepting another of the bonbons from the little crystal box. In the end she agreed, though it was by no means clear from her evidence what she had agreed to. When it was over, Sade had given her six francs and left.

On the following morning, he left Marseille for La Coste. By then, the first evidence of a crime was apparent. Late on Saturday night, two medical dramas had been enacted in the houses of rue St Ferréol le Vieux and rue d'Aubagne. Marianne Laverne's stomach ache of Saturday morning had not improved, indeed it was much worse and alarmed her companions. She was feverish, her pulse was rapid, and it was alleged that she began to vomit black bile and blood. At the same time, her urinary tract was inflamed. She passed water frequently, though with some difficulty. Most alarming of all, it seemed that she was beginning to bring up fragments of her stomach lining.

It would have been little consolation to her to know that another girl, a few streets away, was suffering the first symptoms of a similar ordeal. Marguerite Coste's pains and nausea began later but seemed to worsen more rapidly, perhaps because she had consumed far more of the sugared aniseed pastilles. When their doctors were called, they gave their opinions that both girls were the victims of poisoning. Among general poisons of the irritant type, which this clearly was, the symptoms seemed to correspond closely to those produced by a strong dose of arsenic.

Questions and investigations began. Marianne Laverne and Marguerite Coste had eaten a number of the little sweets that Sade carried in his ornamental box. Marianne Laugier had put them in her mouth as he had ordered but had then thrown them out of the window while he was not looking. She and Rose Coste, as well as Mariette Borelly, escaped the ordeal of their companions. There was no difficulty in finding some of the pastilles. Marianne Laugier had thrown hers into the street where they were easily collected. Mariette Borelly's servant, sweeping the apartment next day, gathered more of them in the broom that had been used as a makeshift birch on Mariette Borelly herself.

As it happened, the two poisoned girls recovered after a week of medical care. They and the others were now anxious to assist the authorities, if only as a means of keeping out of trouble. Poisoning, incitement to sodomy, sodomy itself with the willing Latour and the unwilling Marianne Laverne were included in the depositions, sufficient to draw all the retribution of the law on to the head of the fugitive criminal. If Marianne Laverne had been forced to submit to his unnatural lust then, as the unwilling victim of such an assault, she had no real need to fear being tried for her life. The manner in which events unfolded meant that, of course, the story which spread to the world was that of the accusers rather than of Sade himself.

A description of the criminal was given to the authorities. The picture of a fair-haired, good-looking young man, slightly built, in dress-coat and breeches, carrying a sword and stick was perhaps a little vague. When the witnesses added that he was called the Comte or the Marquis – they could not quite remember which – de Sade, identification was complete. Sade had driven beyond Aix and on to La Coste but he was sought by every officer of justice in the area. Measures were taken to seize his revenues and possessions.

His response to the charges brought in the Rose Keller case told against him now. That callous self-justification at Paris four years earlier suggested that he was certainly capable of having poisoned the girls at Marseille deliberately to heighten his own excitement by a diabolical sexual experiment. An entry in the *Mémoires Secrets* for 25 July claimed that he had already been investigating cantharides, or Spanish fly, by trying out the aphrodisiac on his young sister-in-law, Anne-Prospère, during their winter at La Coste.

Something appalling had happened at Marseille, though the world was not quite sure what. As late as 1834, Jules Janin insisted that the two girls poisoned by the infamous marquis had died the next day. Poisoning for pleasure was, after all, a phenomenon of murder trials. The sardonic use of poison in this manner, whether it occurred or not, was a perfect match for the reputation of Sade. It was certainly to be a device of his fiction. In his sketch for the fourth book of *The 120 Days of Sodom* he notes that his heroes amused themselves by giving one of their girls a powder that would cause her the greatest possible discomfort without killing her. In planning this joke, they contrive "to give Julie a powder, hidden in her food, which will cause her the most frightful belly-cramps. Then they tell her that she has been poisoned. She believes them, begins to howl, and goes almost out of her mind." Another reference is made to a man who never makes love to his wives except by way of sodomy and who is now poisoning the twenty-second of them.

Cantharides was used as an aphrodisiac by some of Sade's contemporaries. It was also used for medical purposes in a homeopathic dose. The Duc de Richelieu impregnated sweets with the powder and gave these to his mistresses. Such bonbons were sometimes called *pastilles de Richelieu*. They were alternatively *pastilles de serail*, a name under which they were said to have been used by Madame du Barry on the girls in her charge so that they might be more active in serving the ageing Louis XV. The doses were small enough to avoid indisposition and scandal, but cantharides remained a poison as lethal as arsenic.

Scientifically, cantharides was known as a substance whose operation was similar to arsenic. In anything more than a minute dose it would set up an irritation so violent as to destroy the lining of the digestive tract and to produce a fatal nausea. In very small doses, it was intended to pass through a woman's body until, when excreted, it set up a milder irritation or excitement in the erogenous areas, allegedly increasing her desire for intercourse. The source of the substance was in the wings of the *cantharis* or Spanish fly, hence the popular name for the drug in England. In France the sweets containing it had been more generally referred to as *pilles galantes* and in Italy as *diavolini*. In its natural form it would blister the skin when applied externally. The prospect of internal use might have deterred all but the most resolute.

Dosage was never Sade's strong point. He was no apothecary and was evidently no true judge of what he was doing. Cantharides could only be used in a far weaker solution than he was now said to have devised and in which the aniseed sweets were said to have been soaked. Yet despite the waggish cruelty of his fictional heroes, there is no convincing evidence that Sade intended to poison anyone at Marseille.

There was a sequel to the outrage, though it was not widely reported. Marianne Laverne and Marguerite Coste rather quickly recovered from their ordeal. Forensic evidence had been employed in such cases as this for a hundred years, at least since Spencer Cowper was acquitted of murder in 1699, when it was demonstrated that a floating body was not necessarily dead before entering the water. As a matter of routine, by 1772, the vomit yielded by Marianne Laverne and Marguerite Coste was analyzed. The two apothecaries, André Rimbaud and Jean-Baptiste-Joseph Auert, made their report on 5 July. They had subjected the samples to the usual tests, mixing each with a chalk solution, adding a distillation of the suspect material to that of copper, then testing the residue in water. None of the changes which would indicate arsenic or a corrosive substance appeared. They were given two grains of the bonbons to examine. One of them burnt without any odour of arsenic. The other, when examined under a microscope and tested, seemed to consist only of aniseed and sugar.

The analysis of the alleged poison certainly contradicted some of the symptoms reported by the doctors. But the analysts did not deny those symptoms. They said only that the substance analyzed "was not the matter which had made the patient vomit". In the two grains of sugared aniseed, they had found nothing sinister but considered that the sample was too small to establish the truth one way or the other.

As in the case of Rose Keller, the most specific evidence failed to corroborate the details which Sade's reputation demanded. The chemical analysis did not entirely acquit him and its accuracy might still be questioned. But it certainly raised the possibility that the bonbons were not the cause of the sickness or, at least, that he had not poisoned the girls after all. He was never brought to a proper trial, though he was captured in the end. Had he been arraigned in person, he might have produced the evidence, which he later described from his prison cell, to show that the girls were not poisoned at all but suffering from the remedies of a pavement quack. Though Sade's unsupported claim might be doubted, it was not contradicted by the forensic examination. The irony was that he was hunted and then held in captivity for most of the rest of his life for a crime which he may well not have committed and which, as a crime, perhaps never existed.

4

Sade reached the temporary security of La Coste early in July 1772, just as the warrant for his arrest on the capital charge of poisoning was being issued. His villagers would remain loyal to him but at any moment he might glimpse across the plain to the east a cloud of dust by the ancient pont Julien, as the constable of Apt and his officers rode out to arrest the fugitive. In the hot Provençal summer, the château above the village rooftops was the scene of hurried consultation and decision.

Renée-Pélagie must go to Marseille and institute an appeal on his behalf before the justices who had charge of the investigation. It would be better if he could be present himself but the risk was too great. At the same time, she must try to buy off the two "poisoned" girls, as Rose Keller had been bought off several years before. It ought not to be difficult with such a pair as Marguerite Coste and Marianne Laverne. Sade and Latour, both facing a death sentence if matters went badly, must go into hiding at once. The only role not defined in this scheme was that of Anne-Prospère. It was unwise to leave her in charge at La Coste to deal with the forces of law when they arrived. Nor was there any role for her at Marseille. Her attitude to Sade seems to have been as unchanged as it had been after the Rose Keller incident. Perhaps it was her suggestion that she should go into hiding with her brother-in-law and his servant.

According to the evidence of his future gaolers, before the first week of July was over, Sade, Latour and Anne-Prospère were on the road from La Coste to the frontier of Savoy, the mainland territory of the King of Sardinia. Once across it, they could think themselves safe with the road to Italy before them. The nearest stretch of the frontier was just above the Mediterranean coast to the west of Nice. This was the direction decided upon. By the time that the constable and his officers arrived at La Coste from the little town of Apt, they found silent and suspicious villagers in the steep and narrow streets. The château contained only the family servants who were certainly not going to aid their master's downfall. The constable and his party rode back down the precipitous cobbles, out under the arch of the Portail des Chèvres and round the flank of the hill to the road that took them back to Apt.

But Sade's escape, however necessary it may have been, killed his hopes at Marseille. Renée-Pélagie had no difficulty in persuading the girls to change their story – perhaps to tell the whole truth this time. They went before the notary on 9 and 12 August and in pious unanimity withdrew all their allegations against Sade. The justices were unimpressed and dismissed these retractions. Renée-Pélagie tried to appeal but without success. Throughout August 1772, the case against Sade and Latour went ahead, while the criers in the hot city streets and village squares announced the identity of the two wanted men and the nature of their crimes. In the absence of the culprits, the trial went ahead with all speed. There was no defence. Sentence was passed on 3 September and forwarded to the high court of justice at Aix-en-Provence. The details of the sentence were confirmed with only minor variations on 11 September.

Sade was convicted of poisoning. Both he and Latour were convicted of sodomy. According to the first formal sentence of the law, they were to be led with ropes round their necks to the cathedral of Ste Marie Majeure, close to the harbour of Marseille. There, in penitents' shirts, their heads and feet bare, they were to kneel with tall burning candles in their hands and ask for forgiveness before the main door of the building. When that was done, they were to be led to place St Louis. Sade was to mount the scaffold, where the executioner would behead him. The more plebeian Latour was to be strangled by the hangman. In order that no consecrated ground should be defiled by the burial of such corpses, the two bodies were then to be burnt and the ashes scattered to the winds. It was an elaborate and rather expensive entertainment, even for a city the size of Marseille. The law required that the central figures should pay for being despatched with such ceremony. The court therefore fined Sade thirty francs and Latour ten francs to help cover the costs of their deaths.

The high court varied this sentence by substituting Aix-en-Provence as the place of execution. In the entire scheme, the only flaw was that the officers of justice had no one in their hands to execute. Rather than postpone the spectacle, it was better to have execution by proxy. So the high court was able to announce that the entire splendid charade had taken place at Aix on 11 September. Sade had been beheaded and Latour strangled. But the executioner had beheaded an effigy and the hangman had strangled a straw dummy that may or may not have resembled Latour. Perhaps it was thought safer to perform a farce of this kind in the tranquillity of Aix than at Marseille, where a large and enthusiastic crowd might run riot if it were deprived of the sight of real blood spouting from severed arteries or the features of a living face contorting under the hangman's attentions.

Sade, Latour and another servant known as "La Jeunesse" were safely at Nice, under the protection of the kingdom of Sardinia. The letters of Sardinian officials, including the governor of Miolans, added that Anne-Prospère de Launay accompanied her brother-in-law as his "wife". The Comte de la Tour, Governor of Chambéry, spoke of Sade having abducted Anne-Prospère, "whom he led to Venice and through part of Italy under the name of his wife, taking those liberties due to him under this title". The documentary evidence assembled by Maurice Heine and Gilbert Lely makes it probable that Anne-Prospère was the woman who was with him. It was suggested by Jean-Jacques Pauvert that if certain undated letters are given the date of 1772, she can be shown to be somewhere else. But this is the chronology of begged questions. Whatever the truth, contemporary witnesses certainly thought Sade's companion was Anne-Prospère. Madame de Montreuil was to write to the Comte de la Tour on 21 July 1773, demanding the return of letters in Sade's possession, "because mention is made in them of her younger daughter, who had been seduced by the Comte de Sade, her brother-in-law". Even before that, Madame de Montreuil had been anxious to get hold of a certain red box inlaid with ivory which Sade had with him in Chambéry. He must not, she insisted, be allowed to abstract any papers from it. Perhaps such papers related to his travels in northern Italy. Their disclosures or comments relating to Anne-Prospère may have inspired Madame de Montreuil's anxiety.

If Anne-Prospère travelled as Sade's wife, she afforded him every intimacy that was due to a husband, as the Comte de la Tour described it. Sade himself posed as the Comte de Mazan, a subsidiary title taken from his lands in northern Provence. News of the proceedings at Marseille filled him with scorn. To those who passed sentence upon him, he returned a derisive salute, the outburst of a man who regarded the Marseille scandal as a fuss about nothing. Though it was fifteen years later, his rage at the absurdity of the legal proceedings and the ludicrous inappropriateness of the sentence still warmed his imagination. His contempt for the president of the high court of justice at Aix was edged with personal vindictiveness as he wrote of himself in the third person, mingling Marseille with memories of Arcueil.

In his story "The Mystified Magistrate", Sade took a literary revenge on the president of the high court. Under the exact date of 1772, he presented himself as a decent young nobleman injured by a whore, to whom he gave a thrashing as an "amusing" revenge. Such was his fictional amalgam of the events at Mariette Borelly's apartment. The contemptible oaf, as he calls the president, made this birching of the young woman a capital crime by talk of murder and poison. His fellow judges were too stupid to argue the point. They conspired to ruin the young gentleman and, unable to lay hands on him, tried to justify their conduct by a sham death sentence.

Few of Sade's contemporaries ever saw his misadventures in quite the same light as he. In the official calendar of crime, the whipping of Rose Keller had been a mere incident compared with the Marseille poisonings. Indeed, the girls of the rue d'Aubagne to whom he gave six francs apiece for their services must have felt hard done by, if they heard of the two thousand four hundred which Rose Keller had coaxed from the Sades and the Montreuils as the price of cooperation. But while the extent of Sade's criminality may have been exaggerated a little in the case of Rose Keller, there is at least a possibility that it was exaggerated out of recognition in the Marseille "poisonings". He had better reason for his indignation there than at Arcueil.

5

There was one actor in the drama who had yet to appear on stage. By 29 August, Renée-Pélagie was back at La Coste, and so was Madame de Montreuil. Madame de Montreuil had organized the buying-off of Rose Keller, in order to save her son-in-law and daughter. She was able to support Renée-Pélagie's efforts to quieten the scandal in Marseille, until they came to nothing. So far as Sade was concerned, the period of grace had expired. Madame de Montreuil made the long journey from the forests and fields of Echauffour to the southern landscape of La Coste in order to be with her daughters. Upon her arrival, she apparently discovered that her younger daughter had eloped to Savoy with the perpetrator of the latest scandal.

The name of the Montreuils had been tarnished by the rumours of orgy and murder now attaching to that of the house of Sade. Madame de Montreuil had reason to feel cheated of the social rewards and the future fame which she had imagined for Renée-Pélagie and the children. As for Anne-Prospére, what future would there be for her, shop-soiled in the marriage market by her scandalous attachment to her brother-in-law? Brooding among the cool summers and winter rains of Echauffour, Madame de Montreuil saw reason for her grievances. Sade was now thirty-two, the head of one of the great families of France. He behaved, even by the most lenient assessment, like a rowdy, womanizing subaltern. Indeed, if the catalogue of poisoning, sodomy, assault and incest were to be believed, it was a good deal worse than any regimental depravity.

Such was the view from Echauffour and the Paris house in rue Neuve du Luxembourg. But there was a further ingredient in Madame de Montreuil's attitude towards her son-in-law and it was the determining one. At the beginning of the marriage she had been doting, then understanding, then cautious. Because her affection and understanding had been rejected, she now grew unalterably hostile in her dealings with Sade. She retained her friendship with the Abbé de Sade and other members of his family, seeing that they were as much the victims of the young criminal's behaviour as she and her husband. The question at issue was whether her son-in-law was criminally evil or whether he was simply a criminal lunatic. Whichever the answer, the proper place for him would be much the same.

By the autumn of 1772, Sade and his companions had set up house in Savoy, near Chambéry. He still called himself the Comte de Mazan but his true identity was hardly a secret. Nor would it be difficult to find him. Anne-Prospère returned to La Coste and then apparently went back to her brother-in-law in Savoy. Anyone who had chosen to follow her would have found the fugitive. For the moment, it seemed that public indignation had cooled and that the interest in catching and punishing him was growing stale.

So long as he was beyond the immediate reach of French law, it was scarcely worth the laborious process of trying to bring him to justice. But Madame de Montreuil now thought it worth doing, if only to separate him from her daughters. She sought the assistance of the Duc d'Aiguillon, foreign minister of Louis XV. The minister listened to her story and then summoned the Sardinian ambassador in Paris, Comte Ferrero de la Marmora. He informed the count that a wanted criminal, masquerading as the Comte de Mazan, was living near Chambéry. It would confer a great favour upon France if the kingdom of Sardinia, or at least its mainland duchy of Savoy, were to arrest the miscreant and simply hold him in prison, securely and indefinitely. "His family is greatly concerned that he should be securely detained, his mind being much deranged, and there is good reason to fear that he may risk returning to France or that he may perpetrate some new madness in Savoy." His detention in a secure château would cost the Savoyards nothing, since the family would have to send money for his food and accommodation. There need be no trial, no extradition and no public scandal. The Comte de Mazan, alias the Marquis de Sade, was to be safely locked up and then allowed to fade from the collective memory of his age.

When the Duc d'Aiguillon put the case in such terms, the Sardinian government was ready to oblige its powerful neighbour. On the night of 8 December 1772, the house near Chambéry was surrounded by soldiers. The Comte de Chavanne and two of his officers entered. They found Sade and his two servants, Latour and La Jeunesse. There was no sign of Anne-Prospère. Sade was taken completely by surprise. He offered no resistance and surrendered the arms he was carrying, a sword and two pistols. Next morning, he was driven to the hilltop fortress of Miolans, high above the valley of the Isère. The strength and solidity of its towers perfectly matched the bleak and rocky landscape over which it looked. Sade was locked in a cell with a distant view of the Alps. Then he was left to think his own thoughts.

Within hours he was made to understand the gravity of his situation. He was accused of no crime and his story was not to be heard. Unless he could save himself, he might remain at Miolans until he died. His fate was in the hands of those who were answerable to no court for their actions. There was no appeal against their decisions. Neither the manner of his arrest nor the appearance of the prison suggested that this was to be a few months' detention of the kind he had endured at Pierre-Encise. In any case, if he was turned over to the French authorities, he might be faced by something worse than Miolans.

Sade tried to persuade the Sardinian authorities that he was an innocent man, the victim of persecution by powerful forces in France. If he was believed, he might be released. He began a series of letters to the governor of Chambèry, the Comte de la Tour, explaining his innocence. Perhaps in time his protests would be heeded. Otherwise, he must escape. There was a moral complication in any plan for escape. Sade was, in appearance at least, an officer and a gentleman. One does not keep an officer and a gentleman locked up like a drunken trooper. Sade signed a parole, which he had no intention of honouring, promising that he would make no attempt to get away. In return for this, he asked for a servant to attend him and for permission to correspond with his family. This was agreed. With the instinct of an old lag, Sade knew that the first privilege is the truly difficult one to win. The rest follow more easily, as if from precedent. He wrote to the Comte de la Tour, explaining that he must have a little money, just sufficient to pay debts which he had contracted while in prison. He also needed to buy a watch. Later he admitted that it was not a watch which must be paid for but gambling debts that were to be settled. While in prison he had played cards with the Baron de l'Allée de Songy, a rather more professional criminal than Sade was ever to be. Not surprisingly, the baron had soon emptied Sade's pockets.

The baron was in prison for a series of crimes, ranging from attempted murder and assault to organizing a gaol-break. He was a gamester and an accomplished swordsman, a swaggering figure who was Sade's only close associate among the prisoners of Miolans. They met in the prison day-room, where the inmates were allowed to congregate and talk together. Sade also earned the privilege of being allowed to walk in the garden, so situated that any escape from it was impossible.

Sade's association with the Baron de l'Allée de Songy was watched by the prison governor. As so often, gambling led to suspicion and quarrels until the two men were on thoroughly bad terms. There was nearly a fight when Sade accused the baron of cheating at cards. The baron's speciality was playing faro, a game so crooked that English law had made it illegal at one time. It required the players to bet on the order in which cards would be turned up by the banker and was designed to empty the pockets of the uninitiated. Colonel Edmund Fielding, father of the novelist, had lost £500 in a few minutes when he played for the first time at Prince's Coffee House in 1718. The opportunities for trickery were almost unlimited and Sade soon realized that he had been fleeced. He also denounced the baron for taking a mean advantage of the valet Latour, who was held in prison with Sade, by making the young man sign promissory notes for the gambling debts he was incurring by playing cards with this aristocratic sharper.

In the early weeks of 1773, Sade found other targets for his displeasure. He raged and swore at the prison governor, the Commandant Louis de Launay, then wrote a high-minded letter to the Comte de la Tour complaining of the prison governor's conduct. Sade announced that he had been brought up as a gentleman and deplored the governor's manner of beginning every word with an "f" or a "b".

To the governor of Chambéry, Sade forwarded petitions for his freedom, demands for visits by his wife, and his first protest against Madame de Montreuil, whom he now accused of seeking his destruction. With the prison governor he was less formal. No less than the spoilt child of the Condé Palace, Sade at thirty-two showed an ill temper that made de Launay fear personal violence. Orders were given for Sade to be kept under lock and key. This provoked more letters in which Sade accused de Launay of being an accomplice in the baron's card-sharping. But such detonations of anger, however therapeutic, achieved nothing. Petitions and accusations alike were turned away. His hopes of freedom seemed to dwindle and die.

On 1 March, the Comte de la Marmora reported to the Comte de la Tour a meeting with the French foreign minister at which Sade had been the topic of conversation. If the foreign minister sounded concerned, there was reason to think that the warnings had been put into his mind, if not into his mouth, by Madame de Montreuil.

Yesterday I saw the minister, the Duc d'Aiguillon, at whose insistence the "Comte de Mazan" is detained. I read to him the letter which Monsieur de Launay, Commandant of the fortress of Miolans, wrote to you after receiving one himself from the prisoner's wife. Monsieur de Launay is beyond reproach. One must excuse the feelings which an ill-informed wife may unfortunately harbour when her trust has been abused by the husband she loves. It is necessary that Monsieur de Sade shall be held more securely than ever, that all leniency shall be withheld, that all communication with the outside world shall be forbidden, and that, above all, his wife shall not be allowed near him.

Commandant de Launay needed no warnings of this kind. He had complained on 5 February of the danger presented by allowing Sade freedom of movement within the prison. He had discovered that Sade had changed all his money into French currency and that he was asking for information about bridges across the Isère. So long as Sade was not locked up in a cell, he might "scale the walls in a moment, despite all my precautions". Perhaps this seemed alarmist, since the walls on the prisoners' side of Miolans represented a long and precipitous drop.

Renée-Pélagie worked from the beginning against her mother's attempt to keep Sade in confinement. Lacking Madame de Montreuil's influence with ministers of state, she took more direct means. In March 1773, three months after Sade's arrest, she arrived in Chambéry with an adviser of the Montreuil family, Albaret. She was dressed as a man and might have had a vague plan of tricking her way into the fortress of Miolans and coming out with her husband. Such an adventure was no more than a figment of a drawing-room novel. She must first trick her way through the military garrison which occupied much of the fortress of Miolans. Then she must penetrate to the heart of the prison itself. After that would come the far more hazardous journey back through the prison and the garrison with Sade.

Even her arrival at the little town of Montmélian, where she took lodgings in an inn on 7 March, was known almost at once to the authorities. The rulers of Savoy had already decided that the Marquise de Sade, like all other visitors, would be turned away. At sunset, Albaret presented himself at the fortress of Miolans with a letter from the marquise and a request that he should be allowed to see the prisoner. He was turned away. Next day,

Renée-Pélagie wrote to the Comte de la Tour, asking to be allowed to visit her husband. The request was refused.

Renée-Pélagie gave up and withdrew from Savoy. Defeated for the moment, she contented herself with writing abusive letters to the governor of the prison. If he was affected by these, he was also consoled by letters of encouragement from Madame de Mountreuil, assuring him that he was earning the admiration of all right-thinking members of the Sade family by keeping the marquis locked up. She knew what a trial it must be to have such a prisoner in one's care but urged de Launay to do his duty and to rest assured of the support of powerful friends.

After his final bout of anger, Sade had appeared to resign himself to his imprisonment. Even the Commandant de Launay thought how much more tranquil and reasonable his charge had become. Indeed, the governor suggested that if only Sade would confide in him, approaches might be made on his behalf to Madame de Montreuil or to the Duc d'Aiguillon. Nothing could be promised but if Sade behaved himself well, it was possible that he might be allowed to live quietly as a free man in Savoy, or even in some remote part of France.

Instead of rejecting such a preposterous way of life, Sade mellowed still further. With the coming of April and Easter, the Commandant de Launay and the Comte de la Tour were impressed by the new gentleness which came over him after he had fulfilled his religious obligations. Here, surely, was proof of the reforming moral influence of their prison system. Best of all, he had patched up his quarrel with the Baron de l'Allée de Songy. There was a room which some of the officers of the garrison had recently vacated and which adjoined the officers' mess. The newly reconciled baron and marquis ate their dinner together there, under the approving benignity of Commandant de Launay's gaze. He had every reason to be gratified by his achievement.

After dinner on 30 April, Sade seemed rather restless. He certainly appeared to have had a troubled night, since the light was still burning in his room at six o'clock the next morning. One of the soldiers on guard became so uneasy that he opened the door to see if all was well. There was no one there. Hurriedly, the door of the Baron de l'Allée de Songy's room was opened to see if he could give some account of where Sade might be. But the baron's room was also empty.

The discovery of the escape had come several hours too late. Like many attempts of its kind, the timing had been more important than any amount of contrivance. Because the room where the two men dined had not previously been part of the prison, a few alterations were needed to make it secure. But as in so many regimes, the château of Miolans was behind schedule in its work on repairs and renovations. A few weeks more would have made the dining-room absolutely secure. Even in its present state, escape from the room itself would have been impossible. But next to it was a little kitchen, from which Sade's servant Latour fetched the food for his master and the baron. It was impossible to get from the dining-room to the kitchen at any other time, the door being securely locked and bolted. The entire plan of escape depended on Latour.

When Sade and the baron had finished dinner, it was assumed that Latour had gone back to the kitchen with the dishes. Instead, he slipped away to the rooms occupied by the baron and the marquis, where he lit the candles. Since the candles would not have ignited of their own accord, those who saw them assumed that the two prisoners were now back in their quarters. Even so, by this time the door between the dining-room and the kitchen had been locked.

While Sade and the baron remained concealed in the dining-room, Latour went to join the other servants for their dinner as usual. Even though a prisoner, he was still his master's servant. No one paid much attention to Latour, the guards relaxing now that the prisoners were assumed to be safe in their rooms. Unobserved, Latour moved past the keys that hung nearby and removed the one that fitted the door between the dining-room and the little kitchen. He made his way back to the dining-room, where Sade and the baron emerged from hiding. The door to the little kitchen was unlocked and then closed again behind them.

There was a small window beyond the kitchen door, constructed as an aperture in the sheer wall of the fortress. Elsewhere the drop might be precipitous but at this point in the defences there was rough, steeply sloping ground no more than a dozen feet below the opening. Sade's military experience had served him well in finding the weakest point of the fortifications. He and his companions scrambled out and dropped down. Waiting for them was Joseph Violon, a Savoyard who had been bribed by

Renée-Pélagie or her associates to assist the fugitives and lead them towards the French frontier.

Both Sade and the baron left notes for their captors. Sade addressed his to the Commandant de Launay and the Comte de la Tour. He sportingly expressed the hope that they would not be made to suffer for his escape and he apologized for leaving them in this unceremonious manner. Only the unremitting persecution he had endured from Madame de Montreuil and the consciousness of his own innocence had driven him to this expedient. With a born sense of the rights of property, Sade had also drawn up in triplicate a list of his possessions at Miolans, which he asked the governor to be good enough to send on after him. Nothing came of this and, at the end of July, Renée-Pélagie presented herself at the fortress of Miolans to demand her husband's property. She left empty-handed.

In his farewell note to his captors, on the night of 30 April, Sade had tempered apology with menace. He claimed, quite falsely, that he was accompanied by fifteen armed horsemen who would die rather than see him recaptured. He advised his correspondents not to attempt a pursuit. Commandant de Launay read the note, dismissed the threat as nonsense, and organized a mounted detachment to search the area between Miolans and the French frontier. But Sade and his party had several hours start, time enough to ride down and follow the valley of the Isère to Chambéry. At that point, there was little hope of catching them before they crossed into France. Grenoble itself was only fifty miles from Miolans and Sade arrived there on the following day. Commandant de Launay forfeited whatever rewards and promotions he might have obtained through Madame de Montreuil's influence but perhaps he was not entirely sorry to be free of the family quarrel.

SEVEN

THE SCANDAL OF THE "LITTLE GIRLS"

1

SADE WAS SAFELY IN FRANCE. More precisely, as Renée-Pélagie was to express it in the summer of 1774, there was a feeling that he might be safe if he chose. Though he was still a wanted man, few of those responsible were inclined to hunt him out unless he should draw attention to himself by some further outrage. This was less surprising than it might appear at a time when the nobility feared the costs of such a prosecution, which they might have to underwrite in their territories, while the judges were apprehensive that they might not be paid for trying the case. Sade had already been tried. If central authority in Paris or at Versailles chose to bring him to justice, they might. The lords of Provence were not inclined to do the job for them.

Such action was all the more to be avoided because it now seemed that the proceedings against Sade at Marseille and in the high court of Aix-en-Provence contained certain irregularities. The case had been brought and concluded with considerable haste. So great was the speed of the hearing and confirmation that it became the subject of a representation to the king in 1777. Why was the evidence not more rigorously examined? No one in authority had stopped to ask why there was no trace of the poison in the specimens of sugared aniseed or vomit which had been submitted for analysis. At the very least, there should have been some further analysis. The evidence that Sade had poisoned anyone remained nil. As for the crime of sodomy, it was attested to by those who had reason to allege it and who afterwards withdrew the allegation. Few of the *grands seigneurs* had any enthusiasm for committing themselves and their money to the pursuit of such a prosecution.

Behind the original trial was the figure of Chancellor

Maupeou, who had been President of the high court of Paris when Sade appeared before its Chambre de Tournelle in 1764 to answer for his treatment of Rose Keller. It happened that Maupeou resented what he regarded as the rival power of the Court of Aides and harboured a personal hostility for its president. That post was held, of course, by Sade's father-in-law, the Président de Montreuil. There was reason to suppose that Maupeou sought to disgrace his rival by ruining the son-in-law. Yet even if this were true, it was Sade who had given the chancellor's malice its opportunity. With the death of Louis XV in May 1774, Maupeou fell from power and another of Sade's enemies was removed.

After six years, the conviction and sentence were quashed. As Sade's counsel, Joseph-Jérôme Siméon, summarized them, the proceedings of 1772 were cankered by judicial and procedural irregularities. There was no evidence whatever that the girls had been poisoned, indeed the evidence was against such a crime. They had been taking the medicines of a pavement quack, a matter not considered by the court. Sade was not officially informed of the proceedings against him, the speed of the prosecution overruling such formalities, yet his absence was taken as confirmation of guilt. But he had every legal right to be absent. Worse still, he had been condemned without even being properly identified as the man who visited the houses in Marseille. One of the girls was merely told that he was the Marquis de Sade, which was far short of proper identification. Sade was condemned on that evidence alone. Of course, this was purely a legal argument. There was no question as to whether Sade had been in the Marseille house of Mariette Borelly. But courts of law do not deal with what happens. Their judgments rely on what can be proved to have happened. In these terms, the case against Sade had never been proved.

For such reasons, Sade now had less to fear from the state than from his own family. A struggle had developed between Madame de Montreuil, as the protector of moral innocence, and Renée-Pélagie, as the understanding wife. During Sade's months in Savoy, Renée-Pélagie had been made guardian of the children, largely on the grounds of her husband's moral incapacity. But her visit to Chambéry and the first unsuccessful attempt to free Sade from his prison appeared to Madame de Montreuil as downright betrayal. Once it was known that Sade had escaped to France, Madame de Montreuil and her husband began to petition the Ministry of Justice. They wanted the miscreant arrested and committed permanently to the Lyonnaise prison of Pierre-Encise. It was suggested that he could be given sufficient freedom of correspondence to manage his estates from within the fortress. This would only be necessary until his elder son came of age, at which point all the property might be transferred to him. As for the proposed inmate of Pierre-Encise, Madame de Montreuil would never consent to freedom for the criminal lunatic whom ill-fortune had given her as a son-in-law.

To counter this, Renée-Pélagie went to Paris to plead Sade's case at court, urging the king's advisers to take no notice of her mother. After the scandal at Marseille, Sade had remarked of his life as a fugitive that:

> the mania of Madame de Montreuil in not wishing to put a stop to this is truly extraordinary. For what does she gain from it? Only to perpetuate the dishonour which this unfortunate matter involves, the dishonour of her daughter and her grandchildren; to cause the most dreadful disorder in the estates; for myself, to make me lead the most sad and miserable existence, for you know very well that there is no pleasure being in a country where you have to be constantly in hiding and playing all sorts of parts in order not to be recognized.

Sade, remaining in Provence, tightened his control over the estates at La Coste and Mazan by dismissing the lawyer who had acted on behalf of his family and appointing another of his own choosing. Gaspard Gaufridy, who had been a child acquaintance at Avignon during Sade's infant visit to his grandmother, was an attorney at Apt, almost within sight of La Coste on the far edge of the eastern plain. For the next forty years, in a correspondence which ran erratically between bonhomie and cantankerousness, Gaufridy was Sade's friend and confidant, an embezzler and turncoat, an old acquaintance and a good-for-nothing laggard. Through the storms of anger and the changes of mood, it was Gaufridy and his sons who undertook the collection of revenue from the estates and the forwarding of the proceeds to subsidize the master's entertainments.

Gaufridy's situation in 1773 was a curious one. He served Sade as a lawyer and he served Renée-Pélagie in her representations on her husband's behalf. But perhaps he guessed how matters would turn out and so he soon contrived to serve Madame de Montreuil privately as well. All the obligations which this represented were somehow reconciled in the labyrinthine conscience of Gaspard Gaufridy.

By the end of the year, it seemed that Gaufridy had been wise to put a side-bet on Madame de Montreuil. An order was at last signed in Paris for the arrest of Sade and his detention at Pierre-Encise. The order was signed on 16 December and implemented quickly. Preparations were made in Paris, evidently in consultation with Madame de Montreuil who may have contributed to the bill of more than eight thousand livres which the operation was going to cost. A troop of mounted men from Marseille, accompanied by four constables, acted as escort to the Sieur Goupil, police adjutant from Paris. On the night of 6 January 1774, they came unannounced to the village of La Coste. It was an easy matter to seal the village off by Portail de la Garde in the east, Portail des Chèvres in the west and rue Basse which offered the other escape to the plain below. With the château rising steep and grim as a stone granary or warehouse above them, the horsemen moved up the narrow cobbled ways and surrounded the building on its high plateau above the rooftops. There was no difficulty in entering. Renée-Pélagie was there and left her own account of the raid in a legal complaint drawn up by Gaufridy.

The ladders were prepared, the walls of the château were scaled. They came in with swords and pistols in their hands. It was in such a state that the police adjutant presented himself to this plaintiff. The fury excited by this action was plain in his face. With the most frightful oaths and the lewdest expressions, he demanded where he would find Monsieur de Sade, this plaintiff's husband. Who could depict her plight in so cruel a situation? She saw such barbarity before her eyes, horror and terror agitating her in turn. She saw and could not disguise from herself that this was the work of her own mother . . .

This plaintiff replied that her husband was not there. That was the signal for the most unbridled violence. The party of men divided, one section guarding the approaches of the château, the other scattering to search every hole and corner with weapons in their hands, ready to crush the least resistance. The implements had been prepared for this and one even saw, in the hands of one of the constables, an iron bar forged at Bonnieux to be used for breaking open doors and furniture. The failure of the search redoubled their fury. Monsieur de Sade's study was the object of the final scene. They seized and cut the family pictures. The police adjutant distinguished himself by breaking open bureaux and cupboards in the study. They seized all the papers and letters that they found. According to the whim of the police adjutant, some of these were devoured by flame. He took the rest without giving any indication to this plaintiff what they might contain, without giving the least account. He gave no reason for Madame de Montreuil's decision in favour of this seizure, which violates both the rights of individuals and the rights of humanity, as well as sacrificing the reputation of Monsieur de Sade to the prejudices of Madame de Montreuil.

The search-party continued its nocturnal rampage. Goupil snatched papers from the hands of Renée-Pélagie and seized an enamelled and gilded miniature. "There was no infamy which was not pronounced against the Marquis de Sade." Some of them admitted that they were there only to carry out a death sentence, the orders of Madame de Montreuil. They were each "to put three bullets into him and take his body back to her".

There was a growing danger, said Renée-Pélagie, that the citizens of La Coste might join battle on behalf of Sade. There were shouts from above of "He's been caught! We've got the bastard!" But they had not. Of Sade himself there was no sign. Though the constabulary were sure that if the marquise was at the château, the wanted man must be somewhere nearby, it was impossible to find him. At last the posse turned its horses and the adjutant's carriage. It remained in the village next day and then headed back towards Apt, one of many fruitless sorties against the fugitive. The lawyer Gaufridy received a hastily scribbled note from Renée-Pélagie. He was to warn Sade of what had happened and tell him to keep clear.

After this fiasco, the Duc de la Vrillière wrote on behalf of the king to the lord-lieutenant of Provence, on 25 March, suggesting that it was useless to try arresting Sade at the château of La Coste. Far better to entrap him somewhere in the neighbourhood, when he was off his guard. The lord-lieutenant replied on 12 April, promising to put his spies to work but adding pessimistically that Sade seemed to be nowhere in the region of La Coste.

As it happened, Sade returned to the château quietly and lived there with Renée-Pélagie and Anne-Prospère during June and early July 1774. If the authorities seemed less than energetic in their search for him, it was perhaps because of the renewed battle in Paris, to which Renée-Pélagie and her sister returned on 14 July, to make Madame de Montreuil seek a withdrawal of the orders for Sade's arrest. It seems to have been during her absence that Sade travelled to Bordeaux, where one of his plays was staged at the theatre, and then crossed into Spain on a journey to Cadiz. By November, he and Renée-Pélagie were again living unobtrusively at La Coste. A further truce prevailed between the hunters and their quarry, so long as Sade lived a quiet life in his remote château. That quietness appeared to last throughout the isolation of the winter months. Renée-Pélagie had written from Paris on 3 September urging that Sade should be advised to stay at La Coste or Mazan. "If he has not followed my advice, show him this letter." The *lettre de cachet* by which he might be arrested by royal authority had not yet been withdrawn. But that was a technicality. The conviction against him at Marseille would first be quashed before the *lettre de cachet* was rescinded.

It pleased Sade to play the role of *grand seigneur* among his villagers from time to time, even when his actions were uncharacteristic. In December 1774, he informed Gaufridy that he had forbidden a group of strolling players from performing a play in the village and had ordered their posters to be torn down. They had intended to present a comedy which Sade considered to be defamatory, *The Cuckolded Husband: Beaten and Happy*. Such an exhibition, Sade remarked piously, would be an affront to religion.

Life at La Coste had a cautious and furtive air as 1774 drew to its close. In December, Sade invited Gaufridy to dinner but stipulated that the meal would be at three o'clock in the afternoon, which was two or three hours earlier than was customary in the eighteenth century. The host explained why.

We have decided, for a thousand reasons, to see very few people this winter. Consequently, I spend the evening in my study. Madame and the womenfolk take up residence in the next room, until bedtime. By this means, when night comes, the château is impregnably locked up, lights out, no more cooking and not even any more food. So it really does put us out not to arrive at dinner-time and inconveniences us in every way.

Sade's study was on the ground floor of the château, looking south-east from the outer wall towards the Luberon range. A larger room next to it was used by Renée-Pélagie and the women. At bedtime, the arrangement on the first floor was a little more unusual. Sade's summer bedroom with dressing-room occupied the north-east bastion that rose rather precipitously above the roofs of the village. Renée-Pélagie and the children had rooms on the other side of the building, beyond the courtyard. Sade's neighbour was his wife's young maidservant, "Gothon", as Anne-Marie Maillefert was known. Though Sade also had a winter bedroom, it was tucked away down the end of a corridor and was still further from his family.

If Gaufridy believed that the winter arrangements at La Coste were proof of a change in Sade's life, the events of those winter nights, as they were revealed in the spring of 1775, came as a profound shock. A girl of fifteen arrived at Saumane and was taken in by the Abbé de Sade. She began to tell him of the things that had been done to her during the previous winter in a certain château where she was kept with a number of other girls. They were all very young and had been employed as servants with the consent of their parents, who ought to have known better. The parents now began to swear evidence against the master, with accusations of abduction. But during that time of their daughters' need such parents had been far off, in Lyon and elsewhere. It was now said that one macabre incident involved the burial of human remains in the grounds of the place where this girl had been kept. Far more important, the girl at Saumane had certain marks on her which had not yet faded. She was living proof of the dark pleasures of a libertine's château during those winter months.

The Abbé de Sade was dismayed, not least because the château was recognizable at once as La Coste and the demented master of ceremonies as his nephew. Sade himself insisted on 27 January 1775 that the girl at Saumane was lying, though he did not explain how she came to have the marks on her body. His explanations went unheard and his uncle was now ready to join those demanding Sade's arrest and imprisonment. Soon after this, a letter came to Saumane from Madame de Montreuil who was now at Lyon, investigating the "Scandal of the Little Girls", as it became known. She confirmed the worst suspicions of the abbé but urged him, for all their sakes, not to let the girl in his care be examined by a doctor. A second fifteen-year-old girl, Marie Toussin, was taken to the convent at Caderousse as a refugee from La Coste. Whatever the truth of the matter, there now seemed likely to be a scandal to equal those of Arcueil and Marseille. This time, to Madame de Montreuil's chagrin, her own daughters appeared to be implicated in the crimes. Renée-Pélagie was both accomplice and victim, in her mother's view. When Sade began to wield the birch or the whip in the orgies at La Coste, Renée-Pélagie was "the first victim of a frenzy that one can only regard as madness".

Madame de Montreuil kept her head, even in the turmoil of accusation and legal threats. The Sades had hired five girls and a young male secretary for the winter. The girls had been obtained by another member of the cast at the château, "Nanon", Anne Sablonnière, a young woman of twenty-four now described as a procuress.

Madame de Montreuil's instructions to Gaufridy on 11 February were unequivocal. Renée-Pélagie had acquired certificates to show that some of the girls at La Coste were in good condition. This would not do. Gaufridy was to choose a woman whom he could trust. With her assistance he was to take the girls from La Coste and return them to their parents, getting some kind of legal discharge which would lay the matter to rest. If the girl at Saumane threatened to make trouble, she was to be reminded that "young women know nothing of the law or the consequence of these matters and she may find herself gravely compromised in all this". Gaufridy was urged to lose no time in going to Vienne and

Lyon to "negotiate". Above all, he was to put nothing in writing. Whatever her feelings about her son-in-law, Madame de Montreuil was a woman of energy and decision. In her priorities, she showed little sympathy for the reproaches of adolescent girls who complained of having been whipped or otherwise ill-treated for Sade's amusement during the long winter nights of La Coste.

For the winter of 1774–5, it seemed that Sade had tried to organize in reality the kind of harem that was to inspire his heroes in the fiction of *The 120 Days of Sodom*. The childhood isolation of Saumane in reality had given way to the adult fantasies of La Coste. In the autumn of 1785, Sade was to combine his childhood winters of Saumane with his winter imprisonment in the mountainous region of Miolans and his season of pleasures at La Coste. The mixture of memories and fantasies gave birth to *The 120 Days of Sodom*, whose heroes had locked themselves and their slaves in the mountain fortress of Silling for a season of pleasure and cruelty, from the beginning of November until the end of February. At the heart of the isolated mountain fortress lay the auditorium, in homage to the private theatre at La Coste. Its mirrored alcoves and pillars, softly cushioned ottomans and throne, the participation of the audience in the drama, made a bizarre essay in theatrical design.

Despite the best that Madame de Montreuil could do, Bruny d'Entrecasteaux, president of the court at Aix-en-Provence, informed the Sade family in May 1775 that the lord of La Coste had abducted the girls from Lyon and that charges were now being brought against him there. In addition to the five girls and Nanon, Sade had apparently made use of Renée-Pélagie's maid, Gothon, the daughter of a Swiss protestant. There was also the boy, whom Sade employed as secretary. In the world of *The 120 Days of Sodom*, every hero has a wife as well as a harem, reflecting the fact that Renée-Pélagie was present at La Coste throughout the winter months and the scandals of the "Little Girls".

Sade produced an explanation for the human remains that had been buried in the grounds of the château. During his travels the year before, keeping well away from La Coste, he had visited Bordeaux and met a ballet-girl, Le Plan, who came back to Marseille and joined the theatre there. The visit to Bordeaux had been eventful, as Sade recalled it in 1785. He had also recognized two of Madame de Montreuil's spies and had given them a good hiding. Another spy at Bordeaux, described as a whore, had received Sade's attention when she was "whipped to teach her better manners and conduct".

The ballet-girl Le Plan had also spent the winter at La Coste with the others, showing tastes that were decidedly perverse. It amused her to use human bones as decoration and she had brought some with her from Marseille. At length it was decided to dispose of these gruesome ornaments by burying them in the garden. As for the other girls, there was Rosette from Montpelier who stayed some months, asked to leave, and was taken away by her friend who worked as a carpenter in the girl's home town. Then there was Adélaïde, who stayed until Madame de Montreuil began to deal with the consequences of Sade's winter sports.

The hazards of employment for the maidservants of La Coste were pregnancy, flagellation and sodomy, as Madame de Montreuil hinted to the Abbé de Sade. But the gloating relish of the heroes in *The 120 Days of Sodom* was apt to be frustrated by life's banalities at La Coste. Nanon became pregnant, though she loyally insisted that she owed this to her husband. And then, unthinkable in the fictional fortress of Silling, a couple of the girls simply ran away. The walls of La Coste were no match for a determined young woman. In any case, on its eastern side there was an open courtyard with nothing more than a driveway and two gates. Bearing the marks of their most recent ordeals, the fugitives had arrived at Saumane and Caderousse. Their parents began proceedings against Sade. The family of the secretary called at La Coste and took the young man away.

Of all the names heard in the winter at La Coste, only Adélaïde reappeared in fictional form ten years later in *The 120 Days of Sodom*, as the daughter of the incestuous President de Curval, who gives her in marriage to the banker Durcet at the beginning of the novel. Her portrait and her experiences suggest the winter days of Sade's harem.

She was twenty years old, petite and slim, slight and delicate in her build, a perfect subject for a painting with the finest blonde hair. There was something interesting about her, an air of sensibility which one saw in every aspect and which suggested the heroine of a novel. Her blue eyes were unusually large, reflecting simultaneously her tenderness and modesty. Her eyebrows were long, narrow, and well marked, adorning a forehead that was not tall but of such nobility that one might have thought it the very temple of decorum. Her nose was straight, rather narrow at the top, coming down in a somewhat aquiline shape. Her lips were thin and lined in full red, her mouth rather large, which was the only fault in this celestial portrait . . . Her breasts were small, very round, very firm and well-supported, scarcely enough to fill one's hand. They were like two little apples which the playful Cupid has brought from his mother's garden . . .

Her belly was smooth as satin. A little blonde mound, lightly haired and seeming to act as the peristyle of the Temple of Venus, invited one's admiration. The way into this temple was so tight that one could scarcely insert a finger without her uttering a cry. However, thanks to the president, the poor young creature had ceased to be a virgin almost ten years before. This true of her here, as it was on that other side of her which was yet to be examined. What attractions that second temple offered, what a sweep of her back, what a shape in those hind cheeks, what whiteness and what blushes! Yet this beauty was small-proportioned . . . Spread this delectable behind and see the rosebud that offers itself to you. So unspoilt, it is the most rosy that Nature can present to you. But what tightness, what narrowness! It was only with infinite difficulty that the president had managed to navigate through those straits, and he had only succeeded in doing so again on two or three occasions.

Like many portraits in his fiction, Adélaïde has a detail and intensity which suggests that she reflects the reality of that winter at La Coste which gave the form to his fiction. In this case, however, the heroine is spared none of the ordeals and is despatched before the end of the novel.

In other respects, fantasy and reality were far apart. Before long, the harem and the regime of sexual tyranny had collapsed at La Coste, as it was never permitted to do in Sade's fantasies. Yet there are moments in *The 120 Days of Sodom* which seem to mirror the reality behind "The Scandal of the Little Girls" during the winter of 1774–5. In the final part of the novel, having tired of other pleasures, the bishop is seduced by the bottom of a beautiful Swiss girl, nineteen years old, a fictionalized Gothon. She is one of the kitchenmaids, rather than a harem recruit, and when the heroes have finished with her she is sent back to her duties rather the worse for wear. At this point the only mutiny of the novel occurs. The cooks threaten that unless messieurs keep their hands off the domestic staff, the service from the kitchens will cease. The bishop, the banker, the president and the duke may own half of France and all the girls within it but they are doomed to starve rather than cook their own meals. The social irony of aristocratic orgies being frustrated by a threatened walk-out of kitchen staff has a plausible echo of events at La Coste and is a reminder of the proximity of Sade's bedroom to that of the Swiss servant-girl.

But the pleasures of *The 120 Days* in reality were soon to be paid for. For the first time in the spring and summer of 1775, Sade found that the world seemed almost united against him. Renée-Pélagie remained loyal. Mingled with threats from the parents of the little girls was even a denunciation from his uncle, the Abbé de Sade, who now wanted his nephew locked up as a madman. On the other hand, the abbé had lost patience with his female fugitive. Now that her marks had faded he wanted to be rid of her, having looked after her, "showing consideration for people who have never shown me any, and with whom I wish to have nothing more to do". He was persuaded to keep the girl at Saumane for a little longer and to make sure that she was examined only by a doctor answerable to Madame de Montreuil. It had alarmed the Présidente de Montreuil to hear that there was an unnamed medical man at Saumane whom the Abbé de Sade might invite to inspect the girl in his care.

In April, Madame de Montreuil urged Gaufridy to see if there were any marks of ill-usage on the girls or whether they were making "childish complaints". To be on the safe side, however, the girl at Saumane must be kept there. What had she said? And to whom? It was not until the autumn that it was judged safe to remove her from the Abbé de Sade. Even then, she was transferred to the care of Ripert, who managed the estate of Mazan on Sade's behalf.

Sade tried to stem the hostility at its source. He urged Gaufridy to write to Madame de Montreuil, assuring her of the respect and

The French Investigator: a modern view of Sade. (*Mary Evans Picture Library*)

The Condé Palace in Paris where Sade was born.

Saumane where Sade spent his childhood with his uncle, the Abbé de Sade.
(*Carol Thomas*)

Le cul est-il juste quand il abandonne la vertu
à de si grands tourments ?.....

"Can Heaven be just when it abandons Virtue to such great torment?" The Horrors
of the Inquisitions. An illustration for *Aline and Valcour*, 1795.
(*Weidenfeld & Nicolson Archives*)

The prison at Vincennes (*above*) as it was when Sade was imprisoned there
and (*below*) as it is today. (*Carol Thomas*)

Renée-Pélagie, Marquise de Sade.

The Marquis de Sade in the asylum at Charenton. (*The Mansell Collection*)

je ne sais point reprendre ce que j'ai donné : on aura
beau vouloir m'enseigner l'art des bassesses, a la bastille,
on ne viendra pas à my former. si les loix *imaginaires* de
cette maison cy, tendent a détruire toutes les vertus et a
inculquer tous les vices il est affreux que le gouvernement le
souffre ; mais il le serait encor bien plus pour une âme honête
de ne pas, dans un tel cas, tendre a la plus parfaite
indépendance.

on payera ce qu'on voudra a Lossinote mais je lui dois
soixante deux livres, et je ne sçais pas signer un mensonge

Ce 3 Janvier 1786.

A manuscript in Sade's handwriting.

A *petite maison* of the 18th century.

Toutes les parties de ce beau corps étaient formées par la main des grâces.

The Beauties of the King of Butua's harem. An illustration for *Aline and Valcour*, 1795. (*Weidenfeld & Nicolson Archives*)

devotion which both Sade and Renée-Pélagie felt towards her. That this was a moral non sequitur seemed not to bother him. He insisted that the Montreuils were the source of all the feeling against him. If only they could be quietened, he had nothing else to fear. Madame de Montreuil was now engaged in her familiar double role of trying to buy off witnesses against her son-in-law while doing her best to have him locked up somewhere from which there would be no further escape.

Early in April, Sade left La Coste to resume his wanderings across France. His journey brought him to Montpelier, perhaps from a refuge on the family estate of the Mas de Cabanes, near Arles. Soon he was at Bordeaux again, then he was at Grenoble. Fugitive travels made him master of the scenic picaresque in *Justine* and his shorter fiction, with a sure touch and a sense of place in his scenes. In his absence there followed rumour, accusation and bribery. Nanon's baby was born and died. She had left La Coste and, according to Renée-Pélagie, had taken some silver plate with her. She was arrested under a familiar *lettre de cachet* and held at the house of detention in Arles. That autumn, Madame de Montreuil was assured that Nanon had been given a talking-to by a lawyer and by the mistress of the establishment. Though Nanon had a "sharp tongue", she was in the charge of those who would make her "tranquil".

Madame de Montreuil had worked hard to bring the complainants and the law to heel. Surely she felt entitled to some respite from the demands made on her by her son-in-law's activities. But already on 3 May, the president of the parliament at Aix-en-Provence had reported that Sade was back at La Coste, once again "giving himself up to excesses of every kind".

As the summer of 1775 passed, Sade could scarcely avoid drawing attention to himself for reasons of a quite different kind. The affairs of his estates at La Coste, Mazan, Saumane and the Mas de Cabanes were in disorder. He had tried to sell the lands on the west side of the Rhône but without success. Creditors and unpaid bills were now a greater preoccupation than the complaints of little girls and their parents. Even Renée-Pélagie was obliged to appear in court at Aix to answer the suits brought against her.

Her financial difficulties increased the dangers to him on all fronts. Where the creditors went, the spies followed. In July there was a sudden raid on the château of La Coste by a party of constabulary from Apt. Sade was very nearly caught but the hunters lacked the tenacity of Police Adjutant Goupil from Paris. Though the château was searched, Sade managed to hide himself in the recesses of a garret until the posse gave up and rode back to town. Whatever his conduct, those to whom he was lord and master remained loyal. Neither the villagers of La Coste nor his own servants offered the least assistance to the hunters. But the Abbé de Sade and Alexandre de Nerclos, Prior of Jumiège, had both sheltered fugitive girls from La Coste and both now demanded Sade's arrest. The prior had earlier given shelter to Nanon, whom three of Sade's servants had tried to take into their custody over the matter of the silver plate stolen from La Coste. The prior had refused to surrender her. And now other voices were raised. The mother of the young man who had been Sade's secretary was in Aix-en-Provence making loud accusations of sodomy. There were creditors whose persistence threatened to bring bailiffs in their wake. The police raid had come closer to capturing Sade than any other of its kind.

Even Sade appeared to realize that his time was running out. As he wrote glumly to Gaufridy during that summer of 1775, "If anyone so much as whips a cat in this province, they all say, 'It's Monsieur de Sade who did it.'"

3

It was time to leave La Coste. Indeed, it was time to leave France. On 19 July, Sade and his servant rode out of the château in their carriage and down to the plain below. On the first two nights of their eastward journey they slept in barns. Then, on 21 July, they began their ascent, crossing the mountains into Savoy. The route they chose was so precipitous that they were told by the villagers there had been only three carriages on it in the past twenty years. Undetected, they came down unannounced into Savoy, crossed the duchy at speed and reached the Italian frontier. Though Sade was now safe from arrest, he was in a country where he understood scarcely a word of the language. As he remarked ruefully to Gaufridy, he had been advised to take an Italian girl as his mistress, that being the only way Italian was learnt.

Under his subsidiary title of the Comte de Mazan, Sade was to spend the next twelve months travelling in Italy. During this period, he kept a journal which, like the journal of his visit to Holland, was addressed to Renée-Pélagie. In its pages he began to express those opinions and tastes which were to win him praise and execration as the most daring or the most vile of authors in modern literature. Condemnation by society worried him very little, however. On leaving La Coste, he wondered whether society and its police forces had done anything to improve human life. They had certainly done nothing to improve his. Egoism, he concluded, is the primary law of nature. It was a proposition with which he felt sure that Renée-Pélagie would agree.

Sade's journey took him by way of Turin, Parma, Modena and Bologna to Florence, which he reached on 3 August and where he was to spend two and a half months. Before he had been there a month, he was writing the first of many letters to Gaufridy, demanding money due from the revenues of the estates. "My dear advocate, you are a charming man but you spend too little time in finding the three thousand francs which I need. Moreover, you will expose me to all that is most disagreeable and inconvenient if you don't get the money to me by the end of August." The same theme ran through his following letters. "Please see that nothing impedes your diligence in sending me the entire sum of three thousand francs." By September, he was at the end of his patience. "In the name of God, monsieur, do me the courtesy of telling me who it is who hangs round Madame de Sade and offers all sorts of absurdities which she forwards to me on the subject of my three thousand francs, for which I have waited so long and with such impatience."

As a traveller, he was fascinated and appalled by what he found in Florence. His voluptuous excitement on seeing the blonde beauty of Titian's Venus in the Medici Palace is reflected in his journal. As for the Venus de' Medici, his prose lingers caressingly and fetishistically on the beauties of her breasts and buttocks. But he was no less enthusiastic over the wax model of a girl, which could be opened up in order to teach anatomy. Like Rodin, the homicidal surgeon in *Justine*, Sade was able to penetrate the secret mechanisms of female beauty. Unlike Rodin, his wilful dissection was bloodless and purely cerebral.

Sade was also much taken by the art of the waxwork, a form

which offered lifelike and three-dimensional representations of horrors that could never be performed in reality. He was most impressed by a series of figures showing the decay of a human being from the moment of death to that of complete dissolution. It was a topic that was to be treated repeatedly, if not obsessively, in both *Justine* and *Juliette*. In addition to this his attention was held by art that was remarkable for its sexual portrayal. He paused to admire the Hermaphrodite of the ancient world and the Priapus on which, as he reminded Renée-Pélagie, pious ladies of antiquity would sit in order to practise their devotions.

Sade's enthusiasm for the portrayal of dissolution and decay was less pathological than it might seem. The new Gothic age was well established by the mid-1770s, in fiction, poetry and art. In England, almost sixty years before, Alexander Pope had identified the poetic taste for scenes of "Repentant sighs, and solitary pains", in *Eloisa to Abelard*, a prospect far removed from the grandeurs and certainties of neo-classicism, preferring,

> Grots and caverns shagged with horrid thorn!
> Shrines! where their vigils pale-ey'd virgins keep,
> And pitying saints, whose statues learn to weep!

In 1794, the taste among middle-class novel-readers for what Jane Austen was to call the "horrid" led one of the English novelists later praised by Sade, Mrs Ann Radcliffe, to use the waxwork admired by Sade for Gothic effect in her *Mysteries of Udolpho*. The plot depends largely on its heroine making the discovery of a body half-eaten by worms in her Uncle Montoni's Apennine castle. The horror and the terror of her situation are resolved at last when it proves to be only a most convincing wax model, as much a trick as her uncle's pretended villainy. Sade's own Italian journey was reflected frequently in his fiction. Rome and Naples were to be recreated in the rogue's progress of *Juliette*. An excursion from Florence to the monastery of Vallombrosa left a striking impression of literary Gothic on his story of the sixteenth century, "Laurentia and Antonio", collected in *Crimes of Love* (1800).

> In arriving in this shadowy retreat, situated at the heart of a dark forest, where the rays of the sun scarcely penetrated,

where everything inspired that religious terror so agreeable to sensitive souls, Laurentia could not help breaking out again in tears. . . . Crime prefers these grim locations. The darkness of the little valleys, the striking solemnity of the forests, surround a criminal with the shade of mystery and seem to inspire him more energetically to the deeds he contemplates. The kind of horror with which these places fill the mind draws it towards those actions which have the same disturbing hue that nature gives to these locales. One might say that the hand of this incomprehensible nature chooses to enslave whoever contemplates her in this mood – promoting the moral perversities which she inspires.

Not surprisingly, this is the place where the heroine is kept imprisoned under a delayed sentence of death, awaiting incestuous rape and writing out a sonnet of Petrarch in her own blood. Such was Sade's fictional essay in Italian Gothic of the sixteenth century.

Perhaps his most unexpected reaction to life in Florence was his disgust at the sexual degeneracy of Italian manners. Though he knew that other eyes than Renée-Pélagie's would read the journal, it seems out of character for Sade to attempt moral ingratiation and rehabilitation by such a form of self-righteousness that he did not feel. In his own right, he condemned the abnormal sexual conduct of actors and their hangers-on in the theatres of Florence. He professed nothing but contempt for those transvestites who took female parts on the stage and betrayed their manhood in real life. In this respect, Sade's outburst might seem odd after the allegations of sodomy made against him and Latour during the Marseille scandal. Perhaps, after all, those allegations were false. In that case the heterosexual Sade's comments on Italy's perversion were of a kind described in the previous century by Samuel Butler, describing the Puritans in *Hudibras* who would

> Compound for sins they are inclined to,
> By damning those they have no mind to.

On the evidence of his writings, Sade's objection is not to sodomy but to men who can perform it only with other men. A man must be able to establish the sexual conquest of women first. Thereafter, he may do as he pleases. A man who cannot fulfil this first obligation with the other sex is less than a man. It may be that this sexual logic also underlies Sade's comments on the Florentines. There is certainly no indication in the journal that he is other than disgusted by the creatures of the theatre. As for the castrati, he remarks that they bring out the true depravity of actresses, who prefer them to unmutilated men because their desire is never appeased by orgasm. As a city of sexual vice, he had as yet seen nowhere to rival this. The streets would have been in complete darkness at night, had it not been for plentiful illumination from the windows of the brothels. These enabled pedestrians to avoid literal pitfalls while luring them into those of the moral kind.

Sade left Florence on 21 October 1775 and made his way to Rome, where he found St Peter's "more theatrical than impressive". He soon visited the places in which many of the most elaborate orgies described in the Italian scenes of *Juliette* were to have their setting. If he was seized by the literary inspiration of making the Pope perform a black mass in the great basilica, as was to happen in his novel, he certainly kept such subversive fantasies out of his journal. Indeed, the only suggestion of his characteristic tastes is in his reaction to the portrayal of the torture of St Agnes. Sade was disappointed by it. The woman in the picture lacked the fear in her eyes which would have made her suffering a great artistic masterpiece.

He spent the rest of the autumn in Rome, lingering beyond Christmas and the New Year of 1776. It was late in January before he moved on. In general, he wrote like many a patrician tourist in the city. He noted the beauties of classical and pagan art, the glories of the Christian successors. When his itinerary was complete, he went on to Naples. During these months, according to Renée-Pélagie, he was leading a life of exemplary uprightness and had been received in audience by the Pope. Naples, however, opened his eyes to the true extravagance and depravity of southern Europe. Despite his enthusiasm for using the birch or the cord whip on the girls of his harem at La Coste, Sade was taken aback by the blood-letting of Marini and the Flagellants in the cause of true religion. He was astonished by the commitment of the people to the trade of prostitution. A mother would offer her daughter or her son for sale, according to the buyer's taste. A sister would tout for her brother, a father for his daughter, and a husband for his wife. Florence and Rome had been, for the most part, moral variants of Marseille or Lyon. Naples was as morally alien as the sexual despotism of Assam, about which Sade wrote to Renée-Pélagie with such relish.

Prostitution in Naples was so universal, Sade reported, that the noblest ladies of the city would hire themselves, provided that the price was high enough. This state of pornocracy was later reflected in his novel *Philosophy in the Boudoir*, when the participants accept prostitution as being in harmony with natural law. Any attempt to suppress it is an affront to common sense. Sade's ideal republic, an irony in which murder, theft, rape and sodomy, as well as prostitution, are sanctioned by law, is a nightmare vision of the moral anarchy which prevailed in Naples at the time of his visit. But it is not these crimes and vices alone which are to be allowed in the kingdom of the new philosophy. The triumph of treachery and moral nihilism is to be the stamp of that new order.

The sardonic tone of *Philosophy in the Boudoir* was absent from his Italian journal. Confronted by the reality of Naples in the early months of 1776, Sade was dismayed by a spectacle of social collapse. What hope could there be for the maintenance of honour, virtue or even physical well-being in the face of such human degradation as he saw on every side?

He remained in the city until May 1776, having to be presented at court as a French colonel in order to conceal his true identity from the *chargé d'affaires*. Renée-Pélagie might insist that her husband had behaved well in Italy. But during this time, Madame de Montreuil and the Abbé de Sade were still trying to quieten the protests and accusations from the previous year. The fifteen-year-old who had taken refuge at Saumane had been examined by the doctor loyal to Madame de Montreuil. This was the victim who had been found honest work in November 1775 with a farmer on the Sade estates at Mazan, where she was less likely to talk to strangers. After so much care had been taken, it was particularly galling that she should abscond in the following July. Worse still, she made her way to Orange and there swore a statement before a judge describing all that had happened. The other fifteen-year-old who had sought refuge at the convent of

Caderousse had left for Lyon in the company of two young people who claimed to be related to her.

But Sade was weary of Naples and was making his way back to France. He insisted that his travels were still bedevilled by lack of money. He had written repeatedly to Gaufridy about this with growing acrimony, demanding that the revenues due to him from the estates should be forwarded. How else was he intended to live? He had been away for almost a year, his protests at the situation in which Gaufridy and Renée-Pélagie had abandoned him growing more strident. There was nothing for it but to come home, whatever the risks. Yet he also mentioned the quantity of objets d'art and antiquities which he had acquired and was packing up for his return. His poverty appears to have been relative.

On 1 June he was at Rome and a couple of weeks later he passed through Bologna and Turin. By the end of the month he had crossed the frontier and reached Grenoble, still disguised as the Comte de Mazan. He sent his servant La Jeunesse ahead to La Coste to see what the situation might be. It seemed safe enough. Sade made his way there and took up residence at the château in the latter part of July, just as the fugitive fifteen-year-old from Mazan was telling her story to the judge at Orange.

4

Despite such revelations, he remained safe for the moment. He survived the summer at La Coste and then at Montpelier. It was in Montpelier, on 2 November, that he negotiated with Madame Trillet the employment of her twenty-two-year-old daughter Catherine as a kitchenmaid at La Coste. Two days later he returned safely to the château with the girl in his charge. He made arrangements to employ another girl for the kitchen, as well as a chambermaid, a wig-maker and a secretary. Only the girl who was to assist Catherine Trillet in the kitchen stayed. But it was not merely a tale of desertions. Among the other girls who now accompanied him at the château was one who had been a "victim" of the scandal two years previously. In the pleasures of La Coste, Catherine Trillet now became known as "Justine", which may or may not have been significant in terms of Sade's most famous novel. Whatever was done to her in reality certainly proved sufficient to create a good deal of trouble for him.

January 1777 was an ominous month. Sade's mother, the Dowager Comtesse de Sade, died at the convent in Paris to which she had retired even before the death of her husband in 1767. But the news came slowly. Before he knew of her death, Sade was involved in a disagreeable incident over Catherine Trillet. All his dealings had been with the girl's mother. At about noon on Friday 17 January, Sade was informed that her father had arrived at the château. Trillet brushed aside formalities and advanced "insolently" upon Sade. He announced that he had come to rescue his daughter from this place of iniquity, which he had been tricked into believing was a respectable house.

Sade had never experienced a direct approach of this kind. He told Trillet that of course he might speak to his daughter. As for taking her away, that was out of the question. It was impossible for her to leave until a replacement had been found to undertake the work in the kitchens. When Sade wrote of the problems caused by kitchen staff in *The 120 Days of Sodom*, he did so from experience. But the argument with Trillet grew more alarming. It appeared that some of the servants who had been briefly at La Coste had returned to Montpelier. They reported that Sade had offered them money if they would consent to indulge his rather extreme sexual whims. Trillet, hearing this, had set off to save and avenge his daughter. Sade dismissed the father's protests as absurd, if only because he had no money left with which to bribe the servants for sexual favours. By this time, Catherine had appeared. Trillet seized his daughter by the arm and began dragging her towards the main door of the château.

Sade had just come down from his study and was unarmed. He put his hand on Trillet to restrain him as they reached the door. He also insisted that the man must go down to the village and wait there while his request was considered. Furious at this command, Trillet broke free, turned round and drew a pistol. He aimed it at Sade and fired. There was no doubt that he was in earnest. As the explosion deafened those in the room, Sade felt the breath of the bullet passing two inches from his chest. While he and his servants took cover, Trillet withdrew from the château and returned alone to the village, shouting abuse as he did so. Intermediaries went between Sade and the outraged father. That evening, at five o'clock, Catherine followed them down there in an attempt to calm him. All too soon Trillet was back, though escorted by four worthies from La Coste. But when Trillet began roaring out threats and shooting into the courtyard of the château on the pretext that he saw Sade moving about in the darkness, the escort scattered.

After some time, Trillet withdrew to the tavern in the little rue Basse, while Sade endeavoured to start legal proceedings against him through local citizens who were also magistrates. It seemed a bizarre convolution of the law for a man who was wanted on a capital charge to bring a prosecution against another. But though the rest of France might be beyond his control, Sade was still lord of the village. When Trillet was confronted by Paulet and Vidal, the magistrates of La Coste, he caused some surprise by insisting that he had "the most sincere feelings of friendship and attachment" for Sade. The reason for this change of view, in Sade's opinion, was that Catherine had given her father money. On the following day, Saturday, the weather was too bad for him to travel. First thing on Sunday morning, however, Trillet left the village.

But, having assured the magistrates of his affection for Sade, Trillet was soon at Aix-en-Provence, swearing an affidavit against him for the debauchery of the past few months and his refusal to release Catherine. It was true that Catherine had declined to accompany her father but legal opinion was that Trillet had every right to withdraw her from the château. When the proceedings ended on 30 January, the court at Aix could hardly ignore the fact that the wanted man was living openly at La Coste. It could scarcely avoid taking measures for his arrest. However, by this time Sade was on the move again.

While the New Year melodrama of Trillet and daughter was playing, Sade returned to the problem of his finances. Since the sentence of death passed on him by the high court at Aix-en-Provence more than four years earlier, he had lost his income from the crown as lieutenant-general of Bresse, Bugey and his other territories. Revenues were due to him privately from his own estates but debtors did not hurry to pay a man who was hunted by the law and badly placed to take action against them. His position was by no means hopeless, since Renée-Pélagie promised that she had almost persuaded Madame de Montreuil to make up the loss. Better still, Madame de Montreuil hinted that she might use her influence to get the death sentence of 1772 annulled. After four or five years, no one truly believed that Sade would be put to death if he was caught. Indeed, if it were ever necessary to examine the proceedings against him, their flaws would be made public.

In these circumstances, Sade and Renée-Pélagie set off for Paris at the end of January. In the other direction came a letter from Madame de Montreuil to Gaufridy, assuring him that she was unmoved by any threats from her daughter or son-in-law and that they would discover how well she could look after herself in a quarrel. At the same time, Reinaud wrote to Gaufridy, one lawyer to another, insisting that Sade was walking into a trap by going to Paris. Madame de Montreuil was planning "a subtle stroke, to gain by cunning what she has failed to gain by force".

The Sades left La Coste with La Jeunesse and Catherine Trillet, who assured Renée-Pélagie that she had not the least desire to return to Montpelier and wanted only to continue as a servant. On 1 February the party reached Valence and a week later they were in Paris. It was only then that Sade learnt of the death of his mother three weeks earlier.

For the moment, Renée-Pélagie went to the Montreuils in rue Neuve du Luxembourg, while Sade had an apartment at the Hôtel de Danemark in rue Jacob and visited his old tutor, the Abbé Amblet. The separation would last only as long as it took to confirm Madame de Montreuil's intention of making a financial settlement and using her influence to annul the death sentence. Yet Sade celebrated his return to Paris by writing a letter to an easy-going clergyman of his acquaintance, apparently during the second week of February. He explained that he was in mourning for his mother. However, he invited his friend to meet him at a discreet rendezvous so that they could resume their evenings of going out together "hunting" women.

On 12 February, Renée-Pélagie was even more confident of the new understanding which existed with her mother. She confessed to her that Sade himself was actually in Paris. Next day, there was a visitor at the Hôtel de Danemark. He was by no means a stranger to either the Abbé Amblet or to Sade. This was Inspector Louis Marais, the officer who had been prominent in the cases of Jeanne Testard and Rose Keller and who had watched Sade's career of sexual offences from its first hint of notoriety. Sade had last seen him on the journey to imprisonment at Pierre-Encise nine years before. Marais was now equipped with a warrant and armed with an escort for the arrest of the fugitive marquis. No charges need be brought. The prisoner was to be held during his majesty's pleasure by *lettres de cachet*, issued on the authority of the new king, Louis XVI. Because there was no sentence, there was no promise of release. Imprisonment under this system might last for a few months or for ever.

Sade was escorted across the city with Marais at his side. They drove through the winter day, towards Vincennes on the eastern side. Dark grey against a grey sky, rose the fortress of Vincennes. Higher still at the centre of its western wall stood the grim tower of the keep. Though it bulked far above the other buildings, foursquare with its rounded turret-corners, the windows were scarcely more than archers' slits. It was night by the time that Marais and his prisoner reached it and half-past nine when Sade was handed over to his gaolers. He was to see precious little daylight in the months that followed. Though he could not know it at the time, he was not to have even the briefest period of freedom for another twelve years, with the exception of six weeks' liberty snatched by his own ingenuity. That apart, when he saw the world outside again, he would find it changed by events that shook and altered the whole of Europe, replacing the stable order of the modern Renaissance world with a new age of Revolution.

EIGHT

The House of Silence

1

RENÉE-PÉLAGIE KNEW ONLY that Sade was a captive in the labyrinth of the prison system. She thought it possible that he was held in the Bastille. There was no means by which she could communicate with him nor he with her. She went to the minister responsible for his arrest and was told to "keep calm". She would be "content" when she knew what had been done. She was also told not to make a fuss by spreading the news. Madame de Montreuil insisted that she had no hand in the affair. "She was not capable of such betrayal." Far to the south, among the gardens and fountains of Saumane, the Abbé de Sade received news of his nephew's arrest from Madame de Montreuil. "I am untroubled at present," he wrote, "and I believe that everyone will be satisfied."

Madame de Montreuil's letters to those involved in the arrest belied her reassurances. "Everything has gone as well and as safely as it could," she wrote on 4 March. "It was about time too! . . . I do not think that Monsieur the Abbé can disapprove of me." After Sade had been in Vincennes almost a year, she was gratified to find her daughter calmer, though still showing a misplaced loyalty to him in his demands for freedom. By then the aim was to remove any stigma from the family by an annulment of the verdict and sentence for the "Marseille poisonings", while keeping him in prison by means of the royal *lettre de cachet*. "I greatly approve of this new manner of proceeding," wrote the ailing Abbé de Sade that summer. "I think it will succeed because the minister supports it and the magistrates are well disposed."

Madame de Montreuil's earliest concern was over any "compromising" objects or writings which the authorities might find at La Coste. She wanted any such incriminating items buried "a hundred feet deep". Worse still, there were people who might compromise the family. When Nanon was at last released from detention it must be in return for her silence. This was now an issue of some concern, since the girl's father was protesting more vigorously and directly against the arbitrary detention of his daughter. Lions, who was Sade's representative at the Mas de Cabanes estate, reported in December 1777 that Nanon had accepted the conditions for her release. She was not to live at Arles nor Lyon, nor in the Auvergne. Nor was she to speak of things which were now "past history".

2

The keep of Vincennes had been built in the reign of Charles V, during the fourteenth century. It housed few prisoners by 1777 but it held them securely. Even by the standards of eighteenth-century imprisonment there was a hopelessness about this bastion on the wooded eastern fringe of Paris. For the men who were enclosed by the monstrous thickness of its walls and in the semi-darkness of the ill-lit rooms, rats, mice and disease were their sure companions. Far worse for a man in Sade's situation was the uncertainty of when, if ever, he would be free again. The thought that the rest of their lives might be passed in such conditions, without appeal to any court or tribunal, broke all but the most resolute spirits.

At the time of Sade's arrival, Vincennes contained another prisoner whose personal notoriety and literary fame were to be a match for his own. Honoré-Gabriel-Riqueti, Comte de Mirabeau and author of the *Erotica Biblion,* was nine years younger than Sade. When the two men met in prison, they showed no sympathy for one another, quarrelling and issuing challenges. But they were both the victims of arbitrary imprisonment under the system of *lettres de cachet.* Mirabeau was later to denounce in print this system whereby members of influential families could have troublesome relatives locked up by favour of the king without recourse to any court of law. As Sade entered Vincennes, the desperate protests of other men who feared they had been "entombed alive" echoed from its dark keep. "You have sent me to a living death," Mirabeau wrote to his father, "a fate worse than any death by execution." Sade was to make the same plea, with variations, many times in the next twelve years. He was thirty-six years old. With the exception of six weeks as a fugitive, he was to spend his life in the great prisons of France until he was fifty.

He was to be allocated Room 6 in the great keep. According to the custom of the prison, his name was not mentioned by the guards. He became henceforward "Monsieur le 6".

He knew that the *lettre de cachet* under which he had been detained must be the work of Madame de Montreuil. Within a few days of being arrested, he wrote her a letter that was savage in its denunciation of her vindictiveness and the cruelty of such vengeance. He also wrote to Renée-Pélagie, begging her to use her influence and to save him from the horror of the oblivion which his imprisonment represented. He asked for access to a court, a chance to defend himself and, if found guilty, the right to be sentenced to a specific term of imprisonment.

He was held in solitary confinement in a room with two very small and heavily barred windows. Between him and the outside world were nineteen iron doors. Sometimes he was taken from his cell to an exercise area a dozen yards square with high walls round it. It seemed to him that they might as well have left him in his dimly lit room but while he was absent it could be searched for subversive writings or any signs of an attempt at escape. The governor of Vincennes had not forgotten that Sade was the gaol-breaker of Miolans. In the great keep, the rules were strictly observed. Few words were exchanged and all unnecessary sound was forbidden. The governor of Vincennes prided himself on having his prison known as "The House of Silence".

Sade's solitary confinement lasted all day, except for brief interruptions when his food was brought. During the rest of the time he sat alone and wept tears of self-pity. Soon the weeping was followed by outbursts of hysterical anger, and by a morose despair. He wrote to Renée-Pélagie and Madame de Montreuil, his letters alternating between accusation and gloom. At length, Renée-Pélagie was allowed to write to him, though these were open letters which the gaolers read. The couple later devised simple ways of coding messages and, on occasion, made use of invisible ink.

The Montreuil family, with a curious mixture of duplicity and concern, tried to placate him. They and Renée-Pélagie would seek leave to institute proceedings to have the death sentence of 1772 anulled. He would then be in no danger of being arrested for the Marseille incident. But Madame de Montreuil suggested an ominous qualification to this. The only basis for a successful annulment of the death sentence would be to argue that the court had failed to take into account Sade's mental state. It might have to be shown that he was insane. Surprisingly, Sade seemed to accept this condition. He joined eagerly in the discussion of the plans for his appeal. He insisted that the girls at Marseille were not innocent victims. They were experienced whores who would have known all about cantharides and had taken Sade's bonbons willingly. He had never suggested sodomy to them and, indeed, none of them had admitted submitting to it herself. Finally, he offered evidence to show that Marguerite Coste's sickness came from the potions of her pavement quack and had nothing to do with the sweets which Sade had offered her.

In this farrago of denials, there was a plausible explanation for the girls' sickness which exonerated Sade. Indeed, it seemed to be supported by the chemical analysis. But Sade was not able to clear himself of sodomy, if only because of his conduct with Marianne Laverne and, possibly, his behaviour with Latour. Despite his enthusiasm, none of his new "evidence" was as valuable as the measures taken by Madame de Montreuil before the hearing of the appeal. She ensured that Gaufridy put the girls through their paces and that when the hearing came on there should be a wholesale retraction of the evidence against her son-in-law. The scandal of Marseille in June 1772 had, according to its witnesses, never taken place.

As Madame de Montreuil noted in April 1778, it was not an easy matter to overturn the convictions for sodomy and poisoning. "What has to be done, regarding the girls in the affair, is delicate and must be undertaken in concert with those who are the principals in the negotiation – or with the secret advice breathed by the justices, which they give you in order to bring the vessel safely to harbour. There are two at the head of the police in Aix who can render great service in accordance with the need one has of them." Whatever the legal position, the Montreuils were spending time and money to ensure that the evidence was now favourable. As Madame de Montreuil wrote candidly on 14

April 1778, "The matter is of too great consequence to take risks with it".

Even Sade's elder uncle, the Prior of Toulouse and Commander of the Order of St John of Jerusalem, added his opinion for the benefit of the judges. "The family punished the libertine as soon as it could," he told them on 28 June. "He will trouble society no more. The king and the government have taken part in the arrangements which are necessary to preserve the honour of a family which has never given cause for reproach. I hope that you will truly contribute to this." It seems unlikely that Sade saw a copy of the letter. A promise that he would trouble society no more was scarcely encouraging.

The preparation of the appeal seemed a protracted process to Sade, as he waited impatiently in Vincennes. After six months in prison he was still buoyed up by the prospect of a successful plea to the court, followed by his release. At last, on 27 May 1778, leave to appeal was granted him by the king, despite the lapse of more than five years since the trial. Sade was still a prisoner in June when he was escorted to Aix-en-Provence in the familiar company of Inspector Marais. It was on a golden Provençal evening, 20 June, that the prisoner and escort arrived at Aix. To Sade, after a year and a half of the gloomy twilight of Vincennes, the promise of liberty in such a place was more alluring than ever.

He was held in prison at Aix during the hearing, though with access to female detainees. On 22 June, the high court of Aix ordered that his case should be presented. Eight days later, the pleadings were put in on his behalf by the attorney for his defence, Joseph-Jérôme Siméon. The judges ruled that the conviction of 1772 should be quashed and that the witnesses should be heard again. On 7 July and the following day, Sade and the witnesses confronted one another in court, gave evidence and were examined. On 14 July it was judged that Sade should be convicted of the lesser offences of libertinage and extreme debauchery. He was sentenced to be admonished by the court for his misconduct and forbidden from visiting Marseille for three years. He was also fined fifty livres towards the expenses of the judicial and penal systems. To one who had just spent sixteen months in the dark keep of Vincennes, it must have seemed like a reprieve from death. Sade was taken back to prison in Aix to await the completion of formalities.

When Inspector Marais came to him again, Sade was prepared to take his leave and walk from prison as a free man. He was told that the original order for his arrest had been rescinded, following the decision of the court. Then, to Sade's dismay, Marais informed him that there was a carriage outside which would take the prisoner and escort back to Vincennes. The order of 1772 had been quashed and the family name had been redeemed. But the *lettre de cachet* which had brought Sade to Vincennes was still in force, unaffected by the proceedings at Aix. The reputation of the Sades and the Montreuils might be vindicated. But Sade himself must return to indefinite imprisonment.

He saw too late the trap into which he had fallen. Madame de Montreuil's concern had never been for him, only for her own reputation. Now that the scandal of 1772 had been laid to rest, it suited her that her son-in-law should remain where he could do no more harm. Sade's indignation at the trick that had been played upon him was tempered by panic and dismay at the prospect of indefinite imprisonment at Vincennes. It was not a matter of being detained until the formalities of his appeal were completed. They had been completed already. He faced ten or twenty years in the grey and dimly lit bastion east of Paris, perhaps an ordeal that would end only with his old age and death.

Accompanied by Marais and four guards, Sade was taken north from Aix on the same day, seeing the vineyards and gorges, the hilltop châteaux and cherry orchards of Provence for what was probably the last time. Inspector Marais tried to cheer him up. The return to Vincennes might be merely a technicality, Marais suggested. Sade guessed, correctly, that it was no such thing. And then, in a most extraordinary exchange, Marais said that the police had no real interest in seeing Sade returned to his cell. A *lettre de cachet* was, strictly speaking, a civil matter, almost family business. Of course, the police escorts could not set him free on their own authority. They had their own jobs and reputations to consider. But if Sade were to escape, as prisoners sometimes did, that would be a different matter.

Soon after this strange conversation, they ended their second day's journey. The prisoner and his escorts crossed the Rhône and came to the outskirts of Valence, where the party stopped for dinner and the night at the Logis du Louvre. Nothing more was said about escaping but Sade complained that he had no appetite for the meal. He withdrew to the room where he was to be kept until morning and where there was a guard watching him. It was after dark when he asked to be escorted to the privy. This was done by the second in command of the escort detail, who was Marais's brother. Presently Sade emerged from the privy and began to walk back to the room, past the guard who stood at the head of the stairs. As he went by, Sade seemed to stumble and the guard instinctively put out an arm to steady him. Sade at once ducked back under the arm and bounded down the stairway in three or four enormous leaps. So far as escape was concerned, it was now all or nothing.

Surprise and audacity favoured him. The officer shouted for his colleagues and the four of them followed down the stairs in pursuit of their prisoner. But Sade had judged his attempt better than he could have hoped. Within seconds of reaching the bottom of the stairs he was through a doorway and into the yard of the inn, at a point where it had an entrance on to the main road. Sade was through it before his pursuers could get near him. The inn was on the outskirts of Valence and by this time at night there was not a light outside. In a few seconds more, Sade had disappeared into the darkness.

Marais and his companions could do nothing but search the immediate area. Perhaps they lacked the enthusiasm to do much else. Sade, who knew the area better than they, made his way down to the Rhône and followed the river bank downstream until daylight. Soon after dawn he came across some fishermen, one of whom was the owner of a leaky wherry. There were negotiations in which Sade tried to persuade them to take him down the river to Avignon, hinting at a generous reward for their services. At length the owner of the wherry agreed and Sade returned to the city of his ancestors, safe from discovery. At six o'clock that evening, 17 July, he stepped ashore at Avignon and found shelter with a friend.

During the period of his detention at Vincennes, there had been a family bereavement. The Abbé de Sade had died at Saumane on 3 January 1778, where he was buried the next day, and the family home was vacant. While it was true that the Abbé had died embarrassed by debts and that he appeared to have sold part of the property to his Spanish mistress, there might still be a bolt-hole for the fugitive. Saumane was subordinate in civil matters to

Mazan and Sade, of course, had been Lord of Mazan. Unfortunately, one of his kinsmen, Jean-Baptiste-Joseph-David, Comte de Sade d'Eyguières, had obtained the lieutenancy of Mazan by pointing out to the king that Sade himself had had his powers suspended five years earlier. But the family had not had the time to purloin Saumane from Sade. That being the case, it might offer a present refuge. Unlike the easier approach to La Coste, Saumane stood high above the valleys on either side, crowning a rocky summit. The walls below the château had been built as if for fortification. Less accessible than La Coste, it was also less likely to be watched by those who hunted him.

But first he had to make for La Coste to equip himself for what was to come. The friend with whom he had sought sanctuary provided him with a meal. Then Sade took a carriage and began driving through the darkness on a road that had long been familiar to him. By next morning he was safely at La Coste. Gothon, Renée-Pélagie's maid who had taken part in the pleasures that led to the "Scandal of the Little Girls", was in residence. So was the housekeeper, Mademoiselle de Rousset, who had welcomed him to La Coste as a girl of sixteen in 1763. Sade half-believed that Madame de Montreuil had relented after all, that the escape had been agreed between her and Inspector Marais. But as news reached him of the search that was being mounted, he withdrew his expressions of gratitude towards his mother-in-law.

He wrote to Gaufridy, describing his escape, and received a letter from Renée-Pélagie which had been prepared for him in case he should ever evade his captors. "Now do you believe I love you?" she wrote to her adored *"bon petit ami"*. She advised caution and suggested that when he wrote to her, the letter should not be in his writing. Whatever messages he wished to add might be written between the lines of another correspondent, perhaps in invisible ink.

It was some weeks before she knew that Sade had escaped and, during this time, there had been what she called "a terrible scene" with her mother. Renée-Pélagie learnt that Sade was not after all to be freed, the news being imparted by Madame de Montreuil to her daughter in a "high-handed and revoltingly despotic" manner. Sade, meanwhile, was urging Gaufridy to put his case to his mother-in-law. Madame de Montreuil equivocated. Sade's fate would depend on how he used his freedom, she explained. He must pay his way and Renée-Pélagie must not attempt to rejoin him. Renée-Pélagie was informed that any attempt to go to Sade would mean his arrest. She at once wrote a warning note to her husband to be forwarded by Gaufridy.

The month that followed his escape was one in which Sade enjoyed the pleasures of freedom all the more for having been deprived of them in the previous year and a half. He truly behaved as though he had got away with it. His intentions were to enlist Madame de Montreuil's sympathy and to live in Provence with Renée-Pélagie. He was no longer a criminal and the law had no reason to trouble him. Were there really men prepared to arrest him? "For my part, I still don't believe it," he wrote. As for the story that Inspector Marais had wept with frustration at his escape, Sade thought it absurd. "Believe me, tears are unknown to that sort. Their expressions of anger are profanities rather than weeping." He even thought that it would be safe for him to go to Aix. Marais and his officers might stir up trouble by arriving empty-handed at Paris, but not at Aix, "where no one will do anything but laugh at them." As for the fears of coachloads of men setting out to arrest him, "It's a farce good enough to make one die laughing."

However, it was perhaps imprudent to remain at La Coste all the time. Saumane might be even safer and it was the place Sade had insisted he wanted to see again. In his years of captivity he was less drawn to La Coste than to this single rocky street with pale houses of Provençal stone above the deep silence of the wooded valleys to either side. The Abbé de Sade now lay in his tomb in the little church at the extreme point of the village with the misty sweep of Provence falling away towards the far-off sea. At the other end, the steep path led up to the château and its gardens, separated from the village and commanding a view of the approaches on every side.

During the weeks at La Coste, however, the intimacy between Sade and Marie-Dorothée de Rousset prospered. There was no suggestion that she shared the tastes he had indulged at La Coste in the winter of 1774–5. Their affection was profound, though they were together so briefly. She was a frequent correspondent in the years before her death in 1784. It was as if, from prison, Sade reserved something of the adoration for "Sainte Rousset" which Petrarch had shown to the family's most illustrious ancestor.

In August, Sade wrote to Gaufridy to report a warning that the authorities proposed to raid La Coste. Why should they do this if they were content to let him escape and live quietly? Having returned to the château, Sade decided that he must leave it and sleep in a barn to avoid a night search. He withdrew to the shelter offered by a friend at Oppède, a neighbouring village. Nothing came of the warning and Sade decided that it would be safe to sleep in the château itself. It was four o'clock in the morning on 26 August when Gothon burst into his bedroom and shouted at him to run for his life.

Sade woke to sounds of men searching the lower floor and cries of confusion upstairs. Scrambling from bed in his nightshirt, he ran to a box-room and tried to lock himself in. In no time at all this locked door was broken open by the hunters and he was surrounded by men who carried swords and pistols. Sade protested but Marais sneered at him, "Talk, talk, little man, you are going to be locked up for the rest of your life for the things you've done in the black room upstairs, where there were bodies. . . ." At this point it seems that Sade was dragged out to the carriage and the witnesses heard no more.

Madame de Montreuil was as unforgiving towards Marais as to her son-in-law. She assured Mademoiselle de Rousset that Marais was dismissed and refused his expenses for first letting his prisoner escape and then for recapturing him in a manner that showed too little respect for social superiors. Abandoned on all sides, the unfortunate policeman was dismissed and died two years later.

3

Bound like a felon, Sade was paraded before the crowds at Cavaillon, then at Avignon and the other towns on his route, men and women pressing eagerly to see what sort of a man it was who had whipped Rose Keller and Mariette Borelly or sodomized Marianne Laverne and done as bad or worse to the "little girls" of Provence. Yet there was time on the journey to write a letter of instruction to Gaufridy. Gothon's wages were to be increased; an inventory of the contents of the château must be drawn up; Mademoiselle de Rousset was to be left in charge of the building; his study was to be locked and the key given to Renée-Pélagie. He wrote like a man who was leaving for ever.

On 7 September, Inspector Marais and his prisoner arrived at Vincennes. Marais said no more about escape. Sade was consigned to one of the dark, airless cells of the massive keep, which Mirabeau later described as having walls sixteen feet thick and opaque glass to dim still further the light from the tiny barred windows. As darkness fell, the drawbridge of the fortress was raised and every door was locked. The stillness of the inner courtyard was broken only by the half-hourly patrol of the night-watch.

Within the prison, whose very existence was supposed to represent law and justice, Sade confronted an infinite variety of cruelties and corruption. Such a system was to be his world for the next twelve years and its cynicism was to condition his first essays in fiction. During this time he suffered the elementary privations of all prisoners. To begin with, there was no fire in winter and the rats were so numerous that he could not sleep at night. When he asked if he might keep a cat in his cell to deter such vermin, he was told without a trace of humour that animals were not permitted within the prison.

The governor of Vincennes, Charles de Rougemont, was the illegitimate son of the Marquis d'Oise and an Englishwoman, Mrs Hatte. "The Bastard Rougemont", Sade called him in his letters, no doubt relishing the thought that the governor's underlings would read the comment as they censored his correspondence, "A Fucking-Jack without a soul." Rougemont had followed the contemporary custom of buying his governorship and therefore expected to make a profit on his investment. This was done by extorting money directly from the prisoners or indirectly from their families.

In English and French prisons alike, prisoners might be obliged to pay for their food and drink. In some cases they even had to pay if they wanted water to drink. The governor would either sell food to them at whatever price he chose to fix or he might sell the franchise for supplying food. A prisoner's family could send in some of the food and drink, as Sade's did, but there would still be a charge for accommodating him. The Montreuils paid eight hundred livres a quarter to keep Sade at Vincennes. In one of the more grotesque practices, when English prisoners were killed by the brutality of their gaolers in 1729, their families were then charged rent for "The Lion's Den", used to chain and beat the men to death. It was an irony beyond the wildest moral extravagance of Sade's fiction.

The winter of 1778–9 was a formative season in Sade's mental development. In his mind he carried the words of his captor at La Coste, who had promised that the fugitive was to spend the rest of his life in prison. Sade's letters to Renée-Pélagie now became more melodramatic. His first appeals for help were again followed by a plea to have some determinate sentence passed upon him. He demanded repeatedly to be told how long he was to be kept in such conditions and "to know the worst". It seemed little enough consolation in the unending loneliness of the little prison room with its high vaulted roof. The gaolers brought his food or visited him four times a day. Only during the seven minutes which this took them was Sade's solitude relieved.

Nothing could be done for the prisoner in the autumn months of 1778. The letters imploring Renée-Pélagie to help him were followed by those in which he cursed and raged, then fell into despair and apathy. He was, he wrote to Dorothée de Rousset, like a victim of Tiberius's tyranny in a nation that called itself civilized. The Roman tyrant was known to grieve when he ordered the death of a favourite victim because he would no longer be able to torture the man.

Three weeks after his new imprisonment began, Sade received his first letter from Renée-Pélagie. At first he was allowed one letter a week, his chief correspondents being Renée-Pélagie and Mademoiselle de Rousset. To "Sainte Rousset" he wrote in terms varying from the flirtatious to the humorously pedantic, like a schoolmaster to a favourite pupil. She had, as she told Gaufridy, "a passionate nature" and the attachment to Sade was profound, if platonic. She came to Paris in November 1778 as a companion to Renée-Pélagie, the two women living in rooms at the Carmelite convent until the tuberculosis from which she suffered drove her back to the warmer climate of La Coste. From there she wrote to Sade, giving him news of the château and of people whom he had known. In the following year he asked her to stop writing to him, though their correspondence was to be resumed. Indeed, it was Sainte Rousset who complained that his letters to her had become abusive and that she felt he might betray to the authorities her secret advice to him. In July 1780, she had also warned him that the bitter abuse of those authorities in his letters was liable to compromise any hope of his release.

After three months of detention, Sade was allowed two periods of exercise a week. These were taken as a rule in the little yard, whose walls rose tall and dark on each side. On these occasions the prisoner walked in silence with one of the guards. Sade supposed that he was not permitted to walk in Rougemont's garden for fear that he should steal the apples. On 29 March 1779, he was allowed an additional hour of exercise each week. These "promenades" were eventually increased to five a week, though they were sometimes suspended for a month or two to punish him for some act of rebellion.

Above Rougemont's power was that of the police, in the person of Lieutenant-General Le Noir. It was Le Noir who dealt with Renée-Pélagie's requests to see her husband. Even when such requests were granted there was often a delay of several weeks, which Sade insisted was the result of the lieutenant-general's obsession with Madame Le Noir's posterior. But for the first three years, Renée-Pélagie was not to see Sade at all. The moral scorn which the prisoner himself felt for Le Noir and his kind was never concealed. "I may have smacked a few bottoms," Sade wrote, "and he has brought a million souls under threat of death by hunger."

Sade was no longer held as a criminal. That being so, books, furnishing, writing materials and clothes, as well as food and wine, might be sent in for him. The world of Monsieur le 6 was a curious combination of darkness and indulgence. His letters frequently asked for pots of confiture or nougat or the lemon biscuits made near the Palais Royal or bottles of a particular wine. Not surprisingly, he began to get fat. By the time that he saw the outside world again he described himself as looking like a portly country priest. Renée-Pélagie also inquired anxiously of her "*cher ami*" what clothes he would need for the winter in the chill prison cell. He had been given a room without a stove, where the cold months were an agony.

"Monsieur de Sade's situation is appalling," Mademoiselle de Rousset told Gaufridy in January 1779. "You can judge that by your knowledge of his character and vivacity. The brief moments of gaiety that he shows from time to time are wiped away for us by storms which pierce the heart through and through like hailstones."

Sade's hope of release was not strengthened by the bitterness between Renée-Pélagie and Madame de Montreuil. Renée-Pélagie at length thought it a matter of pride not to speak his name in her mother's presence. Though she was short of money and not particularly good at managing what she had, she answered all questions on the topic by saying obliquely that her husband had provided for her. Nor was Madame de Montreuil the only person to stand in the way of Sade's liberty. Even when he had been in prison for more than three years and when his case was being "considered", Mademoiselle de Rousset reported the outcome at court privately, though not to Sade. "Monsieur and Madame de Maurepas, two princesses, and several others who have seen the reasons for his captivity have said, 'He is best where he is. His wife is either as mad or as guilty as he, if she dares to ask for his liberty. We don't want to see her.'"

Sade's behaviour towards Renée-Pélagie followed a pattern of increasing desperation. At first he laid all the blame on Madame de Montreuil. His letters protested at the injustice of his imprisonment. Then he demanded again, if he had committed some crime, to have a specific and determinate sentence passed on him. Like many obsessives, he also showed a compulsion over numbers and calculations. A favourite game, though played in earnest, was to use the numbers of months or days he had been imprisoned, in order to calculate the date of his release.

At length, he turned against Renée-Pélagie. Was she truly working for his freedom? Was she not, perhaps, having an affair with some other man? He swore she was having one with a friend, Lefèvre, who had obtained some books for him. When she talked of going to live with Madame de Villet in 1781, as a means of setting up home again, Sade accused her of embarking on a lesbian romance. It was on 13 July 1781, almost four and a half years since they had last seen one another, that Renée-Pélagie was allowed to visit him for the first time. Sade was taken down to the Council Chamber of the fortress, where he and Renée-Pélagie were reunited, the eyes of a police officer upon them. In November, Le Noir told Renée-Pélagie that if she insisted on her right to visit her husband regularly, he would inform higher authority of the trouble Sade was causing by his unbalanced state of mind. This was presumably a reference to her innocent use of the word "*grosse*" to describe the weight she had put on. Sade had burst out in fury on the assumption that she was pregnant. She had, indeed, said that she feared she must look like a pregnant sow. This self-deprecation was sufficient to start the quarrel.

Neither Sade's state of mind nor the facilities available to him had yet moved him in the direction of much prison writing. Yet the first hint of inspiration had come during the night of 16 February 1779, after six months of confinement. He reported a vivid dream, in which he was visited by Petrarch's Laura, who came to comfort him as none of his living family had done. The vision urged him to follow her to the joys of Paradise.

Sade was not apt to be impressed by manifestations of this kind. Yet the experience perhaps caused that change in him which the world was soon to witness. He began to construct a kingdom of his own within the confines of his prison room. He would be the actor rather than the victim, supreme in his own thoughts and imagination. He still wanted his freedom but the letters in which he argued for it began to develop a second preoccupation. If there could be no escape outwards through the massive walls of Vincennes, perhaps there might be an escape inwards. The letters began to carry the more routine demands of a prisoner for books, writing materials, and the candles without which the books and pens would be useless in the gloom of the great medieval keep. These provisions were not a mere anodyne against the slow agony of solitude. They were the foundations upon which a new world was to be built. Day by day in the letters it seemed that he was redefining his own view of himself. He was not to be the weeping petitioner but the heroic and unbroken champion of his own cause. There were those who had expected him to go mad, as other men did after years of such captivity. But he was not to go mad. On the contrary, he was to shock the minds of his bourgeois readers by a terrifying intellectual clarity. He would employ his sanity against his enemies as though it were a weapon of total war. Even if Sade had not yet sought salvation through writing novels, the ideas which were to feature in his fiction were soon to preoccupy him in his letters.

Despite the power of many of his letters, Sade was not invincible. All too often his composure melted like a wax mask and he raged at his guards with a ferocity that threatened physical violence. As a rule his anger was directed at guards or servants but in 1780 Sade turned it against the most celebrated of his fellow prisoners. His outbursts against his captors made them withdraw the privilege of exercising in the yard. Brooding on this in his cell, he was convinced that it was done in order to allow the Comte de Mirabeau to walk there instead. Soon afterwards, the two prisoners came face to face. Sade burst into one of those rages which had been characteristic since he first beat up his Bourbon playmate in the nursery of the Condé Palace. He shouted that Mirabeau was the male whore of the prison governor, Charles de Rougemont, and swore that he would slit the scoundrel's ears when they were both free.

"My name", said Mirabeau coldly, "is that of a man of honour who has never dissected nor poisoned women – and who will write that name of honour on your back with cuts of his cane, unless you are broken on the wheel before then – whose only fear is of having to wear black at your execution in place de Grève." As Mirabeau wrote in his letters, it was bad enough having to share the same prison with a "monster" like Sade without having to endure encounters of this sort. In Sade's works, Mirabeau was to be referred to several times and always as a spy, a knave, a traitor or an ignoramus. The two prisoners remained unreconciled but Sade's periods of exercise in the yard were at length restored.

Apart from such encounters, Sade's contact with the life outside his prison room was through the letters which he wrote and received, all of them subject to prison censorship. In the world beyond the prison, time and mortality overtook those who had once been dear to him but were now seemed almost creatures of the imagination, remote as the characters in a novel might be. Months passed and he was not allowed a visit from Renée-Pélagie. During this time he maintained an untiring fusillade of letters, still protesting his innocence and demanding his release, still cursing Madame de Montreuil as an old whore, showering obscenities on Governor de Rougemont and the "satellites" of the Paris police. Renée-Pélagie replied that if only he would be patient and well-behaved something might be done for him. As time went by, however, this promise was made less often and with less confidence.

Sade heard rumours that he was to be transferred to an island prison, which appalled him. Yet the conditions in Vincennes had weakened his chest by cold and damp. He had begun to cough blood and, like Mademoiselle de Rousset, was in need of a warmer climate. It was proposed to transfer him to the prison at Montélimar, so that he might be closer to La Coste. He could even administer his estates from such captivity and Gaufridy would be able to visit him there. Sade knew only that the prison at Montélimar was far more insanitary than Vincennes and that he had not the least wish to be transferred there. He wanted his freedom, nothing else. If necessary, he would agree to go abroad as the price of liberty. Indeed, he began to cherish the delusion that the king intended to send him abroad as a diplomat rather than an exile, following his father's example.

The discussion of his transfer continued during 1781. Madame de Montreuil claimed that she was indifferent to it. Sade rejected the suggestion of Montélimar but indicated a preference for the fortress tower of Crest, standing above a little town to the east of the Rhône. Better still would be Pierre-Encise, where he might be treated as a brother officer by the commander of the garrison. Nothing came of it. Sade offered again to become a voluntary exile. But his suggestion that he should serve the king abroad in some diplomatic capacity was received without reply.

It seems that he did not know for some time of the blow which struck the Montreuil family on 13 May that year. Anne-Prospère de Launay, the "canoness" whose attachment to Sade had caused such scandal and such pain to Madame de Montreuil, died at the age of thirty-seven. She had never married nor ever entered fully into the life of a religious community. It was probably six or seven years since she and Sade had been together. Like so many of the figures in his life, Anne-Prospère had slipped a little further towards the verge of recollection. If Gaufridy was right in his account of her symptoms, she probably died of appendicitis which turned to peritonitis.

Grief on this occasion was the prerogative of Madame de Montreuil. The death of one daughter and desertion by another, added to moral treason by her son-in-law, had almost destroyed a generation of her family. The youngest daughter of all was married but Madame de Montreuil's affections now fastened on Sade's two sons. Towards Sade himself, she was unrelenting but without passion in her comments. Four years later she remarked wearily that he must stay in prison because, if he was released, he would only misbehave.

The following year, 1782, brought news of damage at La Coste. Storms, during which the wind had increased every fifteen minutes to an alarming strength, brought down plaster and revealed cracks in the corners of the walls. In September the local population had looted the vineyard and killed the young partridges. Mademoiselle de Rousset, her health in decline, moved out of the building and advised the other occupants to do the same.

In consequence of his ill-tempered encounter with Mirabeau, Sade's privilege of taking exercise had been withdrawn for a period of eight months, until the spring of 1781. He sat in his cell and issued embittered protests in the form of letters to Renée-Pélagie. He had already been ill for some time, coughing blood and suffering from piles, when a doctor was at length allowed to examine him. His eyes began to trouble him and he could not see in the gloom of the cell. He asked for an oculist but as yet no oculist had arrived. By the beginning of 1783 he seemed to have lost the sight of one eye. Lieutenant-General Le Noir thought he might be shamming. However, Sade was seen by the oculist Grandjean and prescriptions were made up by an apothecary. The cause of the complaint was put down to too much reading and writing in the ill-lit room.

Whatever the state of his eyes, the letters from his room came with greater frequency and volume. The theses of his innocence were bluntly stated. "I am a libertine," he announced, "but I am no *criminal* and no *murderer*!" As if to show the truth of this, he began to detail his sexual longings and philosophical beliefs in parallel. When Renée-Pélagie, like Mademoiselle de Rousset, wrote back ominously that his present state of mind and the topics which obsessed him would not assist his release, he replied with considerable indignation. "I respect all tastes and all fantasies, however bizarre they may appear." And thinking of Renée-Pélagie's own beauty, he promised that when he was released the first thing he would do would be to kiss her eyes, her breasts, her bottom, and only then would he rush to his bookseller to buy volumes of Buffon, Montaigne, Dorat, Voltaire and Rousseau. Sex and literature had at last been brought into balance, it seemed.

His own predilections were advanced proudly in his letters. In one of them he energetically demolished the philosophy of Madame de Montreuil on the inviolability of the female anus, recalling to Renée-Pélagie the warm passion of nights at La Coste. At this point, remembering that she was the Marquise de Sade, a woman of noble blood by birth, the mother of two grown-up sons, it seems that she had no desire to be reminded of what had happened in the past and certainly not to discuss it in the present. She replied to her husband that if he persisted in such outbursts, which were read by the prison censors, she would refuse to receive any more of his letters.

But Sade was into his stride as a correspondent. The great pleasures of his life in prison, he explained eagerly, would be to cut off the testicles of Albaret, that minion of the Montreuil family who had accompanied Renée-Pélagie on her journey to Miolans when Sade was a prisoner in Savoy; to have a beautiful woman posing naked in his cell as the Callipygian Venus, drawing the veil from her behind while looking back over her shoulder; to blow up the powder-magazine of the fortress, and finally to open a parcel with the horrid thrill of finding that some-one had sent him a pair of skulls. As for Madame de Montreuil, he now had proof that she was a whore as well as a hypocrite and that she had presented her fool of a husband with any number of bastards. One would never find a creature more abominable, he had written on 3 July 1780. Hell had never "spewed up" any-thing like her. It was from such material that ancient preachers had fashioned the figures of the Furies. Nor had he forgotten his other female persecutors. In January 1783 he once more regret-ted the passing of the good old times, when a nobleman who suf-fered injustice at the hands of whores was entitled to turn his sword against them.

Then, as self-pity broke over him once more, he begged Renée-Pélagie to consider whether his parents would ever have treated her as her parents were now treating him. "In God's name come to me!" he implored her. But that winter passed and he saw nothing of her. He raged against his principal enemy once more.

Madame de Montreuil had been known to masquerade as a woman of the camp and had sold herself to common soldiers. Anticipating the themes of his own novels, Sade commented on the irony by which such criminals as she should have the power of judging and punishing the poor wretches who inhabited the dark and insanitary cells of Vincennes or the Bastille. Whatever retribution he might deserve, Sade prayed God that he might no longer be punished by a family whose principal members were a bawd, a monopolist and a sodomite.

However bitter the tone of the letters, their style was not that of a man who any longer hoped for liberty. On 28 April 1782, after four years of captivity, Sade recognized plainly the hopelessness of his situation. He wrote yet again to Renée-Pélagie. This time he signed himself, "The Prisoner Sade".

5

His correspondence expressed little interest in the great public events which constituted the history of France during his years of imprisonment. When he commented on the news of his own family, it was usually to announce displeasure of some kind. There was a squall of temper at the beginning of 1784, when he heard that his elder son had dishonoured the family by accepting a commission in an infantry regiment rather than joining the cavalry. When Renée-Pelagie was free was allowed to come and see him again, he wrote to her afterwards with all the prudent suspicion of a careful and respectable bourgeois. He urged her not to parade herself in public like a slut, nor to go about the city on foot like a street woman. He felt so sensitive on these topics that he wrote in the same terms to one of Renée-Pélagie's female friends, so that she might keep an eye on the thoughtless Marquise de Sade.

Though his moods and letters might be erratic, by 1784 Sade had not gone mad in his dim cell at Vincennes. His dark *alter ego* matured in irony and bitterness, asserting its power in the realm of imagination, until at times it seemed to rule his personality. "I tell you", he wrote to Renée-Pélagie, "that prison is a place of evil. Its solitude gives power to certain obsessions. The derangement which such a force brings about grows more rapid and inevitable." A century later, from the isolation of another prison cell, Oscar Wilde made much the same point. "The mind is forced to think," Wilde wrote in his petition to the Home Secretary, and he added that in a prison cell "it becomes, in the case of those who are suffering from sexual monomanias, the sure prey of morbid passions, and obscene fancies, and thoughts that defile, desecrate, and destroy." But Sade came to terms with these horrors more robustly than Wilde could do. It was understandable that a man might draw back in disgust from the dark dramas that taunted the mind. But it was possible, too, to revel in what a later prisoner still, Jean Genet, called "the festivals of an inner prison".

There is no clear point at which Sade becomes a writer rather than a correspondent. There is a change in his letters during several years of his detention, the private anger transformed into moral scepticism which seeks a public audience. He had long been a stylist of energy and perception in his correspondence and in his travel journals, even a tentative dramatist. For the moment, his letters continued to harp on the same personal grievances. Governor de Rougemont is trying to poison him on Madame de Montreuil's orders. His health is deteriorating. He has lost the sight of one eye. It is four years since he asked to see a doctor again, and still no doctor has appeared. It was certainly true that in his middle forties, after eight or nine years of imprisonment, Sade had begun to look like an old man. His hair was white and his face was set hard with the experience of Vincennes.

"Monsieur de Sade writes furious letters attacking the whole world," Renée-Pélagie reported in October 1783, "not least against those who keep him where he is. He promises to avenge himself. That is not the way to advance matters. I have written to him. I hope he will reflect on this and become calmer."

Yet it was for Sainte Rousset in the last three years of her life that he now reserved his finest letters. What emerged from the pages of this correspondence was the vigorous exercise of a strong intellect, particularly in matters of philosophy. But he seldom surpassed the letter written to her in January 1782 on learning of the death of Gothon, the Swiss servant-girl whose room had been conveniently next to his in the château of La Coste. He ordered that the ceremonies of the Church should be performed for this convert from Protestantism, as she had lately become at the time of her marriage. But her death also moved him to a superb Sadean funeral oration, in which even his denunciations of Madame de Montreuil took on a new grandeur and a rhetorical sweep.

> The eagle, Mademoiselle, must sometimes leave the seventh region of the air to come down and perch upon the summit of Mount Olympus, on the ancient pines of the Caucasus, on the cold larch of the Jura, on the white rump of Taurus and sometimes even near the courses of Montmartre. We know from history (for history is a fine thing) that Cato, the great Cato, cultivated his field with his own hands. Cicero himself laid out trees in the beautiful alleys of Formio — I don't know whether anyone cut them down. Diogenes retired into a tub. Abraham made statues of clay. . . . And in our own days, Mademoiselle, in our own august days, do we not see the famous Présidente de Montreuil leave Euclid and Barême in order to discuss salad oil with her cook?
>
> There you have proof, Mademoiselle, that man has done well and has raised himself. Yet despite this there are two fatal moments in the day which remind him of the sad state of brute creation. . . . And those two moments are (if you will forgive me, Mademoiselle, for expressions which may not be noble but are truthful), those two dreadful moments are when he must fill himself and when he must empty himself. One might also add the moment when he learns that his inheritance is destroyed or when he is assured of the death of his loyal slaves. Such is my situation, lovely saint, and such will be the theme of this sad epistle.
>
> I grieve for Gothon. . . .

So he did. What followed was better than anything in his formal eulogy for Marat and Le Pelletier during the years of the Revolution. Of course, it would not do for anyone but Sainte Rousset and perhaps not even for her. "Gothon had, they say, the most beautiful — Dammit, what can one call it? The dictionary has no synonym for the word and decency forbids me to write all its letters. . . . Well, to tell the truth, Mademoiselle, she had the most beautiful c . . . that had escaped the mountains of Switzerland in more than a century — a secure reputation."

If this was an outrage on her memory, it was one that only Sade could have devised. If it was an honest compliment, it was one that only Sade could have paid.

Almost at once, on 26 January, he followed this with a letter on the absurdity of judgment and punishment in a world where there could be no absolute moral standard. It was a vision of pure materialism, in which mankind became "Miserable creatures thrown for a moment on the surface of this little muck-heap – where it is laid down that one half of the herd must persecute the rest. . . . You who decide what is a crime and what is not, you hang men in Paris for what would win them crowns in the Congo." In Sade's view, it is Newton rather than Descartes, Copernicus rather than Tycho Brahe who must be the teachers of men. But Mademoiselle de Rousset was ready for him in her practical way. Men were not hanged in Paris for acts which might win a crown in the Congo, she assured him. They were hanged in Paris for being stupid enough to think they were in the Congo.

Sade had read Voltaire, whom he regarded with some disapproval because of the philosopher's ambivalence towards Christianity. He had also read a good deal of Rousseau and, on 18 January 1779, Mademoiselle de Rousset wrote to him in Vincennes to assure him that *Émile* was still safely in place on its usual shelf in his library at La Coste. But Sade had been imprisoned prior to Rousseau's death and the publication of the *Confessions*. When Renée-Pélagie tried to send him the copy he had requested in July 1783, it was impounded by the authorities at Vincennes. He assumed that the decision to withhold the *Confessions* was Renée-Pélagie's and his impatience was expressed to her later that month. Why forbid Rousseau, when she allowed him to read Voltaire? "Jean-Jacques" was to him what Aquinas was to her and her "fellow bigots". He continued to demand the book, having assured her in July that Rousseau's philosophy of nature represented to him a strict morality and was one of the few influences that might improve his own conduct.

Sade was soon to show Nature as a far more malevolent power in human affairs than Rousseau could ever have imagined. Yet Rousseau's politics, the social contract and the enlightened republic, matched a good deal of Sade's political philosophy as it later developed. Above all, it was the influence of Rousseau on his own nobler instincts which Sade pleaded now. His anger cooled in the second letter of July 1783. He assured Renée-Pélagie that he kissed her bottom in imagination, as he had promised to do when first asking for the book. Since his letter was read by Rougemont's minions before being sent, this compliment was likely to cause Renée-Pélagie embarrassment and annoyance rather than gratification, as Sade must have known. Prisoner though he was, Monsieur le 6 had not entirely lost his power of retribution.

Sade had also seized on the work of the philosopher La Mettrie, author of *L'Homme Machine*, published in 1748. La Mettrie's views were, in essence, simple and exercised considerable influence on the characters of Sade's fiction, if not directly on their creator. Man, according to La Mettrie, must be defined exclusively by scientific observation and experiment. The conclusion of this method can only be that a human creature is a machine, as dependent on motion as the machinery and instruments of the new scientific age of the seventeenth and eighteenth centuries had proved to be.

The science of anatomy as well as that of mechanics had been in the forefront of seventeenth-century advance. The consequence was to bolster both materialist philosophy and the Christian optimism of those like Samuel Clarke who saw in such discoveries of order and harmony a vindication of faith and systems of belief. La Mettrie steered a middle course, allowing that the existence of God and the immortality of the soul were probable, though not scientifically demonstrable by his system. This qualification did not save him from having to leave France and seek refuge in the more tolerant intellectual society of Leiden.

Until 1783, Sade still presented himself as an abstract philosopher rather than the author of plays and novels. "The pineal gland", he wrote laconically to Renée-Pélagie, "is where we atheist philosophers place the seat of human reason." He had taken La Mettrie's system, though that of Epicurus and other materialist philosophers familiar to him from his education would have done just as well for his purposes. Philosophy, of whatever kind, was to become the material of his art. Like Henry Fielding in England forty years earlier, Sade had become one of the most erudite and well read of contemporary novelists.

6

For more than ten years, Sade had tried his hand at writing plays for the public stage and had apparently succeeded in getting one of them produced at Bordeaux in 1773. Perhaps this was the one he had written in 1772, while a fugitive, sending it to Renée-Pélagie in order that she might copy it out. At the end of 1780, after three years as a prisoner at Vincennes, he was working as a dramatist once more. His novels were to record the private sexual melodramas of his solitude. But the plays which he wrote offered a public image of Sade the loyal subject, moralist and entertainer. *Jeanne Laisné: or, The Siege of Beauvais* was an attempt at patriotic tragedy, written in 1783 and sent to Renée-Pélagie on 26 March that year. *Oxtiern: or, The Downfall of Lechery* was to show him as the cautionary moralist. Such pieces as *The Boudoir: or, the Foolish Husband* were bland comedies of a kind already too familiar on the stages of Paris to offer Sade much scope for originality. With few exceptions, his plays were rejected, revised, and rejected again by the theatres of the revolutionary period. Though there was an element of misfortune in this, Sade's plays seldom showed his style at anything but its most lacklustre.

Having occupied himself by writing plays in his prison cell during 1781, he began a piece in the following year which was intended to show what "an atheist philosopher" might do. This was *A Dialogue Between a Preacher and a Dying Man*. In one respect, the topic was no longer original. The deathbed of the virtuous unbeliever, scorning the comforts of religion and "superstition", was already something of a cliché in the thought of the Enlightenment. Nor is there anything new in Sade's use of La Mettrie's arguments to show that life may be viewed as a mechanical process. The merit of the piece is that of Sade the writer rather than Sade the philosopher. The preacher, rather than his beliefs, becomes the butt of the joke, the tables being turned on him by the dying man. To add injury to insult, in a characteristically Sadean ending, the death of the virtuous atheist prompts six beautiful women to enter the room. They take the preacher in their arms and proceed to teach him the true "corruption of nature".

Sade in his *Dialogue* also confounds La Mettrie and the virtuous atheists of Enlightenment mythology. The dying man remarks to the preacher that crime and virtue are mere processes of nature, an argument which insists that such terms as vice and virtue, crime and morality, are meaningless in a mechanistic universe. La Mettrie and the materialists had been uneasy on this point. Their various hopes rested on a belief in God being some-how compatible with a rational or unsuperstitious explanation of the universe. At least, if religion must go, it would be replaced by the moral instincts of rational benevolence. But what, Sade inquires, if it were not? The consequences of his *Dialogue* brought discomfort to virtuous atheists and true believers alike.

Sade himself, either as atheist philosopher or devil's advocate, explored the principal consequence. The logical substitute for what he was apt to call a Supreme Being was the new romantic deity of Nature. If that were so, the morality of human society was to be imitated from Nature. But it was plain to any observer that Nature cared nothing for the absurdity of human conven-tions, particularly as they affected crime and punishment. Indeed humanity itself had no universally agreed conventions. As he had illustrated to Renée-Pélagie and Anne-Prospère, there were coun-tries in the world where it was thought natural for a man to poss-ess a harem whose members were no more than beasts of burden and whom he might kill off with no more sense of doing wrong than if he ordered the slaughtering of cattle or of sheep. If religion was deposed and Nature installed in its place, by what moral code was one nation's conduct to be preferred above another's? It seems plain that in this new natural order the laws of a nation, derived democratically or by despotism, must be merely the fashions of the hour with no more moral authority than the dic-tates of the dressmaker or tailor.

More specifically, Sade was to point out during *Philosophy in the Boudoir* and much of his later writing that murder and rape are natural acts. They are among the most common in the animal king-dom. No code of nature punishes them. Indeed, the animal committing them is more likely to prosper than the one who does not. In a system based on religion over nature, the moral prior-ities would, of course, be different. But if Nature is to be the moral imperative, it is surely absurd to preserve a social code by which murder and rape are regarded as crimes.

It was not surprising that religion's believers and unbelievers alike ran for cover under the cold hail of such a fusillade. But Sade allowed his audience no respite. If Nature was the supreme authority, he insisted, it mattered nothing whether a man copulated with a woman to have a child by her or in some other fashion. If no further procreation whatever took place, the human race would become extinct. But the end of mankind or of all life on earth was of little importance to the natural universe. By this argument, even if Sade had tortured Rose Keller in the manner of some of the most lurid descriptions of the scandal, or had he murdered the girls of Marseille by slow poison, Nature would neither allocate blame nor exhibit grief. True, the human stock would be diminished but bodily decay would furnish matter for the creation of life in some form.

The essence of this philosophy was shocking, preposterous, and in some respects comic. But granted the premise of Nature as moral arbiter, it was not easily refuted. Sade's natural world, illustrated in a novel like *Juliette*, is unpalatable enough to send the tentative unbeliever back to religious orthodoxy, if only as the more preferable of two terrors. No less than John Milton in *Paradise Lost*, but with a good deal more ambivalence, Sade the novelist claims that his fiction is intended to justify the ways of Providence to mankind. The cruelties of that fiction are then a grandiose and Swiftean irony. The terms in which its heroes announce the delights of sodomy or incest, and the pleasures of murder, the savagery with which they denounce the folly of virtue or compassion may fit this interpretation. Moreover, in creating such characters, Sade was portraying the world primarily as he thought his own experience showed it to be, rather than as he imagined it in fantasy.

In his life, no less than in his fiction, Sade was to present the same duality, the same ambivalence. Without any apparent sense of hypocrisy, he professed religion as he did when narrator of his fiction. He assisted at mass, opposed cruelty, upheld both the king and the republic which succeeded him, and supported established institutions. He also led a life characterized by publicly unacceptable sexual desires, which he indulged in fact and fantasy.

Taken at face value, Sade's writing was to show a lack of philosophical consistency. There are horrors in his fiction evidently used as moral irony. But even in the light of such evidence his work did not express a continuing and unmodified belief. Erratic in temper and imposed upon by the circumstances of his life, he was not well placed for such consistency. Whether as a fugitive from justice, a prisoner seeking favours or an aristocrat caught in a revolutionary terror, he was too often obliged to react to events rather than to control them. In this respect, the Revolution was the great political determinant, more profound in the disillusionment it brought him than in the realization of the hope it had kindled.

If he mocked the moral standards of royalist France in *The Misfortunes of Virtue*, he just as surely mocked the violence and corruption of the new order, its treachery and carnage, in the pages of *Juliette: or, The Prosperities of Vice*, where the Friends of the Revolution become the Friends of Crime. If the reader turns from this later novel feeling, once again, that any alternative is preferable to the world it portrays, this is perhaps a reflection of Sade's privately expressed view that the old order of church and king could hardly have been worse than the eight years of tyranny and hunger, the madness and butchery of the Terror, which marked the darkest periods of the brave new world between 1789 and 1797.

But Sade's philosophical allegiance was to count for little by comparison with its form of expression. In the two centuries which followed, few of his readers cared about the mechanistic hypothesis of La Mettrie or the free thought of the Enlightenment. He survived, much talked of and less read, as an author of erotic cruelty and sardonic obscenity. For the few who regarded him as a materialist philosopher using the literary devices of pornography to embody his views, there were many who saw him as a pornographer self-justified by philosophical pretensions. His philosophy appeared variable and ambiguous: only in his obsession did he remain true to himself and his reputation.

7

His years at Vincennes took their toll on those who might have exerted a contrary influence on Sade. Among the women in his life, both Anne-Prospère and Gothon had died before their time. Now, on 28 January 1784, Mademoiselle de Rousset succumbed to tuberculosis at La Coste. It was probably two or three weeks before Sade heard the news. Perhaps it was kept from him for longer than that. Renée-Pélagie had lost whatever affection she may have felt for her rival in Sade's affections. Her response on hearing of the death was to order that any possessions of the Sade family which might have found their way into the dead woman's keeping should be retrieved at once. It was as though Sainte Rousset had been the procuress Nanon making off with the silver plate.

Whatever Sade's own feelings at such a loss, the world beyond his prison walls had grown less real to him than the truths of his own writings. In 1783 he had written to Renée-Pélagie that the darker side of his nature was establishing a rapid and permanent ascendancy in his thoughts. But before he could give full literary expression to such moods, he was informed at the beginning of 1784 that he would be leaving the fortress of Vincennes. It was almost six and a half years since his imprisonment had begun in 1777. Apart from his six weeks as a fugitive in the summer of 1778 he had seen nothing of the world in that time. 1784 was a leap year and 29 February was the date of his departure. It was far from being the date of his release. He left the great fortress in the custody of Inspector Surbois. At nine o'clock that evening, he was a prisoner of the Bastille.

NINE

NIGHTS OF THE BASTILLE

1

THE REASONS FOR SADE'S TRANSFER to the Bastille corroborated the worst that had been said about life at Vincennes. Conditions in the ancient keep had become so bad that the authorities had decided to close it down. Yet though the Bastille was soon to become the most famous and notorious of all prisons in history, it was little better than Vincennes. The building was in part a prison and in part an administrative centre. Proposals for its closure and demolition had been approved in principle before the first murmurs of the Revolution. Even in 1784, Sade was one of a handful of men held there. By 1789, the number had dwindled to seven. They were held, as securely as in the keep of Vincennes, in the four corner towers. When Sade arrived there, the appearance of the building seemed a match for its reputation. Beyond the first drawbridge, separating it from the artisan streets of the St Antoine district, stood the high fortress walls with the round towers at their corners. Then came another bridge to the inner buildings. Sade's cell had been picked out for him. By a fine irony of the gaoler's imagination, it was in the Tower of Liberty. On its platform were thirteen cannon, used to fire salutes on days of national celebration.

The Bastille was less harsh in some aspects of its regime, though Sade insisted in his letters that conditions were worse than at Vincennes. Renée-Pélagie was now allowed to make regular visits to him, bringing the clothes, food, books and candles which he needed. By 1787, she was able to see him once a fortnight. There were no more raids and searches of his prison room, which he had experienced at Vincennes. No longer did the guards burst in to seize his books and papers on the pretext that he might be engaged in subversive literary activity. The furnishing of the cell was sparse at the Bastille, Sade being allowed an old carpet on the stone floor and a camp bed to sleep on. Nevertheless, the decoration and furnishing of the room were of his choosing and paid for by his family. The room was about sixteen feet square and the same in height, its walls washed with chalk and its floor made of brick. Sade chose wall hangings and carpets to cover this shell. On 14 October 1788, Renée-Pélagie wrote to Gaufridy, explaining that money was needed to buy new wall hangings, a bed, a cover and a mattress.

During his five years in the Bastille, Sade continued to put on weight, though it was Renée-Pélagie's health which caused greater concern. Sometimes she suffered so badly from piles that it was impossible for her to make the journey by carriage to the Bastille. In addition, she had begun to accumulate fluid and her sight was deteriorating. From time to time, she reported that her health had improved. Yet in November 1788 she wrote that she had totally lost the use of her legs, though she had been reassured that this was temporary. She relied greatly on Sade's servant Carteron, "La Jeunesse", until his death in 1785. Thereafter, it was her daughter Madeleine-Laure who was her companion: "a great sluggard", her mother called her, who could not even write a letter.

Meantime, from his confinement on the second level of the Tower of Liberty, the prisoner demanded chocolate and white nougat, dried fruit and pots of jam, peaches in eau-de-vie, candles and notebooks of Holland paper. He had also begun to assemble a considerable library of books in his room, most of which naturally reflected his literary interests as an author. From the time of his transfer to the Bastille, his demands were more specifically for books of history and travel. He would write to Renée-Pélagie for volumes containing information on English history or on Spain and Portugal. When he did so, it was in the impatient manner of one who needs the material for some immediate purpose. He insisted that he must also have novels like Henry Fielding's *Amelia*, a dark landscape of social pessimism, which would scarcely have appeared on the list of the general reader. *Amelia* proved difficult to get and Renée-Pélagie spent some time in this quest. Yet it was the great English example of a world in which the wicked prosper and the good suffer, until the last minute. Perhaps there was reassurance for Renée-Pélagie in

Sade's impatient enthusiasms. However greatly he might complain of the worse conditions in the Bastille, his transfer had spurred him into a new phase of activity.

2

It was in his room in the Tower of Liberty, high above the roofs of working-class St Antoine during the autumn evenings of 1785, that Sade began the composition of his most ambitious work. *The 120 Days of Sodom* was to be variously judged as one of the vilest books ever written or as a masterly revelation of the darker fantasies of a human mind.

Its manner of composition was almost as remarkable as the details of its narrative. Sade did not intend that anyone else should read the novel in 1785. Perhaps it was to remain secret for ever. As a rule, he wrote in a bound volume, which would be difficult to conceal. To overcome this, he managed to glue together small sheets of paper, each about five inches wide, until he had produced a scroll almost forty feet long. Then, in his exact and tiny script, he began to write on the evening of 12 October.

The great wars which imposed so heavy a burden on Louis XIV drained the wealth of the Treasury and the people alike. But these circumstances also showed a swarm of parasites the way to prosperity. Such men are always on the watch for public calamities. They do not endeavour to mitigate these but rather seek to create and foster them, so that they may profit more fully by the misfortunes of others.

As usual, Sade the narrator distanced himself from the profligacy and the cruelty of his protagonists. Yet it was from a class of villains and profiteers with a place in reality that he took his four heroes: the duke, the bishop, the banker and the judge. They were to retire to the château of Silling for the one hundred and twenty days of the four winter months, with their wives, daughters, harems and every aid to luxury. From the beginning of November until the end of February, they would live this life apart. Thirty days would be devoted to the "simple passions", which numbered a hundred and fifty. Then would come the thirty days of the hundred and fifty "complex passions". The third quarter of the novel's plan contained one hundred and fifty "criminal passions", and the final part an equal number of "murderous passions". While the heroes indulged these passions with the members of their harem, they were to be entertained by one of the four procuresses, who would tell the story of her sexual adventures, illustrating a passion which was then being performed in reality.

Like the heroes of his narrative, Sade turned to the delights of the château of Silling after dinner, writing every evening without interruption from seven until ten. He sometimes wrote much later than this, correspondence to Renée-Pélagie being timed at one o'clock in the morning. In his new nocturnal fiction, the whipping of Rose Keller, the orgy at Marseille, the winter of the Little Girls at La Coste acquired a new dimension of imagination, as he inscribed the first part of his novel on the long scroll of paper. The solitude of his prison room was high above the city tiles and chimneys of St Antoine as the château of Silling stood high on its winter peak. When each evening ended, Sade once again concealed the scroll of paper in the wall of his room, behind the brightly coloured hangings which he had chosen. In the secret universe of his skull, he had committed acts of the most monstrous kind, which no eyes but his own would ever witness, even though the crimes were confided to paper. So long as its hiding place remained undiscovered, his deeds would be as secret as those of his heroes.

It was as if, on these autumn evenings, the cell in the Tower of Liberty became the auditorium of Silling, the rounded wall matching that of the novel's interior where the victims waited chained or tethered until the procuress who sat where Sade now was had finished telling her story. "The reader will recall our description", Sade added, "of the pillars in the auditorium. At the beginning of each session, Aline is fastened to one and Adélaïde to the other. Their backsides face the heroes' alcove. A table stands close to each pillar, covered with assorted instruments of discipline." Other groups of girls, meanwhile, were to carry out the orders of the men whom they served.

Despite the unremitting display of sexual deviations, it is the creation of a world of his own, beyond the power of gaolers or judges to impair, which Sade regarded as his greatest achievement in the novel. An imagined landscape lay around him which he saw at times as more important than reality. "I am here alone," he wrote, "I am here at the end of the world, hidden from all eyes and beyond the reach of any creature. There are no more restraints and no more obstructions. There is nothing here but God and conscience." When the evening's work was finished, he had only to roll up the manuscript and return it to safety in the wall of the room.

The "passions" planned by Sade, whether simple or murderous, complex or criminal were thought grotesque enough, even when the unfinished novel was at length discovered and published almost a hundred and twenty years later. Apart from every form of intercourse that his brain could devise, as well as systematic and meticulous forms of punishment, there were dinners at which the girls performed as human milk-dispensers; tricks to make these beautiful captives think that they had been poisoned or were about to be hanged; a strongly anti-erotic preoccupation with digestion and excretion; a variety of murders that seemed by no means always sexually inspired. If there was much in the narrative that seemed unappealing or repugnant, Sade had an answer to this objection with the publication of *Justine* in 1791. Fiction is not to be confused with fact, nor fantasy with reality. Clément confronts the heroine of the later novel as "Thérèse" with the reason for this assertion.

> You claim it is extraordinary that things which are in themselves filthy or disgusting can produce in our senses the stimulation necessary to the fulfilment of delight. But before being astonished at this, my dear Thérèse, you ought to consider that objects have no value in our eyes which they do not hold in our imagination. It is therefore entirely possible, in the light of this unvarying truth, that we can be sensibly affected not only by whatever is most bizarre but also by what is most vile and most fearful.

In a more moderate dose, this was the principal ingredient of the fashionable eighteenth-century taste for decorative Gothic, whether in art or literature.

Sade's invention, as he began his narrative, seemed vigorous, if disordered. But by the end of November, when he had finished the first of the four books of *The 120 Days of Sodom* and had sketched out the remainder in note form, it was evident that something had gone fundamentally wrong with his work. There was no lack of time for writing. Had the remaining three books progressed as quickly as the first, he would have completed a major novel by the winter's end. But he was contented with a list of notes to remind himself how the novel ought to be rewritten, though he added that he could not manage to reread the first complete book. It would be possible to conclude that Sade was prevented from doing this by the weakness of his eyes. A more realistic judgment is that he had lost enthusiasm for an intractable project.

As a fictional narrative, *The 120 Days of Sodom* lacked the more conventional creativity of Sade in the stories of *The Crimes of Love* and the sharpness of moral satire in *Justine*. Despite the easy sweep of its historical opening, the dramatic setting of Silling and certain of the incidents, it was obsessive and repetitious in its chronicling of the simple passions. The first book in itself is the length of a major novel, though sustained by little more than the elaboration of vomiting and excreting. The manner of its composition and concealment suggests that Sade wrote it for himself rather than for an audience. It remains less valued as a work of art than as a novel about language and ideas, or as a precursor of Krafft-Ebing and Freud. But it is neither scientific nor comprehensive. Its obsessions are restrictive and, as fictional narrative, tedious. To Sade, it was a private and secret document, hidden in the wall of the Bastille. As public fiction or as art, he exceeded it in imagination and skill in almost all his other novels and stories.

To treat the whole of such a composition as though it were a novel intended for publication may be unjust. Yet Sade writes at first as if with an audience in mind. He warns his reader, apologetically, to prepare for "the most impure tale that was ever told", an apology of the kind that appears elsewhere in his works, though the horror of the château of Silling is initially more evident than the impurity. As well as the auditorium in which the orgies and displays are staged, there is a remote dungeon, equipped for more sinister deeds. The Duc de Blangis, master of Constance, who is a "Roman beauty" of twenty-two, and of several younger women and boys, is driven to orgasm by a mere description of what lies down there.

Despite the ferocity of sexual violence, the château of Silling is an ordered society, as much subject to rules and regulations as the Collège Louis-le-Grand, or great prisons like Vincennes and the Bastille. The four heroes have one "wife" each, apart from the harem of boys and girls. Such a wife is available to serve the hero in any manner from the beginning. But the members of the harem are not to be used in any way that is beyond the limit reached in the daily description and demonstration of the passions. Sade's obsession with moral system and order, including its inversion, was never more plainly shown. School and prison contributed as much to *The 120 Days of Sodom* as any moral waywardness of his own.

Bourgeois respect for *propriété privé* is no less evident at the château of Silling than in the soul of bourgeois France. Even before the harem loses its first virginity, its members are shared out. Each of the masters has his colours. A boy wears the appropriate colour. A girl must not only wear it but do so in such a way as to indicate the manner in which she is reserved. In the case of the Duc de Blangis, for example, Fanny, Sophie, Zelmire and Augustine wear his colour on the fronts of their coiffures. Rosette, Hébé and Michette wear them "where their hair fell downwards on the napes of their necks".

The narrative is most effective in the setting and anticipation of the threatened horrors. Like many self-proclaimed Gothic terrors, it collapses in bathos as the threats become reality. When Sade gave up the attempt to continue the narrative, he listed some of the mistakes he had made in writing the first part. Stating the obvious, he found that he had not been "sufficiently reticent" in describing some of the grosser functions of humanity and that he had allowed the practice of sodomy to monopolize the discussion too often. After that, the project was at an end.

With the long scroll of his abandoned work hidden in the wall of his room, Sade resumed the role of public novelist. The most immediate influence came from England, particularly from the novels of Fielding and of Richardson. *Pamela, Clarissa* and Fielding's four novels were among the volumes that he had with him. Of these, Fielding's *Jonathan Wild*, a satire on moral inversion, was more closely akin to Sade's *Justine* than any other work of its time. Fielding, forty years before Sade, produced a perfect parable of social irony, in which criminality is to be admired and encouraged, while virtue is justly punished.

3

The first attempt to write a philosophical novel in the evenings of the Bastille was different in kind to either *Justine* or *Jonathan Wild*. *Aline and Valcour* occupied him during much of the period between his abandonment of *The 120 Days of Sodom* on 28 November 1785 and the appearance of the new novel in Sade's catalogue of his manuscripts in October 1788. It is a novel of considerable length and he was certainly at work on it by 25 November 1786, when he wrote to Renée-Pélagie asking for information about Spain and Portugal for the sections of his novel set in those countries.

Aline and Valcour was written in the form of letters, at a time when Sade had been greatly impressed by Richardson's use of this form. The letters are exchanged between Aline and Valcour, their closer happiness being frustrated by Aline's father. He intends to marry the girl to an old rake who happens to be a crony of his. As in Richardson or Laclos's *Les Liaisons Dangereuses*, the action is minutely detailed. Indeed, Sade insisted that Richardson was a general model for writing of this kind. As in Richardson's *Clarissa*, the triumph of the rake over the innocent girl at one level is as certain as the ultimate vindication of her virtue. Unable to marry Valcour, her true love, Aline takes her own life rather than submit to the legalized whoredom of a marriage to the depraved Dolbourg. Like a true heroine of the age of Sensibility, Aline in dying commends herself to God and to the one human love she has known. The main story of the novel is more explicit in its details of sexual intrigue than Richardson but less so than Laclos.

A good deal of the principal narrative reflects the work of more conventional novelists, both English and French. The most Sadean ingredient is the adventure of Sainville and Léonore, which forms a long interpolation in the tragedy of Aline and Valcour.

This subordinate story reflects Sade's enthusiasm for the oddites of social and sexual behaviour in remoter parts of the world. He had taken an interest in the accounts of Captain Cook's Pacific discoveries and had read the descriptions of those voyages as they were published. Their appearance coincided with Sade's writing of *Aline and Valcour*. In his novel, Sainville and

Léonore lose one another and then travel to the more distant areas of the world in their mutual search. This fictional device was the basis of Sade's essay in moral geography, drawn from a panorama of primitive civilizations.

Sade's enthusiasm found expression through Sainville's description of the African kingdom of Butua. The royal harem consists of 12,000 superbly beautiful women, the tallest and most mature of whom form the palace guard. A second class consists of women between the ages of twenty and thirty who undertake routine duties in the palace itself. A third class contains girls between the ages of sixteen and twenty, while those used most often by the king for his pleasures come from the fourth class of slavegirls who are all younger than sixteen. Sainville's informant is an expatriate Portuguese nobleman, who assures him that when the King of Butua takes a fancy to such a girl he sends one of his men to whip her. This, like the handkerchief of the Sultan at Constantinople, is a flattering summons to her master's bed.

Sainville is intrigued and even amused by these stories, until he suspects that the succulent cut of the joint which the Portuguese count carves for him is taken from the judiciously roasted hips of one of the harem favourites. But as Sainville is informed, one must live according to the laws and moral customs of the country, no less in Butua than in Paris or Lisbon.

In a narrative of this sort, Sade's gift for moral paradox and anomaly was given full scope. Nor does he miss the opportunity for a commentary on superstition and belief. Léonore, despite having blackened her face as a disguise, is seized in the barbarous territory of Sennar and condemned to death by posterior impalement in a public arena. Nothing, it seems, can save her. A command is given that the unfortunate young woman is to be stripped for her ordeal. But she has blackened only her face and her would-be executioners are startled to find that her bottom is pure white. Terror strikes the ignorant savages who find themselves in the presence of this supernatural creature. Léonore escapes with her life and, having survived the comparable hazards of rape and torture in the cellars of the Inquisition, returns to France.

If Sade had written nothing more sensational than *Aline and Valcour*, he might have avoided notoriety. Though the novel was extravagant in some of its episodes, its sexual drama was seldom as explicit as *Les Liaisons Dangereuses*, which Sade read at this time. The irony of Laclos's protagonists was more than a match for Sade's. Yet the incident in *Les Liaisons Dangereuses* when Valmont writes a letter to the virtuous Sophia, lying in bed with a young trollop and using her naked body as his writing desk – even breaking off to make love to her – is entirely Sadean. So too is Valmont's satisfaction in seeing Prévan "cruelly punished for a crime he did not commit".

In *Aline and Valcour*, Sade returned frequently to examples of the absurdity encountered in trying to lay down universal moral laws. It seemed plain that what was regarded as virtuous in one part of the world would appear abhorrent in another. Sainville's acquaintance Zamé is dismayed to find that a girl in France is praised for her virtue in becoming a nun, while a man who commits sodomy is executed for his crime. They have both renounced the processes of procreation, says the puzzled savage. By any standard of logic or natural law, it follows that both must be regarded as virtuous or as vicious.

Sade might lack the system and subtlety of a philosopher. Yet, as a novelist of ideas rather than of character, he had found a theme which was to serve him well. A virtuous act was to seem meaningless in nature. Moreover, in a universe ruled by what the world called "vice", this so-called virtue was out of tune with the natural order and dealt with unsympathetically by human society. There were two possible deductions from this. Either morality and religion were denied by the very principles of nature, or else the sufferings of virtue were permitted by God so that virtue might appear more admirable in distress during this life and might be infinitely rewarded hereafter.

4

Despite the sufferings and degradations of his heroine, it was virtue triumphant which Sade depicted at the end of his next novel. *The Misfortunes of Virtue* was, at face value, a vindication of religion and morality. For the reader who saw the book as an essay in irony, the narrative showed religion and morality as mere superstitions. It offered instead a particular and rational pleasure to be found in persecuting and torturing the innocent. This pleasure was all the more intense when the victim was a beautiful young woman.

Whatever Sade's precise purpose, he now followed this argument to a point which rationalists and philosophers of the "Enlightenment" had on the whole baulked at. He insisted that morality, severed from its religious or metaphysical source, must wither like a flower cut from its root. In that case, there was no higher law for the moralist to invoke than the law of nature or human instinct. In the natural world of *Juliette* or *The 120 Days of Sodom*, it was a matter of moral indifference whether a man's instinct moved him to love and cherish a girl or beat and murder her. To suggest that one instinct was, by nature, more criminal or virtuous than the other was plainly and logically absurd. Indeed, if the ultimate and divine authority were no longer the basis of human conduct, such terms as "virtue" and "crime" could have no true significance except as descriptions of local and variable customs.

Sade also played devil's advocate in the world of his fiction. Mankind might retain God and divinely sanctioned morality or it might dispense with them. But there could be no compromise, no wistful appeal to the natural benevolence of humanity. To construct a humanist ethic without divine sanction was as absurd in logic as it was repugnant in theology. A world without God and without divine sanction for morality resulted in those scenes which were to make *The 120 Days of Sodom* and *Juliette* among the most scandalous books of their century.

The true heroes in this new world of fiction were to be those who derived most pleasure from sexually abusing, torturing and murdering their victims. In such a society, hypocrisy and treachery were necessary and admirable qualities. Revolutionaries and radicals may continue to denounce kings and tyrants, seeking to overthrow them in order to establish a new democracy or a people's republic. But such activists, in the world of Sade's fiction, are motivated by a carefully concealed jealousy of the secret police, the torturers and the executioners who serve the existing tyrant. As Borchamps remarks in *Juliette*, "It is the jealousy of seeing despotism in other hands than their own. Once they have seized power, you may rest assured that they will no longer abominate despotism. On the contrary, they will make use of it to procure themselves the greatest pleasures."

At another level, Sade expressed a philosophy common to eighteenth-century fiction. In his conclusion to *The Misfortunes of Virtue* he deduces from the horrors of the story a godless and immoral society, where man's only hope is as the creature of a divinely ordered universe. Social morality may be destroyed, in this view. It can be maintained only on the basis of divine authority. The ambition of eighteenth-century rationalism, even in the hands of Voltaire, was its desire to reject established religion and yet to be spared the social consequences of such rejection. Somewhere, in the middle ground, there was to be a nebulous and inoffensive Supreme Being or a soft-hearted religion of Nature. In Sade's demonstration, this middle ground is the least tenable of all. God and moral chaos appear as the true alternatives. That Sade ultimately chose one or the other would be a comforting but facile conclusion. He retained a novelist's ability to patronize the best and the worst without giving final allegiance to either, voicing the possibility of divine order while a darker *alter ego* rushed forward to the pleasures of moral anarchy.

The Misfortunes of Virtue formed an interlude during the composition of *Aline and Valcour*. It was written in a fortnight and completed on 8 June 1787. It was a short, witty, philosophical novel, phrased in those moral ironies at which the age excelled. Sade was a latecomer to the tradition. Henry Fielding in *Jonathan Wild* (1743) had shown that public greatness was merely a superior form of criminality. It is Fielding's hero who has most in common with the triumphant villains of *The Misfortunes of Virtue*. Samuel Johnson in 1759 had demonstrated the vanity of human wishes a second time in *Rasselas: Prince of Abyssinia*. In the same year, Voltaire's *Candide* demolished the philosophical optimism which held that all is for the best in this best of all possible worlds. The successors to the eighteenth century produced nothing comparable to these short ironic fictions until Samuel Butler's *Erewhon* in 1872. Butler's satire on Darwin and the evolutionary theory depicts a later Sadean world in which the sick and the unfortunate are savagely punished, while the criminal is treated with sympathy and concern.

The strength of Sade's short novel, like those with whom it may be grouped, is in the panache and brevity with which it drives home its single moral. It was to appear, revised and extended, as *Justine* in 1791. Later still, it became the overblown narrative called *The New Justine* in 1797. This third version was padded out with long-winded elaborations of the arguments and with intrusive sexual rituals and narrative episodes, which add nothing much to the existing plot, though destroying something of the original vivacity.

In *The Misfortunes of Virtue*, the heroine appears as Sophie and in this character tells the story of her tribulations. The narrative is not burdened by the overwriting of Sade's *New Justine* and, in consequence, the series of moral grotesques who are Sophie's persecutors appear more sharply defined. They include the homosexual Bressac with his hatred of women and his plan to murder his aunt; Rodin the surgeon, who practises his skill for amusement only and enjoys cutting up girls alive; the monks of Ste Marie des Bois with their harem of little girls. Though Sade's own obsessions always inform the drama, they do not overwhelm it. Sophie is tied to a forest tree and whipped by Bressac before she suffers every form of sexual indignity at Ste Marie des Bois, though the specific acts are alluded to rather than described with the detail of the later versions. Predictably, the villains observe her sufferings with sardonic amusement. Father Antonin consoles Sophie by remarking that the pain she suffers is not wasted, since it prepares him for his pleasures.

The Misfortunes of Virtue was the only version of Sade's most famous story to remain unpublished until the twentieth century. In essence, it was his greatest contribution to European fiction of the eighteenth century. It was certainly the most important piece of prison writing during his years in the Bastille. Unlike *The 120 Days of Sodom*, its style was that of public utterance rather than self-addressed obsession. In the same category as this story of Sophie were the shorter tales and sketches of his candle-lit evenings after dinner in the Tower of Liberty. Some were to appear in 1800 as *The Crimes of Love* and others were to remain unpublished for a century and a half. The shorter stories were often bawdy or melodramatic by turns and drew on Sade's knowledge of French life and tradition. He had travelled the country from the Rhine to the Vendée, from Bordeaux to Marseille and Grenoble, from Provence to Normandy. Combined with this, he had read widely in the history of France and Italy. These stories showed him equally at home in Paris or Provence during the eighteenth century and in the châteaux of the Loire two hundred years before.

In *The Crimes of Love*, Sade devised Gothic fictions that were far more to the taste of his time. In other stories, there was drollery and innuendo. "The Mystified Magistrate" was his revenge on those who had judged him. An elderly magistrate is subjected to a series of elaborate but well-deserved bedroom humiliations to prevent him consummating his marriage to a young woman whose lover wants her returned. Its tone is closer to Chaucer or Boccaccio than to Sade's sexual melodramas. When sexual eccentricities appear in such tales, they are presented light-heartedly rather than in earnest. "Augustine de Villeblanche", for example, is the story of a lesbian being reformed by a male lover. This ingenious fellow dresses up as a young woman in order to be picked up by the heroine. She is so enraptured by his lovemaking that, even though she discovers the trick, Augustine is entirely cured.

Some of Sade's stories written in the Bastille were the work of a single evening and are little more than jokes in literary form. "The Self-Made Cuckold" describes an unfaithful husband who is offered a mistress by a go-between. The woman's body, her face remaining concealed, is carefully unveiled for him. The client and the pimp gloat over her naked beauty. Only afterwards is the predictable truth revealed – that this naked beauty was the client's own wife. Sade had read Beaumarchais and used as his story a device similar to that which brings happiness at the end of *The Marriage of Figaro*. Elsewhere, the device of the wife disguised as a mistress was soon embodied by Delacroix's painting of the Duc d'Orléans showing his naked mistress to the Duc de Bourgogne but, in veiling her face, concealing the truth that she is actually the Duchesse de Bourgogne.

As in his novels, Sade's own predilections run through these fictional jokes. "The Happy Husband" is the story of a beautiful but innocent young girl whose father arranges a marriage for her with the depraved Prince de Bauffremont. The girl's mother is horrified by this, knowing the prince's reputation for sodomizing his female partners. Before the marriage the good woman instructs her daughter that when her husband comes to her on the wedding night and approaches to make love to her, she is to say, "Why, sir! What sort of a girl do you take me for? You cannot imagine that I shall allow you to do such a thing. You may do

whatever you like elsewhere – but you shall not do it there."
Unknown to the bride or her family, however, the prince suffers a
bout of conscience before the wedding. He resolves to mend his
manners, if not his morals, and to treat his beautiful young bride
in the most orthodox fashion. To his surprise, when he
approaches her in bed, she greets him with the words her mother
has taught her. Astonished but delighted, the prince turns her
over, swearing that he would not dream of displeasing her, least
of all on their wedding night.

It is not hard to see why Sade should have cherished the
ambition of becoming known as "the French Boccaccio". Like
The Misfortunes of Virtue, these tales were written for a general
audience. Though some of them were bawdy, they lacked the
greater obsession and the self-indulgence of his more secret
writing. Moreover, he was the storyteller now rather than the
philosopher of natural morality. When he touches on the great
questions of the universe, he usually does so in the most conventional manner. Christianity, he says in "The Philosophical
Teacher", is the most sublime part of all education.

6

In a change of mood, Sade retired to the secret world which had
opened upon the château of Silling and *The 120 Days of Sodom*.
In 1787 he composed his poem "The Truth", denouncing all
forms of religion, virtue and morality. Only Nature is admirable,
thriving on so-called "crimes".

> Nature allows all, by its murderous laws:
> Incest and rape, all theft and parricide,
> All Sodom's pleasures, Sappho's lesbian games,
> All that destroys and sends men to their graves.

In case there should ever be a reader of this secret poem, Sade
made sure that his own approval of such "Nature" was not in
doubt. He planned a frontispiece to the poem. It was to show a
man sodomizing a naked girl and plunging a knife into her body
at the conclusion of the act. After ten years of solitude in his prison room, he remained possessed of two contrary voices, even

when they were not contradictory. The public voice spoke through *The Misfortunes of Virtue* and his shorter tales. It was from *The 120 Days of Sodom* and "The Truth" that the murmurs of chaos rose.

By the autumn of 1788, Sade was occupied with a new project. It showed plainly that he had now begun to see himself foremost as a writer. Acting as his own bibliographer and critic, he was drawing up a catalogue of his literary work. Significantly, he excluded from this such private or secret writings as *The 120 Days of Sodom*, either because they belonged to the realm of obsession rather than literature or perhaps because his great experiment in this *genre* was not yet complete. Yet in whatever style he wrote, he had endured eleven years of imprisonment and found his role as a writer of fiction. He had achieved a clarity of vision that was to make many of his readers shiver. He was no longer the pathetic victim of the Montreuils or the system of *lettres de cachet*. He was the Prisoner Sade, as he had been "Monsieur le 6". But the Prisoner Sade now faced the world with, as it were, fifteen manuscript volumes tucked under his arm.

7

Even before his compilation of this *catalogue raisonné*, external events had begun to overtake the literary plans of the prisoner in the Tower of Liberty. The young Louis XVI, one of the most reluctant monarchs ever to ascend a European throne, was almost at the end of his authority. It was not the revolutionary spirits of the Enlightenment who presented the most immediate challenge. Even Sade was to nourish private monarchist sentiments long after the Bourbons had been swept away. Other figures of the Enlightenment also showed a greater attachment to justice than to democracy. Voltaire, the most vigorous opponent of tyranny, was prepared to uphold the rule of the king. Every man, in Voltaire's view, had to serve. It was, therefore, better to serve under a lion of good pedigree than under two hundred rats of the common kind.

In 1788, the immediate threat to royal authority came from the French nobility, which had lost a good deal of power in the seventeenth century. The weakness of Louis XVI seemed the moment to restore the *status quo*. The time appeared well chosen. Confronted by a revolt of the nobility, which demanded new rights and immunities for the courts of justice that it constituted, Louis could look nowhere for support. In the end, the king conceded the case for reform. Thereupon, the commons demanded parity of representation with the nobility.

Louis XVI afforded the most dramatic illustration of de Tocqueville's comments on the absolute ruler's limited compromise which leads, as if by a law of history, to full-blown revolution. The democratic appetite was stimulated rather than appeased by the election of January 1789. Under the reformed electoral system about half the population of France was entitled to vote, which was considerably greater than the franchise in England immediately after the 1832 Reform Bill. The post-election assembly, or Estates General, proved far more resolute and intransigent than any of its predecessors. When locked out of its chamber at Versailles on 20 June and barred from entry by royal troops, the members held an impromptu meeting on the indoor tennis court and took the Tennis Court Oath to carry on the nation's business, with or without the blessing of the king.

During the early months of 1789, Sade was not a spectator of such events, still confined to his room in the Tower of Liberty, high above the humble rooftops of faubourg St Antoine. Yet Renée-Pélagie wrote a letter which Gaufridy received on 11 April, assuring him that the rebellion he feared in Provence was no worse than that in Paris where the areas of St Marceau and St Antoine were "the theatre of revolt". Looting had broken out and cavalry was needed to control the unrest. The soldiers had fired on the mob, she reported. Some of the demonstrators had been hanged and some imprisoned. By the time that she wrote again on 11 May, the revolt had been dealt with but there were troops everywhere.

It was plain by June that the king could not longer control the experiment in democracy which had been imposed upon him. More troops were moved into Paris as a precaution. There was an affray in place Louis XV, later to be known as place de la Concorde, when cavalry was ordered to clear the crowds. Political instability was made worse by economic failure. The price of bread rose all the more sharply with the arrival in Paris of starving workers who hoped to escape the famine prevailing elsewhere. The nobles, jealous of their privileges, the bourgeois political reformers and the hungry crowds in the streets had little enough in common to begin with. But by the end of June, it seemed only a matter of weeks or days before the misery of the poor provided fuel for middle-class political ambitions.

The situation of the poor in the eastern quarter of St Antoine was particularly bad. Since early May, there had been further demonstrations against the authorities. It was no longer a secret, even to the prisoner in the Tower of Liberty, that the city was close to insurrection. Indeed, one of Sade's more recent privileges had been permission to receive newspapers and almanacs. In a *coup d'état*, the seven prisoners in the Bastille would have little significance for the insurgents, though the building itself was both a symbol and an office of the Bourbon regime. Sade none the less concluded that the present period of public disorder represented his best chance of freedom after twelve years as a prisoner.

On 2 July 1789, he improvised a megaphone from a funnel that was used for emptying slops and gained the window of his room. Below him, the nearer streets were crowded with local people in the summer afternoon. Using his megaphone, Sade hailed them and began his harangue. According to witnesses, he shouted that the guards had been given orders to kill all the prisoners in the Bastille and that they were even now preparing to cut the throats of the inmates. "I stirred up the spirit of the people from my window," he wrote, "I drew them together below it. I warned them of the preparations being made in the Bastille and urged them to tear down this monument of horrors. All that is true." His words rang across the square and the crowd began to pay attention. As there was a response to this and a murmuring of interest, Sade urged them to be quick, if they intended to attempt a rescue.

Not surprisingly, he was seized by the guards and pulled away. The governor of the Bastille was informed of the incident. He consulted the king's minister and it was agreed that Sade was "very dangerous to have here" in the present state of the city. It seemed best to send him to a place from which his ravings would not be heard – the lunatic asylum at Charenton on the south-east fringe of Paris, not far from either Vincennes or the Bastille. Arrangements were made at once. On 4 July, Sade was taken from the Bastille after a period of five years and transferred to Charenton. Ten days after that, the citizens of St Antoine belatedly heeded his advice and stormed the Bastille.

The other prisoners in the great fortress were set free by this most famous of revolutionary acts. Ironically, Sade remained in his new confinement at Charenton long after 14 July. He was not a prisoner of the *ancien régime* but the inmate of a lunatic asylum. It was the purpose of the revolution to set political prisoners free. Lunatics were another matter entirely. Moreover, his continued detention was ensured by those whom he described as "the Montreuil scoundrels". He accused them of being responsible for his detention in the madhouse of Charenton for nine months after he left the Bastille.

His transfer to Charenton had been at gunpoint. Sade's manuscripts and his personal possessions remained in the Bastille, where they were plundered or destroyed in the assault of 14 July. Some of the manuscripts were recovered and some were already in Renée-Pélagie's possession. *The 120 Days of Sodom* was safe but unlocated in the wall of his room, never to be found again during his lifetime. He was never again to see *The Misfortunes of Virtue* nor most of his short stories. Sade later referred to the "tears of blood" which he had shed over so many lost works.

Soon after his transfer, his remaining Sade uncle, who had been prior of Toulouse, suffered a stroke on 21 August. The Commander of the Order of St John of Jerusalem remained between life and death for another month in his Paris house at St Cloud. He died on 28 September. It seemed that whatever money he left was to go to Sade's younger son, while his sister-in-law, Madame de Villeneuve, helped herself to the contents of the house.

Sade had seen almost the last of Renée-Pélagie. On 11 May, she described herself as "beginning to be old and infirm" at the age of forty-seven. As the disorder in Paris grew worse, she wanted only to be free of it. On 8 October, she escaped from the city in a carriage with her daughter and a maid, "in order not to be seized by the common women who were taking others by force from their houses to go and fetch the king from Versailles, making them go on foot through the rain and dirt". By this time the shortage of food was worse and there was a belief that the king's presence would attract supplies to the capital. On 24 October, Renée-Pélagie was apparently safe at Echauffour. "I am in the country," she wrote, "not because I fear being hanged from a lamp post nor for fear of the man with the big beard who cuts off heads, but in order not to die of hunger and because I have not a sou."

In the autumn of 1790, the National Assembly met in Paris. It was much preoccupied with rights and democracy, though most of its members had no more intention that their nation should be a full democracy than had their English predecessors after the Glorious Revolution of 1688–9. In his present circumstances, Sade was not likely to qualify for privileged treatment by reformers or revolutionaries. He remarked that the only difference made to his life by the revolution was that the attendants at Charenton beat and robbed him with less compunction. The persecution of the innocent and the triumph of the persecutors was intended to be merely a device of his fiction. Sade was outraged when it happened in reality and when he was cast in the role of victim.

At the beginning of 1790 there had been no sign that he was likely to be released from Charenton. He was almost fifty years old and as far removed as ever from a world he had last seen when he was thirty-seven. But the wheel of fortune spun with rapidity, as it did for so many thousands during the revolutionary period. In Sade's case, it brought him unexpected good news. On 2 April 1790, he was informed that he was free to leave the asylum. No one had bothered about his individual case but an amnesty had been decreed for all those imprisoned under the system of *lettres de cachet*. It was discovered, with some misgivings, that Sade belonged in this category. However, he was not entirely master of his destiny. They warned him not to go to Renée-Pélagie. She was now cured of her attachment to him and had given orders that he was not to be received at Echauffour or at the convent in Paris where she had lodged. In well-worn clothes and with little money in his pocket, Sade was released from the elegant building at Charenton in its leafy park. He turned his steps westward along the Seine into the eastern streets of Paris. His destination was the office of Monsieur de Milly, a lawyer who had managed his affairs in the city.

TEN

CITIZEN SADE

1

SADE FOUND HIMSELF at liberty in a world that seemed about to move towards benevolence and rationality. France aspired to a state of constitutional monarchy, a democratically elected National Assembly and a king who exercised the functions of head of state without being an absolute ruler. In art and politics, Parisians during the summer of 1790 breathed the air of freedom. But freedom was to be sustained only by the mutual respect of Louis XVI and the forces of reform. It was not surprising, as disorder grew, that Louis and Marie-Antoinette considered wistfully whether a counter-revolution with the assistance of Prussia or other great powers might not make the king master of the situation once again. Such a dream of authority restored was not merely a reactionary ambition. There was now anarchy in much of France, where royalist and insurgent factions fought one another, and where the revolutionaries fought among themselves.

For Sade, the immediate problem was physical and financial survival. On 2 April 1790, the day of his release from Charenton, he was offered bed and board by Monsieur de Milly at his home in rue du Bouloir. Four days later, Sade moved into a room in the Hôtel du Bouloir, in the same street. He wrote at once to Gaufridy, as his attorney at Apt, asking for three thousand francs from the revenue of the estates in order to live for the immediate future.

Sade was soon to discover that his income from La Coste and the other lands in Provence had come under threat with the first acts of revolution, even though the properties themselves had not yet been confiscated. The loyal Costains, who had shielded their lord when he was hunted by the police, were now democratic and egalitarian citizens, conscious of their rights and resentful at what had been withheld from them under the old regime. Their tradition of dissent was now to work against Sade, as it had once favoured him. There would be no songs of welcome or ribboned shepherdesses on his return. Sade wrote to another friend, the lawyer Reinaud at Aix, in May 1790, assuring him that he had no intention of visiting Provence in its present mood. "There are important matters to be resolved here and the fear of being hanged on a democratic gallows will delay me until next spring." It was no mere irony. Gaufridy was soon forced into hiding as a royalist sympathizer and the agent of a former aristocrat.

For the immediate future, Sade hired rooms with such money as he could salvage from Gaufridy's remittances. In his letters to the attorney, he cursed the Montreuil family and lamented the loss of most of his fifteen volumes of manuscripts in the plundering and burning of the Bastille. Renée-Pélagie had managed to save a few of them but had then taken it upon herself to burn those which she considered improper. Sade had also passed her secret messages and papers during their prison meetings, all to no avail. On his release from Charenton, he had gone to the convent Ste Aure, her last address in Paris, only to be turned away as an unwelcome visitor. Even before the end of April, she had begun proceedings for a separation. But it was the loss of his manuscripts which brought his anger upon the handsome woman whom he had married thirty years before, who was now running to fat and going blind.

It was soon agreed that he and Renée-Pélagie should separate. In the division of the spoils, he would have owed her a capital sum of 160,000 livres, the money which she had brought into the marriage. There was nothing that Sade could sell to raise the sum, in the present political uncertainty, and so it was agreed that he should pay her 4,000 livres a year and that she should receive the capital sum from the proceeds of the estate at his death. On 13 June 1790 she wrote calmly and sensibly of their parting.

> On my part, it comes after careful and difficult reflection over a period of time. If Monsieur de Sade searches his heart, he must acknowledge the reason which has decided me and must feel that it could not have been otherwise. As for scandal, he is the master of it. I would rather not say what he will force me to say

if I have to justify myself. But if he forces me to do that, then I will say it.

Before long it was clear that Sade could not pay 4,000 livres a year nor, indeed, anything at all. Desperate for money after three months of liberty, on 23 June he wrote again to his attorney. It was the first of many letters in the same vein to Gaufridy.

> Along with your letter, I received one from Lions [at the Mas de Cabanes]. He tells me that the sheep have not been sheared. Fuck the sheep, for all I care, my learned friend! Do you think that my butcher and my baker can be paid by being told, "Gentlemen, the sheep have not been sheared?"
>
> Oh, yes, yes, you may laugh, learned friend. I am content to make you laugh but send me my money regularly or you will put me to the greatest hardship and the cruellest difficulties. I cannot wait more than another fortnight. It is now 23 June.

On 14 July, Sade did his republican duty by attending the celebrations for the first anniversary of the Revolution. It had been an orderly occasion, only one man killed and two injured when a cannon misfired. Yet the crowd was so densely packed that Sade had stood there in the rain for six hours without getting wet. All the same, he reported, the steady downpour on this republican occasion made one wonder whether God might not be an aristocrat.

Four months after his release from Charenton, Sade fell in love as he had perhaps never done with Renée-Pélagie or her sister. His new mistress was Marie-Constance Quesnet – Constance, as Sade called her: "Sensible", as he nicknamed her. Like so many of his women, she was an actress. Though hardly more than half his age, Constance was married to a husband who had now gone to America, leaving her with their son. It was impossible for Sade to marry her during Renée-Pélagie's lifetime but he did the next best thing. The couple lived together in contented domesticity for the rest of Sade's life. They were separated only during those months when Sade was confined in the prisons of the Revolution, where Constance was refused access to him, and at the beginning of his final confinement in the asylum at Charenton. He described her as "a good and honest bourgeois, loving, gentle and intelligent". She shared with him the small allowance that her husband made, while he provided her with food and lodging. If her affection for him succeeded in prolonging his life until he could get his hands on his money, he proposed to provide an income for her. He subsequently stipulated that she should have the use of Saumane after his death.

There was no suggestion of Sade's more extreme sexual predilections in their relationship. Sometimes he spoke of her as a respectable matron and sometimes as a daughter for whom he felt a father's affection. Constance can scarcely have been unaware of Sade as the man who had flogged Rose Keller or tried to sodomize the girls at Mariette Borelly's apartment in Marseille. He read the manuscripts of his books to his new mistress, so that she was equally well informed as to his literary preoccupations. In 1791, when *The Misfortunes of Virtue* was judiciously "peppered" as *Justine* to warm it for the market, it bore Sade's dedication to Constance. He had described her to Gaufridy as a young woman of sensitivity and feeling. In the dedication to *Justine*, he calls her an honour and an example to her sex, "detesting the intellectual trickery of immorality and irreligion, fighting such things incessantly by word and deed". By this account, she was a fit companion for Sade as moralist in his ambivalent fiction, a witness for his sincerity when he swore that he depicted vice only in order to make religion and virtue shine immaculately.

Having assumed the responsibility of a new family at a time of great difficulty, Sade turned to the ways of making his living. He had begun courting actors and those with influence in the theatre almost as soon as he was released from Charenton. By the end of 1790 he and Constance were living in rue Neuve des Mathurins, in chaussée d'Antin, running north from the centre of the city. The little house was not on the street but was reached across a garden from the buildings that fronted the road. Sade described himself living there with Constance like a portly priest in his presbytery. His family's title and former wealth, far from assisting him in Paris under the new regime, were to make him the object of suspicion as an aristocrat. Moreover, the estates in Provence were obliged to pay "patriotic" levies to the new order. On 12 June 1791, Sade urged his representatives to "fight rather than pay or, as you say, fondle them well so that they don't bite us".

The bourgeoisie of Provence was not in a fighting mood. Sade still pursued his own financial salvation in the world of the theatre. He had a number of plays already finished, some written in prison, and the system for submitting them to theatres was now more egalitarian. The author read his piece to the members of the company, as had usually been the case, but these members then voted upon it. Sade had an early success when his comedy, *Love's Misanthrope*, was accepted by the Comédie Française in September 1790. By the spring of 1791, no less than five more plays had been accepted for production at other theatres. It seemed that the dramatist of the new order might now solve the problems of the impoverished ex-aristocrat. But though the plays had been accepted, time passed and nothing more was done. There were explanations and postponements. In the end, not one of the plays was produced and no money was paid.

Even the few plays of Sade's which were produced later were beset by a variety of misfortunes. *Oxtiern: or, The Downfall of Lechery* was put on at the Théâtre Molière in October 1791. But the most powerful character was the villain of the drama, provoking an outburst of hissing and demands for the curtain to be rung down on so distasteful a performance. When Sade himself appeared on the stage at the end of the evening, he was applauded but it was thought best to postpone any further appearance of the play until the following season.

Before *Oxtiern* could be staged again, Sade's theatrical career was ended by a new wave of revolutionary patriotism. His play *The Suborner* was the cause of the trouble. It was produced at the Théâtre Italien in January 1792 and survived until its fourth appearance on 5 March. It then encountered a house that had been well packed with political vigilantes in their red bonnets. The behaviour of these members of the new audiences had become a cause for complaint in the theatre. But what had once been ill-mannered or anti-social in their conduct was now dignified by such terms as "revolutionary" and "patriotic". It would have been a brave man, in the circumstances of 1792, who complained of them.

When Sade's play began at the Théâtre Italien on 5 March, the red-bonnets behaved as though the curtain had not gone up. They continued talking and shouting loudly enough to drown the words of the actors. The din grew in the auditorium until the actors gave up all attempt to continue. They had thought the play unobjectionable and could not understand, in their innocence, how they had offended the purity of the Revolution. It seemed that those who prevented the performance of Sade's play could hardly have objected to its contents if not a line of it had been heard. But the play was objectionable because Sade had written it, no matter what it contained. However diligently he might support the new political order, he was an aristocrat, or an ex-aristocrat. All performances of plays by such men were to be prevented as a matter of civic duty.

Even on their literary merits, some of Sade's plays would have stood little chance of success. But the disturbance at the Théâtre Italien was seen as a general warning to actors and producers that they had better leave his work alone. The nation stood upon the brink of a period in which the guillotine had never been busier. It took no more evidence than such a play as this for the head of an actor or a manager to be locked in the "keyhole" while the blade was hauled up and then released to shear him at the neck. Sade's writing was "unpatriotic", though the play which he continued to submit unavailingly for the rest of his life was his "patriotic tragedy" *Jeanne de Laisné*. Its only performance had been when Sade, as an inmate, was invited to read it himself to the officers of the Bastille in the council chamber of the great prison. He was never to see another performance of his work in the theatres of Paris.

Sade's disappointments were summed up in a circular letter which he sent to the directors of the major theatres of Paris during 1795. He offered them his plays and described the misfortunes which had attended each of them. The Théâtre Louvois had been about to produce *The Prevaricator* when Sade discovered that he was not going to be paid and withdrew the piece. *Sophie and Desfrancs* would have been performed at the Théâtre Français had not the company been disbanded. His comedy, *The Boudoir*, was a single vote short of acceptance at the Théâtre Français and was accepted unanimously at the Théâtre Italien. However, Sade had felt obliged to withdraw it when the director insisted on adding a musical accompaniment, "which would have ruined it completely". As for his other unperformed works, *Jeanne de Laisné* was filled with "true patriotism", while women swooned at a mere reading of *Henriette and Sainville*.

All Sade's efforts to establish himself in the theatre were fruitless. If there were to be an income to support him for the rest of his life, it would have to come from La Coste or the other lands. He wrote repeatedly to Gaufridy, demanding the payment of whatever could be raised in order to save him from destitution. By the spring of 1791 he said bluntly that he could not pay Renée-Pélagie her money. Indeed, he assured Gaufridy that he now went to bed without dinner or supper. Gaufridy's letter, telling him that the advocate had written "in strong terms" to Lions at the Mas de Cabanes for the money that was owing, had left Sade's butcher and baker unimpressed. Nor was there any enthusiasm for letters of credit from Provence.

Whatever his apparent support for the revolutionary order, Sade had not come to terms with its effects at La Coste. Republicanism was more active there than in Paris. At first his former tenants were pleased to hear that Citizen Sade was behaving in a manner befitting a supporter of the new republic. He was assured that his property would be safeguarded during his absence so long as his conduct warranted this. But Sade was not to be curbed in his private opinions by promises of this kind.

In May 1791, he denounced the revolutionary "brigands" who had arrested his aunt, Madame de Villeneuve, in Provence. He was soon embroiled in a family struggle over who should inherit her estate when she should die. He accused the Montreuils of greasing the way for his younger and least-liked son, thereby cutting Sade out altogether. Faced with the outrage of 1791, he demanded Madame de Villeneuve's release. Nor was that the only republican effrontery from which he suffered. It was suggested that he might like to finance the rebuilding of walls at Mazan on behalf of the citizens. Sade swore that he would undertake nothing to benefit such "thieves" and "imbeciles". As he wrote to Gaufridy, the Revolution was becoming a haven for cheats and time-servers rather than a paradise for patriots. For an honest man like himself, it was even dangerous to suggest the removal of the remains of his great ancestress, Petrarch's Laura, from a church which the "barbarians" proposed to demolish, for fear of being accused of "aristocratic" behaviour.

Sade seldom bothered to keep his indignation to himself. In April 1792 he wrote to the president of the Club de la Constitution at La Coste about the threat of patriotic vandalism at the château.

If one single stone is taken from the house which I have in your area, I shall go to our legislators, I shall go to your brothers, the Jacobins of Paris. I shall demand to have carved on it, "A stone taken from the house of the man who brought down the Bastille. The Friends of the Constitution stole it from the home of the most unfortunate among the victims of royal tyranny. You who pass by, stick that in the history of human perversity!" . . . Brutus and his allies had no such "masons" and arsonists in their company when they restored to Rome the precious liberty which tyranny had taken from her.

Sade's honest indignation was commendable but it turned the republicans of La Coste against him as surely as it displeased the red-bonnets in the pit and gallery of the Théâtre Italien. There was no probability that he would ever again receive much income from his estates. Gaufridy, a royalist sympathizer, had been obliged to go into hiding for his own safety. Sade had already warned him that an informer, the daughter of Soton, had arrived in Paris from Provence in the summer of 1791. The young woman had a grudge against the elders of La Coste and was eager to do her patriotic duty by denouncing Gaufridy, the curé of the village and a number of others before the National Assembly. She had reason to hope that orders for their arrest and execution would be issued.

Informers and their kind thrived in the third summer of the Revolution. Sade saw the young woman and recognized her for what she was. He described her in his warning letter as "a little bitch", evil-minded as could be. Worst of all, the "slut" appeared at his lodgings with a soldier, threatening to add Sade's name to her list on the grounds of his behaviour at La Coste almost twenty years before. Sade left her in little doubt as to the pleasure he would find in administering to this fair revolutionary the thrashing of her life.

Whatever protection the château of La Coste may have enjoyed as a result of his protests proved to be short-lived. On 17 September 1792 the first of two mobs entered the gardens on the plateau above the village. They broke into the building itself and began to loot it, carrying away whatever they could and smashing whatever was too heavy to steal. Books and pictures were of little interest to them but they found more promising booty in the wine cellars, which were summarily ransacked. The furnishings of the main rooms were destroyed without compunction. Even beauty was now suspect as an emblem of former aristocratic privilege.

The looters discovered Sade's study and his private rooms with their unusual decorations. There was said to be an elaborate frieze "depicting the administration of an enema". Sade's bedroom was reported to be painted with obscene frescoes illustrating scenes that were later to find a place in the story of *Juliette*. Various instruments of penance and torment were found. There was no doubt in the minds of the looters that these had been used to torture the fifteen-year-old girls during the winter of 1774–5 as well as the young women who accompanied them. Rumour and allegation began to spin a web strong enough to draw a man before the Committee of Public Safety and thence to the guillotine. The looters of La Coste were able to enjoy the emotional luxury of plundering and destroying like common thieves while feeling a moral self-righteousness in cleansing their village of such past abominations as the *Juliette* frescoes and the enema frieze.

Sade wrote privately and bluntly to Gaufridy that he worshipped the king but hated the abuses which had existed under the old order. The only revolution to which he would give his support readily would be one designed to bring about a constitution on the English model. He was an aristocrat, as much by temperament as by breeding. The thought of rubbing shoulders with the revolutionary mob seemed to him profoundly unappealing. The adherents of that mob he systematically dismissed in his letters as fools or petty criminals. But not all of them were so foolish or petty. In July 1791, he assured Gaufridy that there were middle-class revolutionaries whose only interest in the process was to advance their own careers. Being men of profession and intellect, they exploited the political turmoil to gain wealth and power in precisely the same spirit as the sycophants of the court had sought favour with the king and the nobility. As Sade later remarked in *Juliette*, such men and women have not the least interest in any welfare but their own. A revolution is no more than the means of transferring wealth from the pockets of the previous rulers to their own.

It was not expedient for Sade to announce such political truths in a more public style. Instead, he matched public conformity with private denunciation, rather as he was overtly the author of plays and novels while secretly the writer of *The 120 Days of Sodom* and its kind. But mere conformity was no longer enough, so long as he stood in danger of being denounced as a former aristocrat. Citizen Sade must work for the Revolution, to which he owed his liberty.

2

In May 1790, Paris had been divided into "sections" as the new basis of the city's government. Sade lived within the section of place Vendôme, later known as the Section des Piques. He became an "active citizen" of his section in July 1790. Some months later, at a section meeting, he was asked, "Will you be our secretary?" It was a modest enough compliment, since many of those present lacked the qualification of being able to write. However, Sade agreed to the appointment and took up his pen on behalf of the Revolution.

To secure his position still further, he became a member of the National Guard, even undertaking a certain amount of guard duty. But this support for the new regime was still at a time when most Frenchmen expected nothing more radical than a peaceful change to a state of constitutional monarchy. Despite his membership of the National Guard, it was as secretary and author that his abilities were most in demand. The section appointed him as one of the commission for the administration of hospitals, in which role he drew up their observations on such matters. Most of this work was humdrum, involving little more than the record in his own prose of other men's bureaucratic decisions.

Sade had at length acquired a certain public influence and a position of power within the Section des Piques. By chance, the Montreuil family came within the jurisdiction of the section, though soon stripped of authority and fearful of being denounced. With improbable speed, as the Revolution gathered pace, Madame de Montreuil and her relations were obliged to look for protection from the son-in-law who had appealed to them in vain during his years of imprisonment.

Sade did not denounce them but he later took an aggressive initiative in family affairs. Madame de Montreuil and Renée-Pélagie favoured keeping his two sons abroad. The young men might join the ranks of royalist *émigrés*, some of whom were now gathering under Sade's kinsman, Louis-Joseph de Bourbon. When the time came, they might support a Prussian invasion of France with a view to restoring the king's lost powers. In September 1791, Sade heard that his elder son, Louis-Marie, had gone abroad. With some heat, he threatened to denounce the Montreuil family as enemies of the Revolution and as *émigré* sympathizers. They were certainly both and he left them to fret as to whether he would carry out his denunciation or not. In the end, he did not.

As a pamphleteer and propagandist of the new order, Sade's first production was prompted by the attempted escape of Louis XVI and Marie-Antoinette from Paris in June 1791. Evading their guards, the royal party headed for the German frontier and had reached Varennes before its members were recaptured. It was bad luck which prevented the escape from succeeding but the incident was a turning point in revolutionary sentiment, the constitutional monarch brought back to Paris and soon a prisoner awaiting trial. Had Louis XVI escaped, there seemed no doubt that he would have rallied the *émigrés* and the armies of the European powers to put down the rebellion in his own country.

When the king returned to Paris in some ignominy, Sade took the opportunity to publish *An Address to the French King from a Citizen of Paris*. It was less than a denunciation, however reproachful. In it Sade accuses Louis of having betrayed the trust placed in him by the French people, but he never suggests that France ought to be other than a monarchy. He insists that all men are equal in the sight of God and, to that extent, the position of the king must be that of first among equals. "France can never be ruled except by a king. But the king's rule must be agreed to by a free people, and he must remain faithful to their law."

In the ill-judged flight to Varennes, Sade accepts that it is the king's advisers rather than Louis himself who must bear the blame for the damage done. The task of the monarch is now to win back the affection and trust of the nation, which remains ready to forgive him. Yet Sade warns Louis that there can be only one party in France, the party of freedom. The abuses of the former Bourbon monarchy cannot survive in the new age of reason. Of these abuses, Sade writes, "Being works of darkness, like the actions of the Prince of Hell, they live only in the dark night of prejudice, fanaticism, and slavery. The torch of philosophy blazes forth and they are eclipsed, vanishing before its beneficent fire like the thick vapours of an autumn night before the first rays of the sun."

These clichés of revolutionary prose were all too soon to sound like cynical propaganda as new forms of prejudice, fanaticism and slavery replaced the old with ferocious efficiency. Yet Sade was the victim rather than the oppressor in that situation. Indeed, though his style in the address is freed from the bureaucratic prose of reports on hospital administration, it seems unlikely that he can have believed by the autumn of 1791 in his more optimistic prophesies made for the benefit of the king. But the brave political experiment which the nation had undertaken was not yet tarnished beyond hope. To invoke the dangers ahead might be to incur them. As for his public voice, personal prudence suggested that Sade's hortatory tone had better be sustained loudly for the time being.

More than a year later, in November 1792, after the most savage blood-letting of the September Massacres, Sade was still preaching revolutionary democracy in his *Ideas on the Manner of Sanctioning Laws*. But he spoke and argued in accordance with the instructions given him by the vigilantes of the Section des Piques. Sade now praised those men who had seized power from the more royalist revolutionaries in August. The new men were leaders whose actions had now led to the abolition of the monarchy and were to ensure the execution of the king two months later. Sade's view of monarchy is irreconcilable with the constitutional ideas he had voiced in the summer of the previous year. He explains that under a monarch, the representatives of the people are mere petitioners. In a republic, however, the representatives have no duty but to represent their electors. They are not to draw up constitutions nor pass decrees without reference to those who have chosen them to do so. They are empowered only to propose new laws and submit such proposals to the people, whose democratic choice remains absolute.

Sade's other work as political author for the Section des Piques was routine enough. There were "fraternal addresses" to similar bodies, encouragement for the growing tyranny of the revolutionary regime in its hunt for the enemies of the people, and strong opposition to the raising of an army of six thousand regular soldiers in Paris. Such a military adventure would be far too expensive and, as Sade wisely pointed out, a professional military force is easily made the tool of counter-revolution.

There was a predictable irony in Sade's role as a citizen of the Revolution. His personal reputation suggested he might have taken the opportunity to torment or abuse the victims of the oppression, while enjoying the sanction of the law. Instead, his revolutionary activity was confined to the production of material some of which can scarcely have interested him much. Indeed, it was often dictated by others. On being released from Charenton in 1790 he soon discovered, as he wrote to Gaufridy, that the greatest good consisted in being able to exist independently of others. Such a choice was no longer open to him when the Revolution extolled the stern duty of collective action above the self-indulgence of individualism. For Sade, the tedium of solidarity replaced the life of intellectual independence.

In his private comments, one of Sade's more illuminating reactions was to the September Massacres of 1792. Following the revolt of 10 August and the final overthrow of royal authority, there was a state of anarchy in Paris, which the city Commune seemed unable to control. Indeed, its enemies judged that it had acquiesced in the most brutal acts. This brutality was inspired more generally by a sense of desperation and a desire for vengeance on those who would defeat the Revolution by external means, as the Prussian army under the Duke of Brunswick took Verdun and began to strike towards the capital. In a determined move to defend the city, the Commune armed its citizens. It found too late that many Parisians were intent on settling personal scores rather than in offering resistance to the invaders.

There was a massacre of priests by the self-appointed executioners who led the mob. The prisons were opened to the rioters. Their purpose was not to free the inmates but to drag them to summary justice. The knives and sabres of the butchers, working on men and women alike, turned such places of detention as Bicêtre and Salpetrière into slaughterhouses. For the time being, the king and queen were spared. Yet the queen's friend, the Princesse de Lamballe, who was rumoured to be Marie-Antoinette's lesbian partner, was brought out to be lynched by the mob. A single sabre-stroke from behind took off her head, which was then mounted on a pike and held up to the windows of the queen. For some hours, the body of the princess was dragged about the streets by men and women driven beyond rationality in the excitement of shedding blood. The executioner cut off her breasts and then cut off the vulva, which he wore as a moustache to the great amusement of his followers. As he cut away the pudenda, he said jovially, "The whore! No one shall ever thread his way into her again!" Such was one glimpse of the reality behind what was sanctimoniously referred to as "the stern justice of the people" after three years of the new order.

Reality at its most bestial had overtaken the excesses of Sade's fiction in the scenes that filled the prisons and the streets. Had he truly been possessed by the fantasies of his novels and been inclined to give substance to them, there was never a more propitious moment. He might have flogged or tormented a score of women in the service of the new Revolution and in the name of justice. If slaughter made him squeamish, he need only have ill-treated his chosen victims as others did. But he chose not to. Instead, he noted the behaviour of those who meted out justice of this kind. He observed that their political superiors were motivated by little more than a greed for power and a longing for the opportunities which it would give them to indulge their secret vices and cruelties.

"Nothing", he wrote to Gaufridy after the massacres, "can equal the horrors which were committed." Whatever his views on religion, he lamented the deaths of the murdered priests, particularly that of the Archbishop of Arles, "the most virtuous and the most respected of men". Given Sade's experience of the Revolution and his private reactions to such incidents, the brutalities of *Juliette* are apt to appear as a moral fable rather than a sexual enticement. There was a fragment of ambiguity in this. In the manuscript, where Sade described the horror of the massacres, the words "but they were just" were added between the lines. Why? Sade shows no other sympathy for the justice of indiscriminate slaughter. The addition was perhaps an attempt to protect himself in case the letter should be opened and examined before reaching Gaufridy.

Further evidence of Sade's attitudes followed early in 1793, when he was appointed as a judge of the revolutionary court, being promoted to chairman of his court in July the same year. In a sardonic letter to Gaufridy, he warned the lawyer either to send him some money or expect a death sentence. The grim little joke was not likely to be appreciated. Louis XVI had gone to the guillotine in January and Marie-Antoinette was to follow him in October. Denunciations and executions grew in number as the discarded experiment in constitutional monarchy degenerated into terror.

In the circumstances of 1793 Sade's position as a judge was at least unusual, perhaps unique. It also brought him within the shadow of the guillotine. Despite his thrashing of Rose Keller and the scandal at Marseille, despite the triumph of homicidal villains in his fiction, he was opposed to capital punishment on moral principle. It was also a rational principle, since he claimed that all punishment which is not directed at reforming the culprit is illogical and abhorrent. Among the blood-letting of the day, he stood for peace and order, tempered by humanity. The dark dramas of cruelty which inspired his narratives seemed to be locked away in his mind until the political crisis should pass. His brother judges noticed that, where it could be done, Sade made great efforts to establish the innocence of those denounced and brought before him. He was almost "unpatriotic" in his anxiety to save such defendants from the customary sentence of death.

His behaviour certainly belied the legend of the monster who had done such things to Rose Keller or Mariette Borelly and her companions. But Sade went further and placed himself in mortal danger. On 6 April, at a meeting of the Section des Piques, he encountered his father-in-law, the Président de Montreuil. They had not seen one another for fifteen years but now the old man was desperately playing the part of a loyal republican. "I foresee the moment when he will invite me home with him," Sade commented laconically. On 13 April, when Sade reported to Gaufridy that he had been appointed as an examining magistrate, he added that Montreuil had been to see him. Their roles were reversed in the most improbable fashion. The disgraced judge of the former regime and his family were of precisely the type to be denounced and dragged to their executions. The old judge came to beg protection from the new. A denunciation was expected at any time. Sade could scarcely have chosen a more dangerous subject for his clemency.

Despite the clamour for blood, there was a list of families

vindicated by the new regime and removed for a while from the peril of being condemned as enemies of the Revolution. To this list, on his own authority, Sade added the Montreuils. "Such is the revenge I take upon them," he remarked.

Perhaps it was this favour which finally brought him into conflict with authority. His colleagues had watched him closely and with growing disapproval for his tendency to "moderation". Moreover, the Committee of Public Safety began to hear that the former Marquis de Sade was guilty of undermining their political philosophy. He had apparently suggested that the heaven on earth which their tyranny was intended to establish would prove "impractical". It was concluded, perhaps with justification, that he had assumed the mantle of a revolutionary only to save his own skin and that he had worked against the new rulers from the start. He began to attract notice of the most sinister kind.

3

As a writer of fiction during the years after Varennes, Sade appeared only to give further cause for suspicion. His literary reputation was to be impressed on his contemporaries by two novels published after his release from Charenton. The first of these gave ammunition to purists of the Revolution as surely as to the censors of the former regime. At the age of fifty, when he emerged from confinement, he had yet to see a play performed in Paris or a book generally published. However, he offered *Aline and Valcour*, as well as a version of *The Misfortunes of Virtue*, to Girouard, a young publisher who was also to publish Sade's *Address to the French King* after the attempted escape to Germany.

Girouard was doubtful about *The Misfortunes of Virtue*, though he saw that it might form the basis of a best seller now that the first phase of the Revolution proclaimed the freedom of the press. At present, it stood in no danger of censorship. If anything, the story was a little tame. Perhaps Sade would consider reworking it, describing in fuller detail the sexual ordeals of the heroine? Girouard was no revolutionary, if anything he was inclined to monarchism, but no one could fault his commercial sense in the case of *Justine*.

By June 1791, just before the king's disappearance from Paris, the revised novel was in the press as *Justine: or, The Misfortunes of Virtue*. Sade wrote to the lawyer Reinaud, explaining that the book had been "warmed up" at Girouard's insistence. He urged Reinaud to burn it rather than read it in its present form. He also confided to his correspondent that he intended to deny authorship of the novel, if by chance his name were ever to be associated with it. Three times in public and privately for the rest of his life, Sade denied that he had written this "infamous book". Perhaps a denial was prudent in the political circumstances of 1791 and in the light of his attempts to find employment as the curator of a museum or a library. On the other hand, he may simply have felt that he had suppressed the earlier version with its purer philosophical strength in favour of a quick commercial success. He certainly needed the money and the gratification of seeing a major piece of work published after so long a period of disappointment.

Whatever the moral objections to the new version might be, they were augmented by the literary misgivings of current taste. In this view, the new characters and incidents impeded a clear and direct narrative, which might be paired with a philosophical novel like *Candide* or *Jonathan Wild* or *Rasselas*. The simple theme of virtue ill used and vice rewarded was now cluttered and obscured by repetition or self-indulgence. The elaboration of scenes detailing rape, sodomy or sexual cruelty might be abhorrent. An equal error of judgment was the development of long and repeated justifications of vice by its proponents, rather than the original form in which the events spoke more for themselves and the commentaries were more succinct.

When it appeared, *Justine* attracted little interest for its philosophical content, though it revealed moral truths about society past and present. If the antics of the revolutionary mob and some of the sentences sanctioned by the former regime had not convinced men and women of the connection between lust and brutality in the chain of human passions, perhaps their response to Sade's novel remedied this. Indeed, the children of the Enlightenment formed a willing audience for the novel's heroine, who now masqueraded as "Thérèse". The devotees of Liberty, Equality, and Fraternity skimmed through pages in which the virtuous girl suffered under the whips and branding-irons of her persecutors, such vigorous and unnatural use being made of her body that she remained technically a virgin through an improbably long part of the book. At the dawn of a new age of mechanical invention, Sade's imagination matched that of industrial technology. As a demonstration of "La Femme Machine", no detail was omitted of how the judge Cardoville had corrosive sublimates inserted in the heroine's body and sewed up the orifices with wax thread or of how the surgeon Rodin dismembered the vital workings of his victims. Somehow, all this was to be reconciled with the moral pretensions of 1789. If the September Massacres belonged to the same world as the Rights of Man, then the readers of *Justine* might embrace Sade's fiction with an equal enthusiasm for freedom and justice.

Girouard was sufficiently pleased with the book's success to undertake the publication of *Aline and Valcour* as well. Its popularity was less assured but it was puffed as being "by the author of *Justine*". Sade was gratified that this long and picaresque tale of moral paradox should appear. He had no reservations about being announced as its author. It was to be issued in six volumes and Girouard began the printing at his shop in rue du Bout du Monde. But his royalist sympathies made him an object of suspicion and then the victim of denunciation. Before the printing of the six volumes could be completed, he was arrested. The novel was published after some delay in 1795, though still bearing the date 1793. Girouard was never to see it. He was condemned and, on 8 January 1794, he went to the guillotine. It soon seemed likely that the author himself would not live to see his book in print.

4

While *Justine* brought him notoriety and his "moderation" as a judge drew suspicion upon him, Sade also found himself threatened by the conduct of his children. He had not seen his two sons during his long imprisonment and they behaved more like the descendants of the Montreuils than of the Sades. The suggestion of the Montreuils that they should enlist abroad against the French government had come to nothing. But the younger son had gone to Malta, for which he offered the excuse of doing his duty as a member of an order of chivalry. Louis-Marie de Sade, the elder brother, resigned his commission as a staff officer. He began to travel about France, studying drawing and botany. The regime took a stern view of their conduct and listed both young men as *émigrés*. Any member of such a family who could not be readily accounted for was apt to be listed as an *émigré* and an enemy of his country by the new zealots in office. In the bureaucratic madhouse of this regime, Citizen Sade himself was to be cited as an *émigré* at La Coste in 1797, merely because he happened to be doing his republican duty in Paris.

Like other tyrannies before and since, the new republic decided that those members of a family who remained must be punished for the crimes of those who had fled. By August 1792, this increased the danger to Sade himself. He wrote two official letters. The first was an attested letter, in which he ordered his sons to return home. The second was a warning to the Montreuils that unless they also ordered the brothers to return, he would denounce the président and his family to the National Assembly. The cankered roots of fear and betrayal spread through even the closest relationships.

In practice, it made little difference to the two families. Fears over the reprisals that might be suffered by the relatives of *émigrés* were now overtaken by the terror of a general witch-hunt for enemies of the people among former patricians. Ancient and successful houses like the Sades and the Montreuils were among the first to be investigated. Not only was there a gratifying sense of civic duty in bringing such privileged delinquents to justice, the property of these criminals was forfeit and might, with a little judicious manipulation, pass into the pockets of the agents of social righteousness. Sade's estates were confiscated while he was in Paris rather than Provence. Though he was proved beyond all doubt to be in France, there was no enthusiasm for rescinding the order.

For a little longer, he was spared. The creation of the Committee of Public Safety in April 1793 and the concentration of power in the hands of its members seemed at first an attempt to control the anarchy of revolutionary government rather than to rule by sheer terror. Indeed, the assassination of Marat by Charlotte Corday in July 1793 inspired a famous funeral oration on behalf of the Section des Piques in Sade's *Address to the Spirits of Marat and Le Pelletier* in September that year.

To praise such men was an act of prudence in respect of the rulers of France. Marat, the dead hero, had believed in repression and the shedding of blood as the means of establishing a virtuous and just society. Sade, as a dutiful philosopher of the new autocracy which had emerged through the Committee of Public Safety, praises Marat's selfless political fanaticism. The example of Marat, in Sade's view, disproves egoism as a universal law. In this Sade distinguished himself from a number of the most prominent voices in his fiction who had demonstrated that egoism was one of the few truly universal laws. Le Pelletier, who like Marat had fallen by the hand of an assassin, is then praised for his courage in voting for the death of the king. Those who remembered Sade's public argument two years earlier that limited monarchy was the only practical means of governing France may have found his conversion to regicide somewhat less than convincing. But it is Marat on whom Sade places greater importance, comparing him with the stern fathers of the Roman republic, generally to Marat's advantage.

Sade as public orator was ill-matched with Sade the imaginative narrator. Moreover his praise of such heroes of the revolutionary government was to do him little good. In July 1793 a new member had joined the Committee of Public Safety. Like Sade, he was a man of breeding and family, even having been educated at the same school, the Collège Louis-le-Grand. He had no sympathy for Sade's destructive themes in fiction, yet Maximilien Robespierre saw the problems of the Revolution with the devastating and homicidal simplicity of a Sadean hero. There the similarity ended. Contrary to Sade's fictional hypothesis, religion and virtue were to be the foundations of the new order, though they were not to be confused with the religion and virtue fashionable before 1789. Worse still, all that had seemed most revolutionary in Sade's fictional heroes was deemed to be reactionary. In his rise to power, Robespierre had denounced atheism as "aristocratic" and ordered the worship of the "Supreme Being". This was a term by which Sade had frequently described the deity in his novels, though for quite other purposes.

The words of Robespierre acquired an almost hypnotic authority over the minds and will of many Frenchmen. "The essence of Republicanism is virtue," he proclaimed. "The Revolution is a period of transition from the rule of crime to the rule of law." Sade, in *Juliette*, saw the process in reverse and described the triumph of such organizations as the "Amis du Crime". The world of "transition" was in reality a paradise for the criminal and the psychopath. But Robespierre intended to enforce religious morality by statute. He proposed a new code of law, the first article of which should lay down that the French people believed in the existence of a Supreme Being and the immortality of the soul. "Nature is the true priest of the Supreme Being, the universe is his temple, and virtuous conduct is the means by which he is worshipped." It was hard to imagine any man with so pure an ambition to overturn the old order and yet differing so absolutely from the mouthpieces of Sade's novels.

Robespierre's intentions presented an immediate difficulty. In a country the size of France, there were a good many people who had no wish for a mass conversion to this Deism of the romantic revival, its themes sounded by Thomas Paine and Wordsworth as plainly as by Robespierre. There were men and women who were content with Christianity or some other faith, or with no faith at all. Many of them, like Sade, were sceptical that human nature was compatible with the ambition of creating a virtuous republic. But Robespierre was not daunted, since if virtue was the supreme goal, even enforcement by terror was not too high a price to pay. A corrupt body politic must be bled before it could be cured.

So the cure was attempted by wholesale denunciations, per-functory trials and executions on the scale of a massacre. Men and women died by dozens, scores and hundreds, many of them scarcely knowing why. As Robespierre's ally Couthon remarked, the guillotine was no longer a punishment but the most effective machine for exterminating the enemies of society. In the summer of 1794, the executions which had been running at a hundred a month rose to two hundred a week. In June, the law had been altered so that suspicion rather than guilt became the basis of conviction. In order to proceed more quickly, individual trials were replaced by mass indictments of as many as sixty people at a time, upon whom verdict and sentence were pronounced.

It was under the shadow of this reinforced regime of terror that Sade lived with Constance in rue Neuve des Mathurins. They were both at home on the morning of 8 December 1793, when two men presented themselves at the door. One of them,

Marotte, was a commissar of police; the other man, Jouenne, was also a police officer. They had a warrant for the arrest of Citizen Sade, issued by the Revolutionary Tribunal, as the court was called. He was to be indicted and tried for counter-revolutionary activities.

Sade replied that he would obey the command of the Tribunal, having no alternative. He seemed bewildered by the arrest because, like so many victims, he had believed himself to be a loyal worker for a regime which now proposed to butcher him in the name of unreason. He was not told whether his crime was to have two sons who were *émigrés* or whether the virtuous republic feared corruption from his most notorious novel. Indeed, he soon discovered that neither of these was the true cause. He was charged with having sought employment for himself and his two sons in the king's royal guard, late in 1791. Even had this been true, France remained a monarchy in 1791 and the National Assembly still recognized the king as constitutional ruler and head of state. There had been nothing unworthy, let alone illegal, in seeking such employment. But times had changed and actions were now examined in a new light. Retrospective criminality was a theory which kept the guillotine busy. Moreover, the Tribunal was busily searching out other "crimes" to bolster up this first accusation against the former lord of La Coste.

In the deepening nightmare of political terror and distorted reason, Sade's arrest was entirely logical. A man who once sought royal employment was suspect. Sade was not alone in being charged with the crime of seeking a place in the king's guard. It was impossible to disprove and sufficient to hold him in prison while his case was more thoroughly investigated.

Sade was held for some time in the former convent of the Madelonnettes, without yet being informed of the other charges that would be brought against him. He wrote to the Section des Piques and also to the Committee of Public Safety. He complained bitterly that after thirteen years in the prisons of the king, he had welcomed the Revolution as his liberator. And now, after only four years of freedom, he was imprisoned by the very cause that he had always supported. He had even expressed his approval of the execution of Marie-Antoinette in the previous October. Much good had it done him.

While Sade was writing these letters in the crowded prison, his apartment and papers were being scrutinized. Among his manuscripts, the searchers found remarks and opinions which must have given them a quite different view of this revolutionary judge.

In the early months of 1794, Sade was shuttled from one prison to another while awaiting trial, to the Carmes house of detention, to Saint-Lazare and at last to Picpus near Vincennes. It was on 27 March that he was transferred to Picpus, another former convent which had been converted into a prison after the increase in arrests during 1792. His age and apparent ill-health was one reason for the move, though his cell was within a few hundred yards of the open space in which the guillotine had been erected. It had been moved here from place de la Concorde, when the inhabitants there complained of the constant stench of blood. In its new location a large lead urn collected the blood under the platform and was brought to Picpus each evening to be emptied.

Sade was spared little by way of sight or sound of the daily executions. He had no reason to doubt that in the next few months he would join the men and women who queued up to die bravely or abjectly beneath the guillotine's blade. While he was confined like this, the law was changed to make suspicion enough for a capital conviction. It was scarcely an encouraging development. How good a view Sade had of the guillotine may be doubted. Yet he wrote to Gaufridy that he had seen 1,800 men and women go to their deaths, bravely or in terror as the case might be, to satisfy Robespierre's taste for virtue.

Then, on 24 July 1794, the Section des Piques forwarded evidence against their former secretary and judge, naming him as plain Aldonze Sade. On 26 July, he was charged by Fouquier-Tinville, public prosecutor of the Revolutionary Tribunal, with having been in treasonable correspondence with enemies of the republic. He was charged additionally with having been unpatriotically lenient as a judge in allowing enemies of the people to escape death. He was denounced as having been an active member of the Section des Piques only in order to save himself from the stern and necessary justice of the Revolution against former aristocrats.

He was not to be given the luxury of an individual trial but

would make his appearance and receive his sentence simultaneously with twenty-seven other accused. The culprits would be
condemned in the morning and brought back to Picpus in the
carts in good time to be guillotined the same afternoon. Twenty-
three of the twenty-eight accused appeared before the Revolutionary Tribunal that day. By nightfall, twenty-one of them were
dead – ex-nobles, ex-priests and ex-officers. One man was
acquitted. A woman fell into convulsions on arriving at the hearing and was taken to the Conciergerie for a later appearance.

But in Sade's case the procedural anarchy which the terror had
failed to reduce to order was to operate in his favour. On 24 July,
when his comrades of the Section des Piques offered their fabri-
cated evidence, he had less than three days to live. Then, on the
morning of 27 July, the escorts came to the prisons to take the
accused to the Revolutionary Tribunal. Five of the twenty-eight
men and women could not be found. Perhaps there was confusion between Aldonze Sade and Donatien-Alphonse-François
de Sade. More probably they looked for him in the wrong prison.
This was an understandable mistake, since there were now 8,000
prisoners in Paris, despite brisk business at the guillotine, and the
extra improvised prisons were not well organized. While twenty-
one men and women died under the guillotine that afternoon,
Sade and four others had still not been tried.

Sooner or later, he would have been unearthed. But fortune, to
whom he had paid tribute in his fiction, came to his assistance.
On the very day when he should have been tried, the gathering
revolt against the Reign of Terror grew to open resistance. It
came several hours too late to save those who had gone to the
guillotine that afternoon. Yet during the evening, those troops
who were positioned on place de Grève outside the Hôtel de
Ville, protecting Robespierre and his colleagues in the building,
began to withdraw. In the small hours of 28 July, there was no
protection left. At that point, the forces of the National Conven-
tion moved in to arrest the leaders of the government. Next day,
Robespierre and his brother, Saint-Just, Couthon and their companions went to the guillotine.

On 24 July Sade had faced certain death within a few days.
After 28 July, by a combination of improbable events, it seemed
that he might be safe after all. For months before that the
"Throne in Reverse", as the swivel-board of the guillotine was

called after Louis XVI had been strapped on it and tilted backwards, had been in daily use. If Sade had watched the afternoon executions, the last moments of the victims and the spouting of blood as the heads were severed before the faces of those who were soon to take their turn, it must have occurred to him that nothing in his fiction had yet equalled such ghastliness. Perhaps it was a test of Sade's abrasive sanity that he emerged from the horror of such a spectacle and the prospect of his own fate with his intellect and spirit unbroken.

In Picpus, no less than in the Bastille, he turned to the inner world of his writing. It was evidently during the early weeks of his confinement that he embarked upon a new novel, *Philosophy in the Boudoir*, which at face value appears to revel in sexual cruelty, justifying vice and brutality on the grounds that such things are "republican". At another level, it appears as an ironic denunciation of the "virtuous republic" of Robespierre with its false vision of nature, built upon misery and slaughter.

The book takes the form of seven dialogues which are intended to convey to a young girl the truth about sex and politics. This dialogue form had been common in French erotic writing, though *Philosophy in the Boudoir* offers few enticements. In a similar form, however, Michel Millot and Jean l'Ange had produced the comparatively innocent *L'École des Filles* in 1655. Also issued in England in 1688 as *The School of Venus*, it records an older girl enlightening a younger cousin on the truths of sexuality. About 1660 Nicolas Chorier's *Dialogues of Luisa Sigea* increased the number of actors and introduced a certain sexual perversity. Sade's dialogues are, in part, a development of Chorier's technique. In two letters written to him in Vincennes during August 1781, Renée-Pélagie confirmed that she was trying to get him a copy of *L'École des Filles* from his bookseller Mérigot. In the following month, Mérigot was still waiting for the book, as well as for some volumes of Rousseau. Despite Sade's assumptions, this was further proof that the authorities at Vincennes, rather than Renée-Pélagie, were the censors of his reading.

The young innocent, whose education is to be undertaken, is Eugénie. She learns the pleasures of her own sex from Madame de Saint-Ange and those of mankind from Dolmancé. Easily persuaded by her mentors, she submits readily to being sodomized and even to being whipped by her lover. Madame de Mistival, the girl's mother, arrives to save her from such horrors. But Eugénie is so enthralled by her education that she assists in the stripping and violation of Madame de Mistival before, literally, booting her out of the bedroom.

At the level of sexual incident, there is little that Sade had not employed before and, indeed, little that could not be paralleled in Robespierre's France. Gilbert Lely cites a scandal that occurred as Sade began to write his novel. The scandal involved the abduction of several young women at Nantes by fugitive slaves from the United States who had come to join the army of the Revolution. After a few days of multiple rape, the young women were set free. They complained of having been used in every imaginable way, sometimes by more than one man at a time, and of the youngest having been partnered by about fifty men on the last day. Though there may be exaggeration in such stories recorded by Émile Camperdon and others, the new order and the anarchy of the times enabled certain men to improvise harems from the girls they had seized. Lesbianism, which Sade elaborates more fully in the character of Madame de Saint-Ange, was also a fashionable topic of scandal. For political reasons, supporters of the Revolution had suggested that Marie-Antoinette and her close female friends were lesbians. More lurid were the stories of the so-called sect of Anandrynes with its elaborate rituals of female love. But as the title of Sade's book suggests, it was "philosophy" rather than the mere mechanics of fictionalized sex which was at the centre of the narrative.

Taken simply, the book debunks virtue and all religion except the religion of evil. Kindness or philanthropy is to be despised as merely encouraging the repressed to rebel. To do evil, or at least to avoid doing good, is the only conduct which can offer satisfaction. Dolmancé, as if anticipating Nietzsche, attacks Christianity for its benevolence and its consequent slave morality. Cruelty and vice, rather than benevolence and virtue, correspond most accurately to the true law of Nature. What, after all, is the result of an attachment to virtue? Who was more self-consciously a disciple of virtue than Robespierre, whom Sade attacks in his argument? Who was more passionately an advocate of Nature as a moral pattern than Robespierre? From his prison, Sade was presented with a living example of the "virtuous Republic" in action as he watched the leaden urn emptied of its contents each evening.

With a coolness that suggests Jonathan Swift at his most savage, Sade shows that the true ideal of the virtuous republic has yet to be realized. Only when France fully reflects Robespierre's religion of Nature will perfection be attained. Abruptly, in the middle of the fifth dialogue, Sade introduces a bizarre political harangue. "Frenchmen! One more effort, if you truly wish to be republicans!" The ideal republic of natural morality is described in terms of its attitude towards so-called crimes. There must be no more capital punishment. Indeed, there must be no more punishment at all for murder, since Nature does not punish the killing of one creature by another. Nor is theft to be punished, except in cases where the state punishes the man who has been robbed.

The ideal republic must also follow Nature in its attitude towards sexual conduct which has been traditionally discriminated against. Not only must it tolerate prostitution but enforce it upon all women, even in their childhood. Where, after all, does Nature forbid it? If a man is attracted by a woman, the law will compel her to present herself at a publicly provided brothel. There she must submit to whatever act the man wishes, even at the cost of her life. Such is the example which the natural world suggests. The fact that she may prefer another man is no excuse. Nature makes no provision for such preferences. A female animal is taken by the available and dominant male.

Adultery will no longer be an offence. Marriage, which is an absurdity in terms of the natural world, will have been abolished and all children will be the possessions of the state. However, incest must be permitted since there is no taboo against it in the animal kingdom. Homosexuality and sodomy between the sexes is also to be regarded as normal conduct for the same reason.

Sade insists that it is not a valid objection to his argument that such a universal republic might soon lead to a decline and to the eventual extinction of the human race. Why should that matter? Nature cares nothing whether an individual lives or dies. Nature, as universal phenomenon, would be very little affected by the extinction of the entire human species.

Had Sade intended his hypothesis to be read without irony, it would have foundered upon fallacies. It requires the deification of Nature, in a manner which would defeat the purpose of his attack on Robespierre for creating a religion of Nature. Sade's device, however, is to use a phrase like "the Law of Nature" as though it were akin to "the Law of Contract". Nature has no laws except those governing scientific phenomena. It is, in that respect, not so much the giver of laws as the subject of laws formulated by human observation. In that sense, the laws do not exist in Nature but in human science.

To read Sade's argument with no perception of irony, however, would be extremely difficult. The ideal republic requires yet more murder, of which he seemed likely to be an early victim. It also requires theft, which he was to experience in the confiscation of his remaining estates. Upon such a road lay Robespierre's progress to Utopia. Once that goal was reached, who but a hypocrite would argue that such lesser aberrations as incest or sodomy must not be equally allowable?

Whatever Sade's intentions, *Philosophy in the Boudoir* reads like a libidinous parody of Plato's *Republic*. That Sade truly felt an enthusiasm for murder among the stench of blood and the procession of the condemned seems as likely as that Swift, after his *Modest Proposal*, felt an appetite for infant flesh. Moreover, Robespierre had been the target of his literary vengeance and Robespierre was now dead. The Reign of Terror did not end at once. For a little longer Sade was left in apprehension that he might be found and dragged out to his trial. He waited for a month. Then, on 22 August 1794, the Committee of Public Safety received his petition asking to be set free. The Section des Piques was consulted and agreed that Sade should be given his liberty. On 15 October, just over ten months after his arrest, Sade was released from the Picpus prison into a city from which the terror had at last been lifted.

A good many citizens had been arrested and survived to be released after Robespierre's fall. The Montreuils had been protected by Sade until his own arrest, then they too had been seized. As it happened, they were luckier than he in being released three months earlier. But the old judge never recovered from his confinement or the shock of finding his world turned upside down. He died in January 1795, six months after his release. It was more than two years before Renée-Pélagie wrote to Gaufridy with the news. By then she was able to report that Sade's adversary, Madame de Montreuil, was still "doing well".

ELEVEN

THE FRIENDS OF CRIME

1

THE HARDSHIPS WHICH HAD GREETED SADE on his release in 1790 were in no way as severe as those awaiting him in the autumn of 1794 as he left Picpus. When he returned to Constance at the house in rue Neuve des Mathurins, it was to find six thousand francs in debts with no means of paying any of the sum. He was destitute rather than poor. Almost a year before, on 14 November 1793, he had drawn up his accounts for Gaufridy's benefit. All the rents of his land were added together. He deducted the republican taxes, the allowance of four thousand francs a year to Renée-Pélagie and one thousand annually to Constance as his "natural and adopted daughter". The result was that he had one hundred francs a year to live on. It was a hopeless situation.

Matters were soon to become much worse. Sade's property had become the subject of sequestration orders by the new regime. After the fall of Robespierre and the liberalization of this policy, it was possible to have such orders lifted. But this could not be done without payment. Worse still, Sade was an absentee landlord. In 1797, he was still listed as an *émigré* in the Vaucluse, though his name had been removed from the list in the Bouches-du-Rhône. Whether it was mere malice or error which cast him as a traitor, there was reason enough for his tenants to withhold their rent.

As a further complication, the crypto-royalist Gaufridy had withdrawn to Toulon, the tacit supporter of an attempt to restore the Dauphin as Louis XVII. Republican Justice overtook him there. Gaufridy was imprisoned as an enemy of the people from Apt and appears to have escaped death only by means of a false identity paper which named him as a resident of Toulon. Released like Sade in 1794, he and his son were living obscurely somewhere in the Luberon. It was in November 1795 that Gaufridy returned home at last to find Sade's latest demands for money awaiting him.

Having returned to Constance, Sade begged for employment from those who might provide him with it. For the time being, he begged in vain. He had already tried to find employment as the curator of a library or museum. Though he was not successful, it was best that he should not be known as the author of a novel whose pornographic reputation had reached such proportions. The reasons for disowning *Justine* multiplied year by year.

His plays were rejected on all sides but *Aline and Valcour* appeared in 1795. The printing had been abandoned after the arrest and execution of Girouard, since the victim's goods had been confiscated by the state. But Girouard's widow had applied to have the sequestration order lifted and Sade saw his chance of having the novel published.

For Sade, the winter of 1794–5 was the worst. In the society of the Revolution, idealism was foundering, the economy had failed and France was ringed by hostile powers of monarchist Europe. As though all this were not enough, the early months of the new year brought one of the most bitter winters for a century. Sade was too poor to provide for himself, let alone for Constance and the child. The house in rue Neuve des Mathurins was unheated, since they had no money for fuel. The cold grew so intense that Sade's ink froze.

He wrote letters to Gaufridy and to Gaufridy's sons which were almost hysterical in their desperation, denouncing the family as thieves and liars who were keeping his income from him. On the death of one of those sons, Sade put aside his more bitter accusations of indolence and negligence against the lawyer. Yet even his condolences were laced with reproof. "However, my dear and good friend, while we weep for the dead, we must must not allow the living to die – and that indeed is the point to which your appalling negligence has brought me. Send me my money, I beg you!"

It seems that the letter had some effect as the sequestration orders on Sade's property were lifted. On 26 August, in a letter to Gaufridy, Sade referred to a sum between seventeen and eighteen thousand francs which the lawyer had sent him for that year. It was presumably with the aid of this that he completed the publication of *Aline and Valcour*, as well as paying off the six thousand francs of his immediate debts. In addition, he had the unpublished manuscript of a novel written in prison at Picpus with a full view of the guillotine and the vats of blood being brought back each evening to be emptied down the prison drain. There still remained an open market in erotic and pornographic books, that area of liberty which the Revolution had permitted at first and had not yet regulated. *Justine* and a host of lesser novels covered the bookstalls of Paris and the shelves of booksellers in other French cities. There was a considerable public for those darker sexual dramas which Sade had so far published only in his first book. However, he turned to his prison writing in *Philosophy in the Boudoir* and began to prepare it for the press.

When the book appeared, later in 1795, Sade took several of the more routine precautions to distance himself from it. He decided that this novel and *Justine* were written by the same man, but that the man was now dead. *Philosophy in the Boudoir* appeared with erotic illustrations to encourage those who might not have much enthusiasm for the role of Nature in human society. It was duly announced on its title page as a posthumous work by the author of *Justine*. To clouds its origins still further, it bore the imprint of having been published in London, "at the expense of the Company".

If Sade expected a steady income from the book, he was to be disappointed. He wrote to Gaufridy that La Coste, and anything else that still remained, was to be sold. Madame de Villeneuve, Sade's aunt, expressed interest in Mazan during 1795. When negotiations began, however, it proved that she did not intend to buy it outright, merely to offer fifteen thousand francs for a lease during her lifetime. Few people had money to spend on such estates and, in any case, the political situation in the 1790s scarcely made them an attractive investment. Sade, who had been hoping to sell Mazan outright for about seventy thousand francs, refused his aunt's offer. Madame de Villeneuve broke off the negotiations, telling him that he was not the only one short of money. Sade now spoke vaguely of retiring to Saumane but showed no inclination to do so as yet.

It was in the following year that he at length managed to sell the ruin of La Coste with its land and other buildings to Joseph-Stanislas Rovère, an opportunist politician of the new order who had been born nearby at Bonnieux and done well out of the Revolution. Sade's principal concern was that his creditors, including Renée-Pélagie, should not have time to get their hands on the money. To avoid this, he quickly reinvested it in two smaller properties near Paris, at Malmaison and Granvilliers. Unfortunately, he had not enough money to complete the purchase and so increased his debts by several thousand francs. To Renée-Pélagie, he still owed a hundred and sixty thousand francs, her marriage dowry, which he had promised to pay if La Coste was sold.

Sade was in the worst of financial muddles. There was property in his name but he had no money. He had put down money on Malmaison and Granvilliers but still needed six thousand francs to complete the payment. He was lord of Saumane and La Coste, but he could not pay the bill at the Paris eating-house where he dined. Its owner was soon to sue him for debt. Indeed, his title to Saumane and Mazan was under threat again when his name appeared in the 1797 list of those in the Vaucluse who had gone to join the republic's enemies.

He was able to put a stop to proceedings against him as an *émigré* by getting a certificate of his "uninterrupted" residence in Paris. Yet he must have been uneasily aware that he might still be in trouble because of the conduct of his sons. The younger son, Donatien-Claude-Armand, had been encouraged by the Montreuils to remain in Malta. He was certainly an *émigré*. Sade alone now bore the responsibility for such "unpatriotic" conduct by his children. Ironically, his elder son, Louis-Marie, was actually living in Paris as a student and, for the moment, getting on unexpectedly well with his father. Sade now found him a more agreeable companion, not least by virtue of Louis-Marie's taste in music and painting.

2

After the severe winter of 1795, Sade informed Gaufridy that he was going into the country to finish a book. He did not say how he would live or what he was writing. Perhaps he and Constance were surviving on the proceeds of *Philosophy in the Boudoir*. There was little doubt, in retrospect, that the book he was finishing was *The*

New Justine: or, The Misfortunes of Virtue, followed by the Story of her Sister Juliette, or, The Prosperities of Vice. It was a massive undertaking, which perhaps only the energy of obsession could accomplish. About twice the length of *War and Peace*, it absorbed Sade's philosophical and narrative power, his own journals of Italy and, of course, everything that he had given to *The Misfortunes of Virtue* and its successor, *Justine*. As his literary testament, it was the final ironic statement of pure and absolute revolution, extending over morality, sexual conduct and every other area of human behaviour, as surely as it extended over politics and government.

In the original account of *The Misfortunes of Virtue* and in its first rewriting, Juliette had been a mere literary device to facilitate the autobiography of her sister as Sophie, Thérèse or Justine. Left to the mercy of the world at an early age, the two sisters had gone their separate ways. Juliette, briefly described in the earlier versions, has taken to every kind of vice and made a fashionable marriage. Having disposed of her husband, she remains young, beautiful and rich. At this stage, on a journey through France, she encounters a young woman of obvious virtue who is a prisoner, condemned to death and on her way to execution. Juliette persuades "Sophie" or "Thérèse" to tell her story. This narrative of virtue persecuted and triumphed over by vice is so detailed and circumstantial that Juliette at last recognizes Sophie or Thérèse as her younger sister Justine.

Even in its last and most elaborate form, the story has much in common with a cautionary tale of the pre-revolutionary period like *Candide* or *Rasselas*. The innocent hero or heroine, naïve and trusting, journeys through the world, suffering trials and disillusionment from which the reader may draw a moral. In this case, Sade permitted his victim to emerge from her ordeals with her belief in virtue as immaculate as Robespierre's.

But now there was a post-revolutionary tale to be told, of a kind which neither Johnson nor Voltaire could have anticipated. *Justine* was a story of suffering which, in the last extremity, might have been blamed on Providence, but which concentrated on the story of the victim. Yet since 1790 Sade had ample opportunity to see the minds and hands of the revolutionaries at work. Under the former regime there had, of course, been men who tortured or killed their victims with the sanction of the law and in its service.

But the worst of it had been done, as a rule, in secret. The Revolution had brought torture and murder before a more numerous audience and, as in the dismemberment of Madame Lamballe, it seemed that the torturer rather than the victim was the central figure. Even in the case of a death-machine like the guillotine, the device itself was more memorable than all but a few of its victims.

In Sade's new and massive fiction, the emphasis was removed from the virtuous victim and placed instead upon the triumphant cruelty of the oppressor. *Juliette: or, The Prosperities of Vice* offered the world a revolution that was unmasked and absolute. The true and admirable revolutionaries, as Verneuil explains in *The New Justine*, are men like Tiberius and Nero who are prepared to overthrow all moral values rather than be content with substituting one political regime for another. It is no longer enough that Nature should be indifferent to morality, announces Noirceuil in *Juliette*. Crime is Nature's first law and the only "system" upon which the universe can operate. As Madame Delbène explains to the young Juliette, there can be no true happiness except in the systematic pursuit of crime. "Do unto others as you would not have them do unto you." In political reality, it is entirely legitimate for the strong to oppress the weak, since that is Nature's law, as Dorval explains it to Juliette. On the other hand, it is legitimate for the weak to unite against the strong, if they are able to do so. This does not make their cause more virtuous or natural. Indeed, a sensible tyrant will take measures against them and will, as one of the heroes of *The New Justine* advocates, seek ways of controlling or exterminating such "vermin".

With hardly a flaw in its monolithic obsession, the story presents the theme through the ten volumes of its twin novels. There are occasional glimpses of an alternative view but they are rare. Having relied so much on the philosophy of La Mettrie, for example, the narrator attacks him for failing to understand that crime is the only means of sustaining man as a machine. And at least once, in the case of Noirceuil, the reader is told not to take La Mettrie's views seriously, because he is a man whose speciality is to use ingenious arguments in favour of ludicrous propositions.

Yet while the obsession may remain more or less intact, the logic of the narrative does not. At one moment, belief in a divinity and a system of morality of any sort is said to be an absurd superstition. Yet Juliette and the principal male character, Saint-Fond, hold such beliefs. Saint-Fond believes in a supreme power of evil as surely as any Christian child believes in a benevolent deity. He also finds the doctrine of eternal punishment believable and admirable. Juliette also believes in a Supreme Being of evil and it is unsurprising that she should oblige Pope Pius VI to celebrate a black mass in the basilica of St Peter. There is little in the creeds of the two characters which differs much from old-fashioned satanism and not much that would give encouragement to the rational benevolence of the Enlightenment.

Sade's intentions in the novel may be questioned, particularly since he strenuously and repeatedly denied that he had written it. However, as a narrative fiction, it is calculated to sway the reader to precisely the opposite views to those put forward by Juliette and her colleagues. They may amuse or divert but they do not convince. The most enlightened despotism of eighteenth-century Europe or the most bigoted form of contemporary religious belief was bound to seem infinitely preferable to the moral revolution outlined in Sade's fiction. The triumph of crime and the extinction of the human race are presented as unappealingly at a metaphysical level as the diet of faeces consumed by the cannibal Minski when described in a culinary farce.

Sade's achievement is to repel rather than to attract by his descriptions in *Juliette*, not least in his mockery of revolutionary values. It is plain from his letters, for instance, that he strongly disliked the extreme doctrines of the Jacobins. In *Juliette*, there is a sly reincarnation of the Jacobin "Society of the Friends of the Constitution" in the "Society of the Friends of Crime".

Parts of the narrative move at the level of surreal farce. Minski, for example, not only feeds on the most beautiful girls of his harem but makes them provide the furnishings of his dining-room. Their naked bodies are linked together to form chairs and tables, as well as to hold candles and to support the china and porcelain from which hot food may be eaten. Sideboards, formed by these interlocked and naked girls, waddle awkwardly towards the diners when wine is called for. The comic vision of self-propelled furniture shuffling obediently about the room is tempered by the sardonic humour of cruelty. The table is said to shudder when dishes hot from the oven are laid upon the assorted breasts and bottoms which form much of its surface. Minski's guests have an appetite much the same as his own and the dinner begins with a serving of "gammon of boy". By the end of the festivities, Minski has washed down this cannibal feast with thirty bottles of Burgundy.

Such episodes in Sade's fiction are less reminiscent of erotic novels than of fairy tales, which Havelock Ellis believed serve a similar purpose for children to that of pornography among adults. Minski is like the ogre of nursery reading, the archenemy of the giant-killer. He belongs to the race of fairy-tale monsters rather than to that of adult libertines. Minski is a tyrant who views his victim with a promise to "grind his bones to make my bread".

On another occasion in the narrative, the dark humour of *Juliette* is entirely subservient to gleeful cruelty. When the heroine and her companions travel south from Naples, they enjoy the hospitality of a beautiful widow and her three daughters. They seize these innocents and subject them to a dark drama, using every form of suffering and sexual indignity which one of Sade's criminal heroines might be expected to devise. The woman is made to assist while her daughters endure rape and sodomy and they, in turn, assist when she is the subject of such villainous attentions. Finally, she is ordered to torment her daughters while the "heroes" of the incident caress her buttocks with their stilettos to leave her in no doubt of what awaits her. This incident and a great many more like it were to determine Sade's reputation for more than a century. It mattered little to his successors whether he was friend or enemy of the Revolution, whether his aspirations in religion and morality were genuinely revolutionary or reactionary. The manner of his fiction was no more, in this view, than a narrative of sexual cruelty.

3

When *Juliette*, prefaced by *The New Justine*, appeared in ten volumes in 1797, it also contained a hundred illustrations. Sade's work had never been more vividly presented nor his obsessions more luridly detailed. The novel was published in the year when the power of the Directorate over the French Republic was proclaimed in the *coup d'état* of September. Law and order were at last to be imposed upon the tumult of liberty and equality. It was only a first step towards the consolidation of autocratic power, confirmed two years later when the Directorate itself gave way to First Consul in the person of Napoléon Bonaparte. For the time being, Sade was content to have five copies of his novel specially bound and sent to the members of the Directorate. Unsurprisingly, this generosity in the case of such a book was later to seem foolhardy.

In the bookshops of Paris, novels to suit all tastes could still be bought. Though it was doubtful how much longer this tolerant policy could survive, neither the author nor the publisher of *The New Justine* and *Juliette* seemed to run any risk of prosecution.

But while the authorities might be unmoved, there was soon public disapproval. Restif de la Bretonne, who had already published highly coloured accounts of the scandals at Arcueil and Marseille in his *Nuits de Paris* (1788), now turned his attention to Sade's literary delinquencies. Restif himself had enjoyed a certain success as a pornographer, but he now claimed that Sade's fiction was bringing disgrace and even dishonour to the profession. Sade was "a monster". To prove the point, Restif published his *Anti-Justine* in 1798. It was an attempt to show that a man could write a perfectly adequate pornographic novel without resorting to the excesses which Sade had chosen. Restif duly deplored the sexual violence of Sade's fiction as well as the grossness of its sexuality. He offered the world instead his own little pot-pourri of multiple copulation, lesbianism, incest and sodomy.

By this means, Restif was able to combine self-righteousness with profit. In order that the controversy selling his own book should be kept alive he continued to denounce Sade as the author of the unspeakable *Justine*. As it happened, Sade's authorship of the novel was not universally acknowledged. In April 1798, the periodical *Le Cercle*, in an obituary notice of Citizen Langle, swore that *he* was the author of the book. But the *Journal de Paris* commented scornfully that everyone knew the true author to be "a certain Monsieur de Sade, who was set free from the cells of the Bastille by the Revolution of 14 July". There was some further general embarrassment when it was discovered that Monsieur Langle, the subject of the obituary, was still alive.

Three days later, Sade wrote to the *Journal de Paris*, complaining of the "insult" it had offered him and adding: "It is *false*, absolutely *false* to say that I am the author of the book entitled

Justine: or, The Misfortunes of Virtue." Sade warned his readers that he was determined in future to take every means of legal redress "against the first person who thinks he can name me as the author of this evil book, and get away with it".

In the following year, 1799, it was Sade's turn to be the subject of premature obituary rumours. Once again, he was described as the author of *Justine*. He wrote angrily to the *Ami des Lois* that they had killed him and libelled him with equal falsehood in both respects. "I trust you will be good enough to display in your paper both this proof of my existence and my most absolute denial of being the author of the infamous *Justine*." To the editor of the *Tribunal d'Apollon* he wrote a letter which promised that he would print the truth of his continuing existence on the shoulders of the editor with a stick. "It is a falsehood", he added, "to say that I am the author of *Justine*." And now that the dangers of revolutionary zeal had receded, he signed himself as the former Comte de Sade.

This was by no means the end of the matter. In 1800 he published a collection of his shorter fiction, which dated from his years in the Bastille. There were four volumes, containing eleven novellas and a prefatory essay on fiction, *Idée sur les Romans*. The fashionable themes of the Gothic as well as the romantic taste for sensibility ran through these tales, combined with dark sexuality and the motive of incest. They were a good deal more powerful than the milk-and-water Gothic of English fiction which the circulating libraries offered to the schoolmiss and her mama. At the same time, it would have been hard to sustain a charge of obscenity or even indecency against them. Sade called his collection *The Crimes of Love*.

However innocuous they might seem by comparison with Sade's other fiction, these volumes were soon denounced. Villeterque reviewed them in the *Journal des Arts, des Sciences et de la Littérature* on 22 October 1800. "A disgusting book," he wrote, "the work of a man who is suspected of writing an even viler novel." Villeterque made no effort to review the book impartially and seemed clearly intent on making capital out of Sade's reputation as the author of *Justine*. Sade replied, dismissing Villeterque as a hack who had not read the book he was reviewing. As for *Justine*, "I challenge him to prove that I am the author of that 'even viler novel'."

Sade's constant denial of his authorship was perhaps intended to distance himself from a darker *alter ego*. But there was a more immediate threat. On 18 August 1800, a complete edition of *Justine* was seized by the police at a binder's workshop. They found girls of fourteen employed in collating the pages of the text with the obscene engravings which were to illustrate the volumes. Though it was the illustrations rather than the text which caused official outrage, it had been plain for some time that the brave libertarian experiment of 1789 was being overtaken by a self-righteous and patriotic cleansing of literature. With the advent of Napoléon as First Consul, the talk was not so much of liberty and equality as of firm government and moral regeneration. In order to divert the attention of the authorities elsewhere, it was prudent to deny any connection with a book that would surely be one of the first casualties of repression. Sade had spent fourteen of the last twenty-three years in prison. He made every effort, however vain, to avoid going back.

4

In 1796, the year of his sale of La Coste, Sade waited in such despair for the arrival of money in Paris that he distributed a circular letter to all hotels in the area of rue de la Paix, appealing for a banker or merchant by the name of François Perrin from Marseille, evidently the expected bearer of money from Provence. Indeed, in the following year he set out for Provence himself, seeing it for the first time since his escape from Marais and his weeks of freedom in 1778.

In April 1797, Sade and Constance had moved to a house at St Ouen in northern Paris, 3, place de la Liberté. Almost at once, they left for Provence. Instead of the slightly built scapegrace nobleman in his thirties, he now appeared as a portly white-haired old gentleman. He visited Gaufridy at Apt and the new owner of La Coste. At Mazan, he found the bailiffs waiting to discuss the matter of his unpaid taxes. By June he had withdrawn to Saumane. From this high retreat among gardens and fountains, he issued a challenge to the Registrar of Carpentras, Noël Perrin. What had this Jack-in-Office meant by stealing – "Yes, stealing is the word, citizen!" – Sade's rents? "Don't tell me you have dared to present to the nation's coffers the income of a man who was never an *émigré* in his life. It wouldn't be accepted. That money has gone into your pocket. Oblige me, citizen, by returning without delay the sum that you have pilfered."

There was more in the same style. On 8 July, Sade found himself charged before the Tribunal Correctionelle at Avignon with defamation. The unfortunate Perrin complained that he was only doing his job, since Sade's name had still been on the list of *émigrés* for the Vaucluse. Four days later, Sade went from Saumane to Isle-sur-Sorgue and signed a public retraction of his insults. He agreed to pay the fifteen hundred francs demanded by the court.

He took Constance to stay with Gaufridy at Apt and set out for the estate of the Mas de Cabanes, crossing the Rhône at Beaucaire. It was his intention to sell this property as well but nothing came of it. Renée-Pélagie, still owed a hundred and sixty thousand francs by Sade, was well aware that she was unlikely to see any proceeds of such a sale. Writing to Gaufridy, she warned him to put a stop to it immediately.

Sade and Constance spent almost five months in Provence. By the time that they returned to St Ouen in October, the *coup d'état* by the Directorate was a month old. Whatever remained of the great republican Revolution seemed to have degenerated into bureaucratic absolutism. Yet Sade's preoccupation in the autumn of 1797 was still with the inclusion of his name on the list of *émigrés* in the Vaucluse. Not only was his property still technically under sequestration, he might be called to answer before a military tribunal under a proclamation of 5 September. It was not until the following year that the matter was settled.

5

By the autumn of 1798, his predicament was worse than ever. He was unable to get his hands on any money from Provence and he still owed six thousand francs on his purchase of property near Paris. He and Constance left their house at St Ouen. She went to stay with friends and Sade looked for lodgings where he could find them. He stayed for a while with a tenant-farmer near his newly acquired but mortgaged property. It seemed best to sell the property but that was not possible and the farmer stopped feeding him. He made his way to Versailles early in 1799, with Constance's son and a servant. They lived in the garret of a house, while Sade earned forty sous a day at the theatre. He gave subsequent instructions that letters for him were to be sent to an eating-house at 100, rue de Satory, so that the world should not know of the "appalling place" where he now lived.

So far as his family was concerned, he swore that Constance was "an angel sent from heaven" and his more favoured elder son Louis-Marie was now a scoundrel, who came to visit his father in misery and did nothing to help him. Sade had intended that Constance should go to Renée-Pélagie and tell her of his plight. An intermediary had made the approach and a date had been agreed. It was then, according to Sade, that Louis-Marie had intervened to put an end to the proposed visit. Constance came to the garret instead with food in her pocket, smuggled from the friends who had given her shelter. "Send me the means to live!" Sade wrote to Gaufridy in July 1799, "or you shall suffer the greatest misfortunes as your punishment. They shall fall on you. The Supreme Being is just. He will make you wretched as you have made me. I hope it will be so. I pray for it every day."

Next day, there was another letter. It was written by Constance to Gaufridy, apologizing for Sade's outburst and begging forgiveness. "Forgive a man who is in despair and who has exhausted every means of survival in the past two years." But this apology did nothing to prevent Sade's further rage at Gaufridy's conduct. "Today is Sunday. When going to mass, have you at least asked God to forgive you for the way you have torn me, taunted me, tortured me as you have for the past three years?" However ingeniously he might have juggled philosophies of atheism and moral relativism in Vincennes or the Bastille, Sade's instinctive frame of reference on these occasions was Deist, if not Catholic.

In October 1799, he wrote an official letter to a deputy of the National Assembly, Goupilleau de Montaigu, in which he tried "to offer my talents to the Republic and to do so with all my heart". Behind this lay an attempt to find a home at the Théâtre Français for his unperformed "patriotic tragedy" on the subject of Jeanne d'Arc, *Jeanne Laisné*, written in Vincennes early in

1783. Yet though he described it hopefully as "able to stir a love of country in every heart", the play was not to be performed. His only success was on 12 December when his play *Oxtiern* was performed in the theatre at Versailles with Sade himself playing the part of Fabrice, who frustrates the cynical lechery of Oxtiern. It was in this role that Sade spoke the lines containing the conclusion of his play at Versailles. "I have made the best use of my money by punishing crime and rewarding virtue. Can anyone tell me where else I could have got a higher rate of interest?"

As the winter took its hold on the little garret where Sade and his two companions lived, forty sous from the nearby theatre did little to save them. It was on 26 January that Sade's letter to Gaufridy carried a simple message. "Dying of cold and hunger in the hospital at Versailles for three months." At the time, Sade had been in hospital for only a month but his illness may have predated that. Only his admittance to the hospital had prevented him, as he told Gaufridy, "dying at the street corner" from cold and hunger. Now, almost sixty years old, he was officially classified as "destitute and infirm". However, he recovered sufficiently to return to St Ouen with Constance, only to find two bailiffs in the house. They were there to arrest Sade for debt and consign him to prison. His creditor was evidently Brunelle, the eating-house proprietor of rue de Satory at Versailles, who claimed to have fed Sade during the past year.

By this time, Sade was under surveillance by Commissioner Cazade, investigating his status as a possible *émigré*. It was Cazade who intervened to allow Sade until the end of the month to settle the debt. By a further stroke of fortune, the means to pay had been found. In the Bouches-du-Rhône, the sequestration order on Mas de Cabanes had been lifted. Sade appeared once again to be a man of property.

6

The wheel of fortune spun and Sade found himself relieved of the worst poverty. By the autumn of 1800, *The Crimes of Love* had been published and there was a little money from that. Moreover, the *coup d'état* of November 1799, which had brought Napoléon to power as First Consul, now began to work in favour of families like the Sades. On 16 January 1801 Sade received an amnesty, as a former aristocrat and *émigré*. The order of sequestration was lifted on all his remaining property in the Vaucluse. For a while, he was able to remain in the house at St Ouen with Constance.

This relief was short-lived. On 6 March 1801 he went to the office of his publisher, Nicolas Massé, to discuss business. While they were talking, two men appeared and identified themselves as police officers. The Prefect of Police, Dubois, was informed "that the former Marquis de Sade, known to be the author of the infamous novel *Justine*, intended to continue publishing an even worse book under the title of *Juliette*". Dubois ordered his men to search the premises, having been assured that Sade would be there with the manuscript of the novel. The detail and accuracy of this police information already suggested that it must have come from Massé or someone close to him.

The premises were searched and manuscripts were discovered in Sade's own writing, including *Juliette*. Sade found himself under arrest for the seventh time in thirty-eight years. He and Massé were taken to the Prefecture, where Dubois described the sequel. This involved not only the interrogation of the two men but a search of the house at St Ouen, where Constance was awaiting Sade's return.

The seizure of the manuscript was important but the book had been printed and the aim was to discover this edition. The publisher was promised his freedom if he handed over the printed copies. He led our officers to an uninhabited building known only to himself. They took away a very considerable quantity of copies, enough to suggest that this was the entire printing.

Sade, being questioned, identified the manuscript but insisted that he had only copied it and was not the author. He maintained that he had been paid for copying it. However, he did not know the people who had the original.

It is difficult to believe that a man who has had a considerable fortune would become the transcriber of such appalling books as a means of earning a living. One cannot doubt that he is the author. His study was hung with large pictures depicting the principal obscenities in the novel *Justine*.

For a while, there was some doubt in the literary world as to whether the cause of Sade's arrest was *Juliette* and works of that kind or whether it was his alleged authorship of *Zoloé and the Two Acolytes*. This was a pamphlet published in 1800, mocking Napoléon and Joséphine, though also deriding William Pitt as a man who could be easily bought and sold. There is no evidence that Sade was the author of the pamphlet. The account of Dubois, as well as Sade's own statements, make it clear that it was his fiction which had brought the police to Massé's office. A far greater curiosity of the police raid was the speed with which Massé was set free. There was strong reason to suppose that Massé had done a deal with the authorities, facilitating the arrest of Sade in exchange for his own immunity. At all events, it was Sade who now disappeared into the prison of Sainte-Pélagie and then into Bicêtre.

Constance swore that she would never desert him, though the future looked extremely unpromising. After more than a year in prison, Sade wrote from Sainte-Pélagie on 20 May 1802 to Fouché, "Sade, Man of Letters, to the Minister of Justice". He denied being the author of *Justine*, "in the name of all I hold most sacred". He demanded that he should be tried for writing the novel. If convicted, he would submit to his sentence. If acquitted, he must be set free. Since he was already in prison indefinitely, he had little to lose. Nothing happened. Until the next year he waited in his prison while the great issues of war occupied France and Europe. Then, in February and March 1803, he was reported to have made indecent suggestions to young men who were serving a short sentence for disorderly conduct and who were on the same corridor.

The doors of Sainte-Pélagie opened but only for his short journey through Paris to Bicêtre, one of the worst prisons in the city. Yet Bicêtre housed criminal lunatics and had been under the benevolent superintendence of Philippe Pinel. In a rejection of the traditional and barbaric treatment of the mad, Pinel extended the revolutionary doctrine of liberty by unchaining them and treating their condition by "moral therapy". His patients were no longer to be feared, nor ridiculed, nor pitied, but understood. Moral therapy was the means by which the sane would enter the minds of the mad and endeavour to lead them. In the year of Sade's arrest, Pinel had publicized his ideas in his *Traité sur l'aliénation*. His theory, quickly taken up in England and elsewhere, was a perfect match for the contemporary climate of romantic sensibility and humanitarianism. Bolstered by a physiological science in the new fashion for phrenology, it marked the greatest transformation in the science of mentality since the middle ages.

Perhaps it was not surprising that Sade's stay at Bicêtre was short and that the outcome of it was more humane than he might have expected. The question of whether he was mad or not might have been endlessly discussed. He was obsessive and he cherished visions of sexual violence. But a century and a half later it was to be ruled in the English courts that such things and what had by then become known as "sadism" did not constitute insanity. To other contemporaries Sade's rationality, however unwelcome its conclusions, was evident beyond question. Was he not being locked away because the truths he deduced from human conduct were unwelcome to political leaders, moral evangelists, the sanctimonious young and the self-righteous old?

Under the circumstances, it was not surprising that his family should reach a compromise with the authorities. It was scarcely fitting, now that aristocracy of a sort was rather fashionable again, for the sixty-three-year-old Marquis de Sade to end his days in the physical squalor of an institution like Bicêtre. Whatever Sade's own financial plight, there was enough money to have him taken care of in a modest style. A sum of three thousand livres a year was agreed for his keep. He would be held in conditions of complete security and his family would take no part in petitions for his release. As befitted his rank, he would have a private room and the use of the garden. He would be allowed visitors and Constance would be free to live with him. Dubois reluctantly sanctioned the transfer, describing Sade to the minister as being in a state of "chronic libertine dementia". Yet Dubois resented the transfer of Sade to more comfortable quarters and complained that his state of constant sexual obsession should not be regarded as true lunacy. But the decision had been taken at a higher level. On 27 April 1803, the prisoner left Bicêtre for one more short journey through the eastern fringe of Paris to the hospital of Charenton-Saint-Maurice.

TWELVE

CHARENTON

1

CHARENTON SEEMED A HUMANE SOLUTION. Yet, ominously for Sade, it classified him irrevocably as a lunatic. Even so, he would live in a style that most of his countrymen might have envied, while society would be protected from any more of his outrageous thoughts or fantasies. Whatever problem he might present would soon resolve itself. He had already far exceeded the average span of life among his contemporaries and it seemed unlikely that his existence would be much prolonged. In the meantime, the medical men who specialized in criminal lunacy could scarcely have wished for a more promising subject.

Charles Nodier, who saw Sade transferred to Bicêtre, described him at the time as being enormously obese,

> awkward in his movements, which prevented him from employing the remains of grace and elegance, whose traces were evident in his manners and language. The tired eyes still held a certain brilliance and acuteness, which shone from time to time like a fading spark on dead coal.... He was polite to the point of obsequiousness, affable to that of unctuousness. He spoke respectfully of everything that deserved respect.

Sade had little say in his final transfer on 27 April 1803, though Charenton was infinitely to be preferred to Bicêtre. He would still be subject to surveillance, to searches of his room for undesirable manuscripts or books. He would not be permitted to move freely among the other inmates. But such restrictions would be far less than in a prison. Apart from those who visited him from the world outside, Constance would be free to run errands to the city, bringing him back the books he wanted or such comforts as they could afford.

Naturally, he continued to petition Napoléon and lesser men for his liberty, though his tone was increasingly wistful rather than indignant. The essential freedom for Sade, as one of the true gaolbirds of the eighteenth century, had always been in his own mind and its liberty of expression. Nothing affected him more violently than encroachments upon this. He soon found himself the subject of a disagreement between the director of the asylum and the forces of law. The director of Charenton, the Abbé de Coulmier, held views on mental illness which were as enlightened and humane as Pinel's. Dubois, on the other hand, felt that justice had been thwarted by Sade's transfer. The police therefore exercised their privilege of raiding Sade's room in the asylum and seizing whatever suspect manuscripts they could find. Sade was left in a state of almost incoherent fury.

Yet the Abbé de Coulmier proved to be a man of culture, as well as an agreeable acquaintance. His belief in the cure of alienation by therapy, which he shared with Pinel, extended to a hope that the theatre offered one of the best therapeutic possibilities. Whatever anti-clerical views may have been expressed by the heroes of Sade's fiction, their author unreservedly admired men like Coulmier or Father Massilon, whose sermons he read with enjoyment and whom he saw as distinguishing priests who were humane and intelligent from fanatics and bigots. To the surprise of many and the indignation of a few, Sade returned to the sacraments of the Church. Inspector Dubois was appalled to hear that the infamous author had been allowed to take Communion on Easter Day 1805. Because there were visitors to the chapel, it had been a semi-public occasion. Such a sight, Dubois insisted, was bound to inspire horror in those who saw it and might well have led to a riot.

So far as his own books were concerned, Sade continued to deny authorship of those works in which the darker dramas of his imagination had been described. He now presented two literary personalities to the world. In the first of these, he was the author of *Aline and Valcour, The Crimes of Love, Oxtiern*, numerous unperformed plays, and political pieces including the funeral oration for Marat and Le Pelletier. A good many of those political pieces had, of course, been written on the instructions of the Section des Piques. Those who encountered him at Charenton were convinced that this was the true Sade. The author of *Justine*, in whatever version, as well as *Juliette*, was nowhere to be found.

Having his own well-stocked library in the asylum, Sade turned to the writing of historical fiction. The results were a little dull and not at all pornographic. But he must have assumed by now that his manuscript of *The 120 Days of Sodom* had either perished with the Bastille, in whose wall it was hidden, or else had been committed to the flames by Renée-Pélagie along with whatever else she found objectionable among his prison writings. When, in his room at Charenton, he began to devise a new fiction of this sort, he was not repeating himself but trying to restore a lost work.

It was in the spring of 1806 that Sade began once more to embody the darkest dramas of his mind in fiction. First of all he acknowledged himself as the author of *Justine* and then, as though all his earlier work had been lost, he salvaged fragments and characters from it. He blended these with new material in a narrative of monstrous proportions which took him, by his own account, thirteen months to write. When it was finished, evidently filling about a hundred notebooks, he entitled it *The Days at Florbelle: or, Nature Unveiled*. Set into the main body of the fiction were two stories told by the principal characters, "The Memoirs of the Abbé de Modose" and "The Adventures of Émilie de Volnange". For the main adventures at the château of Florbelle itself, Sade revived characters he had last used in *Philosophy in the Boudoir*. Madame de Mistival was doomed to torments and execution (over which even Sade drew a veil), while her daughter, the fifteen-year-old Eugénie, entered enthusiastically into the practice of every form of sexual aberration. There were episodes which reached a new extravagance even in the scale of Sade's writing, and in which naked women fought wild animals, as though at a Roman spectacle.

In June 1807, soon after the work was finished, the police raided Sade's room at Charenton. They took away a number of manuscripts, including that of his *Days at Florbelle*, alleging that they were blasphemous and obscene. The notebooks containing the novel were added to the collection of Sade's manuscripts in police custody, some of which dated from the raid on Massé's premises in 1801. Sade never saw his confiscated papers again. After his death, matters were settled by his younger son Donatien-Claude-Armand. This younger son, intent on restoring the good name of his family, went to the Ministry of Justice and requested that all such mansucripts as *Days at Florbelle* should be burnt. The authorities agreed. In the presence of the anxious young nobleman, the notebooks went into the flames. The same fate was reserved for some of Sade's manuscripts which Donatien-Claude-Armand discovered in the possession of the Bibliothèque Royale, later the Bibliothèque Nationale.

The sixty-seven-year-old inmate of Charenton might rage as he pleased at this interference in the life of a man of letters. He was in no position to challenge a police search of his room, which would certainly be approved by his family. He would never again be given the chance of completing, let alone publishing, such a narrative as *The Days at Florbelle*. The police were convinced that he was not merely composing a tale for his own amusement; there was, it seemed, a plot to smuggle the completed novel out of Charenton. That would not have been difficult with Constance's assistance. It was then to be sent to Germany and published at Leipzig. Once that had been done, the copies would flood back into France to join the few remaining volumes of *Justine* and *Juliette* that had not been seized from booksellers' shelves. His own family would be no less resolute than the police in trying to prevent a literary outrage of that kind.

On the other hand, there was no official prohibition on Sade writing innocuous novels and publishing them if he could find someone willing to issue them. Such work would at least occupy his mind in wholesome activity. His family had no objection to the starving libertine author of the 1790s being transformed into a literary hack of the new century. The seizure and the eventual destruction of *The Days at Florbelle* signalled the end of his libertine career. From the final bonfire, however, one notebook survived. It was stolen by a benevolent policeman as a present for a friend, a souvenir of the "monster" of Charenton. It contained Sade's notes on his novel, just sufficient to give an outline of the story and some indication of characters and incidents.

For the moment, his guardians led Sade into gentler ways. There had always been something of the antiquary in his nature, as far back as his visit to Dijon in the aftermath of the Rose Keller scandal, when he had spent part of the summer exploring Burgundian archives. As he passed from his sixties into his seventies, the attraction of historical episodes as the subject of fiction appealed to him strongly. As early as the autumn of 1807, after the seizure of his manuscripts, he had begun to plan an historical novel. It was *The Marquise de Gange*, which was published without interference in 1813. It was based on a true story whose origin was in the mid-seventeenth century, during the minority of Louis XIV. The tale presents an innocent and persecuted girl, Euphrasie, Marquise de Gange, against a background of darkness and threatened violence. It had much of the appeal to be found in Gothic novels of the late eighteenth and early nineteenth century, including the writing of the English "Queen of Terrors", Ann Radcliffe, whom Sade much admired. Tormented by the family of her husband, the Marquis de Gange, the heroine is imprisoned, abused and eventually forced by her persecutors to swallow poison. The echoes of *The Misfortunes of Virtue* seem unmistakable, except that in this case heaven strikes down the guilty. The voice which speaks throughout the narrative is that of Sade as public author and moralist.

Following *The Marquise de Gange*, Sade wrote *Adelaide of Brunswick, Princess of Saxony*, in the autumn of 1812. He was now seventy-two and the novel shows that his intellectual powers were markedly weakened. Nor was he much helped by his choice of subject. The characterization is indecisive and the wanderings of the heroine through eleventh-century Europe soon become tedious. The novel remained unpublished until 1954, by which time it had acquired the merit of being a Sadean curiosity. There is, of course, not the least indecency or impropriety in it. Sade's moral is that mankind is rescued from misery only by God's blessings.

A weakness of narrative was also to characterize Sade's last fiction, *The Secret History of Isabelle of Bavaria, Queen of France*. From the spring of 1813 until the autumn of 1814, he was occupied with the writing and revision of this story. Sade presents the queen, in the late fourteenth and early fifteenth centuries, as being something like a real-life Juliette, jubilant in evil of every sort. In her private life, she seeks satisfaction in brothels. In public, she lends herself to a variety of crimes. She assists in the overthrow of Richard II of England and in the death of Jeanne d'Arc. France, meanwhile, suffers the rage of civil strife and the disasters of foreign invasion. With the triumph of Henry V at Agincourt, the nation beomes little more than a pawn of England's sovereign and his policy. But for all the sensationalism of its subject-matter, it is not hard to see why this novel also had to wait until the 1950s for publication.

Sade's most famous occupation at Charenton was the production of plays. It may well have offered a more complete release of his emotional energies than the writing of historical fiction. To posterity, moreover, Sade on stage as director had a movement and glamour absent from Sade the creative writer alone with his thoughts. But the facts do not support the legend. According to Hippolyte de Colins, a cavalry officer who visited Charenton, the idea that plays were principally produced or acted by the inmates was quite false. The production and acting were done by professionals, though some of the inmates like Sade were allowed to play minor parts. For most of the patients, therapy consisted in watching drama rather than in taking part. Colins himself doubted the value of the experiment, fearing that the excitement of the performance was calculated to make the mentally ill more disturbed rather than more tranquil.

Perhaps some of the guests who visited Charenton for these performances may have appreciated the Abbé de Coulmier's progressive views more than the patients themselves had done. Sade certainly invited a number of his acquaintances to the theatre there, including on one occasion Madame de Cochelet who was lady-in-waiting to the Queen of Holland. But it seems that Napoléon's ministers soon began to share Colins's misgivings over the effect of dramatic excitement on the mentally ill. In 1813 further performances of this kind at the asylum were forbidden.

Sade remained devoted to Constance and she to him for the rest of his life. Among his own family, the only member for whom he still felt true sympathy was his elder son, Louis-Marie. Not only was Louis-Marie a patron of music and art, he had even written and published the first volume of a *History of the French Nation*. The young man was an agreeable visitor and might be persuaded to use his influence to obtain his father's freedom. So he might have done. But Louis-Marie was also a patriot and a soldier. He had rejoined the army as France stood against the powers of all Europe. He fought in Napoléon's eastern campaign and was present at the battle of Iena in 1806. The following year, he was mentioned in dispatches. It seemed likely that he would fulfil all the unrealized military ambitions of his father in the 1760s. Then, in 1809, he was one of those sent to police the politically restless Italian provinces of Napoléon's new empire. On 9 July, he was ambushed and killed, near Otranto in Apulia.

It was the end of Sade's hopes. His fate was now to be decided by the censorious younger son, Donatien-Claude-Armand, which put paid to the prospect of release from Charenton. There was, of course, Sade's daughter, Madeleine-Laure, who played little part in his life. She never married and died in 1844 at Echauffour, where she was buried with her mother. Donatien-Claude-Armand was to be his father's heir and in 1808 had decided to marry his cousin, Louise-Gabrielle-Laure de Sade. From his room in Charenton, Sade denounced the match and tried to forbid it. His family reminded the authorities that he was a man whose name had once appeared on the regime's list of *emigrés*. It was absurd to suppose that any action would be taken against him now but it showed how little he could be trusted. The marriage took place without his approval.

After all this, Renée-Pélagie herself died at Echauffour. She was one of the saddest figures in the story of Sade's life and never more so than in her decline. The handsome bride of 1763 had deteriorated from stateliness to corpulence and from that to a form of dropsy. She had also gone blind. It was a long time since Sade had seen her, but the death of his "chère amie" affected him profoundly. Now seventy years old, he had been remote from her for twenty years. Yet the abrasive novelist of middle age who had debunked the folly of compassion was now an old man who wept in his asylum room. Sade was easily moved by the thought of those who had once been close to him. He noted in his private journal that he wept bitterly in 1807 on the fortieth anniversary of his father's death. When Constance was taken ill, he was in tears again at the thought that she might not recover.

Happily she recovered after all. By now she was a comfortable middle-aged lady, going to and fro between Charenton and Paris on her own business or running errands to the city for the elderly nobleman who was her companion. From time to time there were threats that Sade would be sent back to Bicêtre unless his

behaviour improved. Good behaviour had never been characteristic of him. It may have been the thought of separation from
Constance which induced him to check his temper on such occasions and do as his captors ordered. It seems unlikely that these
threats were ever made in earnest. The Sade family remained
opposed to any such move. Donatien-Claude-Armand, now
effectively head of the house, abominated his father's works. Yet
there was a considerable difference between being the son of a
man who was in hospital and the offspring of a convict.

Even in 1809 Sade still hoped that he might be released from
Charenton. He was partially blind and suffering from gout, the
two contemporary scourges of old age for those fortunate enough
to reach it. He also complained of rheumatism. On the strength of
such ill health he wrote to Napoléon and asked for his freedom.
The request was considered and a decision made. Sade must
remain in the asylum for the rest of his natural life. Once that had
been decreed, there was little point in further appeals. Sade and
Constance might make plans for the time when he would be free
once more but these would never be more than daydreams.

The most remarkable feature of Sade's final years at Charenton was kept secret long afterwards, until the publication of his
asylum dairy in 1970. One of the employees at Charenton was
Madame Leclerc, an assistant in the administration of the hospital. This woman had a daughter, Madeleine, who was twelve
yars old when she first attracted Sade's attention in 1808. There
is no indication of any sexual relationship between the twelve-
year-old girl and the sixty-eight-year-old marquis at that time.
When Madeleine was a year or two older, however, her mother
evidently allowed her to become Sade's mistress, if his account is
to be believed. In the arrangement of Sade's quarters at Charenton, Constance had a bedroom of her own, so that Sade was able
to receive the girl in his own room at whatever time he chose.
Madeleine worked as a seamstress by day and paid her visits in
the evening. Perhaps the explanation for the willingness of
Madame Leclerc to sanction the arrangement was explained by
Sade's connection with the theatre and references to the hope of a
stage career for her daughter. Yet it was not merely a matter of
opportunism. When Sade and Constance made their fanciful
plans for life outside Charenton, Madeleine joined in, insisting
she would never leave them.

By the autumn of 1814, Madeleine was seventeen and Sade was seventy-four. Whatever the reason, he had found her a willing pupil in his pleasures. The details which he confided to his diary concerned her state of mind, her behaviour and even such trivial personal observations as the shaving off of her pubic hair. With Constance to run his errands and care for him while Madeleine shared his evening enjoyments, with food and drink, his own library and visitors, Sade managed to combine martyrdom and self-indulgence in a manner that was peculiarly his own. Those who came to see him were sometimes greeted, as Sade had greeted the Archbishop of Paris, with formal praise and welcome. On other occasions he was more relaxed, a rather stout but respectable old gentleman who swore that stories of his authorship of such books as *Justine* were downright calumnies. Dr L.-J. Ramon, who was at Charenton in the last weeks of Sade's life, could not credit that the proud and rather morose old man whom he passed from time to time could be the most notorious author of the past quarter of a century.

On 27 November 1814, Madeleine Leclerc visited him as usual. He had not been particularly well for a week or so and he complained to her about his discomforts. But his young friend endeavoured to take his mind off his troubles. When she left, Sade noted enthusiastically in his private diary that he had enjoyed an evening of complete "libertinage" with her. She promised to come to his room again on Sunday or Monday, which would have been 3 or 4 December. On Thursday 30 November, Sade noted that a bandage had been put on him, possibly for the gout. On Saturday, the day before Madeleine Leclerc's next proposed visit, Donatien-Claude-Armand appeared and spent some time with his father. When he left, he asked Dr Ramon to spend the night in his father's room. The young doctor seemed only too ready to oblige a visitor of such rank and influence.

Later that evening, the Abbé Geoffroy called on the patient and found Sade in an amiable mood. Perhaps the invalid was meditating on Madeleine's visit next day. But Dr Ramon noticed that Sade's chest seemed very congested. In order to give the patient some relief, Ramon helped him to sip a hot herbal infusion. Towards midnight, Sade's breathing grew quieter. Ramon went over to look at him and saw that the old man was dead.

Like so much in his life, the manner of Sade's death was something of an anti-climax. Neither the cliché of deathbed repentance nor the even more fashionable cliché of the virtuous atheist facing extinction without a qualm was to apply to his departure. He had died quietly and unexpectedly, though not with dramatic suddenness. Indeed, he had appointments on the following day with a priest as well as with his seventeen-year-old mistress. Characteristically, he left the rival factions of posterity to make what they liked of him.

Sade had drawn up a will eight years before his death and had included detailed instructions for the disposal of his corpse. His body was to remain for forty-eight hours in the room where he died and the coffin was not to be closed until that period had elapsed. In the state of contemporary medical knowledge, some routine precaution of this kind against premature burial seemed sensible. The body was then to be taken to some thickets on the land that he had purchased at Malmaison after the sale of La Coste and there it was to be buried. He wanted no ceremony and no memorial. The ground was to be planted with acorns so that all traces of the grave would disappear, "as I hope my memory will be effaced from the minds of men, except for those few who were kind enough to love me to the end and of whom I carry to the grave a most tender memory". In more material terms, he left a legacy to his faithful Constance who had now been his companion for twenty-four years. Despite the years of poverty, he had now regained sufficient of his property to make this provision for her.

As with most of his literary works, Sade's will gave rise to fiercely argued ambiguities. He wished to be buried with no ceremony. Did this mean without ceremony or without a ceremony? It was a nice distinction, which his son briskly resolved by ignoring the entire provision. Sade was buried in the cemetery of Charenton, according to the rites of the Church, and a stone cross was erected over his grave. The question of whether he spoke the truth when he claimed that he portrayed vice only to justify Providence, or whether he was truly the champion of vice and crime, remained an open question. The religious ceremony and the stone cross might be a tribute to the moralist or a finely calculated vengeance upon their author by Justine and her sisters in suffering. Whatever the answer, there was an aptness in the disposal of Sade's remains. It seemed entirely in keeping with his works that posterity should never know whether tribute or vengeance was marked by the stone cross at Charenton.

Posterity had not heard the last of Sade's remains. Some years later, it was necessary to exhume the bodies buried in that particular part of the cemetery. Dr Ramon attended out of curiosity when he heard that Sade's turn had come. He managed to possess himself of the skull. Later he submitted this for examination by Spurzheim, the phrenologist, who studied the cranium and delivered his opinion as to the character of the man whose brain it had once held. Spurzheim concluded that there were no signs of excessive sexual desire, nor of belligerence, nor of cruelty. The two most prominent characteristics, in this diagnosis, were benevolence and religious faith. The cranium was "similar in all respects to that of a Father of the Church".

Both the grave and the skull disappeared. The latter was said to have been taken to America, where casts of it were made for the teaching of anatomy and phrenology. These casts were sold as examples of a particular type – benevolence and religous faith – without the students having any idea that they were actually examining the brain-case of the notorious Marquis de Sade.

The eventual disappearance of his grave belatedly fulfilled Sade's wish for unmarked burial. He was unlikely to be without a memorial of a different kind and, to that extent, his will expressed a false modesty. The most elaborate tomb in Notre Dame would not have carried his fame to one per cent of those who knew him as the author of *Justine* or through the universal term "sadism". The unmarked cross was removed from Charenton but Sade had composed his own epitaph long before. It revealed astuteness of a kind that he had seldom showed so plainly, anticipating those qualities in his reputation which were to make him, whether feared or admired, an object of interest and fascination to posterity.

> You who pass by,
> Kneel here and say a prayer,
> Close to the most wretched of men.
> He was born in the last century,
> And he died in our own.

Tyranny, with hideous face,
Made war on him at every time.
Like a foul beast, under the King's law,
It would have torn his life away.
Under the Terror, it rose once more
To bear Sade away to death's abyss.
Under the Consul it lived again,
And Sade remained its eternal victim.

Sade was apt to see himself, with self-indulgent exaggeration, as the central figure in an heroic tragedy of martyrdom. Yet this scarcely diminishes the power of his complaint. The opposed factions who were to debate his heroism or infamy might argue for all eternity as to who was the persecutor and who the victim. But when the opposing propositions were locked in equal force, only the suffering remained beyond dispute.

THIRTEEN

THE BOOKS

LEAVING ASIDE HIS PERIPHERAL WORK as political secretary for the Section des Piques, his ceremonial verses and unperformed dramas, Sade's literary achievements were of two kinds. First there was the public figure of Sade, the successor of Richardson or the rival of Voltaire in *The Misfortunes of Virtue*, or the "French Boccaccio" in his shorter tales. In the same public guise there was Sade the historical novelist of some of the darkest and most bloodstained pages of French history, though this was a genre in which he was least successful. Despite the dark reputation of his moral ironies and erotic cruelties, Sade was often the proponent of a conventional morality, no less in the opening of *Justine* than in the first lines of "Eugénie de Franval", from *The Crimes of Love*, a Gothic tale of incest and retribution.

> To enlighten mankind and improve its morals is the only lesson which we offer in this story. In reading it, may the world discover how great is the peril which follows the footsteps of those who will stop at nothting to satisfy their desires. Let them learn that a good education, wealth, talents, the gifts of nature are only likely to lead them astray when discretion, good conduct, wisdom, and modesty afford them no support or are disparaged. Such is the truth which we shall demonstrate. We hope to be forgiven for having to discuss the monstrous details of an atrocious crime. Yet how can one ensure a revulsion at such moral deviations, if one lacks the courage to present the naked truth?

Then there was the private Sade who, despite such protestations of depicting vice only in order to champion virtue, seemed to be the secret chronicler of cruelty triumphant. The same story, which in *The Misfortunes of Virtue* was said to justify the ways of Providence to mankind, was easily exploited to celebrate the victory of tyranny, crime, and torment over the helpless and the innocent. The world unveiled in *The 120 Days of Sodom* or in *Juliette* was devoid of God, benevolence and morality, whatever pretext of moral instruction Sade might offer as narrator. Alone in this darkened universe, where suffering was the first law, a man must decide between the roles of torturer or victim. There could, in logic, be no other option.

By a philosophical irony, it was in these books in which his heroes most energetically debunked the superstitions of traditional Christianity that, as Flaubert suggested, Sade restored the very pains of hell which were so elaborately depicted in the Middle Ages and which had become so obnoxious to the Enlightenment. "If God did not exist," Voltaire had said, "it would be necessary to invent Him." As though in a scornful parody of this, it seemed as if Sade demonstrated the importance of the pains of hell in a more humane culture. He entertained his readers with accounts of his villains giving the heroine a douche or enema of boiling oil, introducing red-hot tongs into her body or making her swallow live coals. "Using a pair of well-heated tongs, he nips her flesh, concentrating on her bottom, her breasts and her mons veneris." The details happen to come from *The 120 Days of Sodom* but they would be entirely in place in a painting by Hieronymus Bosch or in the theologically approved visions of hellfire. In a different context and in a different age, the mere cruelties of Sade's fiction might have seemed visionary rather than obscene.

It was, of course, an error of judgment to bring forward eternal punishment so that it began in the temporal world and was applied to those whose fault was to be beautiful and virtuous. But that error was generally reserved for those works which he hid, or denied, or omitted from the bibliography of his writings. Perhaps the most significant of these might have been acknowledged by him had it not been first "warmed up" and then expanded further into a monstrous picaresque.

1. *The Misfortunes of Virtue*

Though he was well advanced with *Aline and Valcour* when this shorter novel was written, *The Misfortunes of Virtue* may be taken as Sade's first surviving novel to be completed. Its 138 manuscript pages were written in a fortnight of fictional inspiration during his detention in the Bastille and finished on 8 July 1787. Its sweep and concision give the sense of themes fitting easily into place with the poetic aptness of a philosophical fiction. Novels framed in such a way are apt to flow effortlessly from their author's minds, though Sade's facility was still no match for Samuel Johnson who, according to Boswell, wrote *Rasselas* in the evenings of a single week to pay the costs of his mother's funeral. Despite the notoriety of its later versions, *The Misfortunes of Virtue* remained unpublished until 1930.

In its opening sentences, Sade explains the ostensible purpose of his book.

> Philosophy's triumph would be to illuminate the darkness shrouding those methods which Providence employs to accomplish the destiny of man. This would then lay down some pattern of behaviour, revealing to the wretched two-legged creature who is continually buffeted by her arbitrary whims, the manner in which he must interpret the laws of Providence in his own case. It would show the path he must follow in order to avoid the bizarre dictates of that fate which we call by a score of different names without ever being able to settle upon a single definition.

As in subsequent versions, most of the book is the story which the young, beautiful and virtuous "Sophie", alias Justine, tells her sister Juliette. Rejected by friends of her family and by respectable employers, after her parents' death, she is falsely accused of theft. She escapes from prison when a female criminal, Dubois, sets fire to the building, and becomes an unwilling associate of Dubois and her male accomplices. Sophie evades the gang and is discovered hiding in a wood by the homosexual Bressac and his partner. Bressac involves her in a plan to poison his mother, who becomes his aunt in the later version of the novel. The virtuous girl tries to frustrate this. In revenge, Bressac and his friend flog her and leave her destitute. The murder is committed and Bressac becomes rich. Sophie is received into the house of the surgeon Rodin, who advances the science of medicine by vivisecting girls to observe their reactions to pain. When Sophie endeavours to rescue one of them, Rodin uses a branding-iron, marking her as a thief, and sends her away.

Still a virgin and still virtuous, Sophie finds sanctuary with the fathers of Ste Marie des Bois, near Auxerre. Her misfortunes now have something of the comic inevitability attending Candide's disappointments in Voltaire's novel. The fathers are libertines who have entrapped an entire harem of young girls. Every form of sexual irregularity is practised upon these pupils and, as one of the girls remarks, the only form of penance is the whip. Sophie loses her virginity, though not before being penetrated in every other way. Then she is set free. The harem of Ste Marie des Bois is broken up because two of the fathers have been rewarded with offices of wealth and influence in the Church.

Sophie is next seized by a gang of coiners, including the murderous Dalville whose achievement is to shoot his mistress in such a way that she lingers in agony for a considerable time before dying. When the gang is arrested, the virtuous Sophie is taken as well. After encountering the female criminal Dubois again, as well as one of the fathers of Ste Marie des Bois, she arrives at Lyon, accused of theft, murder and arson. It is then that she is seen by Juliette, Comtesse de Lorsange, herself an unsuspected murderess. Intrigued by the girl, Juliette asks to hear her story. When it is over, she recognizes Sophie as her sister Justine. All is put right and the much-abused heroine is released, though only to be struck dead soon afterwards by a well-aimed thunderbolt. Yet despite the harsh trials imposed on her by Providence, despite suffering and even death itself, virtue alone remains admirable.

Juliette, Comtesse de Lorsange, left the house at once, taking some of the money with her, and ordered her carriage to be prepared. She left the remainder to Monsieur de Corville, intimating that she wished to make certain pious legacies. She sped to Paris and entered the Carmelite convent where, at the end of a few years, she became a pattern and an example to all, as much by her great piety as by the wisdom of her spirit and the extreme propriety of her behaviour. . . . O you who read this story, may you draw from it the same benefit as this worldly but reformed woman. May you grow to believe, as she did, that the only true happiness is in the bosom of virtue, and that if God permits virtue to be persecuted upon earth, it is only to prepare it for a more glorious reward in heaven.

Apart from its role as a philosophical fiction, there was another literary dimension to *The Misfortunes of Virtue*, which was exploited later to boost the popularity of *Justine*. The theme of beauty and virtue in distress ran strongly in European fiction, from the publication of Samuel Richardson's *Pamela: or, Virtue Rewarded* in 1740–41. It was exemplified in Richardson's second novel *Clarissa* (1756) and rather more cynically by Laclos in *Les Liaisons Dangereuses* in 1782. At a more popular level, it dominated the Gothic novel, with which Sade's fiction showed an affinity and for which he expressed his admiration through praise of its writers. He thought even Mrs Radcliffe's "brilliant imagination", as he called it, was surpassed by Matthew Gregory Lewis in the more blatant sexuality of *The Monk*, which called forth an indictment from the attorney-general on its publication in London in 1796.

The connection between the Gothic novel and the fiction of sadism, even within the prudish limits of English culture, was closer than either its readers or providers cared to admit. In 1798 the Minerva Press, a bastion of literary culture for the female reader, published *The New Monk*. The convent of St Clare's in Lewis's novel was unmasked as Mrs Rod's boarding-school for young women, complete with illicit and overheated passion, as well as a flogging-room for retribution. "Who knows what may have been going on between you!" says Mrs Rod to Alice, "I'll skin you, Madam; and we will shortly see whether this love can't be flogged out of you: this comes of your novel reading; away with her to the flogging-room; tell the porter to tuck up his shirt sleeves, for he shall have a whole evening's work of it." Joshua Pentateuch, a Methodist preacher who intercepted the lover's note, remarks, "I have done my duty and should have liked to have done the porter's also."

The New Monk not only shows the subtle interplay of the Gothic and the sadistic in the fiction of the day. It also brings into full light the extent to which English Gothic was merely a hot-house version of the passions and vicissitudes of the middle-class mothers and daughters who had made it such a commercial success. Because it existed for female middle-class readers, the

Gothic novel took their domestic experience and dressed it in extravagant fashion to give a sense of vicarious adventure. Despite gloomy castles set against the forked lightning of Apennine skies, despite sinister sights and distant groans, the tales end contentedly and with propriety. Villains with names like Montoni or Schedoni prove to be no worse than disagreeable uncles or unsympathetic fathers. The heroines are sensible middle-class girls with names like Julia and Emily. The trembling beauty imprisoned in the tyrant's lair is a fancy-dress version of the troublesome daughter sent to bed without supper. The vaults of San Stephano at Naples, woken by the distant cries of tortured victims, are no more than the bedroom echoing to the self-pity of the spoilt and ill-mannered daughter. It was left to Sade and those who had seen something of true political horror to do justice to the genre.

Sade's judgments on the Gothic novel appeared in *The Crimes of Love* in 1800. *The Misfortunes of Virtue* was written two years before Ann Radcliffe's first publication and a decade before her most famous novels, *The Mysteries of Udolpho* (1794) and *The Italian: or, The Confessional of the Black Penitents* (1797). Yet this form of popular fiction had flourished in England at least since the publication of Horace Walpole's *Castle of Otranto* in 1764 and its influence was more evident when Sade rewrote his first novel as *Justine*.

Sade, in 1800, identified the weakness of such fiction for the comfortable middle class of England, its wives and daughters pampered and sheltered from the grosser realities of European life in the last decade of the eighteenth century. "There was not a single person who had not experienced greater misfortune in four or five years than the most famous novelist in literature could paint in a century. So it was necessary to call upon the assistance of Hell in order to compound the interest and to find in the realm of fantasy those things which we know only too well by investigating the everyday life of mankind in this age of steel." The gentility of English Gothic was impossible in Sade's French vision. Moreover, the sensibility of romanticism, the delicate emotions of heroes and heroines in fiction of the later eighteenth century, made such figures in the novel more eligible for the ordeals and torments of a fiercer reality. Sensibility, which Jane Austen was to mock in *Sense and Sensibility*, also made the heroines of literature better suited to Sade's purposes than their robust ancestresses had been.

Sade's descriptions of Ste Marie des Bois or the fortress of Roland may anticipate the scenery of Ann Radcliffe at Udolpho or the vaults of San Stephano in *The Italian*. But for Sade's virtuous and beautiful heroine there is no rescue nor a benevolent revelation that all was well from the beginning. The encircling horror ends in rape or sodomy, the whip or the branding-iron, the reality of Bourbon repression mingling with revolutionary violence.

Even in the milder pages of *The Misfortunes of Virtue*, when Dalville leads Sophie to the château of the coiners, the Radcliffean landscape is a mere prelude to things unknown in milder Gothic fiction. As in the abduction by Roland in *Justine*, Dalville and his beautiful victim pass through mountain gorges until the grim building appears, "perched on the very edge of a most frightful precipice and, balanced as it seemed to be on the sharp pinnacle of rock, suggesting a habitation of ghosts rather than of living beings". Beyond this scenery of romantic picturesque, the heroine is soon a prisoner in Dalville's château. Unthinkable in the domestic Gothic fiction of the bourgeoisie, Sophie is unceremoniously stripped and harnessed to the wheel with the other girls. In this situation, they are unable to avoid the fondling by the other bandits or the thrashings inflicted by Dalville's whip.

In an even greater shock to the sensibilities of conventional Gothic, Sade contrives a certain attachment between the heroine and some of her persecutors, as if to suggest a vein of masochism in Sophie. She is drawn to Bressac, who rewards her by indifference to such affection and has her flogged. He is a woman-hater and a homosexual, the one man in the course of the narrative whom she can never have. She shows a certain attachment to Dubois and even a glimmer of interest in Antonin, one of the fathers of Ste Marie des Bois. Beyond any personal allegiance is her loyalty to her virtue and to the suffering she endures on its behalf. At her first meeting with Dubois, Sophie swears that she would rather suffer any pains which accompany her virtuous conduct than enjoy the wealth of this world which may come from crime. It was Sade's claim that she would be rewarded in heaven. In terms of later theories of masochism, however, it might be wondered whether she did not enjoy a more immediate reward in the pages of his novel.

2. *Aline and Valcour*

The longest of his publicly acknowledged works, Sade's "philosophical novel" occupied him in the Bastille from 1785 until 1788. It was published in eight volumes in 1795, after the printing had been interrupted by the arrest and execution of its publisher, Girouard.

The plan of the novel was that it should contain a series of letters, in the manner of Richardson, describing the ill-starred love of Aline and Valcour, very much in the style of *Clarissa*, which Sade had already read and admired. The situation of the characters is conventional enough. Aline is the daughter of the Président de Blamont. She falls in love with the poor but virtuous Valcour. Her mother favours the match but it is opposed by the materialistic and sensual Blamont. He arranges instead a marriage between the pure-hearted Aline and one of his cronies, a debauched and thrice-widowed financier, Dolbourg. Blamont uses every means to impose his will on Aline, as well as on his own wife, whom he at last arranges to have poisoned by a seduced maidservant of his own. He attempts to bribe and then to murder Valcour. Finally, Blamont and Dolbourg take Aline away to a remote house in order to use further persuasion upon her. Alone and at their mercy, Aline resorts to the one means of remaining true to herself and Valcour: she commits suicide.

The story contains a number of minor female characters, the most interesting of whom is Sophie. Blamont believes her to be his illegitimate daughter but does not hesitate to beat her and to abuse her sexually, thus adding a suggestion of incest which is characteristic of a number of Sade's tales in *The Crimes of Love*, written at that time. In the novel, however, suggestion is confounded when Blamont discovers that Sophie is not his child after all.

Aline and Valcour, in its main plot, is another elaborate account of virtue in distress. The characterization shows Sade at his best and is a creditable attempt to develop the novel of sentiment from the point at which Samuel Richardson had left it. But the long unwinding of the principal story is overshadowed by two colourful travellers' tales, so bizarre in detail and vigorous in telling that they steal a good deal of the reader's attention from the principal characters.

Sainville's tale is something like an extension of the fourth book of *Gulliver's Travels*, debunking the moral conventions of European society by comparing them with those of more primitive civilizations. But it was as though Swift's narrative had been revised in the light of Captain Cook's voyages. Cook even features briefly in the novel when it is thought that the missing Léonore may be on board HMS *Discovery*. In visiting West Africa and Tamoe in the Pacific, Sainville discovers bizarre and barbarous cultures, presented to much the same purpose as Swift had used the Yahoos and the Houyhnhnms in Captain Gulliver's adventures. Sade's characteristic theme is that there can be no such thing as a universal moral code based solely upon the laws and customs of human society. Hence, morality and virtue at this level are a logical absurdity. Sainville is introduced to the customs of Butua by Sarmiento, a Portuguese who has "gone native", as the narrative describes him.

As we talked, Sarmiento led me from room to room, so that I saw the whole of the palace, except for the secret harems, which contained the most beautiful specimens of both sexes, but where no mere mortal was permitted to intrude.

"All the prince's girls," Sarmiento continued, "twelve thousand of them all told, are divided into four classes. He assigns them to these groups when they pass into his hands from the man who chooses them for him. The tallest girls, those who are strongest and well built, make up the detachment which forms the palace guard. The group known as 'The Five Hundred Slavegirls' is made up of a type subordinate to the guards I mentioned. They are usually between twenty and thirty years old, and they are responsible for serving the prince in the palace, as well as looking after the gardens. As a rule they are made to perform menial tasks. The third class is made up of girls between the ages of sixteen and twenty, who assist at the sacrifices. It is from this group that victims are chosen to be sacrificed to the gods. The fourth class contains the most delicately beautiful and pretty girls under the age of sixteen. It is among these that girls are found to provide the prince's personal pleasures. If there were any white-skinned girls, they would be of this kind."

"And have there been any?" I interrupted hastily.

"Not as yet," replied the Portuguese, "But the prince is most eager for them. He employs every means at his disposal to obtain them."

And, at these words, hope seemed to be reborn in my heart.

"Despite the groupings," the Portuguese continued, "All the girls, whatever class they may be in, cannot appease the cruelty of their tyrant. When he chooses one of them, he sends an officer to give her a hundred strokes of the whip. This sign of favour resembles the giving of the handkerchief by the Sultan of Byzantium. It informs the chosen girl of the honour which awaits her. In due course she goes to the palace where he attends her. As he makes use of a great number of girls in one day, a good many of them receive the message I have described to you every morning."

I shuddered at this. "Oh, Léonore," I said to myself, "If you have fallen into the hands of this monster, and since I cannot shield you, can it be that your bodily charms which I worship have been ignominiously thrashed in this manner?". . . .

I followed my guide. He led me into a cottage built rather in the style of the prince's apartments, though much less spacious. Two young negroes served our supper on reed mats. We sat in the African manner, for our Portuguese had gone completely native, adopting the morals and all the customs of the nation among whom he found himself.

A piece of roast meat was brought, and my pious gentleman having said grace (for that superstition never leaves a Portuguese), he offered me a slice of the joint which had been placed on the table.

An involuntary shiver seized me, despite myself.

"Brother," I said, with a disquiet I could not conceal, "swear to me on the word of a European. Could the dish you are serving me be, by any chance, a slice of the hips or buttocks of one of those girls whose blood streamed over your master's altar a little while ago?"

"What?" replied the Portuguese coolly. "Would such trivialities put you off? Do you really think that you can live here without submitting to the customs of the country?"

"You blackguard!" I cried, getting up from the table with my stomach turning, "Your feast makes me shudder! I would die rather than touch it! Is this the hideous dish upon which you dared to ask heaven's blessing? Vile man! When you combine crime and superstition in such a manner, it's clear that you aren't trying to conceal which country you come from! Keep away from me! I should have recognized you for what you are without your assistance!"

I was about to leave the house in terror but Sarmiento held me back.

"Wait," he said, "I forgive your revulsion. Let's attribute it to your habits of mind or your patriotic prejudices. But you take it too far. You must stop making difficulties and adjust to your actual situation. My good friend, revulsion is merely a weakness, a minor defect of our make-up which we neglected to cure ourselves of when young, and which seizes us if we yield to it. . . . I was just like you when I arrived here, full of national prejudices. I found fault with everything and maintained that it was all absurd. The customs of the people frightened me quite as much as their morals. And yet now I behave exactly as they do. We are much more creatures of habit than of inherited nature, my friend. Nature merely created us, it is habit which shapes us. It is madness to believe that such a thing as moral goodness exists. All sorts of behaviour, from one extreme to the other, are good or bad according to the country which makes the judgment. A sensible man who wants to live an agreeable life will adapt himself to whatever climate he happens to be in. When I was in Lisbon, I would have behaved as you do now. Here in Butua, I behave as the negroes do. What the devil do you want me to give you for your supper, if you won't eat the food which everyone else eats? I have got an old monkey, though he'll be very tough. I'll have him grilled for you."

Whether or not such passages are a demonstration of black humour depends much on the reader's prejudices. To those who find flesh of any species as revolting a food as any other graveyard remains, the nice difference between the tastes of carnivores and cannibals may seem comic. To carnivores, however, the humour may be strained. At any level, Sade matches the extravagance of utopian satire to be found in Swift or in Samuel Butler's *Erewhon*. It thrives on the quite illogical preferences of the European meat-eater for cows, sheep or even pigs, as opposed to rats, mice, cats, dogs or even a succulent young girl. The closest parallel is not in Sade's other work but perhaps in Swift's *Modest Proposal* of 1729 with its scheme for making the starving population of Ireland self-sufficient by eating those of their children who have not already been consumed by absentee English landlords.

In allowing Sarmiento to continue Sainville's education, Sade returns repeatedly to his theme of women as a subject race and the absurdity of showing admiration or leniency towards those who become pregnant. Pregnancy, in this view, is a mere bodily function and is no more worthy of praise or blame than digestion or excretion. It is as logical to mock or punish pregnancy as to encourage or protect it. An overpopulated country may see it as a crime against society. It is this view which Butua endorses. A pregnant woman is regarded as an object for mockery and abuse. Pregnancy impedes the woman's other labours which, as Sainville witnesses, include being harnessed to a plough and driven by her husband's whip.

The story of Léonore, separated from her lover Sainville, is full of incident but dull by comparison with his adventures in Butua. The high point of her drama occurs when she is awaiting execution, disguised as an African boy, before the king of Sennar. She and her companion Dom Gaspard, as well as a party of men and women, have committed the capital crime of travelling too close to a temple where "the organ of Mahomet" is kept. The king and his harem have now gathered to watch the entertainment of the executions which are to be accomplished by the anal impaling of the victims with a pike. Dom Gaspard tries to save Léonore by presenting her with her face and neck blackened as a boy from a friendly African nation. The king, however, insists that she must be executed with the others. Nor is he moved by the young Arab women who throw themselves at his feet. The king assures them that he will take "the greatest possible pleasure in seeing if they could endure the torture prepared for them as well as the men". Yet Léonore lives to recall an escape which was as much a surprise to her as it is to the reader.

All my thoughts turned to Sainville. "Oh, unhappy lover," I cried, "I shall never see you more. What will happen here is worse than any knife in a Venetian dungeon. Let me die soon, by all means. But to die impaled!" And my tears flowed copiously, though as Gaspard forgot his own peril in mine his hand never ceased to wipe them away. The same despair prevailed throughout our little group. The men swore and stormed. The women, who were always gentler even during their suffering, merely sobbed and cried. There was nothing but oaths and crying to be heard in that sad room, which no doubt made sweet music in the ears of the executioner who was to sacrifice us. Indeed, he and his women had come to dine in an adjoining room, so that they might listen to us at leisure.

At last the fatal hour arrived when we were to be delivered to death. I could not hear it strike without a shudder and I held fast to Gaspard. It seemed that as he was going to die as well, he might be better able to support me. The king took his place and surveyed the arena of death. The monster watched the execution of two Turks, four Europeans, and of the four Arab girls. There remained Gaspard and I. They came for me first. . . .

The ritual certainly had little enough resemblance otherwise to the way in which one chastises children. But it was necessary to lay bare that part which lies just below the small of the back. This is done so that nothing shall get in the way of the pike being thrust into the place chosen for the torment. Before the eyes of the monarch, everything covering the part required for this act was removed. But imagine my feelings, after they had seen me stripped, when I heard a tumult of cries throughout the entire crowd. The executioner himself drew back from me in horror. Overcome by my own fear, I had never thought of the dismay I should create by presenting a bottom that was perfectly white to match a face that was black as could be.

The terror was universal among them. Some took me for a god, others for a magician. But they one and all fled. The king alone, being a little less credulous than the rest, ordered me to be brought for his immediate inspection. Gaspard was fetched. The interpreters came forward and I was asked what might be signified by my piebald appearance, of which Nature had never before furnished a single example. There was no means of deceiving them. The truth must be told. The king made me wash myself in front of him and put on women's clothing. Unhappily, he found me to his taste in this new guise and informed me that I must prepare myself to undergo the honour of serving his pleasures that very night.

Needless to say, both Sainville and Léonore survive to return to Europe and bring to an astonished Age of Enlightenment the news of those dark practices sanctioned by nature and logic in remoter parts of the world.

3. *The Crimes of Love* and *Stories, Tales, and Fables*

All Sade's work as a writer of short stories and novellas, "The French Boccaccio", may conveniently be taken together. *The Crimes of Love*, four volumes with an essay on the novel, was issued during his lifetime in 1800. The collection *Stories, Tales, and Fables* was not published until 1927. The two titles make up a common stock of Sade's short fiction, from which he drew the more tragic or melodramatic stories for publication in 1800.

Some of his comments on the eighteenth-century novel have already been quoted. He praises English fiction, particularly the work of Richardson and Fielding, "who have taught us that nothing but a profound study of the human heart, that veritable labyrinth of nature, can inspire the novelist". Richardson, in this view, demonstrates in *Clarissa* that fiction needs no facile triumph of the good in order to show men the beauty of virtue and the ugliness of vice. "If the immortal Richardson, at the end of twelve or fifteen volumes, had come to a *virtuous* ending by converting Lovelace and *quietly* marrying him to Clarissa, would the reader have shed the delicious tears, now drawn from every sensitive creature, if the novel had been turned about in that manner?"

Sade, of course, sees the Gothic novel and its extravagant terrors as "the inevitable consequence of the revolutionary shocks which the whole of Europe has felt". But the specific sexuality and horror of M. G. Lewis in *The Monk* is therefore more persuasive to Sade than the more reassuring domestic fiction of Mrs Radcliffe. In another area of revolutionary fiction, Sade glances at his adversary, Restif de la Bretonne, finding in him "a mean, pedestrian style, adventures of the most disgusting kind, always gathered from the worst society: in short, a gift for nothing but long-windedness, for which only the dealers in 'hot pornography' are grateful to him." And with such gadflies as Restif in mind,

Sade protests, "Let no man any longer attempt to credit *me* with the authorship of *Justine*. I have never written books of that sort and I vow that I never shall."

The dark dramas of *The Crimes of Love* vary in quality and achievement. Yet a theme of incest threads them. In "Florville and Courval", the heroine unwittingly becomes her father's second wife and is seduced by her brother. In "Dorgueville", the relationship is again between brother and sister. In "Laurentia and Antonio", a Renaissance tale of the Strozzi family, it is the father who attempts to corrupt his son's wife while Antonio is away at the wars. The most powerful of the stories, "Eugénie de Franval", describes how the heroine is corrupted from childhood by her father to serve his pleasures, which she does at fourteen years old, despite the efforts of a devoted mother to shame them both into virtuous conduct. Eugénie is taught to despise the principles of virtue and to hate her mother as a rival for her father's affection. Like a number of the stories, this "tragic tale" relies on the Gothic trappings of setting and melodrama. The theme of the stories may have seemed shocking but there is little in their descriptions that could be objected to. Their morality is unexceptionable, the guilty and even the innocently deceived perish in the vindication of virtue and the castigation of vice. Sade omitted certain passages from the published version in 1800, though even the account of Franval's first night with his fourteen-year-old daughter seems mild enough compared with the scenes in some of Sade's other published fiction.

Franval, who according to the character which we know him to have was graced with such delicacy only to become a more skilful seducer, soon abused the credulity of his daughter. With all obstacles swept aside, as much by the principles with which he had nourished this open heart by so many instructions as by the art with which he triumphed over it in this last moment, he achieved his wicked conquest. He became with impunity the destroyer of a virginity of which nature and his own title as father had entrusted to him the protection. Several days passed in this mutual infatuation. Eugénie was of an age to experience the pleasure of love. Encouraged by Franval's arguments, she gave herself to him recklessly. Franval revealed to her all the mysteries. He showed her all the ways. The more his homage increased, the better he ensnared his prey. She would have wished to receive that homage in a thousand sanctuaries at the same time. She chided the imagination of her lover for not being wayward enough. She complained of her age and of an innocence which perhaps did not render her sufficiently seductive. And if she wished to be better taught, it was only in order that no means of arousing her lover should remain unknown to her.

Sade also removed from the story, as he had written it during his nights of solitude in the Bastille, the account of Eugénie erotically positioned in a bedroom tableau to be viewed by Franval's fellow conspirator Valmont.

Everything was ready to set Valmont's mind at rest and the encounter took place about an hour later in Eugénie's own room. There, in this richly decorated chamber, Eugénie was on a pedestal, presenting herself as a maiden savage, exhausted after hunting and leaning on the trunk of a palm tree. Its raised branches hid an infinite number of lamps, placed in such a way that their reflections fell only on the charms of this beautiful girl, highlighting them and showing them off as if by the greatest art. This example of intimate theatre, this living statue, appeared surrounded by a channel of water six feet wide. It acted as a defence for the young female savage and prevented her from being approached on any side. At the edge of this moat was placed the chevalier's armchair. A silk cord was attached to it. By moving this cord it was possible to turn the pedestal in such a way that the object of his adoration could be seen from every side. Her posture was such that in whatever way she was turned, she always presented herself agreeably.

The count, hidden behind an ornamental thicket, was able to watch his mistress and his friend at the same time. The examination, according to their late agreement, would last for half an hour. Valmont sat down, enchanted by the scene. He swore that so many charms had never been offered to his sight before. He yielded to the excitements which roused him. The silk cord moved incessantly to bring him delights at every moment. He did not know which to sacrifice to, which to choose. All was so beautiful in Eugénie. However, the minutes passed quickly, as they do in such circumstances. The hour struck. The chevalier abandoned himself and the incense flew to the feet of the goddess, whose sanctuary was forbidden him. A gauze curtain fell and it was time to withdraw.

Eroticism of this sort, let alone scenes of Eugénie's contemptuous rejection of her mother's love in favour of her father's sexual attentions, would have found no place in the gentle English Gothic of Clara Reeve or Ann Radcliffe.

Madame de Franval bribed one of Eugénie's maids. A pension, a promising future, a sense of doing right, won the servant-girl's allegiance. She undertook that Madame de Franval should have proof of her misfortunes on the next night.

The time came. The unhappy mother was shown into an adjoining closet of the apartment where her treacherous husband outraged heaven and his own marriage vows every night. A few candles were left burning on a corner-table to illuminate the crime. The altar was prepared and the victim positioned herself upon it. The man who was to put her to the sacrifice followed. Madame de Franval had no resources but despair, outraged love, and courage. She burst open the doors which confined her, threw herself into the room, and there fell weeping on her knees before the incestuous couple. She cried at Franval,

"Oh, you who have brought such sorrow to my life, from whom I have never deserved such treatment, whom I still adore despite the injuries you have done me, see my tears and do not reject me! I beg for mercy for this poor girl. Deceived by her own frailty and by your enticements, she hopes to find happiness in the very bosom of shamelessness and crime. Eugénie! Eugénie! Will you plunge a dagger into that very breast which gave you life? Do not be drawn deeper into a punishment which is still hidden from you! Come to me! My arms are open to receive you! See your unhappy mother on her knees, begging you not to outrage honour and nature at the same time! But if the pair of you refuse me," continued the forlorn woman, placing a knife to her heart, "see how I shall escape the injuries which you intend to inflict upon me. My blood shall spurt upon you, and you will have to consummate your crime on my sad corpse!"

Those who had begun to understand the scoundrel Franval might easily believe that his callous soul would resist this sight. What was inconceivable was that Eugénie should remain unaffected by it.

"Madame," said the depraved little girl, showing the cruellest indifference, "I assure you that I regard the slanders you direct against your husband as being complete nonsense. Is he not the master of his own actions? And if he approves of my conduct, what right have you to blame me? Just think of your own fun and games with Monsieur de Valmont. Did we disturb your amusements then? Kindly allow us to enjoy our pleasures, or else don't be surprised if I ask your husband to ensure that you leave us alone."

Franval does not have to be asked. Having dragged his wife out of the room by her hair, he throws her down the stairs and leaves her to be found, unconscious, by one of her servants. Some months later, he instructs Eugénie to poison her. But vice is punished at last, when Eugénie dies of remorse and Franval himself commits suicide. The climax of the story is superbly and darkly coloured, Franval returning through the dark forest in his search for his wife and daughter, the funeral bell tolling through the storm. "Night continued to veil the forest . . . a mournful chant was heard, the pale light of torches abruptly pierced the gloom, throwing a glimmer of horror which can only be imagined by sensitive souls." Two coffins are being borne to their burial. Eugénie has poisoned Madame de Franval on her father's instructions and has died soon afterwards. Franval is in time to seize his dead wife's body in his arms and then stabs himself in the moment of capture.

"Eugénie de Franval" contains some of the finest writing of all romantic Gothic and stands high among Sade's fiction. He wrote the story in the first week of March 1788 during his confinement in the Bastille. In its destruction of Madame de Franval's maternal sensibilities, it anticipated the more violent and explicit events of Philosophy in the Boudoir, even by bestowing the same name on the eagerly corrupt young heroine of both stories. But while Philosophy in the Boudoir belonged at face value to the literature of moral subversion, "Eugénie de Franval" belongs to the tradition of moral Gothic. Despite its more detailed accounts of the crime of incest, the lesson of the narrative is that the sins of the criminals will find them out.

Sade's *Stories, Tales, and Fables* are, for the most part, the comic counterpart to the melodramas of *The Crimes of Love*. The twenty-six pieces which make up the collection range from short anecdotal tales to more fully characterized stories. A few of them are dark and shadowed, as in "Émilie de Tourville: or, Brotherly Cruelty", but a good many more are light and sardonic, like "The Mystified Magistrate". It was in this latter story that Sade, writing in the Bastille, chose to avenge himself upon judges, magistrates and lawyers. These men, in his view, had shown prejudice, dishonesty, spite and downright asininity in dealing with the alleged crimes of which they found him guilty. The law being an ass, Sade pilloried it in the person of Monsieur de Fontanis, president of the high court of Aix. Sade describes this "species of animal" as "pedantic, credulous, stubborn, vain, cowardly, garrulous, and congenitally stupid ... having the thin face of a bird, the gross voice of Punch, emaciated, tall, scrawny, and stinking like a corpse."

It it to this old fool that the Baron de Terozé marries his younger daughter, leaving her dragoon lover, the Comte d'El-bêne, quite distraught. But the young man and his friends swear to prevent the consummation of the marriage by any means necessary and to make Monsieur de Fontanis only too glad to seek an annulment.

At first the bridegroom's drink is doctored, so that his bladder floods the bridal bed copiously before he can lay hands on his young wife. Then the girl manages to prolong her preparations until the magistrate falls asleep. Unknown to him, his bed is hoisted twenty feet into the air. When he gets up in the night to relieve himself, it is only to fall headlong on to another bed prepared below him. He is assured that such a thing cannot have happened and at length accepts it as a delusion. He is next precipitated into a pigsty, treated by a bogus doctor for twelve days, and is then tricked into sleeping with an elderly negress in the belief that she is his own wife. Sade even adopts a trick from *The 120 Days of Sodom*, when the magistrate sits on a privy whose seat has been coated with a powerful glue, so that he cannot get up. One of his tormentors, under the pretext of freeing him, places the flame of a spirit-lamp under him. Inspired by the flame, the wretched magistrate leaps with such strength and with such assistance from his tormentors that he leaves a neat and decorative circle of skin on the glue-covered seat.

Predictably, the annulment is sought and the young heroine is free to marry her lover. In the light of Sade's later imprisonment, it is hard to begrudge him a literary vengeance on this type of the magisterial Jack-in-Office. But the most revealing passage is one in which Fontanis is sent to drive some troublesome ghosts from his father-in-law's château. The "ghosts" are, of course, the young conspirators in disguise. They haunt the bewildered magistrate with declamations of his own crimes and perversions, until they seize and beat him. The last of Monsieur de Fontanis's delinquencies had been committed by the law against Sade himself in its proceedings against him.

The crimes of Fontanis are recited.

In 1750, he condemned a poor man to be broken on the wheel, his only crime being that he refused to hand over his own daughter for the use of the judge.

In 1754, he promised to save a man's life for 2,000 crowns. The man could not raise the money and so he had him hanged.

In 1760, hearing that a man in the town had spoken disparagingly of him, he sent him to the stake the next year for sodomy, although the poor fellow had a wife and a horde of children, and all the evidence was against his guilt.

In 1772, a young man in the province had been presented with something disagreeable by a courtesan. And so he chose to take an amusing revenge upon her by giving her a sound thrashing. But this contemptible oaf of a magistrate turned the sport into a "crime". He persuaded his legal brethren that it was a case of murder, of poisoning, and they all followed him in this absurd judgment. They disgraced the young man, they ruined him, and because they could not lay hands on him, they endeavoured to raise contempt for him by a bogus sentence of death.

In the last of these judicial outrages, Sade recasts the injustice done to him by the high court of Aix after the scandal of the poisoning at Marseille. The "ghosts" discuss what they should do to Fontanis, loudly enough for their victim to hear. Should they break him on the wheel, as one of them suggests? Should they incline towards hanging or burning at the stake, which some of the others favour? In the end, the leader of the ghosts decides to show "leniency and moderation", ordering a mere five hundred strokes of the whip in a suitably Sadean settling of accounts.

When the conspirators return and meet Fontanis, they pretend that they too have suffered at the hands of the ghosts, though not so badly as he. They encourage him to lay a legal complaint against the ghosts before his colleagues, "who have traditionally taken such an interest in corporal punishment". He must show his stripes to the court, as Demosthenes once bared the breasts of a beautiful client before the judges. Above all, he most show his posterior state to the Paris judges, who are famous the world over for the interest which they took in the state of Rose Keller's bottom in 1768.

Of all Sade's stories in this posthumously published collection, "The Mystified Magistrate" is the most successful as a political satire. It combines the zeal of personal vindictiveness with a flair for carefully staged farce, which might have been a useful embellishment to some of his own dramatic work. Here and in a number of the shorter pieces there is evidence that his ambition to be the French Boccaccio of the late eighteenth century was not far beyond his abilities.

At another level to *The Misfortunes of Virtue, Aline and Valcour* or the shorter pieces, there existed a world of Sade's secret fiction. It was secret in the sense that it had either been hidden, as in the case of *The 120 Days of Sodom*, or else disowned, as was to be the case with *Justine* and its derivatives. There was, of course, no doubt of his authorship. He privately admitted writing *Justine*. *The 120 Days of Sodom* was written in his own hand and elements of it occur in his other fiction. In 1801, the police seized a copy of *Juliette* in his own handwriting when Massé's office was searched. *Philosophy in the Boudoir* was described as being by the dead author of *Justine*, a novel which the living Sade still publicly denied writing. The first major undertaking in this world of secret authorship was *The 120 Days of Sodom*.

4. *The 120 Days of Sodom: or, The School of Libertinage*

The unfinished manuscript of *The 120 Days of Sodom* occupied Sade's evenings in the Bastille during October and November 1785. It was evidently based upon sketches which he had made during the summer and early autumn. The long manuscript roll hidden in the wall of the room survived the sack of the great prison but was apparently never seen by Sade again. In the aftermath of the Bastille's destruction, the manuscript was found in the ruins of Sade's room by Arnoux de Saint-Maximin. It remained in the possession of the family of the Marquis de Villeneuve-Trans until the end of the nineteenth century, when it was sold to a German collector. A transcript was published privately in Berlin in 1904, as part of the new literature of sexual pathology. According to those who issued it, the edition was intended only for scientists, medical men and lawyers. Not until 1931 did the first volume of a more scrupulously accurate edition appear in France under the supervision of Maurice Heine. This, too, was a limited edition. For another thirty years the unfinished novel remained like *Das Kapital*, Krafft-Ebing's *Psychopathia Sexualis* and Freud's *Interpretation of Dreams*, one of that select class of books which are more talked about than read. In this role, it was to feature in Aldous Huxley's novel *After Many a Summer* (1939) as a literary joke. Jeremy Pordage, cataloguing the library of a millionaire hypochondriac in California, discovers a completed version of *The 120 Days of Sodom* published in the eighteenth century with illustrations. Its original owner in England had disguised the volume by having it bound as *The Book of Common Prayer*.

In reality, there was no more than Sade's unfinished manuscript. The cast of the drama enacted in the château of Silling is headed by the four libertine heroes, aged between forty-five and sixty. They consist of the Duc de Blangis, his brother the Bishop, the Président de Curval, representing the judiciary, and the banker Durcet. They are accompanied by their four daughters, Constance, Adélaïde, Julie and Aline. There are four experienced courtesans to amuse the company by their stories and four bawds to rule over the twin harems. The first harem contains eight girls between the ages of twelve and fifteen, the second consists of eight boys of the same age. There are also four strapping young men to act as sexual proxies when the heroes are exhausted. As a preliminary, the four heroes arrange an ingenious set of marriages involving themselves and their daughters.

The Duc, Julie's father, became the husband of Constance, Durcet's daughter.

Durcet, Constance's father, became the husband of Adélaïde, the Président's daughter.

The Président, Adélaïde's father, became the husband of Julie, the Duc's elder daughter.

And the Bishop, Aline's "uncle" and father, became the husband of the three other girls by yielding the same rights over Aline to his friends and retaining the same rights to her himself.

These principal actors and the rest of the company set off in good time to be at Durcet's château of Silling on 1 November, the first of the hundred and twenty days of their winter. The château, like its successors in *The Misfortunes of Virtue* and *Justine*, is one of Sade's Gothic masterpieces.

To get to the place, you must first go to Basle and there cross the Rhine. Beyond that the road grows narrower until the point where you must leave your carriage. Soon afterwards, you enter the Black Forest and penetrate some forty-five miles into it by a difficult and tortuous road which would be quite impossible to follow without a guide. At this stage, you see an evil-looking hamlet of charcoal-burners and gamekeepers. The village belongs to Durcet and marks the beginning of his estate. As the inhabitants are all either thieves or smugglers, Durcet found no difficulty in making friends there. His first and express command to them was that they should allow no person whatever to approach the château with effect from 1 November, which was when the company would all be gathered. . . .

After passing the charcoal-burners, you begin to ascend a mountain almost as high as the St Bernard and a great deal more difficult, since you can only reach the top on foot. It is not

277

that pack-mules do not go there, but the precipices on every side of the path are so great that a rider faces a very real danger. Six of the animals who bore the supplies and the food perished there, as did two labourers who chose to ride a pair of them. It takes a good five hours to climb the mountain, whose summit offers another remarkable feature. Such are the precautions taken that this new barrier is impassable by any creature except the birds. Nature's whim has left a crevasse one hundred and eighty feet wide, dividing the north and south ridges of the summit. Once you have climbed the mountain, it is no easy matter to get back down. Durcet had joined these two parts, over a precipice a thousand feet deep, by a fine wooden bridge, which was destroyed as soon as the last of the convoy had crossed. From that moment, there was no further means whatever of communicating with the château of Silling.

The château itself is surrounded by a moat and a defensive wall. Yet in the heart of so much that is Gothic and menacing lies the sudden luxury of elegantly equipped and richly furnished harems. These have been prepared for four months of every kind of sensual indulgence. Their centrepiece is the auditorium, where the courtesans tell their stories and where the heroes' mistresses sigh or weep according to what is required of them. Sade's description of the room has a hint of the intimate theatre at La Coste.

It was semicircular in shape. In the curved wall were four recesses, lined with large mirrors and each containing a fine ottoman. These recesses were so angled that they each faced the centre of the straight wall, where there was a throne, raised about four feet above the floor and with its back to that wall. This was for the storyteller. In such a position, she not only faced her listeners in their four recesses, but since the distance was small and did not separate her from them by too much, they would not miss a word of her narration. Indeed, she was placed rather like an actress in a theatre and the listeners in their recesses were rather as one might be in an amphitheatre. At the foot of her throne were steps, upon which sat those who were chosen for the orgy, brought there to satisfy any sensual yearning stirred up by her stories. These several tiers, like the throne itself, were upholstered in black velvet with a gold

278

fringe, similar to the rich material of the recesses, though that was dark blue.

At the back of each recess was a little door, leading to an adjoining closet. This closet was for use when, having summoned some seductive creature from the steps, one did not wish to perform in front of the others whatever act had prompted the summons. But these closets were provided with a couch and with devices for perpetrating every sort of indecency.

On either side of the central throne, a single column rose to the ceiling. These columns were intended for fastening a slave when some misbehaviour presented a case for correction. All the instruments necessary for discipline hung from hooks on the column. The imposing sight they offered was quite enough to maintain obedience, a quality so important in pleasures of this kind. It is the imposition of obedience which gives sexual indulgence much of its attraction to the heart of a persecutor.

There appears to be a timeless and detached air about this luxurious amphitheatre set within a forbidding fortress, high up among the most desolate and inaccessible peaks of Europe in the middle of winter, sometime in the first quarter of the eighteenth century. It is a fantasy whose horror goes beyond anything that *The Mysteries of Udolpho* or, for that matter, *The Misfortunes of Virtue* might offer. Yet the themes of Sade's experience were illustrated by it. The topography is a compound of the hilltop château of Saumane during childhoold winters with his uncle, the Abbé de Sade, of German memories of the Black Forest and the villages of charcoal-burners from his military service and travels. More powerfully still, it suggests that other refuge high in an impregnable fortress, the room in the Bastille's Tower of Liberty, where he wrote this section of his novel with the dark streets and rooftops of faubourg St Antoine below him. The auditorium itself is a mixture of theatre and of remembered gilt and plush from childhood in the Condé Palace.

Perhaps the more striking topography is that of the mind of Sade the prisoner. Nowhere was "the imposition of obedience" more cherished than in the regimes of the great prisons of France. The minutiae of regulations and their correctness is reflected and sardonically mocked by this narrative. This bitter parody rather than the creation of an erotic vision is his chosen plan in the first book of the novel. The narrative has little erotic appeal to readers whose excitement is not triggered by sexual cruelty nor by the lesser outrage of practices which are, in sexual terms, unappetizing.

Yet the first book of the novel is not merely a panorama of cruelty. Indeed, there are incidents which seem far closer to what is Chaucerian or Rabelaisian. The opening of the twentieth day is an illustration of this. It involves the Duc de Blangis, his eighteen-year-old wife, Aline, with her "pert little face, snub nose and lively brown eyes", and one of the young slavegirls, Sophie, described as a charming and bashful fourteen-year-old. Aline is, of course, entirely at her husband's disposal. According to the rules, Sophie is to remain untouched for some time to come, since the simple pleasures of the first month do not include wholesale intercourse. The misadventures of the nineteenth night in the château of Silling, reported next day, though they may reflect Sade's sexual preferences, might almost have occurred in *The Reeve's Tale* or in Rabelais.

An amusing incident had occurred during the night. The Duc was incapably drunk and, instead of finding his way to his own bedroom, he had got into bed with Sophie. Despite all that the youngster could say, for she knew well enough that what he was doing was against the rules, he refused to budge. He insisted that he was in bed with his wife, Aline, which was where he should be. But he was allowed certain pleasures with Aline which were as yet forbidden with Sophie. When he told her to position herself so that he might enjoy himself in his favourite manner, and then when she felt the Duc's large hammer determined to force an entry through her tightly closed back gate, the poor young girl cried out with alarm and fled naked to the middle of the dormitory. The Duc followed, cursing her dementedly, still believing she must be Aline. "Little sod!" he swore, "It's not the first time you've had it, is it?" And then, thinking that he had caught up with her and that she had come to her senses, he fell on Zelmire's bed and took this young girl for his own. The same procedure was repeated, for the Duc was now determined to get to the bottom of the matter. But Zelmire, seeing what he had in store for her, followed the example of her companion. She gave a cry of fright and ran for her life.

Sophie, having been first to escape, saw that there was no means of restoring order in this confusion except by fetching some candles and calling someone with a cool head who could put matters to rights. So she went to look for Madame Duclos. But this bawd, who had made a pig of herself at the orgy, was stretched out senseless in the middle of the Duc's bed. There was no help to be got from her. Sophie was desperate, not knowing who to turn to in such a situation, and hearing all her girlfriends calling for help. She risked going into the room where Durcet had got Constance in bed with him, and whispered to her what had happened. Constance, moreover, risked leaving the bed, despite the efforts of the drunken Durcet who tried to hold her back and swore that he must have her again. She took a candle and went to the girls' dormitory. There she found them all in their nightdresses in the middle of the room, the Duc pursuing first one and then another, all the time believing that it was one girl, who was Aline and who he swore had turned herself into a witch that night.

At length, Constance persuaded him of his mistake. She begged him to allow her to lead him to the right room, where he would find Aline eager to submit to whatever he might demand of her. The Duc was very drunk and had honestly no intention of doing anything but sodomizing Aline, so that he let Constance lead him away. His beautiful bride received him and they retired to bed. Constance withdrew and calm returned to the girls' dormitory.

There was great amusement next day over the night's adventures. The Duc maintained that if, by mischance, he had happened to take a virginity, he could not have been made subject to a fine in that case because he was not in command of his faculties. However, the others assured him he was mistaken in this and that he would have been fined very heavily. Then they went and took breakfast in their harem of little girls, who all confessed that the Duc had given them a real fright.

Setting aside the Duc de Blangis's individual proclivities, the incident combines much that is Chaucerian with the unmistakably eighteenth-century "stage business" whose theme might be described as "The Mistakes of a Night".

It was perhaps as well that Sade never went on to embody the notes he made for the criminal and murderous passions in the form of fiction. Even in the twilight world of erotic cruelty, it is hard to see how such chapters as the breaking of a victim's arm or the amputation of a toe could have been a triumph of literary imagination. Cruelty may shock or revolt. On the scale which Sade proposed for his final book of the novel it faced greater dangers. Page after page of such incidents, however appalling in themselves, might become tedious by repetition. Worse still, the incidents might appear ludicrous. The Jacobean blood-tragedy of post-Shakespearean drama, the Gothic novel, the Victorian melodrama in England or *grand guignol* in France move dangerously close to unintended farce. In John Webster's *The Duchess of Malfi*, for example, the horror of the scene in which the duchess is strangled, as is her maid, and then has to be strangled a second time when she revives, provokes giggles from audiences in even the most accomplished productions.

In Sade's case, the twentieth century has employed similar or identical ideas to his own for the purposes of satirical writing or surreal comedy. A mainstream novelist like Evelyn Waugh invokes memories of incidents which two centuries before were characteristically Sadean. In *The 120 Days of Sodom*, on the twelfth day of the murderous passions, Sade's notes indicate that one of the sexual athletes who stands proxy for the heroes on occasion is put to death. The chosen method is that of sawing off his head, which takes a little while. To the twentieth century this method is more likely to recall the black farce of Mr Prendergast, teacher-turned-prison-chaplain in Waugh's *Decline and Fall* (1928), whose head is sawn off by a criminal lunatic for whom he has obtained permission to do fretwork in his cell. The news spreads among the prisoners by the use of improvised lines during the singing of "O God our help in ages past" in the prison chapel. Like the victim of the saw in *The 120 Days of Sodom*, "Poor Prendy 'ollered fit to bust/ For nearly half an hour."

Whether it would have pleased Sade to find that his more perverse suggestions were so comically undermined by an English Catholic with claims to be the most accomplished novelist of his time is open to question. Yet who is the victim of the saw but Prendergast? Who is Sainville at Sarmiento's dinner in *Aline and Valcour* but Basil Seal in *Black Mischief*, searching for Prudence in the African jungle and being told by his stomach-patting host after dinner, "You and I and the big chiefs – we have just eaten her"? Who is Fontanis in "The Mystified Magistrate" but Gilbert Pinfold, whose *Ordeal* consists of being tormented by disembodied voices reciting his misdeeds and perversions and then announcing that he must be physically punished for them? The parallels may be coincidental, yet they serve to show that even at the most intense moments of *The 120 Days of Sodom*, Sade is precariously perched on his mountain peak of Silling, above a precipice of laughter which threatens *grand guignol* in all its forms.

5. *Justine* and *Juliette*

When Sade rewrote *The Misfortunes of Virtue* as *Justine* (1791), and as *The New Justine*, prefacing *Juliette* (1797), the essential structure of the novel remained unaltered. Yet even the 1791 version acquired enough new characters and incidents to mask the plainer outline of the eighteenth-century philosophical tale which it had once been. The tone of the narrative is not altered. The philosophy of the villains still harps on the futility of virtue and the indifference of nature to the sufferings of humanity. "Let us now make this wicked girl submit to the sentence of death which she deserves," says Bressac of the heroine. "Such a trivial murder, far from being a crime, is merely doing what the moral order requires."

Among the characters introduced in the 1791 version, Saint-Florent seems an echo of Saint-Florentin, the king's minister who had supervised the imprisoning of Sade after the Rose Keller scandal. He is rescued by the heroine after being attacked by bandits and rewards her with a brutal assault. Monsieur de Gernande is a true romantic vampire with a mania for opening the veins of women, filling bowls with their blood and sometimes causing their deaths in the process. The legal profession is further represented in a long orgy at the end of the novel by Monsieur de Cardoville. He is the judge in the heroine's case and visits her with his friends for a little enjoyment. The unfortunate victim is stripped and made to mount an armchair, her knees on its arms and her elbows resting on its back, for what she later calls "an orgy of cruelty".

Other parts of *The Misfortunes of Virtue* are expanded and embellished. The ordeal of "Thérèse" and her companion Suzanne at the coiners' château includes orgies in a secret vault, where the girls are required to undergo the ordeal of being hanged and cut down at the last moment. This was, according to Sade, an experience from which the subjects received intense sexual excitement by the compression of the spinal nerves and which was eagerly practised by the ancient Celts.

The episode of Ste Marie des Bois is also expanded to include more elaborate orgies and a fuller description of the villains and their harem. Some of the incidents, though they add little to the story, reinforce the sexual obsessions of Sade's tyrants. One of them is almost hysterical in his anger at a girl who has become pregnant. She thereby creates life rather than destroying it and makes her body less available as a means of pleasure to those who possess her. A woman of thirty-six at Ste Marie des Bois is punished for being three months pregnant by having to stand on an eight-foot-high pedestal, which is so narrow that she can only balance on one foot. She stands naked with her other foot in the air, trying to maintain her equilibrium with a balancing rod. Mattresses are arranged on the floor to break her fall, intended to bring on a miscarriage, but the masters of the ceremony have covered these to a depth of three feet with "brambles, holly and thorns".

Such elaborate devices are liable to defeat their purpose, as literary aids, by inherent absurdities. This applies, for example, to Clément's enthusiasm for what he calls "horse-riding". In this, he is carried round the room on a girl's back, in the manner of a parlour game rather than an orgy. By the introduction of such contrivance, the novel, in the later versions, loses its directness and form as a tale in the style of *Candide*, though its obsession with beauty in distress is reinforced. Yet the reinforcement is too much a matter of repetition and of elaboration that is apt to appear comic. In that respect, the sufferings of virtue are less convincing than they might be when menaced by the type of unspecified horrors which threaten Ann Radcliffe's heroines in *The Mysteries of Udolpho* or *The Italian*.

Certain deficiencies in the 1791 version are even more marked in *The New Justine* of 1797, which is double the length and padded out by the device of letting some of the original characters tell stories of their own experiences and by introducing those long harangues on the politics of immorality which grew to become the bane of his imaginative writing. It is also filled with minor characters who burlesque both cruelty and benevolence at the same time. After Rodin, for whom surgery is a hobby rather than a profession, comes Monsieur de Bandole, whose great contribution to the advance of Sadean medicine is to make childbirth and its labours more difficult for the patient.

The New Justine of 1797 filled the first four of the ten volumes which it shared with *Juliette*. Yet it is *Juliette* which marks a greater development of Sade's fiction. The philosophy of this later work is not essentially different but it is a more profound examination of vice rather than of virtue. While the luckless Justine suffers all the pains of virtuous conduct, her sister celebrates the deaths of her parents by eagerly embracing a career of vice and crime. She is delighted by the lesbian orgies of her teachers and soon makes the acquaintance of the most depraved male criminals, who also happen to be respected and influential citizens. These characters created by Sade are as much moral parodies as some of his women are physical caricatures of their own sex, like Madame de Volmar whose clitoris is so well developed that she can even sodomize other young women with it.

Noirceuil, one of Juliette's first protectors, puts his wife to death in order that he shall be free to marry the daughter of Saint-Fond. Saint-Fond inherits Juliette and finds, in her company, particular pleasure in the sufferings of the poor and the humble. He admires the Inquisition, Machiavelli and all forms of despotism and tyranny, while despising religion, virtue and compassion of any kind. From this master, Juliette is transferred to the English lesbian, Madame de Clairwil, and makes the acquaintance of a true revolution in morality by the Society of the Friends of Crime.

By now Juliette is well equipped for marriage. The virtuous Monsieur de Lorsange redeems her and becomes her husband. The marriage lasts for two years, during which Juliette gives birth to a daughter. But, repenting of her wifely frailty, she poisons her husband and sets off for Italy in company with the Abbé Chabert of the Friends of Crime.

Much of the second half of *Juliette* is taken up with Sade's account of a criminal progress through the principal cities of Italy. It derives something, both in topography and viewpoint, from his own journal of Italian travels, as well as reflecting the experience of Italy shown in sixteenth-century rogue histories like Thomas Nashe's novel *The Unfortunate Traveller* (1594). Nashe, no less than Sade, showed that the world had seen in "The Sodom of Italy", an example of "the art of atheism, the art of epicurizing, the art of whoring, the art of poisoning, the art of Sodomitrie". Indeed, a stage-reading of parts of *The Unfortunate Traveller* at the Playhouse Theatre in Oxford proved so objectionable that it was banned by the Lord Chamberlain's curious edict in the 1960s.

Though Sade's plot lacks the pace of Nashe's, impeded by sermonizing on behalf of crime and against virtue of any sort, the Italian episodes are by far the most interesting part of the novel. They include the fairy-tale figure of Minski. This grotesque, born in Russia, lives in a castle on an island. But the island itself is in the middle of a volcanic lake on the top of a mountain, not far from Florence. Minski is, in the literal sense, a giant. Yet his vices, cruelties and appetites are also on a scale to give him the character of an ogre in a nursery tale. His inclusion in a child's story, however, would be compromised by his possession of a harem of two hundred girls, who provide his pleasures as well as his food and furnishings. He invites Juliette and her companions to dinner.

"No special preparations have been made for you," said the giant. "If all the kings on earth came to visit me, I should not alter my routine one jot."

For all that, the setting and contents of the dining-room are worth describing.

Minski gave a sign and the table came towards us. Moving from the corner of the room, it took up a position in the centre. Five armchairs likewise moved to take up their places round it. A pair of chandeliers lowered themelves from the ceiling and hung above the middle of the table.

"A simple device," the giant remarked, drawing our attention to the construction of the furniture. "As you will see, the table, the armchairs and the chandeliers are made up of groups of girls, tastefully arranged. My dishes will be laid, piping hot, on the backs of these creatures, my candles are inserted in their holes, and my backside, as well as yours, will be supported by the pretty faces or white breasts of these young ladies, when we take our places in our armchairs. So, kindly raise your skirts, ladies. And be good enough to drop your trousers, gentlemen. It is written that flesh must repose upon flesh."

"Minski," I said to our Russian host, "Surely the girls must get very tired, especially if you happen to spend a long time at table?"

"The worst that can happen," said Minski, "is that a few of them snuff it. But the gaps they leave are so easily filled that I never give the matter a second thought. . . ."

A dozen naked girls, twenty to twenty-five years old, laid the dishes on the living table. Since the plate was silver and very hot, and therefore burnt the upturned breasts and bottoms, a charming rippling motion was produced, like gentle sea-waves. A good score of entrées or roast dishes adorned the table. Wines of every sort were laid on sideboards, each formed by a quartet of girls, which came across at the slightest beck and call.

"My friends," said our host, "I should have warned you that we eat none but human flesh here. Every dish that you see is composed of it."

"Then let us sample it," said Sbrigani. "To recoil from such things is absurd, a mere defect bred in us by force of habit. All kinds of meat are made to feed man, and nature offers them for no other purpose. Eating a man is no more extraordinary than eating a chicken."

With that, he thrust his fork into a well-rounded gammon of boy and took a good two-pound helping on his plate. Then he ate it. I followed his example. Minski encouraged us and, since his own appetite was a match for his passion, he had soon emptied a dozen dishes.

Minski drank as heartily as he ate. He was already on his thirtieth bottle of Burgundy when the next course was served, though he washed that down with Champagne. Aleatico, Falernian, and other fine wines of Italy accompanied the dessert. A second thirty bottles had entered the cannibal's guts when, his senses being inflamed by so much physical and mental debauchery, he announced that he wished to unbutton himself.

Minski the monster is Sade's most notable achievement among the characters of *Juliette*. The grossness of his physical appetites is matched by his size, so that he speaks almost apologetically of having a sister who is a mere dwarf of six feet. Apart from his sexual extravagances, he appears repeatedly as an ogre of the nursery adapted to adult fiction. *Juliette* and *Jack the Giant-Killer* have more in common than might appear by reputation. Once again, the promise of "I'll grind his bones to make my bread" is a match for Minski's culinary philosophy.

In order to perpetrate cruelties on a grand scale, Minski's sumptuous bed-chamber with its "libertine frescoes" is equipped with some of the more extraordinary mechanical devices of Sade's fiction, as if to remind us that this was the age of mechanization in industry, from Arkwright's loom to the Spinning Jenny.

At the end of the room was a huge alcove lined with mirrors and containing sixteen black marble columns, to each of which a young girl was tied with her rear view exposed. By means of a pair of cords at the head of our host's bed, like bell-pulls, he could inflict a different form of suffering upon each of the sixteen subjects presented to him. This lasted until he let go of the cord. . . . He gives a tug upon the cords and the sixteen victims, all yelling in unison, receive their different injuries. Some are pricked, or burnt, or whipped. Others are nipped, cut, pinched, scratched and so forth, with such violence that the blood runs freely.

"If I pull harder," Minski remarks, "as I sometimes do when I feel in the mood for it, then these sixteen whores die before my very eyes as I haul away. I like to go to sleep thinking of how I can commit sixteen simultaneous murders at my slightest whim."

Minski takes a fancy to Augustine, who is one of Juliette's companions. He insists upon making use of her then and there. But his size proves fatal to the unfortunate girl. Nonetheless, at the moment of his orgasm, the giant wrenches upon the two cords. Instantly and simultaneously, the sixteen girls attached to the black columns are stabbed, shot, strangled or otherwise disposed of.

After the encounter with Minski, the fantasies of the novel grow still more extravagant. In Rome, Juliette is received in a private audience by Pope Pius VI, who is overwhelmed by her intellect and her beauty. He confesses that he is a conscious hypocrite who believes nothing of religion and is willing to celebrate a black mass in St Peter's in return for Juliette's favours. The novel continues at this level of personal lampoon until the rogue's progress passes through Naples. There is a pause to throw the victim of an orgy into the flames of Vesuvius. Then Juliette returns by way of Venice to France and Noirceuil.

At the climax of the book, Juliette arranges Noirceuil's marrage to a seventeen-year-old girl. During the wedding celebrations, the bride is made to skate naked on a frozen lake outside the château, while men armed with firecrackers and whips line the edge to spur her on. A Sadean marriage is usually of short duration. In this case, the girl is retrieved and vivisected. Juliette gives Noirceuil her own daughter and soon assists him to roast the girl alive. Inspired by this, the pair of criminals then poison the town water supply, though they are disappointed that the death toll reaches only fifteen hundred. The novel ends with Noirceuil becoming prime minister of France and rewarding his profligate friends by giving them wealth and positions of power in the state.

Because of its length, *Juliette* displays the weaknesses of Sade's fiction more fully than most of his other writing. Even as a picaresque or a revelation of the underworld it is overblown. During his imprisonment in Vincennes and the Bastille, Sade had with him a copy of Fielding's political parable *Jonathan Wild*, devoted to the proposition that the qualities of greatness and moral cynicism are identical in the successful politican as prime minister and in the gangster as murderer, betrayer and thief. In a tenth of the space that Sade uses, Fielding demonstrates his proposition with unflawed irony and wit, demolishing the moral pretensions of public life with a strength and conviction beyond anything in Sade's picaresque. In *Juliette*, the political and philosophical speeches are insufferably repetitive and inordinately long, even by the standard of Sade's earlier books. There is no characterization in depth, since the figures of the plot are mere tropes of vice or virtue. Ironically, even when Sade succeeds in creating a creature of fantasy, like Minski, it is the sexual ingredients of the tale which prove least interesting. Minski the cannibal and his surreal dinner-party or Minski's multiple-murder machine eclipse the most extravagant orgy that he or his creator can devise.

6. *Philosophy in the Boudoir*

The last of Sade's unacknowledged writings, *Philosophy in the Boudoir*, was published in 1795. Its title page sustained the disguise of being a posthumously published work by the author of *Justine*.

The seven dialogues in the book make up the education of the fifteen-year-old Eugénie de Mistival by several male libertines and by Madame de Saint-Ange, who combines a promiscuous heterosexuality with an enthusiasm for lesbianism. Although Eugénie is introduced to almost every form of sexual practice, there is a good deal less violence than in most of Sade's comparable narratives.

The most powerful writing in the book is Sade's long political parody in the fifth dialogue, "Frenchmen! One more effort if you truly wish to be republicans!". This praise of murder, theft, prostitution, incest and sodomy as being the only true bases for the good life has already been discussed. Whether it was intended to amuse or outrage its readers, its incongruity is demonstrated by the manner in which those who preferred to regard Sade as a radical political thinker were to take this part of the book and publish or discuss it on its own, purging it of the sexual gymnastics by which it is surrounded.

The remainder of the book is predictable enough, as Eugénie progresses rapidly through the stages of sexual initiation. Only the final dialogue brings a surprise, a new and unexpected participant in the activities. Madame de Mistival, still a beauty in middle age, comes to look for her daughter and is at once conscripted into the drama, though protesting her virtue. Eugénie, who has by this time been turned into a model of depravity, is delighted. When Madame de Mistival kneels imploringly before her, as that other Eugénie had seen her mother kneel in *The*

Crimes of Love, the impudent daughter turns her back and invites Madame to kiss her behind. The others strip Madame de Mistival and there is great hilarity when they discover the marks of a conjugal whipping upon her. She is shared by Dolmancé and her own daughter, is beaten unconscious and then beaten back to consciousness again, to the delight of her wicked child. Finally, on Eugénie's suggestion, the much-abused woman is sewn up and kicked out of the room.

Like Marx or Freud, Sade still owes the survival of his name to his reputation rather than to the texts in which he expressed his ideas. That reputation had a firm basis in his misdemeanours. Yet this in itself directed attention to his more covert publications, to the private fantasies and the secret worlds which were confined in the château of Silling and its rivals. As a child of his time, Sade is perhaps more accurately represented by *The Misfortunes of Virtue, Aline and Valcour* or the shorter fiction of *The Crimes of Love*. For better or worse, it was as the author of human nightmare that his name was to be admired or execrated in the next two centuries. The story of Sade does not end with his death. Indeed, it is arguable that the longer and more curious part of that story began only after the pious burial of his remains in the cemetery of Charenton during the winter of 1814. The world at large was soon to hear with horror of the atrocities attributed to him by nineteenth-century moralists and to realize with incredulity that there were nonetheless men and women who aspired to be the disciples of such a monster.

CHAPTER

FOURTEEN

THE DEVIL'S DISCIPLES

1

WILLIAM BLAKE WAS TO BE CREDITED with an allusion to Sade in his poem "The French Revolution" (1791). If so, it was one of many judgments made by those who knew the man rather than his works, though Blake sees the prisoner of oppression rather than the infamous author. The Bastille received him,

> . . . and the den nam'd Horror held a man
> Chain'd hand and foot, round his neck an iron band,
>   bound to the impregnable wall.
> In his soul was the serpent coil'd round his heart,
>   hid from the light in a cleft rock
> And the man was confined for a writing prophetic.

Blake had not read Sade. In 1791 even the writings of the Bastille were known at best by rumour rather than by publication. Nor was Sade imprisoned for his writings, though it might make him more acceptable as a hero of romantic revolt if that belief gained ground. Nor was he chained and bound. Rather, he was allowed the means of authorship, not to mention small luxuries from the outside world and communication with it by visits and letters. But his reputation attracted verification from neither friends nor enemies.

The first half of the nineteenth century was less concerned with Sade the romantic revolutionary than with Sade the defiler of the innocent and the corrupter of European sensibility. Jules Janin, in a famous article in the *Revue de Paris* in 1834, combined self-righteous denunciation of Sade and all his works with a breathless eagerness to discuss them. In this, he was characteristic of his age. So strong was the public interest in

Janin's article itself that it had to be reprinted as a special pamphlet.

According to Janin, the writing of Sade was responsible for killing more young innocents than the murderous passion of Gilles de Rais. "Be warned by me, whoever you may be. Do not touch these volumes, for you will never enjoy a night's sleep again." Not that Janin shows much sympathy for those who "soil the eyes and the heart" by reading Sade. He promises them that they will be haunted by the terror of the experience ever afterwards.

But neither readers nor writers were deterred from Sade by such warnings as this. A number of prosecutions testified to the circulation of his works. In France, *Philosophy in the Boudoir* was condemned in 1814, *Justine* in 1815 and *Juliette* in 1821. Indeed, *Juliette* made its appearance in the English courts at the end of the reign of George IV, when George Cannon was prosecuted in 1830. He appeared in the Court of King's Bench on charges of obscene libel in respect of Sade's novel. The edition was in French and the extracts cited in the indictment had apparently been chosen to show a certain indignation at Sade's libels on English womanhood, including as they did the antics of his English lesbian, Madame de Clairwil. The fact that the passages were in French caused the jury some problems. However, the Treasury officials put their heads together and concocted a highly spiced translation for the trial, revealing an unsuspected talent for pornography on the part of the attorney-general and his subordinates. The unfortunate George Cannon, who had more coyly issued the book in French, went down for six months.

Interest in Sade was not so easily suppressed. For lack of his own novels in England, there appeared such imitations as *The Inutility of Virtue* (1830), tracing the vicissitudes of a young woman born in Naples and trying to make her living as a singer. Though Henry James was later to describe Sade as "all but unnameable", he was named a good deal. In 1843, in the *Revue des Deux Mondes*, Sainte-Beuve endeavoured to dispel the myth that Sade's influence had been suppressed. His article suggested that there were two great sources of inspiration in modern literature. "I dare to affirm, without any fear of being contradicted, that Byron and Sade (forgive me for putting them together) have perhaps been the two great inspirations of the moderns. One of them is well advertised and visible, the other is hidden – but not too hidden." Editions of Sade were certainly appearing. The Italian critic Foscolo reported seeing one prepared for the Paris trade by a country printer. The proofs were being corrected by the man's daughter, a girl of eighteen or twenty, who was placidly superintending these pages of vice and crime.

That the flamboyant hedonism of Lord Byron and the dark spirit of Sade should be thought of as the major sources of inspiration for modern literature cast a certain shadow on the more genial poetic landscape of a collection like Wordsworth's and Coleridge's *Lyrical Ballads,* published in the year after *La Nouvelle Justine* and *Juliette*. In mid-Victorian England, Swinburne was to profess himself a disciple of Sade, whose work was known to the more rebellious spirits of the age by the 1860s. Henry James was intrigued by the reaction of Tennyson, as Poet Laureate, when the name of the reprobate marquis was mentioned. It occurred at a luncheon party given by the Tennysons at Aldworth. James was escorting Mrs Richard Greville, who made some reference during the meal to "Laure de Sade". Tennyson seized on this. He launched at once into a passionate denunciation of "the scandalous, the long-ignored, the at last all but unnameable author" of *Justine*, a book which Tennyson listed in his tirade. But the lunch party was made up of men and women who listened, as James put it, without embarrassment and with "the blankest grace". These were not the rebels of Victorian society and they had no idea what their host was talking about.

Among a new generation of writers there was a determination that Sade should not be forgotten. On 15 October 1861, Algernon Charles Swinburne, then twenty-four years old, wrote to his friend, Richard Monckton Milnes, MP, later Lord Houghton. He reminded Milnes of a promise that Swinburne was to be lent a copy of *Justine*. Milnes had an unrivalled collection of obscene books and pictures, as well as statuettes, at his country home of Fryston Hall in Yorkshire. Almost all this material had been smuggled into England from the continent. For this purpose Milnes employed Harris, the manager of the Covent Garden Opera, whose back was so curved as to conceal quarto volumes and even statuettes without once attracting the notice of the officers of Her Majesty's Customs. But Milnes was a man of importance in English politics. He also used his influence to have books and *objets d'art* sent to him by way of the British Embassy in Paris in the diplomatic bag. These arrived for him at the Foreign Office, having travelled in close proximity with dispatches addressed to Lord Palmerston.

Sir William Hardman, a mutual acquaintance of the two men, heard that Swinburne was about to get his hands on Milnes's copy of *Justine*. He was appalled at the damage which the book might do, though Hardman revealed his own knowledge of the contents. Yet, in Swinburne's case, his predispositions were deep-rooted and may have required less stimulation from his schooldays at Eton then he claimed. Without any assistance from Sade, Swinburne was evidently able to contribute to the underworld of Victorian literature. He was the author of "Reginald's Flogging" in *The Whippingham Papers* (1888) and *The Romance of Chastisement: or, Revelations of the School and Bedroom* (1870). Life, rather than literature, provided him with the material for such ventures.

Yet the copy of Sade was borrowed from Milnes at last. In August 1862, the painter G. P. Boyce went round to Swinburne's lodgings in Newman Street. He found Swinburne, Dante Gabriel Rossetti and a group of friends preparing for a reading of *The New Justine* to be given by Swinburne and Rossetti. There was some unease over the book, whose effect was, as Swinburne put it, to drive "curates and curates' pupils to madness and death". Indeed, the reading had scarcely begun when there were sounds of unbridled hysteria from the room. Swinburne explained this afterwards.

> I quite expected to add another to the gifted author's list of victims. I really thought I must have died or split open or choked with laughing. . . . One scene between M. de Verneuil and Mme d'Esterval I never thought to survive. I read it out and the auditors rolled and roared. Then Rossetti read out the dissection of the interesting Rosalie and her infant, and the rest of that refreshing episode: and I wonder to this minute that we did not raise the whole house by our screams of laughter.

Swinburne's response to the worst that Sade could do was, "Is this all?" For sheer finesse in sadism, the marquis fell far short of the Victorian public school system. Swinburne's obsession with

Sade as a figure of myth became tedious to his friends and readers alike. He even addressed Milnes as "My dear Rodin", and was apt to announce literary insights into Sade's work with all the pomposity of absolute decrees. In 1865, he thundered to the world that Sade alone "saw to the bottom of gods and men", a phrase which in the light of their shared enthusiasms was received with a certain hilarity.

Such zeal for discipleship was ultimately self-parodying. When on holiday in France with George Powell, a Welsh squire and devotee of Wagner's music, Swinburne encountered Guy de Maupassant, who reported that the friends had renamed the house "Dolmancé Cottage", after the hero of *Philosophy in the Boudoir*, while the driveway was now designated as the "avenue Sade".

Swinburne was by no means the most evident parody of Sade in the nineteenth century. The library of Richard Monckton Milnes owed much to the supply of books from Captain Frederick Hankey, who lived in Paris at 2, rue Lafitte. This house, near boulevard des Italiens, looking out on the Café Anglais and the Opéra Comique, had acquired the nickname of "the clitoris of Paris", in tribute to a series of illustrious tenants. Hankey had been a page at the court of Queen Victoria, an officer in the 6th Dragoon Guards, and had retired to Paris in the 1850s. His father, General Sir Frederick Hankey, was Governor of Malta. His brother, Thomson Hankey, was first a director and then Governor of the Bank of England.

Fred Hankey had an appearance that seemed appropriate in an admirer of Sade. He was slightly built with yellow hair and blue eyes, a pale and sinister figure with skin so fair and transparent that his veins were disconcertingly evident. The collector Henry Spencer Ashbee thought him like Sade "without the intellect". Sir Richard Burton knew him as the friend who begged for a girl's skin to be brought back from Africa, stipulating that it must be removed from a living subject to enhance the excitement of its texture. Burton sensibly regarded Hankey as a joker and the skin was never sought. Subsequently, he dedicated the seventh volume of his translation of the *Arabian Nights* to Hankey and his mistress, Annie. Hankey's murderous fantasies were offset by his objections in reality to the taking of human life and to the kill- ing of animals for food. His appearance may have been less a

sinister pallor than the result of attempting to survive on a vegetarian diet in an age before the isolation of such necessary
supplements as vitamin B12.

Others who met Hankey in Paris were less tolerant of his
eccentricities. The Goncourt brothers encountered him at the
opera and withdrew shuddering. Hankey made no secret of the
sadistic amusements which he had enjoyed in London. He spoke
of the visits made to the brothels of Mary Jeffries in company
with brother officers, where the great sport was whipping girls of
fourteen or fifteen. Mrs Jeffries was at length prosecuted in 1885
and fined £250. Hankey was to live on in the European imagination as the prototype of the sadistic Englishman rather than as
the disciple of Sade. His reputation gave something to the character of the Marquis of Mount Edgcumbe in Gabriele D'Annunzio's novel *Il Piacere* (1889) and to "Sir Arthur Glocester" in
Joseph Péladan's *La Vertu Suprême* (1900).

In D'Annunzio's novel, Andrea Sperelli – the child of pleasure
who gives the story its title – loves Elena Muti and loses her to
Mount Edgcumbe, a morally degenerate English aristocrat to
whom she sells herself. Mount Edgcumbe's tastes are exemplified
by his enthusiasm for the pictures of Francis Redgrave. The
impulses of such art, whose examples are described in the novel,
are "one a priapus and one a skeleton, a phallus and a rictus".
Mount Edgcumbe also has a library of erotica, including
Petronius, John Wilkes, Aretino and Andrea de Nerciat. The gem
of the collection is a richly ornamented and illustrated set of
Sade. "This is the portrait of Elena by Sir Frederic Leighton,"
says Mount Edgcumbe to Sperelli. "And see here, the complete
Sade. . . . You certainly won't know this edition. It was produced
for me by Hérissey, using eighteenth-century Elzevir type on
Imperial Japanese paper, in an edition of only twenty-five copies.
The Divine Marquis deserves such glory."

But Mount Edgcumbe's possession of Elena leads him deeper
into the Sadean world. Like Hankey, he belongs to the clientèle of
Mary Jeffries's brothels. D'Annunzio describes "the elegant
houses of Anna Rosemberg and of Mrs Jeffries, the secret rooms
hermetically sealed, padded from floor to ceiling, where the shrill
cries which torture wrings from its victims are deadened". There
was also something of Sade's sexuality in the passions of
D'Annunzio's dotage during the 1920s. The old man's

passionate affairs were matched by the procuring of women from Milan or elsewhere to perform his perverse wishes in the monumental and overfurnished grandeur of the Vittoriale, a First World War bi-plane suspended from its ceiling and a decommissioned naval cruiser *Puglia* embedded as a surreal promenade in his gardens that overlook Lake Garda.

Paul-Jean Toulet, in *Monsieur du Paur* (1898), saw the reflection of Sade's image in male and female, France and England. His Sancta Cecilia is a sinister private school for girls run by Miss Welkinson in the gloomy town of Sambridge. A number of pupils with no close relatives or with families in the colonies enter there and are never heard of again. After Miss Welkinson's departure, a macabre room is found where bedframes are equipped with leather straps for holding the victim. A coachman who glimpsed something of the goings-on will only hint at them, "showing a mixture of disgust and lewdness". The landlady of the Merry Robin recalls the visits of Dr Welkinson, the mistress's brother, and of a certain "French lady". The French lady herself contributed a girl of fourteen or fifteen to the harem and visited Sancta Cecilia once a week in company with a decayed English "Mylord". "The landlady noticed that on coming back from the school the French lady was always in a state of extreme excitement and yet at the time appeared exhausted." The bodies of two girls are subsequently discovered.

At one level, the tale is a direct descendant of Gothic horror, without the fancy dress. As in Ann Radcliffe's fiction, the crimes are suggested but not described. Yet, like D'Annunzio and Péladan, Toulet's version of English sadism also bore the imprint of Mary Jeffries and the white-slave scandal of 1885, known to Europe through W. T. Stead in his *Pall Mall Gazette* editorials, "The Maiden Tribute of Modern Babylon" and "Strapping Girls Down". That Stead went to gaol while Mary Jeffries was merely fined convinced the Europeans that English self-righteousness and hypocrisy remained fertile ground for Sade's legacy. In *Monsieur du Paur*, it seems that a succession of pupils at Sancta Cecilia have been tortured and at least two have died of it. In the end, however, the English police take no action. Even the witnesses are not questioned. The moral might be summed up by the title of another French view of the subject, contemporary with Toulet, Hugues Rebell's *Le Dessous de la Pudibonderie Anglaise – The Underside of English Prudery*.

Sade and the phenomenon of his conduct were commemorated elsewhere before the term "sadism" was instituted by Krafft-Ebing in his *Psychopathia Sexualis*. The word was first used in the eighth edition of the *Universal Dictionary* in 1834, where it is defined as "A fearful aberration of debauchery; a monstrous and anti-social system which revolts against nature". There was subsequently a curious book of anecdotes, *Aus den Memoiren einer Sängerin*, purporting to be the sexual autobiography of Wilhelmina Schroeder-Devrient, one of the great prima donnas of her age. The book bears the date 1868 on its title page and was certainly issued in time to be included in Ashbee's *Index Librorum Prohibitorum* nine years later. Madame Schroeder-Devrient's performances as Léonore in *Fidelio* and her singing of the part of Venus for Wagner in *Venus and Tannhäuser* assured her fame long before her death in 1860. According to the book, her enthusiasm was principally for the lesbian extravagances of Sade's writings, though there is a chapter whose title carries the word "sadism", in which the masochism of a female convict is the centre of interest. The curiosity is not that Madame Schroeder-Devrient was an admirer of Sade – there is no evidence that she had ever heard of him – but that when her character was used posthumously for these purposes, Sade's reputation was regarded as the hallmark of such perversity.

The plainest influence of Sade in the nineteenth century was naturally and directly on the literature of his compatriots. The Goncourt brothers might shudder at the spectre of Fred Hankey but they never ignored the suggestive presence of Sade. In Gustave Flaubert, they found "a mind unceasingly haunted by Sade, whose mystery exercises an inescapable fascination over him". Flaubert indeed acknowledged Sade as "the one ultra-Catholic writer". It was a judgment that might have stunned most of Sade's critics in the previous century. But, as Flaubert pointed out, Sade exalted those very theologies and institutions which the Church had tried to disown or modify in a more gentle age. The Inquisition and its tortures, the suffering promised by medieval visions of hell and even a contempt for the flesh were unappealing to the more humane Catholicism of modern Europe. What was Sade but a traditionalist on behalf of torment, a man at odds with the heresy of humanitarianism?

Flaubert's judgment displeased both sides. The Church had no wish for an ally with Sade's ability to juggle sodomy and lesbianism or to stage a papal black mass in St Peter's. Nor did the enemies of the Church wish to seem ridiculous by conceding that their greatest iconoclast might have been working against them all the time. Both factions preferred to see Sade in such terms as Baudelaire's. "One must always return to Sade," Baudelaire noted, "to observe mankind in its natural state and to understand the quality of Evil."

Sade and his works were reflected by novelists of the nineteenth century who did not mention him by name. Jules Barbey d'Aurevilly was born before Sade died and, in a collection like *Les Diaboliques* (1874), writes as he could scarcely have done without Sade's example. Among such Sadean titles as "Le Bonheur dans le Crime", the most famous of the stories, "À Un Diner d'Athées", is Byronic and richly allusive to literature and history. Like Sade, its hero enters the Revolution an atheist in religion and emerges an atheist in politics. Barbey d'Aurevilly writes of the misty isolation of his native Normandy, the stained-glass gloom of candlelit churches. He was an anti-democrat, anti-liberal, almost the ultra-Catholic whom Flaubert saw in Sade. His story of a man who seals his wife's genitals with boiling wax, the narrator carrying their baby's heart in his belt, owes more to Sade than to Byron or Poe. A piece like "Le Plus belle Amour de Don Juan" recalls something of Sade's short fiction. Its girl-child insists that her mother's lover has made her pregnant. The cause of her conviction is that she sat in an armchair, still warm from his use. His warmth engulfed her. "Oh, mama! It was as if I had fallen into the fire. I wanted to get up but I could not. My heart failed me. I felt – well, there – I felt, mama, that I had – that it was a baby!"

The reputation of *Les Diaboliques* was further secured with the addition of illustrations for its stories by Félicien Rops in the 1882 edition – "the so bizarre Monsieur Rops", as Baudelaire called him. The murdered woman of the atheists' dinner sprawls naked on the table by candlelight and the sallow child mistress of Don Juan clasps her hands nervously between her narrow thighs. Yet despite this suggestive embellishment, Barbey d'Aurevilly had served those who saw Sade's continued literary presence as reactionary rather than progressive. In contrast, other novelists by the end of the nineteenth century wrote in a nihilistic Sadean style, few more so than the political anarchist of the Third Republic, Octave Mirbeau, whose *Jardin des Supplices* appeared in 1899. The novel begins with a symposium on the importance of murder in society. "Murder is the very basis of our social institutions and consequently the most absolute necessity for civilized life. If there was no murder, there would be no more need for governments of any kind, by virtue of the undeniable truth that crime in general and murder in particular is not only their excuse for existing but their sole reason."

Mirabeau's speaker, like a protagonist of Sade's fiction, insists upon the connection between a desire to make love and a desire to kill. "I have been told this in confidence by an honourable murderer who kills women – in the course of rape rather than robbery. His sport consists in making his own spasm of pleasure coincide with the death spasm of the other party. 'In such moments,' he told me, 'I feel like a god creating the world.'"

Governments approve murder, Mirbeau's speaker insists, by legal executions, colonial exploitation, war, hunting, racial persecution. . . . People enjoy the murder of other species, calling it "sport", the slaughterhouses are busy providing meat, fairgrounds are thronged by those who wish to "kill" lifelike targets with rifles. The poor strangler is a victim of social hypocrisy. The women whom he dispatches in his "sport" are as greedy for blood and slaughter as any man. "Why else do women rush to spectacles of bloodshed with the same frenzy as to sexual pleasure? Why do you see them in the street, at the theatre, at the law courts, at the guillotine, stretching their necks, opening their eyes wide, greedy for scenes of torture, relishing the fearful pleasures of death until it makes them faint?"

The novel is devoted to the portrayal of an English female sadist, Clara, whom the narrator meets on his voyage to the Far East, after his failure in the general elections of the Third Republic. It is she who introduces him to scenes of oriental torture and execution, death by sexual caress or by a rat eating its way through the victim's entrails. Yet these are the horrors of a waxwork show. By contrast with Sade and despite his own part in the Anarchist movement, Mirbeau writes like the political dilettante that he was.

Among Sade's other literary descendants who were Mirbeau's contemporaries was Georges Joseph Grassal, a right-wing sympathizer of Charles Maurras and Action Française as well as an enthusiast for Nietzsche. He wrote under the name of Hugues Rebell. Rebell was prolific as poet, novelist and essayist of the 1890s, a translator of Oscar Wilde. His work in tribute to Sade's influence included the collection *Femmes Chatiées*, his pseudonymously issued *La Femme et son Maître*, describing the fate of European women sexually abused in the harem after their capture at Khartoum, and *En Virginie*, a novel about plantation slaves. Rebell also published a bitter attack upon the English judges and their "petty Calvinist morality", on the occasion of Oscar Wilde's imprisonment. A further target for his scorn was England's indulgence in sadism under the moral disguise of punishment. But Rebell's own career was even shorter than Wilde's. Pursued by creditors and bailiffs, he left his slum lodgings in Batignolles and was reduced to sleeping on the floor of a room in the Marais, while its female occupant and her soldier lover occupied the bed a few feet from him. He died in 1905 at the age of thirty-seven.

Writers like Barbey d'Aurevilly, Mirbeau, Rebell, even D'Annunzio and Péladan, bore out Sainte-Beuve's claim for Sade's influence upon the post-romantic movement, "hidden – but not too hidden". Despite Swinburne's acknowledgement of Sade elsewhere, the same might be said of his attempts at fiction in *Love's Cross Currents* (1905) and the incomplete *Lesbia Brandon*. The underworld of literature and the most prestigious European novels converged at that point.

The time was at hand, however, when Sade's presence need no longer be concealed. Of all European novelists, none gave a clearer interpretation of sadism as a moral phenomenon than Marcel Proust in *Du côté de chez Swann* (1913). The narrator sees through an uncurtained window a pair of lesbians in a lamp-lit room. Mademoiselle Vinteuil is the daughter of the dead composer and music-master. In the preliminaries to love-making, she sits upon her friend's knee on the sofa, her dead father's photograph placed on a table, as though he were made to watch. Though Mademoiselle Vinteuil appears the seduced innocent, she has coached her partner in the words and suggestions heard. So the other woman offers to spit on the photograph of the "ugly old monkey". Such "daily profanation" is carefully rehearsed. There is no physical violence in the scene, not even to the extent of spitting on the photograph. Yet Proust sees in Mademoiselle Vinteuil the truth of "what is nowadays called a sadist".

It is possible that, without being in the least inclined towards "sadism", a girl might have shown the same outrageous cruelty as Mlle Vinteuil in desecrating the memory and defying the wishes of her dead father, but she would not have given them deliberate expression in an act so crude in its symbolism, so lacking subtlety. The criminal element in her behaviour would have been less evident to other people, and even to herself, since she would not have admitted to herself that she was doing wrong. But, appearances apart, in Mlle Vinteuil's soul, at least in the earlier stages, the evil element was probably not unmixed. A "sadist" of her kind is an artist in evil, which a wholly wicked person could not be, for in that case the evil would not have been external, it would have seemed quite natural to her, and would not even have been distinguishable from herself. And as for virtue, respect for the dead, filial obedience, since she would never have practised the cult of these things, she would take no impious delight in their profanation. "Sadists" of Mlle Vinteuil's sort are creatures so purely sentimental, so virtuous by nature, that even sensual pleasure appears to them as something bad, a privilege reserved for the wicked.

Proust's is a classic and well-nigh definitive analysis of Sade's legacy. Sadism, in that respect, is as subversive and sardonic as the darkest satire. It touches the writing of Jonathan Swift and Evelyn Waugh. The use of sexual violence on a victim is not, in this sense, sadistic. Sadism requires a degree of mockery or irony towards its subjects rather than any physical act. In the true sense, Mademoiselle Vinteuil is a sadist, while the drunken wife-beater is not. Sadism also requires a degree of propriety, a "virtuous" awareness in Proust's sense or what Georges Bataille was to call "a sense of transgression", which distinguished pleasure from instinctive copulation.

2

The understanding of sadism, in Proust's account, was obscured in the twentieth century by use and combination. Yet no definition improved upon his. The perpetrators of the greatest evil in the concentration camps or labour colonies of tyrannical regimes have been self-righteous rather than sadistic in the true sense.

The greatest complication was the combination of two terms as "sadomasochism". While it was true that Sade showed elements of both in his own conduct, the use of the neologism yoked together two differing types. In the literature of psychopathology, for example, Havelock Ellis's patient "Florrie" was a suffragette and a writer on art, an example of emancipated modern womanhood, whose compulsions required that she should go to a hotel room with a man she scarcely knew in order that he should whip her there and that she should write letters to the press describing how suffragettes were beaten for damaging property. In the account which Ellis gives of her, any debt to Sade might be doubted. Nor did it follow that the Sadean type and the likes of Florrie were well suited. Despite its reputation, the viewpoint of a modern feminine novel like Dominique Aury's *Story of O* is unremittingly that of masochism. A combination of sadism and masochism was potentially lethal, as the murder of Margery Gardner by Neville Heath in the summer of 1946 was to show.

Even before the nineteenth century was over, "sadism" was adopted as a term that was fundamental in the new science of sexual psychology. To that extent, it might, at length, be lost to literature. Yet so long as that term existed, the reputation of the man whose name it acknowledged would live. From the publication of Krafft-Ebing's *Psychopathia Sexualis* in 1886 it marked a boundary in the new German investigation of sexual pathology. By the scale of immortality, Sade had not waited long. Despite the modernity of Krafft-Ebing's reputation, he was born only twenty-six years after Sade died. His early work for the *Psychopathia Sexualis*, with its smart cocktail-party availability of reference, antedated much of Tennyson's poetry or Matthew Arnold's prose, or even a novel like George Eliot's *Daniel Deronda*.

Yet if Sade was assured of a kind of immortality by the purloining of his name for such purposes, he was also diminished by it. His role in "sadomasochism" was confined and limited by others. Shorn of his political and philosophical significance, he lives in the nursery emotions of a paper like Freud's "A Child is Being Beaten" (1919). With his fellow prisoners Oedipus and Sacher-Masoch, he labours on behalf of theories of infant experience. If he was Freud's prisoner, as he had been Krafft-Ebing's more than thirty years before, he was also the internee of Havelock Ellis in a humane asylum. In "Love and Pain", Ellis left the world with a cameo of Sade the lunatic, remembered by a contemporary at Charenton.

> He told that one of the marquis's amusements was to procure baskets of the most beautiful and expensive roses; he would then sit on a footstool by a dirty streamlet which ran through the courtyard, and would take the roses, one by one, gaze at them, smell them with a voluptuous expression, soak them in the muddy water, and fling them away, laughing as he did so.

Despite the early notoriety of Ellis's work, his vision of a Sade mentally enfeebled by sexual dissipation has far more in common with nineteenth-century preconceptions than those of the twentieth century. It was to be robustly contradicted, from Guillaume Apollinaire in 1913 to Peter Weiss in the *Marat/Sade* half a century later and by the publication of Sade's literary output at Charenton.

Novelists and poets, rather than psychiatrists and critics, saw the truth of Sade and sadism most plainly. Against the simpleminded use of his name in psychopathology, Sade's reputation was more objectively reassessed when manuscripts of *The 120 Days of Sodom* and of many shorter works began to be discovered in the new century. He owed psychopathology a debt, not as a science but as a pretext for the publication of these manuscripts. The twentieth century began with a number of commentaries on Sade, his life and his books, led by Albert Eulenburg, Augustin Cabanès, and Eugen Dühren. The last of these was the pseudonym of Iwan Bloch, the moving spirit behind the first publication of *The 120 Days of Sodom*, which appeared in Berlin in 1904.

Sade had believed that fifteen of his Bastille notebooks were destroyed and he had, as he said, wept "tears of blood" over the loss of them. In the new era of mental science, however, his most extreme sexual aberrations became legitimate subjects of investigation. Texts of his unpublished writings were to be made available to doctors, scientists, lawyers and men of letters. Apart from that, a good many ordinary folk were fired by a curiosity about writing that had remained hidden so long.

3

Whatever the medical interest in Sade, it was overtaken by the underworld of literature in such books as *The Pleasures of Cruelty: being a sequel to the reading of Justine and Juliette* (1898) and *Sadopaedia, being the experiences of Cecil Prendergast, Undergraduate of the University of Oxford: Shewing how he was led through the pleasant paths of Masochism to the supreme joys of Sadism* (1907).

In parallel with this underworld of literature ran a revival of Sade's influence which stemmed from more fruitful sources than the discovery of his manuscripts or imitations of his work in erotic fiction. In 1909, Guillaume Apollinaire, painter, poet and an immediate predecessor of Surrealism, produced a selection of Sade's work and pronounced him the possessor of the "freest mind" the world had ever known. Apollinaire also offered his own tribute in the form of a Sadean slapstick novel, *Les Onze Mille Verges* (1907), in part debunking the military ethic illustrated by the Russo-Japanese war.

As in the previous century, Sade was a symbol of a new revolution in art and literature. During the past fifty years, he had touched the post-romanticism of Flaubert and Baudelaire, Swinburne and D'Annunzio. In the aftermath of the First World War, he was adopted by Surrealism. Its leaders, like André Breton, recognized the great iconoclast as a natural ally. In his own time Sade had been rejected, which in itself made him more acceptable to the new movement. Surrealism contained a belief in revolution combined with a distaste for the classic political dogmas of right and left, after it was evident that the revolutionary regime in the USSR had rejected the invitation to govern on Surrealist principles. More generally, Surrealism saw a duty to outrage the most sacred tenets of bourgeois society, in which it also seemed to follow Sade. The duty was not difficult to discharge. One of many uproars followed the release of Luis Buñuel's film *L'Age d'Or* (1930), in which Sade's Duc de Blangis emerged from the orgies of *The 120 Days of Sodom* in a costume which suggested the iconographic dress of Christ.

Surrealism, like any modern movement, was less interested in its ancestors than in itself. Sade was therefore required to conform to its demands. Even as a figure of myth, he seemed to lend himself equally to the ambitions of Fascism and Communism. Like Nietzsche, he could be made to justify survival by racial superiority in the war of nature, the use of women as objects of authoritarian cruelty, while his heroes were nothing if not supermen above the petty restraints of law and morality. His appeal to Communism and its sympathizers was no less plain. Did he not rejoice in the overthrow of the bourgeoisie and its mercenary values? Did he not show, like Lenin and Stalin, that murder and torture may be the means of cleansing the body politic? Was he not, above all, that purest and most inexorable angel of social justice, the aristocrat turned revolutionary?

To his critics, Sade's role in the totalitarian politics of his successors was to rescue tyranny from being an outmoded tool of reaction and to refurbish it as the legitimate weapon of vigorous revolution.

On the evidence of his writings and experiences, Sade would have felt a robust contempt for institutionalized politics, whether of left or right. Nor would the rigour of his thought and style have matched a good deal of what paraded itself as Surrealism. More interesting were the tributes which the movement paid him, often through the work of its painters. In some cases, this tribute took the form of illustrations of his novels by Hans Bellmer or by Leonor Fini in her pictures for *Juliette* (1944) and *Justine* (1950). Mademoiselle Fini's illustrations have a feminine emphasis. The violence of Sade's heroines and the savagery with which the female victims had been dispatched are vividly represented. Violence in such illustrations is also the characteristic of contemporary artists like André Masson and Hans Bellmer.

At the other extreme, Clovis Trouille's paintings, almost photographic in their representational clarity, dwell much more on the erotic and humorous interpretation of Sade. They are not illustrations but an attempt to relate Sade's work to the twentieth century, recapturing its ironies in terms which are uncompromisingly modern. The painting *Voyeuse* is set in a cinema foyer, decorated with whips and placards of half-stripped girls. A still from the movie *Les Mystères de Sadome* shows an eighteenth-century nobleman leaning on a skull, whip in hand, and choosing which of several bare-fleshed girls shall be his next victim. "No admittance to those under the age of fifty", says the foyer sign, while a young girl draws back the velvet curtain to peep eagerly and furtively into the auditorium. The still from the movie is, in fact, another of Trouille's paintings, *Lust*, in which a Sadean nobleman contemplates his tethered female subjects who are naked but for modern silk stockings. A recognizable ruin of the château of La Coste rises in the background.

Though there is no direct reference to Sade, a similar quality of humour exists in Allen Jones's fibreglass figures of girls as furniture. *Table*, *Hatstand* and *Chair* are three works from 1969. The first consists of a model in gloves, boots, and underpants, kneeling on all fours with a glass surface on her back. The second is a figure in stockings and cache-sex with hands out for hats to be hung. The last represents a supine girl with legs raised to support the seat and back of a chair. Such artefacts may be less outrageous than the female furniture of Minski's dinner-party in *Juliette* but the parallel is striking. Indeed, the female form as furniture had been anticipated within the Surrealist movement of the 1930s by Dali's creations, including his shocking-pink sofa in the shape of the lips of Mae West.

A contrary representation of Sade in modern art is as the figure of heroic resistance, a tragic hero battling against the forces of repression. Among a number of such portraits, the most impressive are Capuletti's painting of Sade the embattled prisoner and Man Ray's powerful Surrealist symbol, depicting Sade as a living edifice, built of the same stone as the prison which holds him. It is this design which was to underline for contemporaries Sade's posthumous reputation of massive courage and indomitable intellect.

In 1939, when including a passage from *Juliette* in the *Anthology of Black Humour*, André Breton made an observation that no longer seemed controversial. Only in the twentieth century, he wrote, had the true horizons of Sade's work been appreciated. In the years that followed this judgment, appreciation was enhanced by the experience of total war and by cruelties which made *The 120 Days of Sodom* seem almost self-effacing in its scope. Yet, within that range, Sade had made a terrifying and accurate diagnosis of human psychology. If it was true, as Flaubert thought, that Sade was the spokesman for an extreme Catholic position, he had stated the fall of modern man with unparalleled force. A modern view of Sade as a writer who wore only the mask of atheism was given by Pierre Klossowski in *Sade Mon Prochain* (1947). More pessimistically, Albert Camus remarked that the history and the tragedy of the modern world began with Sade. In the sense that an awareness of the modern condition stemmed from his writing, this was true.

The experience of the Second World War opened the way for an extensive academic examination of Sade. It was a pale and earnest manifestation by comparison with the colour and imagination of the Surrealists. Yet for a hundred and fifty years histories of France and of French literature had generally omitted all but the briefest references to him. This was made good in post-war academia. The creative spirit of literature also offered its tributes, from poets like René Char, novelists like Georges Bataille, Raymond Queneau and Simone de Beauvoir, critics like Edmund Wilson and Pierre Klossowski and Academicians like Jean Paulhan.

Yet Sade owed most to his admirer Maurice Heine, successively Communist, pacifist and campaigner against the barbarity of bull-fighting. Heine, who died in 1940 as the German army occupied Paris, had rescued many of Sade's manuscripts from obscurity and published them between the wars. Dying before his time, he was able only to sketch out the form of a biography of Sade, in addition to his more intensive studies of such incidents as the Rose Keller case and the scandal of the Marseille poisonings. It was left to his younger friend Gilbert Lely to publish the first systematic account of Sade's life a generation later.

As the flow of academic studies of Sade increased to a torrent, it appeared that much of the earlier work was still the best. Mario Praz in *The Romantic Agony* (1933), a work of imaginative scholarship, had shown the immense clandestine influence of Sade on European literature of the nineteenth century. The post-war industry of academic research into the life of the ever-interesting marquis enabled its journals to devote entire issues to the discussion of his writing. At last, "the all but unnameable" figure of Henry James's anecdote became the subject of a major scholarly colloquium at the University of Aix-Marseille. Despite the criminal proceedings against his publisher in 1956, the time was coming when Sade would be given to the world, complete and unexpurgated. Even the novels which caused such legal difficulties at mid-century were to circulate in mass-market paperback without impediment. Had it truly been decided that he was of such importance to the world that the moral risk must be taken? Or was it simply that the world no longer cared?

It was certainly not through enlightened criticism or university colloquia that Sade's popularity was established in the mass culture of the 1960s. He was the dour and sceptical philosopher of Peter Weiss's play, the *Marat/Sade* – or to give its full explanatory title, *The Persecution and Assassination of Marat as performed by the Inmates of the Asylum of Charenton under the Direction of the Marquis de Sade*. Produced and acted with great accomplishment at a time when the discussion of political ideas was fashionable as the stuff of drama, the conflict between the political idealism of Marat and the wiser cynicism of Sade appealed to a theatre-going middle class.

Those who sought a less demanding vision of Sade were not overlooked. For them, in 1969, there was the American International Films production of *De Sade*, a technicolor romp displaying a good deal of skin but without much resemblance to Sade's life. "De Sade, that long-haired whippie, is now a movie marquis in a film based on the 18th century's eroticist and his kinky pastimes," explained the *Playboy* reviewer.

The filming of Sade's novels presented difficulties in terms of censorship and greater ones still in terms of credibility. Jess Franco's *Justine* in 1968, with Klaus Kinsky as Sade, Romina Power as Justine and Jack Palance as Antonin, was scarcely recognizable as having anything in common with the spirit of the novel. Jacques Scandalari's *Philosophy in the Boudoir* (1970) claimed to be "loosely based" on Sade's book. However, its preoccupation with painted skin, whips and girls in leather trousers formed a basis that was exclusively of the later twentieth century. A more prestigious attempt to give relevance to Sade was Pasolini's *Salo: The 120 Days*, in which Sade's novel was set in the short-lived puppet republic of Mussolini at Salo, on the shore of Lake Garda in 1944. Fascist brutality was combined with memories of Sade's story. It has to be said that the film would have worked just as well without reference to Sade and that some of the odder sexual incidents produced laughter in the cinema rather than a sense of drama.

Any serious attempt to translate Sade to the screen seemed to be abandoned. His fame was relegated to the "De Sade" video series and to single productions like *Monsieur Sade*, the stock-in-trade of Parisian sex shops and a mere exploitation of his name.

4

The true theatre of Sade in the modern world was not to be on the stage or the cinema screen but in courts of law. Human criminality does not change essentially from age to age. Yet it seemed as if certain crimes had shaped themselves to Sade's experience or writing. These dramas were to be played out in court from time to time. Legal argument was concerned with whether sadism at the level of such criminality could constitute insanity. As early as 1907, there seems little doubt that the conduct of Harry Thaw towards Evelyn Nesbit contributed to the verdict of not guilty by virtue of insanity, when he was tried for the murder of the New York architect Stanford White. After their marriage, Evelyn Nesbit was to write of her experiences of being beaten with a dog-whip by Thaw in an Austrian castle during a scene that might almost have come from Sade's own life. After his release from the lunatic asylum at Matteawan, Thaw was involved in a series of scandals involving sexual violence until his death in 1946.

A murderer like Neville Heath, who had proved himself a sadist with certain women, was not so in Proust's sense when he flew upon his final victim with a knife in a drunken fury. As Proust had shown by precept and Sade by example, mindless brutality may be among the gravest of crimes but it is not sadistic. The whipping of Rose Keller or Evelyn Nesbit was, in that sense, the act of a sadist. The murder of Stanford White by Thaw or of a second victim by Heath was probably not.

In 1946, in Heath's earlier murder, it was formally ruled that sadism did not constitute insanity for legal purposes. "Mad as a hatter from a doctor's point of view," was one expert opinion given to the defence. "Mad as a hatter, but I doubt whether within the McNaghten Rules." His earlier murder, appalling though it seemed, was more probably manslaughter. The victim was a young woman who had a reputation as a masochist and whose fate could hardly be explained otherwise. She and her partner had been evicted from a hotel not long before, following a disturbance caused by their activities. Their next encounter, when she was tied to a bed and gagged, ended in her death. It was suffocation rather than sexual violence which caused this. The fact that her partner's fragile equilibrium may have given way under anger or frustration at finding willingness rather than resistance suggests the danger of regarding sadomasochism as a state of emotional compatibility.

Sade's own experience of courts of law produced a drama in the Rose Keller case which was almost a moral fable of society and sexuality. Few of the facts were at issue, yet the stories of the protagonist and victim were irreconcilable. A similar conflict was to be presented almost two hundred and twenty years later in the California trial and conviction of Cameron Hooker for the abduction and sexual ill treatment of a young woman over a period of some years. The facts of the so-called "Girl in the Box" case fitted almost equally the story of a willing slave who, even when set free, returned voluntarily to her captors as part of their household, and that of the victim deprived of liberty until her mind was under their control. As a drama it was more protracted and convoluted than Rose Keller's brief experience on Easter Sunday 1768. Fashionable notions of brainwashing replaced the more urgent persuasives of poverty as an explanation of the victim's conduct. Yet the hearing of two plausible but irreconcilable versions of events illustrated a Sadean paradox, as much a parable of justice in a world of shrill mass media as the Rose Keller case had been in a more ordered world of the *ancien régime*.

5

Sade's destiny was to thrive by notoriety rather than fame. Whether he appears as the corrupter of the innocent, as evil incarnate or as the first great martyr to modern political systems, he is apt to be judged in extremes. He certainly had his share of courage, yet he was not a hero in an easily defined sense. As a martyr, he complained too often and too readily about matters great and trivial. His upbringing had encouraged him to put his own interests before those of others. It was a fault which his irritability and the injustice of imprisonment naturally made worse. If he had courage and tenacity, he lacked patience and compassion.

The contradictions in his character paralleled those in this writing. There was much in him which was sympathetic to the principle of revolution. Yet he remained attached to his aristocratic rights and privileges, even to his lands and possessions. The eager egalitarians were briskly catalogued as "brigands" and "imbeciles". In this respect, he was not far removed from those citizens of the twentieth century who preferred to preach the gospel of world revolution from the discreet distance of bourgeois affluence.

But still his courage remained undeniable. As a judge under the Revolution, he compromised his own safety and survival by showing "moderation" to men and women who might otherwise have gone to their deaths. He put himself at risk even for the Montreuil family, which had done so much to destroy him. If he wrote savagely of his victims and judges in the scandals of Arcueil and Marseille, he readily forgave others with whom he later dealt.

Sade as a philosopher remained an elusive figure. As Matthew Arnold remarked when writing of Wordsworth, the temptation to derive a philosophy from imaginative literature is best resisted. Sade's achievement was inventive and imaginative rather than logical and expository. He showed insight rather than system. Indeed, he was obsessive rather than systematic, repetitious rather than progressive in his reasoning. Like Fielding in *Jonathan Wild* or Voltaire in *Candide*, he took an almost self-evident idea and illustrated it in example after example. Better had he confined himself within similar dimensions to those of his predecessors.

Even as the author of a philosophical novel, he left a question over his work that was to be discussed rather than answered. Did he mean what he said? At face value, he appears the true revolutionary of the modern world, offering an absolute alternative to existing moral and social order. By comparison with Sade, such men as Marx or Lenin, even Robespierre or Hitler, were merely tinkering with the fabric of bourgeois society, enslaved by existing concepts and deluded by such false concepts as economics or nationalism and by moral chimeras.

Some of his successors reversed this interpretation, making Sade the sardonic jester and the great counter-revolutionary. Without returning to Flaubert's view of him or Klossowski's later apology, the evidence of Sade's life lends a good deal of support to such a conclusion. If that argument prevails, then he makes his position clear in *Juliette*. The absolute revolution is a fraud. Revolutionaries who seek to liberate nations from oppression, whatever their slogans may be, are motivated only by envy of the present tyrants. The Friends of Crime in *Juliette* prove to be as much a government-in-waiting as any constitutional opposition or army of liberation. All political movements, in Sade's example, seek power over others. The motive of their search is sexual dominance and cruelty, accompanied by greed and self-advancement. If sexuality is the illustration of Sade's theme, then individual and collective political ambition is the ultimate perversion. That all power corrupts and absolute power corrupts absolutely is the irreducible political truth of Sade.

Historical judgments of his philosophy were further complicated by the possibility, which Michelet insisted on, that he was deranged. It might be doubted that his mania was more pronounced than that of Robespierre or the Duc d'Orléans. Yet even without believing in his "madness" it is clear that Sade's views were variable rather than absolute over the period of his writing. Barbey d'Aurevilly might almost have been writing of Sade when he created his Byronic hero, Mesnilgrand, who had entered the Revolution as an atheist in religion and emerged as an atheist in politics. At his own valuation, Sade moves from satirizing traditional morality in 1787 to a debunking of the new materialist philosophy ten years later. Yet within this shift of view, he maintained one theme which was to discomfit most of his readers in the next two centuries.

It is not the vision of hell or the tortures of the Inquisition which Sade's novels suggest most powerfully. More disturbingly, his alternative theology seems to reaffirm the enduring irrationality of original sin in an age of reason. Sade was the bearer of bad news about the human race. Indeed, his own popularity appeared to confirm this. He was to survive not so much as a hero, nor revolutionary, nor even as a satanic jester. The one undeniable feat of his argument was that he had stood the optimism of the *philosophes* on its head. The self-destructive power of the human race is the supreme power, in Sade's fictional hypothesis. The extinction of that race is neither to be avoided nor even regretted. History is not progress but drift. Like John Henry Newman, Sade sees the "terrible aboriginal calamity" haunting mankind's pretensions. Unlike Newman, he chooses to present the bad news in his fiction as though it were a derisive cosmic joke at the expense of mankind.

On 13 August 1991, the wheel spun full circle from Pauvert's ordeal in 1956. Miss Moyra Bremner, a television presenter, demanded in *The Times* a prosecution of Arrow Books for issuing *Juliette*. With no sympathy for such prosecutions, Miss Bremner urged an exception here. The old chestnut of Sade as model for the Moors Murders was offered, and the need to protect women and children from such examples as parents being forced to eat their infants. By 19 August, Miss Bremner had asked the Lord Advocate of Scotland to prosecute and ban further works by Sade, as inciting child abuse and rape.

Exceptions to a belief in literary freedom are always suspect. The case against banning Sade was powerfully put by Anthony Burgess in the *Evening Standard* on 13 July. He cited murderers who confessed to inspiration from Sophocles, Shakespeare and, of course, the Bible. A good many more might be leafing through *American Psycho* or *The Silence of the Lambs*.

With declining literacy, it would be reassuring if a random dozen jurors could still evaluate an eighteenth-century novel. Without that, a trial could not be fairly conducted within the present law and presumably would go to appeal. The same novel is freely published in Europe and America. That it should still evoke a suppressive urge in Britain, two hundred years after first appearing, suggests that its views had better be answered than censored. Sade may be refuted but, in two centuries, he has not been silenced.

SELECT BIBLIOGRAPHY

1. SADE

Complete Works:
Oeuvres Complètes du Marquis de Sade, Paris, Cercle du Livre Précieux, 1966–7
Oeuvres Complètes du Marquis de Sade, Paris, Pauvert, 1986–8

Individual Novels (available in general paperback series). These include:
Aline et Valcour; Les Crimes de l'Amour; Histoirettes, Contes et Fabliaux; Les Infortunes de la Vertu; Les 120 Journées de Sodome; Justine, ou les Malheurs de la Vertu; Juliette, ou Les Prosperités du Vice; La Marquise de Gange, Paris, Union Genérale d'Éditions, 10/18
Aline et Valcour; Justine; Les Crimes de l'Amour; La Marquise de Gange, Livre du Poche
Les Crimes de l'Amour; La Philosophie dans le Boudoir; Les Infortunes de la Vertu, Paris, Éditions Gallimard/Folio
The 120 Days of Sodom, translated by Austryn Wainhouse and Richard Sever, London, Century Hutchinson, 1990

Diaries and Correspondence:
Cahiers Personnels, 1803–4, ed. Gilbert Lely, Corrêa, Paris, 1953
Correspondance Inédite du Marquis de Sade, ed. Paul Bourdin, Paris, Librairie du France, 1929
Lettres et Mélanges Littéraires, ed. George Daumas and Gilbert Lely, Éditions Borderie, 1980
Journal Inédit du Marquis de Sade, ed. George Daumas, Paris, Gallimard, 1970

2. SADE AND HIS CRITICS

L'Affaire Sade, 1957

Almeras, Henri d', *Le Marquis de Sade*, 1906

Amer, Henry, "Sur le Marquis de Sade", *Nouvelle Revue Française*, November 1958

Apollinaire, Guillaume, *Oeuvre du Marquis de Sade*, 1909

Apollinaire, Guillaume, with Fernand Fleuret and Louis Perceau, "Biblioiconographie des Oeuvres de Sade et Jugements sur lui et son oeuvre", in *L'Enfer de la Bibliothèque Nationale*, 1913

Barthes, Roland, *Sade, Fourier, Loyola*, 1971

Bataille, Georges, *Les Larmes d'Eros*, 1961

——, *La Littérature et le Mal*, 1954

Beauvoir, Simone de, "Must We Burn de Sade?" in *The Marquis de Sade*, ed. Paul Dinnage, 1962

Baccolo, Luigi, *Che Cosa ha veramente detto de Sade?*, 1970

Beliard, Octave, *Le Marquis de Sade*, 1928

Blanchot, Maurice, *Lautréamont et Sade*, 1949

Carter, Angela, *The Sadeian Woman*, 1979

Clement, Henry, *De Sade*, 1969

Cleugh, James, *The Marquis and the Chevalier*, 1951

Dühren, Eugen [Iwan Bloch], *Der Marquis de Sade*, 1900

Doyon, R.-L. *Du Marquis de Sade au Barbey d'Aurevilly*, 1921

Egan, Beresford and Shane, Brian de, *De Sade*, n.d.

Eulenburg, Albert, "Der Marquis de Sade", *L'Avenir*, 1899

Fauville, Henri, *La Coste, Sade en Provence*, 1984

Flake, Otto, *The Marquis de Sade*, 1930

France, Anatole, "Notice sur Sade", preface to *Dorci, ou Les Bizarreries du Sort*, 1880

Gear, Norman, *The Divine Demon*, 1963

Gorer, Geoffrey, *The Life and Ideas of the Marquis de Sade*, 1934

Heine, Maurice, *Le Marquis de Sade*, 1950

Henry, Charles, *Le Verité sur le Marquis de Sade*, 1887

The Inutility of Virtue, 1830 [An English adaptation of *Justine*]

Janin, Jules, "Le Marquis de Sade", *Revue de Paris*, 1834

Klossowski, Pierre, *Sade Mon Prochain*, 1947

Kristol, Irving, "The Shadow of the Marquis", *Encounter*, VIII, No 2, 1957

Laborde, Alice M. *Le Mariage du Marquis de Sade*, 1988

Lely, Gilbert, *Vie du Marquis de Sade*, 1952–7

Obliques, 12–13, Numéro Spécial, 1977

Paulhan, Jean, *Le Marquis de Sade et sa Complice, ou les Revanches de la Pudeur*, 1951

Pauvert, Jean-Jacques, *Le Marquis de Sade, l'Histoire et la Littérature*, 1953

——, *Sade Vivant*, 1986–9

Praz, Mario, *The Romantic Agony*, 1933

Sachez-Paredes, P., *El Marques de Sade, Un Profeto del Infierno*, 1974

Summers, Montague, *The Marquis de Sade: A Study in Algolania*, 1920

Tel Quel, 28, Numéro Spécial, Winter 1967, "La Pensée de Sade"

Weiss, Peter, *The Persecution and Assassination of Marat as Performed by the Inmates of the Asylum of Charenton under the Direction of the Marquis de Sade*, 1965

3. GENERAL

Apollinaire, Guillaume, ed., *Julie Philosophe, ou le Bon Patriote*, n.d.

——, *Les Onze Mille Verges*, 1907

Aulard, F. V. A., *Histoire Politique de la Revolution Française*, 1901

Bachaumont, N., *Mémoires Secrets*, 1859

Barbey d'Aurevilly, Jules, *Les Diaboliques*, 1874

Breton, André, *Anthologie de l'Humeur Noir*, 1939

Bretonne, Restif de la, *Nuits de Paris*, 1788–94

——, *L'Anti-Justine*, 1798

Brion, Marcel, *Leonor Fini*, 1962

Brodie, Fawn M., *The Devil Drives: A Life of Sir Richard Burton*, 1967

Campagne, Jean-Marc, *Clovis Trouille*, 1965

Carlyle, Thomas, *The French Revolution*, 1837

Camus, Albert, *L'Homme Revolté*, 1951

Char, René, *Le Marteau sans Maître*, 1934

Critchley, Macdonald, ed., *The Trial of Neville Heath*, 1951

D'Annunzio, Gabrielle, *Il Piacere*, 1889; rep. Biblioteca Moderna Mondadori, 1951 etc.

Duclos, Charles, *Mémoirs Secrets sur le Regne de Louis XIV, la Régence, et le Regne de Louis XV*, 1881

Dumont, F., *Souvenirs de Mirabeau*, 1950

Ellis, Havelock, "Love and Pain", in *Studies in the Psychology of Sex*, Vol. III, rev. edn., 1913

——, "The History of Florrie and the Mechanism of Sexual Deviation", in *Studies in the Psychology of Sex*, Vol. VII, 1928

Eulenburg, Albert, *Sadismus und Masochismus*, 1901

——, *Sexuale Neuropathie*, 1895

Freud, Sigmund, "A Child is Being Beaten", in *The Complete Psychological Works of Sigmund Freud*, tr. James Strachey, Vol. XVII, 1955

Fraxi, Pisanus [H. S. Ashbee], *Index Librorum Prohibitorum*, 1877

——, *Centuria Liborum Absconditorum*, 1879

——, *Catena Librorum Tacendorum*, 1885

Goncourt, Edmond and Jules, *Journal des Goncourt*, 1891–5

——, *Pages from the Goncourt Journal*, ed. Robert Baldick, 1962

Goodman, Jonathan, ed., *The Moors Murders*, 1973

Hearsey, John, *Marie Antionette*, 1972

Huxley, Aldous, *Ends and Means*, 1937

Hyde, H. Montgomery, *A History of Pornography*, 1965

Jean, Raymond, *Un Portrait de Sade*, 1989

Jelenski, Constantin, *Leonor Fini Peinture*, 1980

Johnson, Pamela Hansford, *On Iniquity*, 1967

Jones, Allen, *Allen Jones Figures*, 1969

Jouy, E., *Galerie des Femmes*, 1799

Krafft-Ebing, *Psychopathia Sexualis*, 1886; ed. Alexander Hartwich, 1959

Lacretelle, Charles, *Historie de France pendant le dix-huitième siècle*, 1844.

Lescure, M. de, *L'Amour sous la Terreur*, 1882

Lindsay, Jack, *Death of the Hero*, 1960

Loomis, Stanley, *Paris in the Terror*, 1964

Mackenzie, F. A., *The Trial of Harry Thaw*, n.d.

Manton, Richard, ed., *The Victorian Imagination*, 1985

McGuire, Christine and Carla Norton, *Perfect Victim*, 1988

Melville, Robert, *Erotic Art of the West*, 1973

Mirbeau, Octave, *Jardin des Supplices*, 1899

Mitford, Nancy, *Madame de Pompadour*, 1954

Mountfield, David, ed., *Illustrated Marquis de Sade*, 1984

Nesbit, Evelyn, *The Untold Story*, 1934

Nicolson, Harold, *The Age of Reason*, 1960

Picon, Gaëtan, *Surrealism 1919–1939*, 1977

Pope-Hennessy, James, *Monckton Milnes: The Flight of Youth*, 1951

Queneau, Raymond, *Bâtons, Chiffres, et Lettres*, 1950

Réage, Pauline [Dominique Aury], *L'Histoire d'O*, 1954

Rebell, Hugues [Georges Joseph Grassall], *Les Nuits Chaudes du Cap Français; Le Magasin d'Auréoles; Femmes Chatiées*, Postface de Hubert Juin, 1986

Richelieu, Louis-François-Armand, Duc de, *The Private Life of the Marshal Duke of Richelieu*, ed. Richard Aldington, 1917

Sadopaedia, 1908

Sainte-Beuve, C. A., "Quelques Verités sur la Situation en Littérature", *Revue des deux Mondes*, 1843

"Sapho, Mademoiselle de", *La Secte des Anandrynes*, n.d.

Sartre, Jean-Paul, *L'Être et le Néant*, 1943

Schonberger, Arno and Halldor Soehner, *The Age of Rococo*, 1960

"Schroeder-Devrient, Wilhelmina", *Aus den Memoiren einer Sängerin*, 1868

Selwyn, Francis, *Rotten to the Core? The Life and Death of Neville Heath*, 1988

Swinburne, Algernon Charles, *Lesbia Brandon*, ed. Randolph Hughes, 1952

——, *Love's Cross Currents*, 1905

——, *The Swinburne Letters*, ed. Cecil Y. Lang, 1959–62

Sydenham, M. J., *The French Revolution*, 1965

Thomas, Donald, *A Long Time Burning: The History of Literary Censorship in England*, 1969

——, *Swinburne: The Poet in his World*, 1978

Thompson, J. M., *The French Revolution*, 1943

Toth, Karl, *Woman and Rococo in France*, 1931

Toulet, Paul-Jean, *Monsieur du Paur*, 1898, ed. Herbert Juin in *Mon Ami Nana*, Union Genérale d'Editions 10/18, 1985

Vezé, Raoul, *La Galenterie Parisienne au XVIIIième Siècle*, 1905

Villiers de l'Isle Adam, Antoine, "Le Sadisme Anglaise", in *Histoires Insolites*, 1888

White, T. H., *The Age of Scandal*, 1950

Wilde, Oscar, *The Letters of Oscar Wilde*, ed. Rupert Hart-Davis, 1962

Williams, Emlyn, *Beyond Belief*, 1967

INDEX